PEEL AND THE CONSERVATIVE PARTY

DEDICATED TO MY AUNT

Mrs. Horace Porter

The Duke of Wellington and Sir Robert Peel

from the picture by Winterhalter. By gracious permission of His Majesty the King

PEEL
AND THE
CONSERVATIVE PARTY

A STUDY IN PARTY POLITICS 1832-1841

George Kitson Clark, Litt. D.

*Reader in Constitutional History at the
University of Cambridge and Fellow of
Trinity College, Cambridge.*

FRANK CASS & CO. LTD.

1964

First published by G. Bell & Sons Ltd. in 1929
and now reprinted by their kind permission.

First edition   1929
Second edition 1964

This edition published by Frank Cass & Co. Ltd.,
10, Woburn Walk, London, W.C.1.

Made and printed in Great Britain by Charles Birchall & Sons Ltd.,
London and Liverpool.

PREFACE TO FIRST EDITION

My object in writing this book is explained in the Introduction. With regard to the material used my most important source has been the unpublished Peel papers in the British Museum. The mass of these is very great, over 300 volumes. They contain a considerable number of letters of importance which have not been published and also a very large quantity of letters whose subject-matter is trivial. Part of these are unquestionably worthless, but there are as well a good many which throw an extremely interesting light on the political habits of the time. I have worked through them systematically from the date 1832 till Peel's death, but before 1832 I have contented myself with looking at selected ones. I have used the privately printed Aberdeen papers, which are also in the British Museum. The most important published authority on Peel is C. Parker's *Sir Robert Peel from his Private Papers*, which prints most of the most important documents to be found in the collection in the British Museum and several—especially to Goulburn and to the Duke of Wellington—which are not there. Three incidents in Peel's life, his passing of Catholic Emancipation, his Ministry of 1834, and his repeal of the Corn Laws are dealt with faithfully in the *Memoirs*, not only with the assistance of documents but also with explanations by Peel himself. The Hon. George Peel's *Private Letters of Sir Robert Peel* is essential for any comprehension of Peel's character, especially as giving the enlightening letters from Peel to his wife; next to these the human side of Peel comes out most clearly in his letters to his friend Croker printed in the Croker papers. There are two interesting sketches of Peel by contemporaries, one by Guizot and the other by Sir Lawrence Peel, a relative. The more modern works on the subject will be found under Peel's name in the bibliography which I have printed at the end of the book. The most recent of these, *Sir Robert Peel*, by Miss Ramsay, came out when this book was about to go to press, con-

sequently I have not yet read it.   I have to thank Miss
Ramsay for having informed me earlier what her
intentions were.

It was Mr. Winstanley of Trinity College, Cambridge,
who originally directed my attention towards the Peel
Papers in the British Museum in 1921.   In 1922 I
started work there and my researches have been greatly
aided by the persistent kindness and courtesy of the
authorities of the Manuscripts Department, to whom I
am very grateful indeed.   My thanks are due to Mr.
F. A. Simpson of Trinity for advice and to Mr. C. W.
Crawley of Trinity Hall for reading the proofs.   I am
under a deep debt to Mr. J. R. M. Butler of Trinity
and Professor G. M. Trevelyan for their encouragement
and criticism during the course of the production of this
work, large parts of which they have read in typescript.
To both of them I desire to give my warmest thanks, but
chiefly do I wish to record what I owe to the constant
help in the writing of the book which I have received
from my aunt Mrs. Horace Porter.   The trouble she
has taken, the sympathy she has shown, have been
very great, and the book has profited immeasurably.
Consequently in gratitude I dedicate it to her.   I need
not say that I myself am responsible for all the theories
and any mistakes that this work contains.

TRINITY COLLEGE

August 30th, 1928

PREFACE TO SECOND EDITION

This book was written over thirty years ago and as was inevitable there have been changes since then. There are certain passages in it which I thought well of then and which I now wish I had phrased differently. There has been much research by other scholars on the subjects contained in it, and I myself have worked on matters that relate to its subject matter, and tried to think them out anew. But it would be impracticable to revise the whole book in the light of more recent developments, and, indeed, I think it is not necessary. The work was, I believe, at that time squarely enough based on direct research on unpublished material for it to remain of use to the student and, I hope, of interest to the general reader. There are however two related subjects on which I think it important to correct, and to add to, what I then had to say.

When I wrote this book I did not give enough thought to the actual organization of the Conservative party, and in particular used the word ' whip ' too indiscriminately. Since then a great deal of work has been done on that subject, particularly by Professors Aspinall and Gash, and it awaits further illumination in forthcoming work by Professor Gash. To their work I would gladly refer the reader, but it has seemed to me important in a short introduction to add something to what I said on the stages by which that organization developed in connection with the other point on which subsequent research by others and myself has cleared my mind, that is the true significance of the resignation of the Duke of Wellington in 1830. For I think it is necessary to grasp the significance of that event and its relation to the development of political parties, in order that what follows should be rightly understood.

I have to thank Professor Gash for his very kind help in clearing up one or two points. He is however not responsible for what follows; I bear the sole responsibility.

G. KITSON CLARK,
    December, 1963.

CONTENTS

ILLUSTRATIONS

INTRODUCTION TO FIRST EDITION

This book is concerned with the problems of a party leader and of his party. Since it was a Conservative party, some attempt must be made to test the reality and practicability of the Conservative principles, which Peel and his followers claimed to maintain. Since affairs were focussed for a time on the changes in the constitution menaced by the Reform Bill, constitutional questions must be involved, especially the question of the House of Lords. None of these problems are obsolete. The House of Lords might become again an important issue, men still claim to maintain Conservative principles, party is still the most important piece of the English political machine. But it would be foolish to forget the fact that 1841 is nearly ninety years ago. Both politics and politicians have changed in various ways since Peel held the stage, and whatever political truths this period holds must often be sought for by grubbing among the redundancies of dead controversies, as a geologist grubs among the extinct volcanoes.

Yet the period presents special advantages. Politics were enlivened by the Reform Bill of 1832 and men's minds were sharpened as the hungry forties approached. The Conservative party which was built up in opposition after the Reform Bill is the classical example of a party which failed, when the test came, to remain united, and while yet in opposition it can be studied without its party problems being obscured by the innumerable distractions and overriding necessities of office. Best of all these politics have been illuminated by a man of genius, for the period will always be remembered for its description in Disraeli's novels and his denunciation of Peel as holding a creed without reality and leading a party without principle.

There is no longer any danger of Disraeli being lightly dismissed as a political adventurer who turned against the man who failed to satisfy him. His case against Peel is important, but it would be obviously unfair to read nothing but *Sybil* and *Coningsby*. This book is intended to describe first how Peel and his party were moulded and scarred by the years before 1832, and then how, after the shock of the Reform Bill, they set about the task of protecting, as they said, the ancient institutions of their country. It was while he was engaged on that task of protection that Peel may have missed opportunities, or possibly followed Conservative principles that did not stand the test of usefulness or time.

In the course of the narrative it is intended to throw some light on the management of a political party in the early nineteenth century, and on the ambitions and desires of some of the rank and file and their differences with their leaders. Most significant of these differences perhaps are those which divided Peel and the Tory Agriculturists, as when Peel refused to assent to repeal the Malt tax in 1833 and 1835—or sometimes over the question of Currency policy—or at other times when Peel's clear and resolute reasoning came into conflict with what men were impelled to demand because of their view of the general needs of agriculture, that is of their own particular interests.

As a nucleus to it all there is a problem of personality, the personality of a man warm to his friends, passionately attached to his home and his wife, yet often to outsiders cold, distant and disagreeable, cautious and yet showing at times the most ardent and ruthless determination, with undoubted limitations and yet endowed with such abilities and integrity as are seldom brought to the public service. For this is not only a study in party politics; it is also a study of Sir Robert Peel.

INTRODUCTION TO
SECOND EDITION

IN an important sense what was discussed in this book began with the resignation of the Duke of Wellingtons' government in November 1830, although for the purposes of this book it was naturally necessary to look back to the history of the years before 1830. The Duke's resignation led immediately to the formation of the reforming ministry of Lord Grey and to the passing of the first reform Bill in 1832. It led proximately to the formation of a new Conservative party in opposition and to what was the first experiment in party politics as we understand them, with a fully organized party in opposition confronting and in the end replacing the party supporting the government. It was with the development of that party and its relation to its leader that this book was mainly concerned.

Without, however, taking account of what followed it, the Duke's resignation was in its own right an event of decisive importance. He resigned because the King's government, though it was still in full enjoyment of the King's favour, was defeated in the House of Commons. This had happened before, since the Revolution, though it had not often happened. In 1782 Lord North, though still supported by the King had had to go after the failures of the War of American Independence; in 1783 Lord Shelburne had been driven out of office by the coalition of Lord North with Charles James Fox. But in 1783 the position had been recovered. By the end of 1783 George III had been able to drive out Fox and North and replace them by the younger Pitt who had the King's favour. After November 1830 there was to be no recovery.

During the storm of the Reform Bill crisis William IV was unable to get rid of Lord Grey. When in 1834 Robert Peel at William's desire did replace Lord Melbourne as the King's first minister he could not wring from the House of Commons the fair trial which he claimed as the King's choice. All that he got was a short postponement of sentence; after a few months in office he had to resign, and King William's best friends became extremely anxious lest the incitements of his brother, the Duke of Cumberland, or his own native excitability should induce him to repeat the experiment, since it would certainly have ended in the same way with possibly worse consequences to follow.

This was in its way the end of the old personal monarchy; the end of the principle that the King, however straitened in choice by Parliamentary necessities and in action by legal restrictions, ought to appoint the executive government of the country. It is true that during the first ten years of her reign old fashioned language was from time to time used about Queen Victoria, and that in all probability she never in her heart felt that her natural will and preferences ought to be completely subordinated to the choice of the nation, particularly when the nation's choice was presented to her in the unpalatable shape of Mr. Gladstone. But these survivals matter little. After 1830 the realities of the constitution had decisively changed; never again would a ministry retain power simply because the monarch wished it to do so.[1]

If, however, the ministry no longer represented the wishes of the King, what was it to represent? Whence was it to draw the authority which would enable it to consolidate sufficient power to enable it to supply the country with a stable and effective government? The classical answer to this question is, of course, that it must draw that authority from a party which has achieved a majority in the House of Commons in the last General Election.

[1]Miss Betty Kemp *King and Commons* 1660-1832 (London 1957). Sir Lewis Namier *Personalities and Powers* (London 1955) pp. 13-38 'Monarchy and the Party System' (Romanes Lecture, 1952).

However this answer implies developments both in constitutional theory and political practice which had not taken place before 1830; nor did the events of 1830 necessarily lead to them. The causes of the Duke's defeat were various and complicated. An underlying cause was no doubt the wastage of the resources on which the King's government had been wont to rely, which had been going since the late 18th century. As well as this, positive potential dangers to government had developed since 1815. On the one hand there was the development of what may be called " Liberal " opinion in the country, and, on the other, the deflation of agriculture from its war-time proportions and also Emancipation of the Roman Catholics, which had antagonized many of the country gentry. But the immediate reason for the Duke's defeat was the fact that he was not the man to handle an admittedly difficult political situation successfully. He had passed most of his life outside Britain and did not really understand the country; though singularly unprejudiced in some matters he was not sympathetic to anything that can possibly be called " liberalism " and among his many fine qualities flexibility was not numbered. He therefore grossly mismanaged the crisis of 1830 and suffered a defeat which probably need not have taken place.[1]

The Duke's defeat was not therefore the result of the victory of one party over another, and the ministry which succeeded his ministry was not, when it started operations, a party ministry. At first Lord Grey's ministry was in fact a collection of men drawn from a wide variety of groups or parties, as parties then existed, their highest common factor being opposition to the late government.[2] What gave it a character that could be translated into party terms was the fact that it sponsored the First Reform Bill, and it was this which gave it a following in the country

[1] A. S. Foord *English Historical Review* Vol. LXII (1947) pp. 484-507. ' The Waning of the Influence of the Crown '. Ian R. Christie *The Cambridge Historical Journal* Vol. XII (1956) pp. 144-154 .'Economical Reform and the "Influence of the Crown", 1780.'

[2] See A. Aspinall *Three Nineteenth Century Diaries* (London 1952) xx-xxix.

B

which prevented the King from dislodging it in 1831 or 1832 when he would have liked to do so. When the bill had passed, the concentration of force behind Lord Grey began to dissipate; nevertheless he and his successors still retained enough power to withstand the wrath of William IV and to retain office, with one short break, till a more congenial monarch came to the throne in 1837.

The Whig government therefore survived partly by virtue of the support for the principles for which they had come to stand and partly through the agency of their own party organization, but not at all because they enjoyed the King's favour. To that extent they approximated to the party government of modern constitutional theory. However, much of the support on which they relied in the country was necessarily different in nature from anything that is operative in modern party politics. Even after 1832 a large part of the electorate was still parcelled out into the territories of different interests and influences, and the Whig governments had to rely largely on the old sources of power, that is on the co-operation of sympathetic noblemen and gentlemen who possessed electoral influence and who in their turn expected favours in the disposal of patronage, upon government influence in certain boroughs, and, where necessary, on what may be called straightforward corruption. Even those who supported the Whigs for more explicitly political reasons often did so without any strong party link, often indeed only because they were preferable to any possible alternative.

In fact what lay behind the Whigs was less of a party than a loose alliance, much of it forged together by techniques similar to those which had been used to organize the support of the King's Government in the 18th century. This condition of affairs continued well on into the 19th century, and it seems probable that the two-party system would not have developed in English politics if it had not been for the fact that the reform bill crisis also produced an opposition party more permanently and extensively organized than the family groups, casual alliances and ephemeral agitations which had been the instruments of the opposition to the crown before 1830.

This party, the Conservative party, was also born in the reform bill crisis, but it continued to develop in the disturbed political situation that followed the passing of the bill. Indeed the organization of the party began to take effective shape in 1835, when Peel had just resigned after his first abortive ministry. The most important agent in this work was F. R. Bonham, who acted as a general agent for the party. He acted under Peel but with apparently significantly little co-operation from him. The party thus created contended successfully in the general election of 1837, and at the election of 1841 achieved a majority with the result that Peel its leader came into office *against* the wishes of the Queen. This was indeed the shape of things to come.[1]

However to understand this party it is necessary to look back to the moment when it came into existence. The story begins immediately after the Duke of Wellington's resignation, and it seems to begin with the disturbance which that event caused—not so much in constitutional conceptions as in certain people's private lives. Readers of Disraeli's novel *Endymion* will remember how the defeat brought unforeseen ruin to Mr. Ferrars who had made his career in government service and had reached an important post outside the Cabinet. Mr. Ferrars' fall in the novel was perhaps more melodramatic and striking than was probable in real life, for he had hoped at one moment to be Prime Minister and in the outcome he was ruined financially. Nevertheless the Duke's resignation must have brought unexpected calamity to several men in subordinate positions in the government. The line between party politicians and the higher administrative officers was still uncertain and several of the men who had to resign in 1830 had no doubt looked

---

[1] N. Gash *Politics in the Age of Peel* London 1953 (passim). N. Gash ' F. R. Bonham; Conservative " Political Secretary ", 1832-41 '. *English Historical Review* V, *LXIII* (1948) pp. 502-522. N. Gash ' Peel and the Party system ' *Transactions of the Royal Society* 5th Series Vol. I (1951). R. J. Hill *Toryism and the People*, 1832-46 (London, 1929).

to spend a lifetime in the King's service, as an ordinary professional career.

A good example is perhaps J. C. Herries. He began his career in 1798 as a Junior Clerk in the Treasury. In 1823 he became one of the Joint Secretaries of the Treasury and entered Parliament. In 1827 he became Chancellor of the Exchequer in Lord Goderich's administration. In 1828 he became Master of the Mint and in 1830 President of the Board of Trade. In fact he worked up from a lowly civil service position to high political office, and till a surprisingly late point in this ascent he regarded himself as less of a politician than a public servant. In 1827, when he had been for four years a secretary of the Treasury and the member for Harwich, he wrote: " I am not in the following of any party. My business is with the public interests, and my duty to promote the King's service wherever I am employed."[1] That is really the language of a civil servant, but the position was equivocal and in the disturbed conditions which followed Lord Liverpool's stroke it was difficult for Herries to keep aloof from party politics. Before the end of 1827 he was in trouble with the Whigs who had joined the administration but regarded him with suspicion. In 1830 he resigned with the Duke.

The resignation of such men probably meant the kind of loss to the country of administrative experience and capacity which nowadays might result from a general resignation of important permanent officials. This was probably the reason why the financial policy of the country took an abrupt turn in the wrong direction after 1830, and remained incompetent and indecisive till Peel took over in 1841. But the Treasury officials had had before 1830 other than financial duties which cannot conceivably fall to any modern permanent officials. Both the Junior Lords of the Treasury and the Secretaries of the Treasury had had the task of organizing the support of

[1] J. C. Herries to Sir Wm. Knighton, 27 February 1827, *Letters of King George IV* ed. A. Aspinall vol. iii p. 200 quoted in Namier *Personalities and Powers* p. 24. (loc: cit:).

those upon whom the King's government had to rely, both in Parliament and in the constituencies. In the early 19th century there seems indeed to have been a growing differentiation between the financial and the political work of the Treasury. After 1809, when Charles Arbuthnot became one of the Joint Secretaries of the Treasury, there was a tendency to concentrate the political work on him, and when Herries was appointed to succeed him he believed he was to take the other—that is the financial—side of the work. But it would be hard to say how absolute was this differentiation of functions in government; moreover it seems clear that other ministers outside the Treasury were also charged with political work.[1]

Since many of the ministers who resigned were in their way professionals it is perhaps not surprising that after they had resigned they should continue in their profession and turn over from the task of organizing the support of the government to that of organizing the opposition. Immediately after the Duke resigned a committee was formed to plan a campaign and influence the press, which included Herries, Joseph Planta who had been a secretary of the Treasury from 1827 to 1830, William Holmes who had been a Whip and Treasurer of the Ordnance from 1820-1830, and Sir Henry Hardinge a soldier who had been Secretary at War and was presumably the link with the Duke of Wellington.

As the Reform Bill crisis developed the need for a wider organization was obviously felt and in June 1831 there was a meeting of fifteen Tory members of both houses of Parliament in a house in Charles Street which Planta had occupied while in office. This meeting included various party leaders, but not Peel, and also most of those who had been or were going to be active in the organization of the party, as for instance Planta, Hardinge, Herries, Charles Arbuthnot, another ex-secretary of the Treasury, Holmes, Goulburn who had been Chancellor

[1] A. Aspinall *The Correspondence of Charles Arbuthnot* (Camden 3rd series vol. LXV, 1941) p. viii. See also A. Aspinall *English Historical Review* vol. XLI (1926) pp. 389-411 'English Party Organization in the early Nineteenth Century'.

of the Exchequer from 1828 to 1830, Charles Ross a Tory M.P. who was to act as a Whip and also Lords Granville Somerset and Lowther, who had been Lords of the Treasury—Lord Granville Somerset continuously from 1819, except during the administrations of Canning and Goderich.[1]

The personal link between the organization of the King's government before 1830 and the organization of the opposition to the Reform Bill was therefore significantly close. This possibly affected their realization of the scope of the work and may have suggested what they should do, but it did not mean that at first they were successful. A certain amount of money was collected and spent, and the house in Charles Street was maintained as an headquarters, but the Reform Bill pursued its triumphant course commanding large majorities both in the House of Commons and in the country. However the very force of the tide, which not only carried the bill into law but seemed to threaten worse things to follow, served to keep the Tories together. It made them disregard, if not to forget, their divisions and it made them perpetuate and extend their organization. In 1832 the Charles Street establishment was replaced by the foundation of the Carlton Club. About the same time Bonham started on his task. He came into Parliament in 1830 and by the spring of 1831 was assisting Holmes and Planta. In 1832 he displaced Holmes as the party's chief election manager, and in 1835 he set to work with an appropriate committee to organize the party in the country. His most important work was not in Parliament but in the constituencies. He was indeed an assistant Whip in the House of Commons between 1835 and 1837, but he lost his seat in 1837 and continued to work where his main influence lay.

The aftermath of the Reform Bill supplied the new

[1]For the organization of the opposition at this period see A. Aspinall *Politics and the Press* (London 1949) pp. 329-340, A. Aspinall *Nineteenth Century Diaries* (op: cit:) p. xxxiv to xlii and p. 27 ff., Lord Ellenborough's Diary from Nov: 26, 1830. See also N. Gash *Politics of the Age of Peel* (op: cit:), pp. 395-401.

party with recruits with various political antecedents. There were Tories who had remained faithful all the way through, and others who had returned to their allegiance when confronted by the Reform Bill. There were also both Tories and Whigs who had supported the Reform Bill but did not like its sequels. The party gained popularity in various constituencies because the Whigs' alliance with O'Connel affronted people who disliked Roman Catholics and Irishmen, and many agriculturists turned back from the Whigs in disgust when they found they were going to get as little from Lord Grey's government as they had done from the Duke of Wellington's government or Lord Liverpool's. Indeed a comparison of the way the counties voted in 1832 with the way they voted in 1841 shows how great in these years was the turnover in agricultural opinion.

As the result of all this it was possible to enlist in the service of the new party a great deal of electoral influence and to draw upon fairly wide-spread popular support, particularly after Oastler's crusade against child labour in the factories had got under way and had been reinforced by the violent hatred excited by the Whig reform of the poor law. What might be lacking was a leader. By now the only possible leader was not the Duke of Wellington but Peel, and it was not clear that Peel wanted to lead. On the day after their defeat Peel called a meeting of 40 official members of the Commons to his house and announced ' first that we were out, and secondly that he meant to retire to private life—to give no opposition and not to lead the party—in short to be his own unfettered man'.[1] Apparently the announcement was not well received by those who had faithfully supported Peel in office.

Circumstances prevented Peel from keeping fully to this bleak resolution. It was impossible for him not to take a leading part in the debates on the Reform Bill. But he was not very co-operative. He took no part in the

[1] *The correspondence and diaries of the late Right Hon. John Wilson Croker* (ed: L. J. Jennings) (London 1884) vol. II p. 77 (Croker to Lord Hertford Nov: 18, 1830).

Charles Street venture, although he seems to have been prepared to make use of the opportunities which Charles Street provided. He was not present at important meetings, and, what was worse, he was inclined to declare that he did not wish to lead the party, that he viewed any possibility of a return to office with growing aversion, and that he would not compromise any of his opinions to gain followers. Indeed he told Goulburn after the reform bill was passed and a new political campaign was in prospect that he could not think beforehand of any point on which he was prepared to concede much, indeed anything, taking, significantly, as his example of a point on which concession was impossible the currency question.[1]

Peel was not to evade his destiny. Indeed it may be questioned how far he really desired to do so. Much of his desire to stand down from the lead in these years was probably the direct psychological result of the bitter crisis over Catholic Emancipation. He was unlikely to detach himself from politics, his interest in them was too profound and he shared with others the fears that the Reform Bill excited, and if he remained in politics he could not avoid leading the party, whether he liked it or not. Indeed circumstances conspired to increase his hold over the Conservative organization. William Holmes had personal connections which might have been dangerous to Peel and he was replaced by Bonham who was entirely Peel's friend. The election of 1832 worked havoc with the old organization. Holmes, Planta, Bonham all lost their seats, the party in the House of Commons was reduced to a dispirited remnant and it would be hard to say who were Whips, so that the situation remained to be straightened out when Peel became Prime Minister in 1834 and appointed Sir George Clerk and Sir Thomas Fremantle to be Secretaries of the Treasury. When he resigned the post of Chief Whip was filled by Sir George Clerk till 1837 when Clerk lost his seat in the House of Commons, after that the post of Chief Whip was filled by Sir Thomas Fremantle.

[1] See below pp. 82-88.

In fact without much effort on Peel's part the party organization passed into the hands of men appointed by him, and the men he appointed, or used, remained personally completely loyal to him. Fremantle remained loyal to Peel to the end, so did Bonham, so did Lord Granville Somerset, who was head of the electoral organization, though too highly placed socially ever to be a Whip. If ever a man had a sword thrust into his hand it was Peel in these years of preparation for his last great government.

Yet his initial hesitation has significance. It is significant personally for it discloses a latent dissatisfaction with his lot, and a latent distaste for his followers which was naturally to complicate his relations with them. But his hesitation also points to an important historical and constitutional issue on which recent research has thrown light. Of recent years it has become clear that the part played in the defeat of the Duke of Wellington in 1830 by a sudden upsurge of liberal and reforming opinion was less than used to be thought. It used to be said that the general election of 1830 was influenced by the French Revolution but Professor Gash has pointed out that in fact the news came too late to influence the elections. Attention has also recently been directed to the importance of the part played by the discontent of the county members and of the Ultra Tories both in the defeat of the Duke of Wellington, and even in the passage of the Reform Bill.[1]

That discontent has a direct reference both to Peel's hesitations about his position as leader, and to his subsequent career. He was, or was to be, significantly involved in all the principal causes of that discontent. The general cause of the agricultural discontent with the government was of course the fall of prices after 1813, but it turned on three particular points—the severely deflationary results of the government's currency policy in the twenties, its

[1]N. Gash in *Essays presented to Sir Lewis Namier* (ed: R. Pares and A. J. P. Taylor, London 1956. ' English Reform and French Revolution in the general election of 1830 ' p. 258-288. D. C. Moore, ' The Other Face of Reform '. *Victorian Studies* vol. V (Indiana University U.S.A., 1961), pp. 17-34.

refusal to reduce taxes, especially the malt tax, which were held to weigh especially heavily on agriculture, and its failure to provide adequate protective duties. The wrath of the Ultra Tories had been kindled later, when, as they believed, the most sacred principles of the Constitution had been most vilely betrayed by the Emancipation of the Roman Catholics in 1829.

Now Peel had been to a large extent personally responsible for the government's currency policy. He was chairman of the committee which had advised the return to a gold based currency, and the act which had effected the reform was called Peel's act. It was a point on which he was both committed and sensitive, as his letter to Goulburn shews. During his brief attempt at government in 1834-5 he was strongly pressed to conciliate opinion in the counties by promising to repeal the malt tax, but though he sorely needed support at that moment, he resisted the pressure.[1] In his last ministry he was under constant attack because he did not give agriculture what was believed to be adequate protection, and he ended his ministry by repealing the Corn Laws. These things set the farmers against him. As far as the Ultra Tories were concerned he was of all men, except perhaps the Duke of Wellington, most closely, and in many eyes most criminally, involved in the Emancipation of the Roman Catholics; and if in the last act he forfeited his position as Prime Minister by his repeal of the Corn Laws in 1846 it seems likely that already he had gravely compromised it in 1845 by his increased grant to Maynooth, the Roman Catholic College in Ireland.

On all these points there had been or was to be particular disagreement between Peel and those who must be his followers, and in these years Peel shews himself to be aware of the underlying possibilities of the situation. Peel's opinions were however not indiosyncratic to himself, they were to a greater or less extent shared by most of the Tory leaders who were his colleagues. Lord Liverpool's government had endorsed the currency

[1]See below pp. 205, 209, 220, 239-41.

policy and had defended it against angry agricultural
attack; the Duke of Wellington had given the authority
of his great name to the Emancipation of the Roman
Catholics, and in his last ministry most of Peel's colleagues
followed his lead over both Maynooth and the repeal of
the Corn Laws. However when they acted in this way
they acted not so much as Tories responsive to the prejudices and demands of a party, and of the groups and
classes in the country which accepted the party label, but
as ministers responsible to King and Parliament for the
welfare of the whole country. As ministers of the King it
was natural that they should put aside what might seem to
be the ignorant and excessive demands of one economic
interest, however important it might be socially and
politically. It was right that they should disregard strong
religious and political prejudices, which, however deeply
grounded in the nation's past, were to be a danger to its
future peace and security.

In 1830, however, the fact that they were ministers of
the Crown had not saved them from defeat, and after
1830 they were no longer ministers of the crown.

They were at first politicians trying to build up a party
in opposition, and after 1841 ministers by the favour not
of a Queen but of a party. To achieve power they had had
to build on the prejudices and interests of those who might
follow them, and they would presumably have to hold it
on the condition that they satisfied those prejudices and
interests. That was the paradox in their situation. They
were party leaders but they had not been educated in the
business of faction but in government, and their party
drew its origins not from the experience of opposition or
agitation but from the experience of government. This
paradox is particularly relevant to Robert Peel the strong
conscientious ex-minister, for whom other men organized
a party which he reluctantly led. Indeed it seems to be
necessary to grasp this paradox in order to see his career
in proper perspective.

G. KITSON CLARK,
    December, 1963.

CHAPTER I

PEEL AND THE TORIES BEFORE 1832

In 1815 the great war stopped. In 1830 the Whigs took charge of the country's destinies, and in 1832 the Bill for Parliamentary Reform was passed and a first step taken on the long road that led, in the nineteenth century, towards democracy. But in the intervening fifteen years the country was ruled by Tories. They had to face the crowd of troubles that follow great wars; they had to face the challenge of disturbing forces in the country and also of disturbing ideas.

For not only had the example and the ideas of the French Revolution managed to find their way into various English minds, but there were also native traditions to be considered. The cause of Parliamentary reform had been agitated before the war broke out, and it had escaped being completely frozen to death in the long winter that followed. At the end of the eighteenth century the Whigs had considered themselves to be the friends of liberty and the people, and when the war was over there still remained some of them who had not been caught up into the Government party. Moreover enlightenment and perhaps philanthropy yawned in the road ahead. Religion had awakened, men's consciences and nerves were being quickened, while science and common sense already intruded themselves on some of the mysteries of government. A desire for Reform was abroad, and reforms were in fact urgently needed. Many of the country's institutions were unjust or absurd, and the most notable corruption of all was the House which was partly elected by irrational franchises and debauched or non-existent constituencies, leaving whole regions and important classes without any direct representation at all.

The men who were opposed to the existing régime differed as widely as the two sides of the sky in their origins and desires. There were the demagogues who

1

directed into political channels the discontent caused by
the acute distress which followed the wars, and were
responsible for a revolutionary fermentation in the first
years of peace. In different parts of the country political and democratic clubs succeeded in coming into
existence in spite of the laws against them. More
important for the future were probably Francis Place, the
tailor who organized the constituency of Westminster,
and William Cobbett, the violent country-bred reformer
who was, among other things, the father of popular
journalism. Aristocrats such as Sir Francis Burdett
had taken up democratic politics, and a little group of
solid men promoted the utilitarian views of Jeremy
Bentham. All these were Radicals, but there were men
of less drastic ideas opposed to the Tories, men of more
or less middle-class origin who had imbibed enlightened
or what were to be called Liberal opinions, and the
remnant of the aristocratic Whigs who held to the
memory of Charles James Fox. Behind the Whigs in
the country were the politically minded Dissenters with
grievances real enough to keep them active in the cause
of reform.

The Whigs and their more immediate allies might
perhaps fill, in Parliament and the country, the rôle of a
respectable Opposition. The clumsy and oppressive
character of the domestic policy of the Tories immediately after the war gave them opportunities, and they
could ally themselves at times with any section of
opinion that happened to be antagonized by the Tory
Government. As a backbone for any opposition to any
Government there was usually alive in those days a
vigorous feeling that taxation was wilfully increased by
the expense of defence and administration and especially by the expense of pensions and sinecures. But
the Whig chance was delayed. The Whigs were themselves disorganized, and impotent and undecided in
policy. They could not gain control of the unre-
formed House of Commons, and after about 1821
the sky cleared, the country grew more prosperous and

men's tempers quieter, and, most fatal of all, the
Government began itself to become enlightened.

For the Tories were nothing worse than a mixed
collection of ordinary men. They wished to protect
their country, were harassed by the fear of revolution,
bewildered by the difficulties of politics and naturally
impressed by the fact that it was important for society
that they should preserve their own interest. They
did not believe in democratic reform, but they had not
less than the ordinary equipment of both conscience
and intellect. It was possible, but it was not necessary,
for a Tory to hold with Eldon, that everything that
existed, however corrupt, should be defended to the
death lest all should fall together. In particular a group
of liberal Tories were gathered round the splendid figure
of George Canning, who was the disciple of Pitt if he
was the enemy of Castlereagh. Consequently after 1821
Lord Liverpool, the Prime Minister, was able to refresh
his Government by able and effective recruits from out
of the Tory Party. The Ministry took up the work of
reform. Robert Peel as Home Secretary set about such
labours as reform of the criminal law. Canning's friend
William Huskisson at the Board of Trade made important if cautious steps towards liberating trade from the
restrictions with which the past had encumbered it,
and Canning himself became Foreign Secretary, defied
the autocrats of the continent and became the cynosure
of Liberal eyes.

Yet though the Tories could satisfy some of the claims
of enlightenment, their position was not secure. They
too had their divisions. Some Tories distrusted reforms,
and some Tories more and more bitterly distrusted
Canning. Worst of all, the question of emancipating
the Roman Catholics from the disabilities still imposed
on them by law split the party from top to bottom. Lord
Liverpool managed to keep these hostile elements together,
but in 1827, when he was removed, the "Protestant"
Tories and Canning's friends found that they could
no longer continue together in the same Government.

The Catholic question had helped to destroy the great Tory Ministry; it was to do further damage. It drew its importance from Ireland. There the restraints on the Catholics hurt the vast majority of the population, and the agrarian outrages frequent among the Irish peasantry were often inflicted in the name of their religious divisions. Ireland had started the century with revolt and rebellion, and the cause of Catholic Emancipation was likely to be pressed forward in connection with Irish Nationalism. In about 1805 the Irish Roman Catholic lawyer Daniel O'Connell embarked on the struggle and became from that time its centre. Perhaps there were moments when the movement could have been placated by concession, but no effective concession was forthcoming. In 1824 the formation of the Catholic Association put the agitation on a national basis. By 1829 the situation had become so serious that the Duke of Wellington and Robert Peel, who were at that moment in power, were forced to concede, although they were "Protestants," the emancipation of the Roman Catholics.

The betrayal of Protestantism made a new split in the Tory Party, and probably deprived it for a time of its most powerful popular appeal. Consequently the Ministry were unable to face the storm which overtook them in 1830. In 1830 distress and discontent came again to a head, especially in the country districts. Liberalized opinion developed rapidly in the country round the Whigs as a nucleus, for Canning had died in 1827. In the summer the people of France got rid of the Legitimist Bourbon régime which the allies had set up when they defeated Napoleon. Inspired by France the cry for Parliamentary Reform became in Britain louder and more definite than ever before. It was a demand which the Tory Government did not attempt to satisfy, and they were turned out that autumn by a coalition of Whigs, Liberals and disgusted Protestants. A Whig Government was formed. In 1831 they produced a Bill for Parliamentary Reform, and in

1832, after desperate Tory resistance and after riots and disorder in the country, it was passed. The Tories were utterly defeated in the elections which followed. They had fallen from their high estate into a condition of utter impotence and humiliation; they seemed to have survived into a world which had no further use for them. After 1832 they had to set out on the rough road of opposition with but little force and no hope at their command.

For a rough road memories and ghosts are not good travelling companions. By 1832 the Tories suffered from too much history; from a past that was too angry and varied to help the unity of the present. It is true that Canning was dead. He had flamed himself out, and the party no longer suffered from the distracting presence of genius. But it still held within it the chief agents in the passage of Catholic Emancipation, the men who had forced an unprincipled compliance with the demands of necessity.

Of course all Tories had a common feeling to unite them in the fear of Jacobinism and Revolution. Fear is a justifiable political emotion, but as a basis for party unity it is perhaps not so satisfactory as belief or hope; and when it is one of the simplest fears, as for life or property, it must override too many other considerations, take up too much of men's attention and dangerously obscure intrinsic differences. Wild animals may cower together from a storm in a common shelter, forgetting their natural antipathies, their growling silenced by thunder. But when the storm abates nature will reassert itself, while an animal of principle will have snarled the whole time.

Most of the Tories had a general belief in the efficiency of the political machine and in the danger of stopping its action, in the goodness of the social fabric and in the disaster of spoiling it, while they had their formulæ about preserving the existing constitution in Church and State. But such beliefs, when generally stated or very vaguely assumed, are but loose bonds for a party;

c

and as for the existing Constitution, there was doubt
as to what were its essentials, when it was being attacked,
or how it was to be defended. Obviously within these
limits Tories of like original ideas could luxuriate into
very different growths, and by their fruits, not by their
roots, would men know them.

So there were some who wished to defend the right on
the sheer edge of principle, and others who believed in
the relaxing doctrines of moderation. Some remembered Canning as a leader, some as a necessity, some as
a sin. There were Free Traders and Protectionists,
gold currency men and inflationists. There were old
High Churchmen, new Low Churchmen, generally
moral and generally careless men, fierce Irish Protestants,
Erastians, and a few of the fashionable ungodly. There
were manufacturers, bankers and agriculturists, independent country members and men who till 1830 had
been usually in office; and to unite them all in the common peril of 1832 was the hard task and high destiny
of one who had been nurtured in office, and who had
quarrelled notably, on a quasi-religious ground, with a
large division of the party that followed him.

§2. 1809–18

Peel was born a Tory. His father, the first Sir
Robert, was a rich cotton spinner with a great admiration for Pitt. The younger Robert came of age and
into Parliament in 1809, with a distinguished career at
Oxford behind him. He was soon pressed firmly and
almost uncomfortably close to the bosom of Government, taking office under Lord Liverpool in 1810 as
Under-Secretary for War and the Colonies. It is said
that the young man sulked a little on first being taken
into that coercive embrace,—it is not unlikely, for he
was not elaborating his own principles or settling his
own destiny. But he did not protest strongly enough to
delay the rush of his good fortune, and he was hurried
on to honour and to his fate. Lord Liverpool, in culti-
vating his intimacy, had admired his qualities, his father's

heart was set on his political career, and he had already proved himself a useful instrument. He spoke and voted on the Protestant side in the debates on Roman Catholic Emancipation, but refused to pledge himself; a refusal in which he could not persist, for in the September of 1812 he was appointed Chief Secretary for Ireland.

It was a responsible position, and Peel was twenty-four; so young that O'Connell complained that he was yet a dandy. He had light reddish hair and a fair complexion, a long nose, finely curved, a long face, rather broad and with strange high cheeks, a high forehead and a strong deep chin. About the mouth, in his portrait by Sir Thomas Lawrence, there is an expression implying contempt or possibly defiance, and about both eyes and mouth there is certainly something high mettled and nervous. He stood more than the ordinary height and was usually elegantly and richly dressed. He was a splendid young man, liked by his employers, appreciated by his friends; but there seems to have been sometimes an awkwardness in his carriage, a stiffness in his manner suggesting that, in superficial matters, he was not always completely at ease.

He was at this time young, able and successful, with not a little of the self-assurance natural to one who had been not only the hope of his family and its heir, but first its good boy and afterwards its success. To his superiors he wrote as one whose opinions were important, and to his contemporaries as one whose good offices might be useful; and as the implication in each case was well grounded, it is not surprising that his accents early took on the full rounded tones, at once confident and guarded, of a mature statesman. The façade was being erected from behind which there was to look out upon the world a man not cold or sly, as other men said, but of genuine and conscious honesty, and, above all, intensely sensitive.

The government of Ireland was at this time no tranquil affair of sleep, routine and memoranda; it was more

like war, and war in which the new Secretary must be a
protagonist. In Parliament he was confronted by the
tedious struggle over Emancipation, an endless series
of mangling blows and indecisive engagements. In
Ireland there was O'Connell and his party and the memories of rebellion, to fill the hands and minds of those
in power, and order had to be kept, agitators prosecuted,
societies crushed. Peel was not tempted to flinch or to
waver, for he had great reserves of strength and of contempt, and his experience stiffened his nature and his
opinions. He saw disloyalty in time of war and agitation in time of peace, and he saw them both from the
Castle in Dublin. He felt the weight of O'Connell's
furious invective, and he resented and despised, as perhaps he suffered. He saw outrages; they were begotten,
it may be, by oppression out of misery, but they were of a
nature to make him feel that among large classes of Irish
peasants there was neither mercy, nor shame, nor faith,
except to accomplices. Moreover he saw what seemed
to be inexorable religious hatred, and he entered on his
duties under a Lord Lieutenant most definitely "Protestant," and with an executive almost wholly opposed to
the Roman Catholic claims.

It was a natural consequence that Peel's views on the
Roman Catholic question should ripen into a most stubborn maturity, and at five-and-twenty he became the
leader on the Protestant side in the battles in the House
of Commons over Emancipation. Here were evils only
to be cured by "gradual and tardy reforms" for which
his experiences did not suggest an easy solution by the
sudden magic of "Emancipation." He had little sympathy for the Roman Catholic Church in Ireland, since
he believed that half the ills of Ireland were due to "Pop-
ish superstition," and he saw the largest part of that
Church in close alliance with O'Connell and his party.
Moreover on general grounds he held the doctrine, then
common, that Roman Catholics could not be loyal to a
state without giving securities, which he knew they were
not prepared to give, but which he thought they did give

to every state but England. He felt that Roman Catholics, once Emancipation was conceded, must be driven by their religion and their hate to press on over Church and State to a Catholic ascendancy, resolutely to be resisted by one born and employed on the side of the Government and the Church. In fact he was carried by his fate to the implication that the Roman Catholics must be refused, for ever, civil equality.

"For ever" are words no man can imply with safety; they belong rather to melodrama than to politics. Peel had chained himself to a rock, and when he broke free his flesh must be torn. He did not change his opinions. Right up to 1829 when he emancipated the Roman Catholics he did not doubt his arguments against them, and even then he felt that they were still valid although he was forced to yield to stronger considerations. Perhaps his official positions helped to keep him steady, for though he resigned in 1818 from his post as Chief Secretary, between 1821 and 1827 he wrestled as Home Secretary with organized discontent in Ireland, contemplating anew from that position the old evils and horrors. Indeed, towards the end, discontent seemed to take on the ugly features of religious warfare, while Emancipation must have seemed like an attempt to quiet the Atlantic with a pannikin of oil, yet a pannikin large enough for the Protestants to drown in it.

Moreover he had taken up his position in his own mind and before Parliament and the Country, and he did not think to alter it. He defended the cause very often in the House of Commons, and there is nothing like battle to make you forget what you are fighting about. To have supported any other policy would soon have required of Peel a violent reversal of opinion in the face of conditions which had never improved, and unfortunately there were clogs on the constitution. There were the King and the Duke of York, the House of Lords and the English Electorate, who till the end never suffered the failing Protestant cause to become desperate enough to screen surrender with necessity.

It was always failing, and it never failed, and it would not fail without a violent transposition of forces.

Thus there was induced, or perhaps demonstrated, a dangerous fatalism which infected too much of Peel's politics. It was the fatalism of private honesty. Perhaps it may be called "Cato's disease." It is the disease in which too often personal dignity and integrity are the touchstones and the question of responsibility is to be solved by individual retirement. When Peel foresaw defeat he talked of resolution and resignation, and adopted the unhealthy attitude of a Cato; a Cato to be forced by the gods to lead their own armies.

But Peel in Ireland must not be thought of as an Orangeman among Orangemen, glorying, rioting and jobbing with an intemperate, overheated and intolerable faction. He had come to a Government, and not to a Party; and he was too morally minded, besides being too much criticized at home, to let Government abandon all its attributes of justice and benefit to the country it kept in order. He was too able a man to be simply the tool of corrupt violence; too able, too honest and perhaps a little too ungenerous. He soon began to show his mettle in administration, with a fine ruthless, methodical vigour, possibly inherited from his father. His reforming ardour was stimulated by his visits to England, where he had to defend before the Cabinet and the House of Commons those things which looked natural enough in Ireland, and yet in London, by some strange alchemy, appeared deformed and indefensible. When Peel turned his attention to Irish administration, it was rather like the severe cold all-intrusive light of morning breaking in on the weird shadows of a haunted wood.

Meanwhile his position and his character were teaching him to dislike some and to despise many of the Government's Irish supporters. For instance, there passed through his hands much of the patronage which was then considered the life-blood of Government, and it was largely left to him to moderate the stream and

Peel and O'Connell

direct it. It was a most unpleasant duty; for in Ireland the thirst was raging, especially for small posts,
the bribery that prepared the way for the Union having
left the palate a little jaded and Irishmen tired of unre-
munerative honours. Men continually pestered Peel,
big with grievances and violent words, demanding patronage which they had not always earned but always
intended to misuse, and Peel grew to think their pleas
disgraceful and themselves ridiculous; indeed he said
that he learned here the chilling caution which he ever
after used in such matters.

It might have been better for him if he had not been
taught so much so early; for these demands were not
entirely unlike the usual desires of the ordinary rank
and file of a party in those days. His feelings dove-
tailed in too well with the natural tendencies of a man
whose nervousness, upbringing and character had made
him paint the background of his world too full of rogues
and blockheads and put into his humour too much
contempt. Contempt is a luxury too expensive for
party leaders.

It may be that this feeling was as yet a mere private
disgust, but there grew close to it in Peel's mind a more
public disapprobation. The Orangemen in Ireland,
armed and organized, endangered peace, doing things
which could not be tolerated by any Government that
was not merely the headquarters of one party in a
civil war. They showed a most exuberant insanity,
and Peel, however much he admired their principles,
or sympathized with their desire for protection, or
believed that the original aggressors were the Roman
Catholics, soon began heartily to desire their quiescence.
He was ready to urge them to restrain themselves, and
to agree with the Government when it tried to restrain
them.

Besides the Orangemen there were the Irish country
gentry. Apparently they spent much of their time in
circulating the most bloodthirsty and unfounded rumours
of plots for massacres and rebellion together with com-

plaints of the Government's failure to protect them.
Again Peel had opportunities for contemptuous laughter.
He sneered and he resented; for while they complained,
they failed to do their duty either as land-owners or
magistrates, and Peel learned that it was better to defend
the peace with forces organized by Government. He
found regular police and stipendiary magistrates more
efficient than the older and more aristrocratic machinery,
and both were perhaps typical products of bourgeois or
governmental conservatism. He was being well educated for his high destiny; he was learning the loneliness
and thanklessness of government, and the unreasonable-
ness of supporters.[1]

§3.   1818–21

In 1818 Peel left Ireland, and the next three years
formed the longer of his two short periods out of office
between 1812 and 1830. It was not unimportant and
it served to bring out some significant symptoms. He
left Ireland a tired man, tired of official dinners, of inter-
views with wearisome people, of long warfare in the
House of Commons, of days and nights of very hard
work, and of being asked to cut down necessary expenditure and yet to maintain efficiency; tired, in short, of
the usual and troublesome accidents of official life.[2] He
declared himself to be surprisingly unambitious. Indeed
he said he really thought he had no further ambition
at all. All that he had was gratified by becoming, in
1817, Member for Oxford University; yet this was
a young man, who was to be so far the sport of circumstances as to become twice Prime Minister of England. He was suffering from the disease of kings
and from the folly of satirists; he found the sceptre
had grown very wearying to the hands into which it
had been thrust, and he despised it because the crowd
admired its glitter. He looked out on the world, and

---

[1] Parker, Vol. I, *passim*. Croker, Vol. I, 46 ff. *Mr. Gregory's Letter
Box*, *passim*. *Diary of Frances Lady Shelley*, Vol. I, 16 ff.
[2] Croker, Vol. II, 116 ; Parker, Vol. I, 237, 286.

realized that he was very rich and was not getting the best that life could afford. Why, for instance, should he not travel? Besides, was there not a stoic virtue in a blameless cultivated leisure, in contempt for the tinselled gauds and dignity of office? The lust for quiet raged dangerously, and he fed it by losing his health and still more by gaining a wife; yet all the time Peel was chained to the car too fast to let him yield even to the temptations of great domestic happiness.

The ship was in harbour, not in dry dock, and it still stirred to the movements of the waves and winds that had troubled it. Happiness and weariness are strong forces indeed, but they cannot make a man entirely deaf or forgetful. Now, as always, Peel was profoundly interested in politics, and in his heart perhaps he knew that they were his profession and his duty and his high destiny. Moreover his friends were interested in his career, and though it is hard sometimes for a man to choose between glory with hardship and the solid joys of obscurity, his friends do not always share his hesitation. Peel might hold back, but his friends talked and intrigued for his promotion. He was an important man, he had made a reputation as Chief Secretary, he was the leader of the Protestants in the Commons. Lord Liverpool could not afford to let such steel lie idle and rusting, he had to attempt to get Peel to give his services in office and in Cabinet, and at last, in 1821 he succeeded.[1]

Even Peel's leisure had not been unoccupied by politics. He had had, in particular, one piece of work to do during that period which was to have a considerable effect on his career. In 1819 he accepted the Chairmanship of the Currency Commission, and he seems to have enjoyed his task. It obviously held a great deal of his attention and he was not at all averse to this kind of calculation. He started with practically no views on the matter in hand; and those which he

---

[1] Croker papers, Vol. I, p. 183 ff. Yonge's *Lord Liverpool*, II. Buck: *Memoirs of the Court of George IV*, Vol. I, p. 102.

developed during his service led him, with the Commission, ultimately to decide in favour of the return to cash payments, and of what became the orthodox monetary policy of the Economists. Indeed, he so identified himself with this result that the Act embodying it came to be called Peel's Act, and his name came always to be associated with the policy involved. He had perhaps hearkened to the voice of Reason, and Reason, when she gives definite answers, may be sometimes a dangerous mistress, not a little seductive to men educated in office where they have a great need of definite answers, and have not that vivid, particularist personal experience which may lead to rebellion against her results. Peel had tried to lift the decision out of the medium of politics, and he rejoiced to feel that his colleagues left their parties at the doors of the committee room. ✗He had tried to solve the problem as if it were a problem in mathematics, and the result was a decision applauded by the opposition and always heartily disliked by the Agriculturists. But Peel heard no warnings for the future.[1]

After the Commission he went back to his retirement, and watched from thence what was happening in Politics. In 1820 and 1821 the political atmosphere was dangerous and depressing, hinting at thunder. It was especially gloomy for Tories and above all for ministers. Distress had followed the Wars, and that child of distress, disorder. The broken fragments of old Jacobinism still lay about to be exaggerated by the timid and, it might be, to coalesce with the miserable. The ministers were chronically weak. They were not at ease with their new master, George IV, and they were starting that pilgrimage through the muck which was enforced by the King's desire to divorce his Queen. Their own party had helped to defeat them over their financial arrangements, and now there were the signs of the growth of a Liberal opposition. Peel watched these things with fear and with interest, and he wrote in March 1820 to his friend Croker that the tone of England

[1] Parker, I, 291 ff.

was more inclined to an undefined change in the mode
of governing the country, was, "to use an odious but
intelligible phrase" more "liberal," than the policy of
the Government.   He wondered how during the next
seven years they could maintain a resistance to Parliamentary Reform.   He wondered whether Whigs and
Tories would unite and carry moderate reform through
together.

In this remark much indeed seems to be foreshadowed,
though it is difficult to say how much—for an exaggerated idea of what is possible in personal consistency
is the great peril of both Politics and History.   In
History it is tempting, by the use of casual remarks and
a knowledge of the future, to docket a man under a
motive or system of motives, to stick him on his pin
and to have done with him.   It is easy to construct
too extensively and too simply upon a casual remark
from the very front of the mind, or upon what is at best
a wayward flickering emotion.   Unfortunately men are
undisciplined enough not to live these straight consistent
lives, full of inevitability and drama, and they are rash
enough not to make all they do or say significant of far-
seeing intentions or deep abiding sentiments; while all
the time politics seem most like a breathless obstacle
race, with the next obstacle usually round the corner.

However, it is true that Peel had by this time grown
strangely infected by a consciousness of the presence
of "Liberalism," to use, as we must, this "odious but
intelligible" word.   He had known it as a name often
upon the lips of the other side, implying the kind of
things which Tories must condemn.   He had known
this thing when he was an administrator with the claims
of order upon him, when the Advanced and Philanthropic made demands which seemed both ignorant
and unsupportable.   He had felt it in the House of
Commons, on those hot excited nights of debate that
he so much disliked, as he sat, nervous, apprehensive,
and sometimes very angry.   He seems to have seen
it elsewhere. He spoke to his friends of it; it was a

modern inconvenience; it would not allow the use of prescription as an argument; it made it especially necessary for his side to be well conducted and always in the right, even if they were Irish Protestants.[1]

In fact, he obviously felt that, unhappily, this intruding principle was not without power, both in the Commons and the Country; and the worst of it all was that its devotees used arguments which a sensible, humane, honest and Christian man could not merely rebut with rhetorical answers without arguments or reasonable concessions—especially a man so sensitive, and one who liked so little to have his humanity, honesty and Christianity questioned. When Fate poisons her arrows, it is often with conscience.

Before he had started his career Peel had not had much time to develop his political ideas, and probably he had not much analysed his Tory assumptions. He had not written novels on which to base his political creed, nor had he wandered through the manufacturing districts looking picturesque and profound. It was not like him, and he had not had time. He went on assuming much, but he learnt something from experience in power, and something also, not from the youthful manufacture of generalizations, or the exercise of profound powers of observation, but from sanity in understanding other men's ideas, and from sensibility in feeling their opposition. These are political attributes by no means to be despised, indeed a statesman cannot well do without them; but they were to fill too large a part of Peel's mind. There was sanity and sensibility and there was also fear, for behind Liberalism, in the darkness, possibly crouched Revolution.

§4. 1821-27

This is probably a true view of some of Peel's thoughts, but it must not be taken to explain too much. The six years following 1821, when he was Home Secretary under Lord Liverpool, with a seat in his Cabinet, were

[1] Croker, I, 170. Parker, I, 90 (March 25, 1813, last para.), 341.

years of confusing events and conflicting emotions, most difficult to straighten out into clear lines of policy. Particular needs and momentary feelings cut across the current till it became as turbid and rough as the pool below a mill-race.

Liberal shapes appeared in the confusion. For instance, there were Peel's legal Reforms. He listened as Home Secretary to the attacks continually made on the state of the law, and with the restless hands of the able and the restless conscience of the abused, he did great work and gained great praise, especially from the other side of the House; and he did not find such praise distasteful.[1] Then there were the beginnings of Free Trade, for which lesson he had no need to go outside the Government, for indeed some of its members were much more infected by the doctrine than were some of the other side. While the Opposition sometimes flirted with Agricultural distress the Government remembered Pitt and sat sometimes at the feet of the Radical, Ricardo. Liverpool and Huskisson were at least dilute Free Traders, indeed Huskisson was a fairly strong mixture, and Robinson, who was afterwards Goderich, was also impregnated. A policy of modified commercial reform was adopted with the aid of Reciprocity Treaties, and in the end even the Corn Laws were touched. Again it was the voice of Reason, and again Peel began to obey, and again her commands were not so readily attended to by all the rest of the Tory Party.

However, in these years Liberalism rallied not so often round Reason or Reform as round a man, a man over whom the Cabinet was continually and passionately divided. When in August 1822 Castlereagh was driven by the miseries of power to madness and suicide, it seemed necessary for the Ministry that Canning should succeed him, and in that September he took his place both as Foreign Secretary and Leader of the House of Commons. Soon he drew all attention to his oratory, his foreign policy, his Liberalism and himself. The

---

[1] Yonge's *Lord Liverpool*, III, 215 (Peel to Liverpool, Oct. 12, 1822).

thunder of his great phrases, the way he stood up to
the Despots on the Continent, the way, it was said,
he stood up to the Tories in the Cabinet, drew Liberal
applause, and, on the whole, strengthened the Ministry,
helping them to draw out from their feeble condition.
Here indeed was a succouring deity, a god to conciliate
Liberalism, and to oppose Parliamentary Reform. Only
such a god has an easier task in a play than in politics,
and is happier in a car than in a Cabinet of men.

Even before this Peel had been forced into a position
of natural and uncomfortable contrast to Canning. They
were both men who might reasonably hope some time
to be Prime Minister, and they were both in the Commons. Canning was the elder and much the more
eminent of the two, yet many men were already prepared
to follow Peel as a Minister in the Commons, and presumably some time as the head of all. More especially
did the Protestants desire Peel, for Canning was odious
to them, a pledged and prominent supporter of Catholic
Emancipation. It was their difference on this subject
that gave its emphasis to their potential rivalry, and might
make others desire to emphasize it still more, as it was
largely this difference that denied to Canning the honour,
which Peel enjoyed, of representing Oxford University
in Parliament. Canning would now come into the same
Cabinet, and men began to talk of Peel stipulating for
an equality of position, of his demanding the lead of
the Commons, if Canning was to be Foreign Secretary,
that thus he might share the mantle of Castlereagh.

Yet Peel did not desire that they should be rivals.
They had already served in the same Ministry, they
had met then on a friendly basis, and in the April of
1822 itself Croker had carried messages of good will
between them. Peel was careful to do nothing hostile to
Canning at Oxford, and there were two seats. Ambition need not divide them, for in all mortal probability
Peel could afford to wait. In the matter of policy
and of principle there was, it is true, their deep sharp
division on the Roman Catholic question. But must

that part them entirely and for ever? Only the wildest
spirits believed that a purely "Protestant" or purely
"Catholic" Tory Ministry could stand in the House of
Commons. It was a question on which all reasonable
men must agree to differ, if they could, while other
things might attract Peel to this great charmer of Liberals.
You may easily disapprove of some of a god's opinions,
or of some of his actions; still you are usually anxious
to be friends. You may need his help, you may admire
the divine nature, or you may fear thunderbolts.

Canning's entry into the Ministry found Peel at his
best, disclaiming any ambition that could prevent Canning from becoming both Foreign Minister and Leader
of the Commons. The personal honesty that he had
made his ideal forbade the violent and selfish ambition
which the suggested stipulations would have implied,
while he was genuinely anxious not to intrigue against
a man so necessary.

It need not detract from all this to say that perhaps
he was not very severely tempted. Canning had declared
that he must have the full inheritance, and most men,
even Tories and Protestants, Lord Liverpool and the
Duke of Wellington, knew that the Ministry must have
Canning. For Peel to have stood out alone against
such men for a distinction which he did not want would
have been both dangerous and foolish. This time his
caution may have saved his honesty most of its trouble.[1]

Yet Canning's entry was but the beginning of troubles.
When the door of the Cabinet room had shut behind him
and the new-comer began to develop himself, some of
his hosts grew hostile, and sometimes lost their tempers.
France, Spain, Portugal, Greece and South America
all supplied subjects for a Liberal Foreign policy, and
for acrimonious contentions. Foreign politics were not
Peel's province, and much of this war was carried on,
it seems, over his head; still he was in the Cabinet, he
must in some way participate. He must develop his
relations with Canning and the Canningites, and those

[1] Parker, I, 320, 327 ff.

relations might help considerably to decide the direction in which his life was to leave the watershed; and unfortunately, at this period, Peel meandered.

He by no means always supported Canning's foreign policy, and he is sometimes reported as personally hostile to Canning himself, or jealous of the promotion of his supporters. He was definitely attached in one important particular to the side that opposed Canning, and he was generally attached to Canning's chief opponent.[1] Nevertheless his relations seem on the whole to have been friendly. Canning admired Peel's honesty and ability, and may not have desired to lose to his enemies the prestige Peel gained as Home Secretary. Peel was found to be "fresh minded," susceptible to new ideas, drawn towards Huskisson's economics, and even in Irish matters to have a healthy distaste for Orangemen; while Canning, on his side, had by no means entirely deserted the cause of order. In November 1825 Canning could write to Peel that there was but one subject on which they did not cordially agree, and in 1827 Peel could repeat the statement, as they finally parted.

It was true; yet whatever Canning was, Peel was certainly a Tory. He felt himself to be one, in a Tory Ministry which was pledged to resist such things as a Reform of Parliament. Even his own reforms had behind them the idea of controlling innovations, and of showing that a Tory could be reasonable. Discipline and order still had his allegiance; he was to show that he could sincerely resist Constitutional Reform; he was to harbour the proper fears of Revolution. He still represented Oxford and so stood in a special relation to the Church; and there was always Ireland and the Roman Catholic question. If he was a nascent Liberal, he would come into his new life with many of the thoughts and most of the livery of the old.

And also trailing crowds of Tories would he come.

---

[1] Buck: *Court of George IV*, Vol. II, 99. Hist. MSS. Commission Earl Bathurst's papers, 543 (Arbuthnot to Bathurst, Aug. 29, 1823).

Tory eyes had already turned to Peel, though some
began to think that he agreed too much with Canning.
He mixed largely in high Tory society and he stayed
at their great houses, though sometimes he wished to
shrink back into his home, and sometimes he did not
like the ways of life he saw.   When he stayed, for instance, at Sudbourne, Lord Hertford's house, he felt
uncomfortable and disapproving, and he went to his
bedroom to write to his wife to congratulate her on not
being asked.[1]   He did not hold aloof from even the
most extreme Tories in the Cabinet; he defended old
Eldon in the House of Commons when Canning abandoned him; Eldon went so far as to ask Peel for advice,
and Peel went with Eldon and Westmoreland to the Pitt
Club dinner where no other Ministers were present.[2]
But most of all he drew into close relations with the other
god of the Cabinet, the Duke of Wellington.

Deaf, silent, abrupt, thin as a lath, covered with all
the honour the nation could give him, without much
pride and without any pose, entirely devoted to the
nation's weal, used not to discussion but to command,
the Duke sat at the Cabinet Board, his hard eye on
Canning, full of dislike, listening to his long harangues,
not always hearing, but always suspecting.   He was
riddled with suspicion, the suspicions of a deaf man who
is not always sure what they are saying, the suspicions
of a soldier matched with talkative civilians, the suspicions of a hero who reasonably expects for his
opinions a consideration that it is impossible to give them.
He often complained that he was neglected, that he was
entirely deserted; and with these suspicions came anger,
breaking out into interminable memoranda and expressions of unmeaning strength, for he had an idea that by
making them stronger he made them plainer.   It was
not that he was a gloomy man; he enjoyed society, talking considerably in his own racy and attractive natural

[1] *Private Letters*, 62.
[2] Parker, I, 360 ff. Buck: *Court of George IV*, Vol. II, 61.   Twiss' *Eldon*,
Vol. I, 555.   But *Diary of Lady Shelley*, Vol. II, 173.

style, and he enjoyed using a jerky playfulness with young women and children; indeed sometimes he sought opportunity for this in rather silly ways. But often he was angry, angry because he suspected, because he did not always understand the needs of politics, because he was an elderly man struggling against what was too strong for him, and because he had great fears. His patriotism had to subdue him again to public service, to send him back to usefulness, grumbling and full of a fatalist's set grief at the constant recurrence of such subjections, yet secretly sometimes proud of them.

In 1819 the Duke joined the Cabinet, on condition that if they went out he was not to be expected to join them in opposition, for he evidently felt that he should be no party man. But he was Tory enough in his fears of revolution, and very soon knew that he must serve his country in menacing weather. The sky was black already, there were short but violent gusts of wind; perhaps there was a storm under the horizon. At one time he foreboded mutiny in the Army, at another he warned a general to keep his troops together so as to be sure of success against any mob, and not to scatter them for police, since some murder and pillage could not be prevented.[1] He felt that the present Ministry must in no case resign, for if their opponents obtained power they would, while in office, so confuse matters that the renewal of executive government might be almost impossible when they were expelled. Perhaps his fears about order at home may have grown dim as conditions improved, but abroad there was usually much to excite them. He was dogged by memories. He was infected by fear of Jacobinism enlisting its forces in every country, and causing another general war. For him the path of constituted authority was the path of safety, and of peace; besides, he had some natural affection for constituted authority. The Duke could be reasonable when faced with a specific question, he could be honourable when interpreting a definite agreement, but these generalized fears are very dangerous, and

---

[1] Duke of Wellington's *Despatches*, New Series, Vol. I, p. 127.

this one penetrated too many of his actions.   Meanwhile the symbol for all truckling to, appealing to and encouraging Liberalism or Jacobinism became incarnate in one man, and him he hated.   This man was Canning.

Of the two gods it was to the Duke that Peel paid his most solemn vows.   The Duke naturally appreciated Peel, as an undoubted Tory, an enemy of the Catholic claim, which the Canningites favoured, a man who had the cause of Ireland at heart and was effective in its service, and a man whom the Duke felt, always, that he could trust.   Both men believed that a purely "protestant" Ministry was impossible, and it was natural that Peel on his side should be attracted by such a leader of so many like opinions and of so great a name.   He drew close, he often wrote to the Duke, he sent him documents about Ireland, he sometimes seemed to lean on his support, and wished him back, when there was crisis at home and the Duke was in Russia.   He named one of his sons after him, and the Duke stood godfather; the two seem often to have met in Society, though Peel could not approve of the way in which the Duke treated his wife. It was natural that their fortunes grew to be bound together with great results for the nation.   It is the natural current of events that brings into uneasy partnership the incompatible.[1]

Meanwhile, if there was nothing else to stop a straight road to Liberalism there were always the questions of the Roman Catholics and of Ireland in general.   They were not always pressing, yet they were always there; and Peel had not forgotten and could not forget the past. He smarted under suggestions that a new Irish Government more "Catholic" in texture would be juster than that had been in which he served.   He was shocked when one of his old friends was dismissed to make room for these arrangements, and he would not believe in the efficacy of the concessions that the new men practised.[2] He still adhered to the Protestant cause, he still was

---

[1] *Private Letters*, 96.   Parker, I, 368, 394.
[2] Parker, I, 307, 342, 417.

anxious for the discipline of Ireland and desired to put
down the agitators and societies that disturbed her. Yet
he was in a mixed Cabinet and he differed over Emancipation with his fellow Ministers in the Commons, and
as Home Secretary was responsible for order in Ireland.

The position was very difficult, and Canning and his
friends were not always quiescent on Irish matters. The
present was embarrassed, the future not hopeful, for
Peel said, though after the event, that he had long foreseen that the Catholic question would drive him out of
office. Peel's "Protestant" way seemed nothing but
an unpleasant blind alley. Unfortunately the alley was
not blind.

At one moment, in 1825, it seemed that the crisis was
come. The House of Commons passed resolutions in
favour of Emancipation and the payment of priests, and
Peel and Lord Liverpool determined to resign. But if
Lord Liverpool resigned, the Ministry was destroyed, for
it depended entirely upon him for its continuance; and
if Peel resigned so must Lord Liverpool, who was equally
committed. Of course it was urged on Peel how disastrous this would be, and he stayed in; he had to stay
in. This time his hand was not forced, nor was the
question settled, for the Lords declared against Emancipation, as did in their debates the Duke of York, the
heir to the throne, while there were hopes for the Protestants from an election. Apparently at this crisis
the Duke of Wellington suggested a settlement of the
whole problem, for to him the question was not one of
rigid, almost religious principle, but Peel felt himself so
tied that he could only offer resignation, and even that
he could not bring off.[1]

The Ministry drifted on to the election of 1826, and
its result was not immediately decisive. In England it
was not altogether unfavourable to the Protestants, but
in Ireland there appeared a new and fatal phenomenon.
The peasants broke away from their landlords, at whose
command they had always before voted, and gave their

[1] Parker, I, 373 ff. Bathurst, 579-85. Duke's *Desp.*, II, pp. 465, 592, etc.

votes to the nominees of their priests. At first Peel
thought that this might be a momentary disease, but
he grew very gloomy. There was distress at home and
religious hatred in Ireland. Men would try in the new
Parliament to force Emancipation through against all
obstacles, and as always when faced with a difficulty,
Peel wanted more facts. He wanted to know about the
dangers from Irish Roman Catholics if Emancipation
were passed, for "when I see it inevitable, I shall (taking
due care to free my motives from suspicion) try to make
the best terms for the future security of the Protestant."
But Parliament would not give the *coup de grâce*, and
in 1827 the new House of Commons rejected Emancipation by 4 votes.[1] By that time Lord Liverpool's
calamity had overtaken him.

There was then, it seems, fair chance for Peel to try
the pains of conflicting emotions. He was a friend of
the Duke, and to a lesser extent, of Canning. He was
a Tory, an enemy of Emancipation, a lover of order, and
yet in some way a Reformer and a supporter of Huskisson's economics. He was held by principle and by the
past, he was susceptible to some of the needs of the
present and the future. Lord Liverpool's Ministry
ought to have been the scene of a pretty tug-of-war with
Peel dragged this way and that in all the agonies of an
interesting and tragic indecision. But very often in
politics men have not foresight, concentration or time
to realize the drama they are enacting. Unlike the
fortunate heroes of plays, they have to think of a thousand things foreign to the question in hand, and thinking
of them they must dismiss their real problems with but
makeshift solutions and stumble on, with their attention
elsewhere, towards their climax.

Peel was satisfied with Lord Liverpool's Ministry, and
with his place in it. It probably expressed his desires
in politics; it certainly satisfied his ambition for the
present, and it was not without its promises for the
future, if it should survive into the future. Emanci-

[1] Parker, I, 412, 413, 422.

pation was not always pressing, and the divisions that were to come may not have always seemed inevitable; and at any rate what is inevitable is not all the time relevant.

It seems probable that these years were happy ones for Peel, though his health was not always good and he still sometimes dreamed of travel. Yet working efficiently was not really unpleasant to him, especially when that work was often widely appreciated. He was happily married; he built a house in Whitehall Gardens; he patronized Art; he enjoyed the society of Sir Thomas Lawrence, and, once at least, he seems to have lived beyond his income. Yet all the time he was serving in a Cabinet which was the scene of the quarrels of gods; and what gods put asunder no man can join. It was a Cabinet undermined by the Roman Catholic question, and one that depended on the thread of an old man's life. In 1827 the thread broke, for in that February Lord Liverpool had a stroke, and was withdrawn from the Treasury into private life and a living death, actually to die in 1828. Nemesis was up with her prey.

§5. 1827–29

Like some long indeterminate winter Lord Liverpool's Ministry managed to persist from February 1827 to the middle of April; but it was no longer a Ministry, it was merely a theatre of war. Behind closed doors, and sometimes in the dark and sordid recesses of George IV's bosom the crisis went on, far too complicated and controversial to be described in this place. In any event the old arrangement was doomed. Canning declared that the Prime Minister must either be himself or his puppet; the Duke could not ultimately accept Canning's supremacy, and Peel wanted the reformation of Lord Liverpool's Ministry as it had existed previously under a Protestant Peer of enough weight to make his office a reality. He felt that he could not remain in office under so eminent a supporter of Emancipation as Canning; his duties would be difficult, and what was

worse, his motives would be doubted.   The old game
was ended, the cards had to be shuffled and dealt again.

Of course they quarrelled over the shuffling, as men
usually do when they suspect each other of cheating.
Irritation, suspicion and intrigue already troubled the
Ministry and did not disappear in the throes of its final
calamity.   Like a fat harlequin the King watched and
confused the drama, it would seem with malicious
humour.   He hesitated in deciding whom to choose for
a Prime Minister; and while he hesitated he was pestered
by pantaloons in the Protestant peers, Newcastle, Rutland
and Londonderry who lectured and bored and bullied
him not to abandon their cause.   However, at the end
the clown was preferred and the policeman disappointed.
The King chose Canning, who was by this time a favour-
ite, and the Duke resigned in a huff over an odd punctilio
and a wild suspicion, even throwing up the command
of the Army.   He was followed by Eldon, Westmoreland, Bathurst and Melville; and Peel felt that he too
must go, though he carefully told Canning that it was
on one fatal question only that they differed.   Lord
Liverpool's Ministry had divided at last, and Peel was on
the Tory side.

The crisis seems to have left him annoyed.   In the
formal letter in which he took his leave, his attitude is
as correct and as intelligible as if he were already in
marble in Westminster Abbey.   But he was still of
ordinary mortal flesh, and he had blood that was often
hot, and ears that could not help listening; he had heard
and believed stories of Canning's intrigues and he
showed some heat in the angry controversy about the
actions and retirement of the Duke and his fellows.
Even in his formal letter taking leave of Canning there
is an undercurrent of annoyance.   Canning had seemed
to underestimate Peel's reason for departure, and Peel
had felt that the old Ministry had been wilfully destroyed.   After all, said he, if they were divided over
Emancipation, they were united against such things as
Parliamentary Reform.   Yet he thought that his mind

was easy.   Remorse was an ill that Peel often avoided.
He had had never a doubt, he said, as to what he should
do in the circumstances, and thinking it over afterwards
he was sure he was right.   He knew he was honest, he
knew he had plotted with no one, his retirement was
not due to ambition, but was plainly demanded by consistency.   His conduct had certainly been intelligible
and, if honour and consistency were all, then all was
right.[1]

But all was not right.   There was pique, there was
principle, there was possibly pride in his mind, but were
there any plans?   The future held, or should have held
matter for thought.   If Peel and the Duke were ever to
form a Ministry that would stand, they must have other
assistance than their present allies could give.   They had
long known they could not form a lasting Ministry from
old Tories and opponents of Emancipation.   Even Peel
and the Duke themselves did not entirely agree on all
topics; for there is evidence to show that they were not
always of one mind on the modification of the duties on
corn proposed in 1828.[2]   Unfortunately man cannot
live by pique alone.   Unfortunately the future might
demand a higher unity from the opposition than could be
got from a common cause for annoyance.

Canning's Ministry, the miserable child of genius
and royal favour, wasted from birth.   Canning himself
had been ill before it came into being, and now that it
crowned his career he was hurrying to add another to
those ghosts for whom crowns were too heavy.   The
thing deserted by so many of the Tories had had to be
suckled by Whigs, and of the Whigs some felt they
had too much principle to join or support it, and they
fiercely attacked it instead.   The members of it were
divided between themselves on Parliamentary Reform,
the King was resolved to prevent Emancipation, and
most of them were pledged to it; in fact, the Duke said
they embodied an untruth.   Still they had their meaning

[1] Parker, I, 448 ff.   Hodder's *Life of Shaftesbury*, I, 96.
[2] Bathurst, p. 640.

and their reason, they had their god with them, and with a present deity men need not care for logic in the services or consistency in the congregation. Canning was their reason for existence, and by the end of August poor Canning was dead.

It was thought by some that the Duke would be asked to form a Government, but the King appointed Lord Goderich, a follower of Canning's. He had been Robinson in Lord Liverpool's Ministry and he was to be Earl of Ripon, for he fled up the steps of the peerage pursued by his reputation. He was not without ability, and though men laughed at him they liked him. But he was feeble and ineffective, with too little energy and too many tears. His task was almost impossible for any man, and his Ministry was from the start the feeblest of all imagined Ministries. As things developed, Peel felt more and more sure that he was right in his retirement. Had he stayed in, his position would have been embarrassing, his reputation embarrassed. He was safe in retirement—retirement not disappointing, but long foreseen as the likely end of his course on the Catholic question, retirement dignified by indifference to seeming royal displeasure—and other men were in trouble over "such questions as Reform, Catholic questions, Repeal of Corporation and Test Acts." In August he viewed the political world, so far as he was personally concerned, with "great complacency," in September he said he had almost become uninterested in politics. He had avoided disgrace, he could never regret his decision, he cared not what happened. It may have been a pleasant pause before great future discomfort.[1]

Meanwhile Lord Goderich rocked his stillborn baby in its cradle, and all his tears could not enliven it. The King and the Whigs both tried to have their will with it, and the difficulties grew more intense. At last in January 1828 Goderich resigned without ever facing Parliament; the King sent for the Duke, and the Duke in his turn sent for Peel to help him.

[1] E.g. Parker, II, 14. Add. MSS. 40,343; 14.

It was a grim summons to receive in that grim season, for it meant that he must turn again and face the troubles that he had avoided with so much dignity. He came up gloomily to London from Maresfield House where he had been living with his family, most loath to leave his wife, most loath to plunge again into politics. "My heart," he wrote with passion, "is set upon Home and not upon ambition." So he came to the destinies of the nation almost like a schoolboy going back to school, and like a schoolboy he could not escape his fate. He came back to the damp streets of London, to his great empty town house to confer continually late and early with the Duke of Wellington.

From the first Peel insisted on one thing. The Ministry could not rest on the rotten foundations of old prejudices and ancient statesmen. He must reunite the old party as it existed at Lord Liverpool's death. For he needed more assistance in the Commons than his present allies could afford; he needed the followers of Canning. And he knew that he needed not only their persons, but also their policy. With the world as it was at home and abroad, with the present position "in respect to Agriculture, to commerce, and to Ireland, no attempt at an Ultra Government ought to be dreamed of." It was the old problem; you could not put a new world into old fetters. Of course it might be that the old problem had outlasted the old remedy; diseases are long and some medicines perishable. Yet Peel prescribed Lord Liverpool's Ministry with its satisfactory relations with Liberalism. The animosities of the last few months should be reconciled in a Cabinet formed under the ægis of the commanding national position of the Duke of Wellington.

But it could not be the old Ministry, for now more places than before must be allotted to Liberals. So Peel wanted the room of some of his old friends, and possibly he did not want their company. The Duke and he thought at first that some of them might retire owing to age or to a desire to relieve the Government

from embarrassment. Considering the usual impor-
tunity of the obsolete, the hope was perhaps desperate.
Certainly it was very generally disappointed. When
Eldon and Westmoreland were left out many old Tories
were angry and Eldon used a word to the Duke about
the Government that he would not put in a letter to a
lady. Peel hardened his heart against the Ultra-Tories.
He criticized them, and he said he did not care for their
dissatisfaction. His task was hard, and he grew weary,
perplexed and dejected, and also determined; indeed
at one time he became almost exalted. He said that
he would lead the Commons alone even without Canning's friends, and fight to the end, and he began to
breathe resolution and dissolution. But at last the trouble
was over, Canning's party was captured and the Ministry
formed. In the Cabinet the Canningites had Huskisson
their leader, and Grant, Dudley and Palmerston, while
Lamb, afterwards Lord Melbourne, was Chief Secretary
for Ireland.[1]

There were others in the Cabinet who would be afterwards of great importance in Peel's life. There was
Goulburn with his dome-like forehead thinly covered, his
pedestrian party ideas, and his good workman-like ability;
Lyndhurst, weak and able, sane and sophisticated, with
the most impressive forearm and finger in the House of
Lords; Aberdeen with his short dark whiskers, pure and
innocent heart and slightly morose appearance, and
Ellenborough with his huge head of hair, his disorderly
mind and his vanity, ability and ambition. Herries was
at the Board of Trade; there were two of the older
men, Bathurst and Melville, and Eldon, Westmoreland and Sidmouth were not included. Peel was well
equipped with a good representative Cabinet. Foresight and insight may be virtues mainly invented by
writers of their own memoirs or of other people's history,
but again it must be asked for the sake of comment, if
not of criticism, was Peel equipped for the future?

[1] *Private Letters*, p. 103 ff. Parker, II, 26 ff. Twiss' *Eldon*, II, 22.
Despatches, Vol. IV.

Peel and the Duke seem to have regarded the quarrels that ended the past Ministry as personal and evanescent; they had been divided on Canning's claims, not on Canningite principles; and the Duke increased the anger of the Ultra-Tories by saying in the Lords that he had had no political enmity against Canning. Both Peel and the Duke were mistaken. Soon controversial matters confronted the Ministry, the future of Greece, the duties on corn, and with them came divisions along the old line, the Duke and his friends against Huskisson and the Canningites. Peel acted as a makeweight—a makeweight often inclining to the Liberal side—and the Duke was sometimes embarrassed and sometimes displeased to find Peel against him. Neither Greece nor corn proved fatal, but these disputes left their mark; they began to excite the distaste of various Ministers, and the Duke grew annoyed that in his Cabinet so many men were against him. He said that he now saw the evil of joining with men with whom he had been recently in disagreement. He was going to show that, if he had learned his lesson late, he had learned it very thoroughly.

The Canningites remained an undigested block in the Cabinet, the allegiance they owed to their dead master still strong enough to hold the most reluctant of them to unwilling obedience. The Ministry was strong; even the Duke had made sacrifices for its continuance, and Huskisson was unwilling that he and his friends should leave it to become old Tory and to maintain abroad old tyrannies. It expressed Peel's desires; he wanted to keep the Liberals, and Palmerston thought at one time that Peel would manage to smooth away the difficulties, he was so right-minded and liberal and "so up with the spirit of the times." It is hard to say that any one's desires were futile, and very much harder to say that they ought not to have been entertained, yet it would seem that the spirit of the living Duke and the dead Canning were still fatal to Peel.

The crisis which ended these divisions was a little absurd, but then it had for its protagonists Huskisson

and the Duke of Wellington, each of whom was quite
capable of absurdities. It arose out of a division in
the Ministry that had been settled by a compromise,
was brought to a crisis by accident, and was aggravated
to a catastrophe by folly, wilfulness and suspicion.
Owing to the miscarriage of a Cabinet compromise over
the franchises of Penryn and East Retford, Huskisson
happened to vote against Peel in the Commons, and Peel
managed to get himself accused of dishonourable conduct. Huskisson often was unwise, Peel was over-
sensitive, and both gave rein to their peculiar follies.
Peel was hurt by the abuse, and Huskisson before he
went to bed wrote to the Duke offering, but only offering, his resignation.

He did not want to go, but he felt that he ought to do
this much, having voted against the leader of the House.
The Duke knew the danger of seeming to treat him
harshly, but he felt that the Canningites might want to
force him to beg them to remain in the Ministry so that
he might remain in their hands. He demanded a with-
drawal of the resignation, and the Canningites declared
there was no resignation to withdraw. It was a vicious
circle, but the circle alone was supplied by immediate
circumstances, the vice had been laid up in the past
months, indeed in the past years, of disagreement. Perhaps Peel might have broken it, but he was annoyed with
Huskisson and for the moment did not regret his going.
Moreover, he did not wish to quarrel with the Duke, with
whom he agreed on the question of recalled resignations.
So do our toys break, and we do not always cry as they
are swept up off the floor. The Canningites, so hardly
secured in January, in May left the Ministry; the mixed
Ministry had been split again, and again Peel was on the
Tory side; and in the end he had been governed not by
policy, but by nerves.[1]

But was it a Tory Ministry that had been left behind?
Parties had been overshadowed lately by personalities.

[1] Bulwer's *Palmerston*, I, 226 ff. Ellenborough's *Diary*, Vol. I, to 133.

The Canningites had showed that they were ready to serve with either party; Lord Grey the Whig was spoken of for the Duke's Ministry; and now the Duke maintained in a memorandum that Huskisson had not left them on any question of principle. Principles, he said, were only dragged in to aggravate these unfortunate differences, and indeed he did not know what the principles might be that should have divided them. "We hear a great deal of Whig principles, and Tory principles, and Liberal principles and Mr. Canning's principles; but I confess that I have never seen a definition of any of them, and cannot make to myself a clear idea of what any of them mean." It is an interesting statement to come from a Prime Minister.

The truth is that the Duke was not conveniently built for use in party politics. He looked too directly to the immediate needs, as he understood them, of Government and the safety of life and property—of order and of peace —to think constantly enough of party principles or to realize in what way others thought of them. Moreover, many of his opinions have an attractively home-made appearance, comparing with ordinary party opinions rather as peasant-made dolls compare with the ordinary manufactured variety. He was not therefore fully equipped with a bundle of sensitive and regular party principles to spread like antennæ over the whole field of politics. When Lord Dudley, a Canningite, was Foreign Secretary in his Ministry, he said of him, "He has no zeal for liberty, that is true, but on the other hand he is quite free from the prejudice of the old Tories both as to Church and State."[1] Prejudice and principle are often but two sides of the same coin.

Nor was the Duke likely to be amenable to the sanctions which usually force consistency. He was too secure in his reputation and too well hidden behind the iron walls of his own self-reliance and the golden walls of the House of Lords to be amenable to public opinion, which he was inclined to regard as usually wilful and always

[1] Duke's *Despatches*, IV, 452. *Letters to Ivy*, Dudley, p. 333.

ignorant. The Duke could not but be a strange party
man. Nevertheless he was a party man and knew quite
well what party it was he wished to retain. He believed
with a kind of desperate assurance in what he called the
Government Party—the great interests, the Church, the
City and certainly the gentry and the landowners. He
believed in the sensible people who would wish not to
lose their property or to have their throats cut for the sake
of a word. Even these were unsatisfactory. Men
would run after principle, men would shirk their political
duties and shelve their political difficulties, by writing
to him. The country gentlemen were greedy but not
steady. Some of them in 1830 even showed a tendency
which the Duke could not understand to coalesce with
the Radicals. In fact, the Duke had a respect, if not
affection, for what must be called the Tory Party, and
consequently, whatever he said, the Duke was really a
Tory after all.

There were great differences between Peel and this
hard compact mass of apotheosized iron. Peel was
younger and more liberal. He was much more exposed
to hurt from the ravages of other men's criticism, his
position was less sublime, his life had been entirely passed
in politics and he was a member of the House of Commons. Moreover, he represented there the University
of Oxford, and so stood in a very special relation to the
Church; and in this connection he delighted. It was
redolent of culture and virtue, it introduced him to
problems of intellectual interest, it was a little outside
the sphere of the ordinary thumb-marked problems and
shop-soiled ambitions of general politics, and yet it was
an honour to him. His time at Oxford had left him with
affection and interest for her, and with one great friend,
Dr. Lloyd, a fat, frank child of nature who was also a
Doctor of Divinity, to whom Peel wrote continually about
general affairs and the most various topics as well. He
toyed with University Reform, he even ventured into
theology, and expressed opinions on Absolution which
Lloyd was forced to pronounce heretical, though Peel

thought he could defend them out of South and Barrow.
He sounded Lloyd as to the opinions of the Church and
University, and when matters respecting the Church
and morals came before Parliament he sometimes begged
Lloyd's research and advice; for though Peel usually
knew the kind of things in that line that he ought to
oppose, he did not always know the arguments against
them.[1]

Behind Lloyd lay Oxford, at that time a town of
mysteries, of grotesque personalities and strange un-
worldly opinions, and behind Oxford the Church.   Oxford's Toryism had been much excited during Canning's
Ministry, but Lloyd felt that then it had been screwed
up to an unnaturally high pitch.   As he once told Peel,
they took there very little interest in ecclesiastical matters
"except as far as they personally concern themselves."
Yet all men dislike finding that their rubbish has been
destroyed by others, and when the clergy lost privileges,
for which they did not care a jot, they discovered afterwards feelings of instinctive irritation.   Lloyd said that
when Peel abolished benefit of clergy they asked what it
was that made Peel so anxious to get rid of it, and the
Bishop of Llandaff put it into a Charge as evidence of the
existing tendency to take all the clergy's privileges away
from them.[2]   But spasmodic irritation is not a power
strong enough to control nations, especially when it is
not well represented in the House of Commons, and by
1828 Peel found himself struggling there against forces
that on many Church matters he could not resist.   Even
known friends of the Church seemed to show a desire to
be reasonable on minor matters, and he himself desired
for the Church's sake to surrender what was useless and
might be dangerous to her.[3]   Split hairs do not twist
into good ropes with which to bind a Parliament, and Peel
found the arguments of theologians of little use in an
assembly of impatient secularly-minded men, restless

---

[1] See Add. MSS. 40,342 and 40,343 *passim*.   Parker, e.g. Vol. I, 322, 385, 438.
[2] Add. MSS. 40,343; 174.   [3] Add. MSS. 40,343; 166; 183.

with the approach of dinner, or dull through its after-effects.

In February 1828 Peel had to submit to a defeat in the House of Commons over the repeal of the Acts imposing Sacramental tests for the exclusion of Dissenters from certain offices. It was not a very serious defeat; the test had been long rendered inoperative, many bishops and Churchmen objected to it as a profanation of a Sacrament, and Peel was enabled to frame and carry a satisfactory settlement of the problem. But Eldon and others were angry, saying that the Church and principle had been basely deserted by the Government; some of the bishops got fluttered, and young men at Oxford could make this repeal a landmark in the secularization of the State.

Eldon was soon to have a greater excuse for anger and the opposition of Churchmen, and others a more notable stage on which to appear futile. In 1828 the question of Roman Catholic Emancipation developed very swiftly. In May the House of Commons voted in favour of Emancipation by a majority of 6. At the end of June the trouble of 1826 developed to its climax and on a vacancy for the County of Clare the peasants elected O'Connell, himself a Roman Catholic, instead of Vesey Fitzgerald, a member of the Government, a landowner of the county and a friend of Emancipation. Throughout the summer trouble went on all over Ireland, huge meetings were held by the Roman Catholics, who assembled perfectly peaceably in military formations. The Protestant Clubs came unpleasantly into notice, and the whole country stirred and seethed with dangerous expectations, which were shared by Anglesey, the Lord-Lieutenant. He talked of massacres, brought evidence of the possibilities of mutiny among the Roman Catholic soldiers, and pleaded almost unreasonably hard for the granting of Emancipation before the fighting began.

Poor Peel was honesty's fool, and mocked by his past consistency. He had conscientiously held up the passing of Emancipation. Yet he was unwilling that the House

E

of Lords should continue to sustain alone the opposition
to it, at the cost of perpetual disagreement between the
two Houses, while he had long been very unwilling that
the measure should be openly prevented by the opposition of the Crown.   An election was impossible; in 1826
there had been an election with full reference to Emancipation, and now it was not certain what chaos or what
representatives an election would produce in Ireland.
Ireland seemed to be slipping and sliding on the greasy
edge of civil war, and yet in the House of Commons
there was a majority in favour of Emancipation, and
the measures necessary to quiet Ireland might be refused
if Emancipation, the obvious concession, were refused
also.   Peel knew from experience how much the divisions on this subject had already hampered the executive
government.

The knot must be cut, Emancipation must be passed.
It might conciliate and quiet the Roman Catholics; Peel
thought it would not, but he felt that its passing would
at least reunite the Protestants.   It could only be passed
by disturbing the equilibrium that had held it up.   There
must be in power a Ministry that could pilot the measure
through the Lords and past the King.   There was only
one Ministry that could do it; indeed, after the futilities
of the last year it seemed as if there was only one Ministry that could exist at all.   The Duke's Ministry must
pass Emancipation, and Peel said he would support it
from outside the Ministry.

And again he could not retire.   In May the Ministry
had been weakened by the loss of the Canningites; by
the end of the year it was to be further weakened by the
loss of Anglesey.   The Duke agreed with Peel on the
necessities of Emancipation, but already he was appalled
by his difficulties, and he became very gloomy.   He
felt that he had made great sacrifices in becoming Prime
Minister, and he was not pleased with his followers'
gratitude; they had been "seeking for curiosities" against
him in the case of the Test Acts.   Now he was called
on to settle at once a problem in which others had found

enough material for years and years of continuous discussion; and as the autumn of 1828 turned into winter,
difficulties began to increase.   Aided by shuffling and
equivocation the King started his last fight for the old
Protestant cause, and the heads of the Church, when consulted, declared against the measure.   The Duke could
not see that Peel was bound to resign, and he knew he
would need him very badly.   He seemed to despair and
Peel began to doubt if the Duke would succeed in carrying the measure without him.   When Peel put his hand
to the plough he neither looked back nor yet always very
far forward—and after all to plough a good furrow it is
best not to look at the hills beyond, nor the heavens
above—so he consummated what many thought was the
first great betrayal of his life; he stayed in office, and, as
a Minister, himself proposed in 1829 the measure to
which he had so long, and with such honest, such conscious, such public-consistency objected.[1]

He can be admired; the necessity was sharp, his
motives patriotic, his actions courageous, and his errors
pardonable.   He could not have been expected to know
for what he was preparing.   Fidelity to party was as
yet not highly developed, and this was a question that
divided his party.   The system of alternative and possible Governments was not in easy running order and it
is instructive to notice how very little, in discussing this
crisis, Peel considered the possibility of the Duke's
resigning in favour of some more consistent supporter
of Roman Catholics.   Peel can be admired and excused.
But at least it was to be shown that even then to sacrifice
party and principle in face of needs however great is to
pay the bills of the present at the expense of the future.
It may be necessary, but it is not cheap.

In 1829 the measure was carried.   The work was
hard, and the abuse terrible.   Peel lost Oxford; he
resigned from the seat, under an honourable scruple,
before he proposed the measure; he allowed himself to
be put forward again and was beaten by Sir Robert

[1] Peel's *Memoirs*, I (*passim*).   Duke's *Despatches*, V, 44.

Inglis. It was hard on him, but men may be forgiven for unwillingness to let the University seem to change its mind in a moment at the bidding of a Minister, and it was on this ground that Newman, for instance, voted for Inglis. Peel lost more than Oxford. His surrender on Emancipation was always afterwards remembered against him, and by men of all parties. Even the dead seemed to accuse him, for he appeared to have abandoned Canning for a principle which he deserted as soon as Canning was dead. Evil opinions of Peel continued to hang about in politics, clinging to him and cloaking him. An awkward shy man often seems to be subtle, and some felt that Peel was sly, deep, ambitious, with a hobby in betrayals. This was monstrously unjust, but it was perhaps natural. The change was very marked and sudden; and though such changes may be in every way necessary, and their agents entirely right-minded and admirable, it is not men's instinct to like them. Men should know by now that consistency is only the luxury of the irresponsible; they should be thankful to those who have strength and courage to eat their words. Yet though men live by treasons they will still dislike the most pure-hearted traitor.

Peel was not pleased with what he had had to do. Yet he was sure that he had been right; sometimes it seems almost as if he was a little exhilarated by the contemplation of the masterful and self-sacrificing spirit that had carried so hard a task to success. It was well that he should have some compensation. Emancipation had lost him Oxford for ever, and possibly the support of the Church. It may have lost him poor Lloyd, who died soon after, killed, it was said, by these turmoils. It had certainly lost him his peculiar connection with the Ultra-Tories.

But had Peel lost all connection with the Church? All his life he was unquestionably loyal to it, and all his life he kept somewhere concealed about him the remains of old Church and State principles. Within the year of 1829 he renewed the grant Lord Liverpool had made for building churches in manufacturing areas. In the past Lord Liverpool had attracted pious Churchmen especially by his great improvements in the use of Church patronage; Peel was a man of unblemished life, and continued Liverpool's purity of motive in his appointments. Besides, at that time there was a wave of morality in all the country, which much affected the kind of demands that were made on a Government.[1] Much of this force was made up of Dissenters who hated the Tories, yet some of it might be available. There were religious men who were already Tory.

There was one young man, for instance, a Low Churchman, who felt that the Prime Minister of this country ought always to be imbued with religious principles, and who was as yet undoubtedly a friend of Peel's and in his party. He was an able and ambitious man who was morbidly sensitive and jealous and something of an egoist, and also entirely, steadfastly, and nobly devoted to his religion. He already dreamed of a public policy founded as immediately as possible on the dictates of Christianity, and, it might be, administered by himself. He was then Lord Ashley, but he was to be better known as Lord Shaftesbury.

Peel was a moral man, attracted by the claims of piety and desirous of its respect. Perhaps he might gain some support from the pious, and perhaps it might be desirable that he should be amenable to their suggestions. Perhaps since he was a Tory it would have been good for him to be a good political Churchman, for it may be that of Established things the Established Church should have been the soul. Yet before he was a pietist, a Churchman, or a Tory, he was a working statesman, and he knew very well that right has to wait on necessity, and that desire must be put through a sieve. In the womb of his sound sense of what was practicable there lay in embryo much good service for the nation, and for the Church itself; and also some tragedy.

[1] Add. MSS. 40,343; 14.

§ 6.   1829–32

A certain saint is reported to have stopped a plague mainly in order to remove a source of most unchristian dissension from among the doctors; and though the motives of the Duke and Peel in passing Emancipation were not entirely parallel, yet the difficulties they had hoped to abolish were almost more in St. Stephen's than on the other side of St. George's Channel.   Now that Roman Catholic Emancipation was passed, Peel felt that they ought to act as if they could count on large majorities in the Commons for schemes for subjecting Ireland to the experience of the blessings and the severities of civilization.   But if he had any hopes he was miscalculating.   The Protestant Tories continued to hold away from the Ministry.

The Duke was not pleased with this result.   He had never expected that the Protestants would still show signs of forming a regular opposition; it was unnatural, and he put it down to the sinister and malign influence of the King's brother, the Duke of Cumberland.   The Duke had not liked being carried away from his own proper party.   He had disliked dismissals and resignations on conscientious grounds, and he is said to have complained that "Men speak to their private friends or their mistresses and get heated as they talk and pledge themselves so that they create a new point of honour to be got over."   Politics are, of course, most inconvenient and embarrassing when they are a steeple-chase over points of honour.   Now that all was over he was anxious to regain Tory confidence and to do nothing more that would alienate it further; nothing at the moment for the Roman Catholics in Ireland; nothing much to gain other allies for his Ministry.[1]

He might have had other allies.   Liberal sympathies had been excited by what the Ministry had done and had suffered, by its resolute economy and by its weakness.

[1] E.g. Duke's *Desp.*, V, 52, 175, 280.   Parker, II, 115 ff.   Duke's *Desp.*, VI, 10 ff., 70, 239 ff.

Whigs and Liberals were still rather inclined to permeate
or influence the Government than to expel it.   There
was an unhealthy tendency towards Group government,
a tendency not only felt by Whigs.   Party unity might
have been lost, and with it among other things the
useful impetus parties may work up in opposition; it
might have meant the forfeiture of the Reform Bill and
also of reunited Toryism.   It is good sometimes that
men should return, scowling and boorish, to their own
traditions, for there are times when union is sterile
and segregation prolific.   But it is well to have real
and lively traditions to which to return.

The danger to the Tory party of adulteration by
Liberals was resisted by healthy feelings of the dis-
honour of coalition and by distasteful memories, by
strange illusions on the part of one man and by a
great weariness on the part of another.   The Duke remembered too well the period of coalition when Huskisson was in the Cabinet.   He admitted indeed that the
group outside his Ministry could turn him out, if united,
but he could not fully believe in the weakness of his
Government.   It is hard for a Government, when it is
conscious it has done right, not to think that it is gathering strength in the country; and it was hard for the
Duke to believe that the Government party would
ultimately abandon his government.   He felt that the
good sense of the country must show it that he had
done right in passing Emancipation.   It is a kind of
despair to trust to nothing more definite than the good
sense of the country.   But it may be that the Duke
was being led by his profoundest political beliefs towards
his profoundest political disaster; and that would be both
intelligible and fitting.   He was inclined to be sanguine,
but was not always happy.   He grew harassed and overworked, and was troubled by the King; and in November
1829 he cried of himself in a burst of discomfort:
"I believe there never was a man who suffered so much,
and to so little purpose."[1]

[1] *Desp.*, VI, 198, 293.   *Desp.*, VII, 24.   Croker, II, 57.

But what of Peel?   His fate is neither so intelligible nor so fitting.   For his desires had been wise and had become futile, and possibly no longer much moved him. The Canningites on whom he had insisted were gone; and ever since they had left there had been talk of how to supply their loss.   Some had thought of Lord Grey and the Whigs, and some of such young men as Stanley, afterwards Lord Derby, and Sir James Graham.   It was suggested that even if Huskisson was undesirable they might try other Canningites such as Palmerston.   But very little was done.   No doubt the Duke's obduracy, the crystallization of the parties in opposition, were in part causes of this, while there was a healthy feeling in the Cabinet that they ought not to let in Whigs. Moreover, at the beginning of 1830 the obscurity of politics concealed to a certain extent the Ministry's needs.   But very soon in that year it was at least patent that Peel needed more help than he got from his Treasury Bench, and that the Government was too often sustained by him alone.   However, Croker declared that Peel was satisfied with his position.   Perhaps he should have said that he was indifferent to it.

It was not that by now the Ministry was sterile, or Peel entirely inert.   In 1829 they gave a regular police force to London, a typical and useful product of Peel's Conservatism.   The Ministry's financial policy might be called Liberal and might forecast a still more Liberal policy for the future.   They practised the most stringent economy.   The new commercial policy was adhered to, and in 1830 Peel, Herries and Goulburn desired to impose an income tax and reduce indirect taxation, and thus relieve the poor.[1]   They had not left behind all Liberalism, they had only lost their Liberals.   But a little Liberalism is not an elixir of life, and Peel seems at this moment to have been more absorbed in the actual measures of the Ministry than in its chance of life, in its administration than in its future.   Perhaps he was suffering from one of his early political maladies.

[1] Ellenborough's *Diary*, Vol. II, 203–17.

For by the June of 1830 at latest the old weariness and discontent were upon him. Listless in decision, disagreeable in discussion, Peel toyed with the destinies of the nation like a tired man playing chess to his own and his neighbour's discomfort. He appeared to Lord Ellenborough, his colleague, to see the difficulties of the Government's position, but not to meet them with energy. He had wanted Stanley for the Ministry, but had wavered much. He was flat; the life had gone out of him, he seemed ill and broken. Desire had failed, except the desire to be gone, and the old dreams and the old resentments seem to have haunted him. He complained of his continual and fruitless attendance at the Commons, and Croker said that some time before he resigned the Duke had got hold of the idea that in any case Peel meant to leave them in order to enjoy domestic peace, perhaps to travel. The Duke was apparently wrong, yet his belief may have been a natural deduction from the tone of Peel's conversation. However, the current of events will not respect disillusionment, or wait for a tired man.[1]

1830 was a difficult year. There was distress in various parts of the country when it started, and since politics may breed on misery even when politics could neither be its cause or its cure, distress had its effects in the political world. The currency question had become exacerbated, and Attwood of Birmingham, who was possessed by a desire for a change in currency policy, turned his large popular organizations in a kind of despair to the cause of Reform of Parliament. There was a demand in the country for reduction of taxation, the country's substance was supposed to be squandered on lazy aristocrats both temporal and spiritual, and there were attacks on expenditure in the House of Commons largely led by Sir James Graham. Politics were doubtful, the Ministry weak, the country gentlemen distressed and discontented, the Ultra-

[1] Ellenborough's *Diary*, Vol. II, 270, 274, 288, 316. Croker, II, 77. Parker, II, 171. *Private Letters*, 126.

Tories still unreconciled, and in the course of the year the demand for Parliamentary Reform grew rapidly and to monstrous proportions.

But it is not intended to describe here the progress of the cause of Reform, nor the gradual crystallization of the party of the Whigs outside the Ministry. At first the Whigs had been less hostile to the Ministry than the Canningites and the Ultra-Tories. They had hoped for comprehension, and perhaps they had feared the success of others. But the Duke was cold and intractable, and to some of the Whigs the Ministry seemed criminally weak. When Lord Grey came up to Parliament in the spring of 1830 he showed great hostility and the Duke was confirmed in his determination not to admit him. The growth of the Reform movement completed the impossibility of Whigs and Liberals joining a Tory Government.

The day for concoctions was over—at least for Tory concoctions. The Whigs were to have a Government of their own, and not merely to dream of adulterating a Tory one. The material Peel had used in building up his Government of 1828 was no longer available. Huskisson wrote to Graham that no one ought to join the Cabinet unless it had been entirely reconstituted, and when the Duke at last brought himself to ask Melbourne and Palmerston they were too much bound to the Whigs to be available.[1]

Canning had been the chief opponent of Reform, but he was dead now, and his followers could mould his opinions to their will and support the Reform Bill, or at least assent to its necessity. Huskisson might have held back from the Bill when it appeared, if he had not been killed in 1830, at the opening of the Liverpool and Manchester Railway, by an engine, possibly in this case the weapon as well as the symbol of progress. Perhaps the ghost of Canning was laid, since it was possible to transfer to the Whigs his friends and his foreign policy. If there were to be Liberalized Con-

[1] Bulwer's *Palmerston*, Vol. I, 361. Parker's *Graham*, I, p. 86.

servative Ministries in the future they must be under
different auspices, and perhaps under a purer tradition.
Confusion and concoction were done with and the
day of reality had come, if any can say what is real in
politics.

Meanwhile there was scene-shifting. Important
features were removed and replaced, and the scene was
prepared for the new act. In May Peel's father died,
and Peel became a baronet and a very rich man, with
an estate and a country house, Drayton Manor, near
Tamworth. Then, in June, George IV was cleaned
away and replaced by William IV, and the Duke felt
that advantage might be taken of this change to effect
another at the head of the State. He wrote a memorandum to Peel.

Except for the Radicals, he said, he felt that the
Opposition was still personal and mainly personal to
him, though "possibly some individuals who vote in it
might be rather more indifferent to certain measures of
Parliamentary Reform than some of the members of the
Government or than the supporters of the Government
in general." The Opposition had till now been dis-
united, but they must now present it with a leader.
Lord Grey must be told that though, unlike George IV,
the new King was willing to have him in the Ministry,
yet that after his behaviour in the spring they could not
let him in. The Duke still thought they would be
strong enough to survive, and if they were not he did
not see the remedy. He thought that a general election
would give them numbers, and that despite Lord Grey
they would get on in the House of Lords; but that
they might need talent in the House of Commons. He
felt that he could never again be Prime Minister with
Huskisson and Palmerston in his Cabinet; he had long
thought that the Prime Minister ought to be in the
House of Commons, and he suggested that Peel should
succeed him in the post.[1]

Here indeed was the future foreshadowed. The

[1] *Desp.*, VII, 106.

future was for Peel, with its leaderships and Prime
Ministerships, and Peel was to be the Duke's link with
the needs of modern Conservatism, a link which the
Duke in his wisdom and self-restraint was voluntarily to
assume and loyally to maintain.   The Duke's suggestion
was reasonable and one that others were discussing.
It is true that among many Tories Peel was particularly
unpopular, while his pedestrian parts and his lack of
any real facility for oratory were distasteful to a generation that was near enough to the classical tradition
in politics to desire rich well-rounded emotions and
glorious eloquence.   Yet he was known generally as a
man of ability and knowledge, whom men might consider a medicine for the sickness of the times, nasty but
necessary.   But at present it came to nothing; the
present was for the Duke, and he could not get rid of it.
Perhaps it would be untrue to say that it was for him
to command, but at least it was for him to precipitate its
calamities.

The Duke hurried on the elections that were due on
the death of the King, and while they were in progress
came news exciting to all and disturbing to the Government.   There was a new French Revolution.   Charles X,
the legitimist Bourbon, was driven out and Louis
Philippe succeeded him, the mob beat the soldiers in
Paris, and men contemplated with surprise and delight
the power of the barricades, or, as it could be called,
the strength of the people.   By popular legerdemain the
Duke got involved in the public mind with the attempt
at violent reaction in France that had been foiled by
Revolution; and, touched by fire from Paris, Reformers
became enthusiastic and urgent, and the cause of Reform
much more likely of success and of much greater importance.

Though the results of the election were confused
they were not really favourable to the Government.
The storm was up now, and beginning to get wild.
There were disturbances in the country, riots and rick-
burning and, worse than all, when Parliament met in

November there were disturbances in London. Reform filled men's minds, and there were offers of moderate support to the Ministry if they would accept some sort of Reform Bill. The Ministry must now make up their mind to fight or run in that matter, or perhaps, if they could, to sidle out of the way.

Possibly Peel had not as yet given very much consideration to the question of Reform. Perhaps at the time of his letter to Croker his mind had been more fluid than it was later on the subject. Perhaps Canning's success and attitude had stiffened him, or perhaps, through inattention, opposition to Reform had slipped from being a matter for consideration to being an article of belief. However these things may be, there seems little reason to believe that he was not sincerely opposed to a scheme of general Reform. In February 1830 he opposed Lord John Russell's scheme for the enfranchisement of Manchester, Birmingham and Leeds in uncompromising terms, and was able to beat it. As the year went on his position became more dangerous. In July he declared that he would not be able to oppose general Reform if there was not shown a disposition to punish individual cases of corruption. In October he said that Reform might be "the all-important vital question."

At the opening of Parliament Reform was not mentioned in the Speech, but it was commented on by the leaders of the Government in both Houses. Peel, though he intimated opposition, was cautious, and the Duke was not. Drunk with his desire for emphasis, in a fine crescendo passage he praised the country's present system of government as it existed, and as an ideal to be aimed at if it did not exist, and declared that while in office he would oppose whatever other people might propose in the way of Reform of Parliament. He had handed Atropos her shears, but the end was not yet; the Cabinet had yet to enjoy a troubled death-bed. There was rioting in London, there was trouble ahead in the Commons over a Reform motion on the part of Brougham, and there came news that Tories were deserting to the rising cause of Reform. It was urged, even in the Cabinet, that the Ministry should at least compromise over the principle of Reform, when that came up, and then perhaps deal with the specific proposals for it separately.

Peel and the Duke refused to play for compromise and, perhaps, safety. The Duke was opposed to Reform generally and fervently, he felt that he could not be sincere about compromise, and that his chief strength was his "character for straightforward manly dealing." He still apparently believed that Reform would not pass in Parliament. Perhaps he was weakening in this, for at the end of the year he confessed that he had been forced to resign to prevent it being carried by storm, and that the country had been in a state of insanity over it. Poor Duke, he was to learn most forcible lessons from that insanity.

As for Peel, he believed that in the end Reform was bound to pass, that nothing the Cabinet could propose would satisfy. It was a question of "Reform or no Reform," and he refused to be responsible for Reform. Apparently he intended to oppose Brougham's motion; at least he would not listen when his colleagues suggested that he need not oppose it absolutely. This too was straightforward and probably desirable, and when men have done what is right and given good reasons, it seems ungracious and idle to plumb their motives further. Yet Peel's actions were tinged with a certain reckless consistency which is founded ultimately on a contempt for the realities of political issues. And perhaps he stood in Thermopylæ partly because he was too tired to go anywhere else.[1]

At any rate, the Ministry was never called on to face Brougham's motion, for before that came on they fell before a coalition of parties on a motion to reduce the Civil List, and in November 1830 Lord Grey came in with a mixed ministry pledged to Reform. The

[1] Parker, II, 156 ff. Ellenborough's *Diary*, II, 315, 426, 432.

old Tory régime was over—and what of the Tory
Party?

The beginning of 1831 seems to be the centre of
indifference for Tories. The party was still divided,
though there were signs of reunion. Many of them
did not trust their leaders, and it was only a few of those
who had been in office with them who wanted to put
them back in power. There was a general feeling of
uneasiness as to what was to happen, while the imminence
of Reform made men not wish to risk another change.
The Duke himself thought that they ought not to
engage in a general factious opposition at present. All
would be right, they would be enabled to get the better
of the Ministry's schemes; after all, "the good sense of
the country is beginning to have its effect." He was
prepared to wait and to trust to damp powder.
Peel was gardening, planting and building at Drayton, tired of politics, tired of power, tired of the party.
When the Ministry fell and he was asked at a meeting of
men who had been in office whether he would lead them
in opposition his answer was damping. 'At the end of
that year apparently he had written to Goulburn of his
distaste for the political game and of his distaste for
reunion with the Ultra-Tories. He excused himself
from attending a political meeting at Stratfieldsaye, the
house of the Duke of Wellington. He was the man
of the future; and yet he was gazing into his future with
resentful and suspicious eyes.[1]
He did not leave politics. For Peel to leave politics
would have been like Peel leaving life. He was
resolved to retain his present immediate party connection; he did not even wish to slight new party
adherents; he only wanted to be cautious. He entertained political guests, he attended party councils, he
remained a leader. He attended the House of Commons, and there his experienced ability had its due
effect, and his friend Croker said that many men, includ-

---

[1] E.g. Parker, II, 170. Ellenborough, II, 441. Croker, II, 77 ff.

ing the Duke, were prepared to look to Peel as head,
although he admitted that many men distrusted him.
He had a good hand, but would he play it out?   Croker
was discontented with some unreadiness in Peel to lead
the whole Tory Party.   But even Croker agreed that
with Reform at the doors they should not turn out the
Government, and it was not likely that Peel in his present
state should have any desire for a change; indeed, so
much did he wish to avoid one that, since the Ministry
was pledged and opinion imperative on Reform, he was
prepared to compromise and accept a moderate Reform
Bill.[1]   His fate was like that of a man who had determined one morning not to get up when he was called,
only to be dragged out of bed when the time came
by the notes of the last trump.   The Ministry produced what Peel could not call a moderate Reform
Bill.

It was a summons to battle.   Politics of late had had
their proper fill of passion.   There had been betrayals,
hopes, quarrels, misunderstandings, divisions and dislikes, indeed all the apparatus that makes men hot and
politics interesting.   But they had been a little confused and parties had been amorphous and divided,
and now there was for a time a peculiarly clear-cut
party division, with the country often on fire to light up
the conflict.

Peel fought the Reform Bill with perfect sincerity.
He spoke against it with ability; he attacked it at the
points at which he thought he would beat it; he had the
right fears and often the right passions.   When there
were riots in November he adopted vigorous language
and vigorous measures, arming his own house against
attack.   He kept his consistency clear and he refused
to have anything to do with the emasculated Conservative
reforms that men were inclined to propose in order to
supplant the Reform Bill.   He refused to have anything to do with those compromises with the Government,
by means of which Lords Harrowby and Wharncliffe

[1] Parker, II, 180.

hoped to enable the Lords to pass an amended Reform Bill and so to evade the crisis. He felt that their efforts were almost certainly futile, that they would not be able to stop the Bill or effectively alter it, and he was probably right.

He felt that the Peers should oppose to the end and force the Government to a creation of peers. He knew the results of this policy. There would be no possibility at all of amending the Bill, the House of Lords would be breached; the peerage would be adulterated, one party, and that the worst, would predominate. Yet peers might be made under any other excuse, while constitutional change would at least have been made difficult. The Government would have been forced into a crime, and when the madness was over they would inherit its odium. The Peers would have remained erect, neither cowards nor accomplices; a rallying point "for the returning good sense and moderation of the country." The example would tell, even perhaps on the new peers that had been created.

It was a reasonable view, fatalistic but dignified. It would have been disastrous from the Tory point of view, had they followed it. In the end the Tories retained their majority in the Lords, and that was of more use to them than would have been courage in an unpopular cause, and their adversaries remained more effectually hampered than they would have been by the odium of a crime with so many accomplices. It is neither wise nor charitable to let your adversary do so much to you that his sorrow afterwards cannot be effective. But probably, as usual, this is but to read history backwards. Probably, like most historical criticism, it may be instructive, but it is certainly unjust. Perhaps Peel was still attracted a little too much by the succulence of stoical virtue. His view of the effect of moral example was perhaps over-simple, too little founded on observed facts, and too much on copy-book psychology; it was a fault fairly common in Peel, and fairly common in his period. Yet his view was reasonable, straightforward, and not

F

the view of an alarmist.   He did not believe, apparently, that serious consequences would follow the Lords' rejection of the Bill, and he did not believe that the extremity of the situation would justify all manœuvres and all surrenders.   Would not so uncompromising a statesman satisfy his party?

Unfortunately the things that had weighed him down before the Reform Bill still intruded upon him.   He was troubled by memories, by fears, and also by happiness. After the Bill had been introduced, Croker was still dissatisfied with the eagerness Peel showed as leader. As the summer of 1831 went on and with it the committee of the Bill, Peel began to show a distaste for lengthy and fruitless struggles.   Sometimes he was away when wanted, sometimes he had even gone to bed.   Moreover, it is hard to combine domestic felicity and political despair.   Peel's wife went to Drayton, and Peel wanted to leave London.   He hated his lonely dinners, his great empty town house with the dead furniture and silent rooms which showed that his wife and children had been in them, and had left them.   At length he warned the ardent and desperate that he was soon going home until the third reading, and they were not over-pleased at what he had said.   In 1832 the same disease affected him.   For the mourner of a broken Constitution, Peel was ungraciously stout-hearted and healthy.   He would admit to dangers, terrible dangers, but he would not seem to feel them; he could make his prophecies desperate, but not his spirits.   Croker found him extremely reluctant to go to the House, though when he was there he spoke ably and firmly.

In this state of things it was not likely that he would give satisfaction to his party.   His sudden departures probably gave rise to suspicion.   His manners, which were often very curious and repellent, his strange past and his difficult present, combined to give life to the legend that he was cold and subtle and ambitious.   Sinister and icy profundities were deduced by many.   Peel was the kind of man to whom men are not easily fair, and boredom was construed into baseness, sulks into stratagems.   Yet it does not seem that his state of mind was peculiarly difficult to resolve.   His past supplied the key; his fears were intellectually conceived, while all the time his estate, his heart and his body would keep on telling that he was now a free man and whispering to him the treason that, except when he was in the House of Commons, he was a happy one.   He was like a tragic actor who just before the curtain went up was told he had received a rise of salary; and his rise of salary was in all probability freedom from office.

He said, more than once, that he regarded his return to office with feelings of growing aversion; but he had suffered not only from power, but also from pledges and party ties.   He said also more than once that, though he would go as far as anyone in adhering to existing party connections, he would be exceedingly cautious in contracting new ones; while on some points his mind was too clear to admit of compromise.   At the end of 1830 he told Goulburn that he would not abandon any one of his opinions in order to conciliate the Ultra-Tories; that so far as abandonment of opinion went, on the currency question for instance he would not "advance one single yard to gain a whole party."   Perhaps it is unfortunate to have so much clear light in the mind as to create a perpetual danger of sinning against it, yet clear opinions are possibly unavoidable and at times even advantageous.   Meanwhile, he remembered what he had suffered on account of pledges and at whose hands he had suffered it.   When in January 1830 Croker asked him to pledge himself against all Reform, he refused: "he said good-humouredly that he was sick of eating pledges."   "I am convinced," said Croker at the end of January, "he wishes to stand alone."   But in politics if you are to stand at all is it not a little hard to stand alone?   Is it not a fairly common misfortune among politicians that they must have colleagues?   Peel did not intend to leave politics, it is true, he only wanted to avoid some of their necessary accidents.

Men and events interfered with Peel's mood. The Reform Bill made inevitable some sort of alliance with the Ultra-Tories who also opposed it, and some sort of alliance was maintained. It was not entered into with grace, or continued without friction, and early in the proceedings the Ultra-Tories are reported to have declared that they did not wish to enlist under a leader who showed such little desire for their company. In the June of 1831 Peel on his part told Goulburn that he agreed to the necessity of cordial union with them so far as the Bill was concerned, but he would consider a party connection very maturely indeed.

Perhaps it was lucky for him that the crisis postponed these mature and difficult considerations. For one thing, he need not run the risk of the final reward of party politics, accession to power. For they could not turn the Government out without fortuitous, unscrupulous and momentary alliance with Irish members or Radicals, nor yet without precipitating chaos; and Peel with some reason was able to sneer at those who thought of such things and yet called themselves Conservatives. The course of events allowed him to remain in politics —almost to return to a united party—and yet to postpone his difficult questions. Yet was he always to be out of office? Was he always to adhere to one half of the Tories and hold aloof from the other? In his letters on these things he had expressed his feeling but not his considered intentions; it is often better to feel than to intend. Perhaps he should have blessed the violence of the moment that cut him off from the consideration of the future; for in such a storm it could not have been right to leave the ship for a cock-boat.[1]

While events forced Peel's hand men interested themselves in his position. The experiences of the Duke's Government had not affected everyone alike; there were some in it unlike Peel in their natures and positions. There were men who had not been so much exposed as Peel, and indeed could not have suffered so much if

[1] Parker, II, 173 ff. Croker, II, 97 ff. *Private Letters*, 132 ff.

they were; men who had not been so highly overpaid by
fortune that they could appreciate the lightness of her
coin, and who were far more unthinkingly attached to
party tradition.   In fact there were the regular official
men of the party, such as form a party's citadel, for their
habits of life give them great loyalty to their leaders,
whom they are near enough to criticize with all the
instructed ferocity of immediate subordinates.   Their
itch for individual paths and probably for individual
ambition has passed away; but they have not been
unsettled by too much need for too much initiative, and
they have a feeling for their party which is tenacious and
lasting.

Goulburn was one of these, a great friend of Peel's,
a man of ability, who had held various offices under
Tory Cabinets and had become a member of the Duke's
Cabinet as Chancellor of the Exchequer.   He was
connected with the West Indian interest, and until the
proposal of Emancipation he had taken the Protestant
side on that question, and had changed with Peel.   He
represented in Parliament the University of Cambridge,
and was supposed to furnish a liaison with the Church.
Another, though less important, was Herries, who, if
he had little fire, had much finance, and whose parts, if
they were pedestrian, were good and, more than that,
useful.   Perhaps these men were second-class statesmen
but at least they were first-class civil servants, and there
are times when commonplace instincts are salutary.
It was natural that Goulburn and Herries should try
to rally their party in its disorder and danger, and to
head their leaders back to the forefront of a reunited
flock.

Goulburn apparently wrote to Peel on reunion with
the Ultras, but found him most obstinately irresolute.
In 1831 Herries suggested a dinner; the Duke saw no
objection, but Peel was cautious, almost wilfully cautious.
He was "sorry that the dinner was still in agitation,"
he presumed that the object was "a formal party union
with the Ultra-Tories."   Right or wrong, this was a

decision that needed more thought than an ordinary
acceptance to dinner.   On a question of a new party
connection "everyone must be at liberty to decide for
himself. I shall certainly claim that privilege for myself
individually." [1]

Meanwhile, the Reform Bill was having its effect on
the Duke of Wellington. It was real tragedy to him,
tragedy with no intrusive happiness, no private consolations. From the start he had felt that such a Bill
would begin a series of misfortunes for his country.
His grand fear was for property, for he had felt that the
protection of property by its influence in the Commons
was one of the chief advantages of the British Constitution, and, by the Bill's light destruction of vested rights,
"a shake will be given to the property of every individual
in the country."   And property not only meant the rights
—the only rights—of the gentry, but also the employment and comfort of the poor.   The Reform Bill would
break the machinery by which order had been kept, the
colonies retained and the country kept secure.   The
turbulence was so great and so unrestrained that gentlemen would not offer themselves for Parliament; the
lower classes would fill the House; lawyers and physi-
cians, demagogues and dissenters, would be returned
and would wreak their hostility on the Church and other
establishments.   The gentlemen of England would
disappear, and with them the honour, glory and prosperity of the country.   In fact the Government as he
knew it was to be altered and he saw signs, misleading
signs, of the class that he mainly trusted being politically
obliterated.   It was natural that he should despair of
the whole future of Britain.[2]

Unfortunately the Duke's hopes were nearly as
stubborn as his fears.   Like an obstinate worshipper
before a broken image at a time when other gods
are triumphing, he still believed in his Government
party.   The public, or rather the gentry, would come

---

[1] Herries, II, 121.
[2] E.g. *Desp.*, VII, 386, 409. Croker, II, 151, 153.

to his help; property and the establishments ought to be on his side. He did not want to be snobbish; he wanted to appeal to all property; for instance, he thought that Herries' dinner "ought to have moderate Reformers and Bankers as managers rather than noblemen and gentlemen." He thought the country was divided as it ought to be, that he had with him property, the Church and all the establishments, religious, commercial, banking, political and the rest; in fact not only the blood but most of the bones of the State. He thought that there were against the Bill nineteen-twentieths of the country—that is of the property and intelligence of the country—and on the other side the mob and the Ministry. It is interesting to compute how many men of substance and repute he was including in the mob.

Something had of course gone wrong to stultify the effect of this division. The country had largely been in a state of insanity; the King had approved of Reform, which made some sort of Reform inevitable, and the Ministry had been weak enough and wicked enough to coalesce with the mob. It was that coalition which overwhelmed the facts of the case; it was that coalition which frightened gentlemen and magistrates into silence. At the end of 1831 the Duke told Wharncliffe that he would not admit any immediate danger that the Ministry could not put down; after all, "the whole country would support them." The "whole country": it would sometimes seem as if politics were largely a system of errors over composite nouns.[1]

As the crisis went on, matters went hard with the Duke, and hurt him. He became gloomy and lost his good humour, he felt mortified and helpless, and he was pelted by the rabble as the figurehead of opposition. For most of the time his course was the same as that of Peel. He declared of himself and Peel that "without much consultation together he and I will generally be found pursuing the same course." Then at the end

[1] *Desp.*, VII and VIII (*passim*).

came a painful, dramatic, and, what was far worse, a very public division.

The course of the Reform Bill did not run to its logical conclusion of a creation of peers by the Government to drive it through a steadfast House of Lords.   In October 1831 the Lords had rejected it on the second reading, but in April 1832 the waverers enabled the Government to pass their new Bill through its second reading in the Lords.   However, at the outset of the committee stage in May the Government was decisively beaten. Lord Grey appealed to the King to create not less than fifty peers, and the King refused.   Grey resigned, but the King considered himself pledged to an extensive Reform Bill.   He sent for Lyndhurst, and despatched him to find out whether an administration could be formed that would relieve him of his difficulties and pledges by passing such a Bill through the Lords.   Lyndhurst communicated with the Duke of Wellington and Sir Robert Peel.

Loyalty or consistency, power or caution, such was the dilemma proposed, and perhaps it was not to be doubted on which horn the Duke would impale himself. He had always been absolutely loyal, if sometimes contemptuous of the sovereigns under whom he served, and he felt that if he now disobeyed his Sovereign's appeal he would not be able afterwards to show his face in the streets.   Loyalty easily vanquished consistency, and perhaps circumstances did not urge caution on him so imperiously as would have been thought.   He had put down so much of the crisis to the wickedness of the ministers, and it seems that he still felt that he had the gentlemen of England behind him.   Perhaps he trusted to this if he ever looked forward to the time when his extensive Reform Bill was passed and came into action. But probably he kept his eyes on the crisis, or felt that with the exorcising of the Ministry the madness of the country would vanish away.   As with other soldiers, his political world was one where power is often effective and politicians can be the entire and original causes of harm; it is not the world usually demonstrated by history. .He determined to give his aid to the King's project.

With Peel, however, things were different. He had always wanted to be thought honest—that was what made him so bitter and resolute when men declared that he was not. At the time of the passing of Emancipation he had required a strong conscious, rather contemptuous inward sense of right to bear him up; now he had not that stiffening, only memories of his past position and its pain; and he had always had a strong belief in the need for personal consistency. What he was asked to do was strangely like what he had had to do on the Roman Catholic question without the necessities and duties of office to force and excuse his actions. At a meeting on the subject at Apsley House with the Duke of Wellington, Lyndhurst and Croker, he declared in a tone of "concentrated resolution" that he was not going to settle the Reform question by passing so extensive a Bill as now must be passed. He talked of "the advantages to the country that public men should maintain a character for consistency and disinterestedness which he would for ever forfeit if a second time he were on any pretence to act over again anything like his part in the Catholic question"; and from this they could not move him.[1]

So by this time, he was provided by his nature with a tender skin, and by his past with old stripes. The lesson on consistency that he would seem to have learnt might be useful, for he was going to meet again like temptations. For ideas about party politics were still a little undeveloped; irresponsible and therefore insensitive branches of the legislature continued to exist with power, and those together with the dead weight of the fear of admitting Radicals into the Government were to make the system of alternating parties work too slowly and clumsily for the swift current of modern affairs.

Peel had been deprived of the position he had occupied

[1] Croker, II, 154 ff.

on the Roman Catholic question, and with it of some of his credit. He had not been deprived of his loyalty to the cause of order; and he had not been deprived of his sincere love of the Church, though perhaps the pressure of circumstances, the passage of time, and their original soil might render these beliefs a little sterile. His party feelings were genuine but not always alive, or at least of themselves they were not capable of putting out new growth. He was fixed in the political world, but he had learnt to suspect the necessary ends and instruments of politics; he shrank from pledges, office, and from some part of his followers. He was odd but honest, sulky but sensible, intelligent and courageous and apt to be the host of uncontrollably clear ideas. He was remarkably well educated in the business of government, and he had learnt much of the economics of the time. But he had not learnt the lesson of the invigorating legend of party.

The attempt to construct some sort of Tory ministry to pass a Reform Bill failed from the start, as it was bound to fail. Yet it seemed to some that Peel had passed sentence of death upon it, and it was remembered against him. The explanations that he and the Duke gave in Parliament were full of respect for each other and showed an uncomfortable contrast of views. The Whigs returned to office and the Duke and his friends determined to abstain from voting on the Bill's further stages. The Bill was passed, no peers were made, the new world was born, and into it were whirled two parties that had been merely formed to quarrel about its birth.

CHAPTER II

WHIGS AND TORIES—1832

The tragedies of history are its epilogues. Too often they run into prologues. Too often they spoil dramatic effect and men's reputations. It is from them that statesmen sometimes learn that by settling one problem they have raised others which they are not likely even to wish to satisfy, or that they have had the punishment and privilege of producing children whom they do not understand. Yet though political epilogues may be bewildering, contradictory, disappointing or dull, they can hardly be overlooked, and attention must be paid to the years immediately following 1832 which form in some way an epilogue to the first and great Reform Bill.

The Bill was an instrument of a change both important and difficult. It was broad in effect and the herald of new ideas, and to make matters more troublesome it was slightly deceptive. It was a revolution, and yet it had not effectively altered all the active machinery of the constitution. The Lords had seemed to be beaten, yet Peers had not been created nor any continuing power secured over them; neither had any perfect doctrine been developed of the subordination of the King's wishes to those of his Ministers, as the history of the next few years was to prove. The House of Commons had, for the moment, been very greatly increased in power, prestige, and importance, but it had not been made supreme. Yet the Bill was supposed by many to be the beginning of a new era.

They are elusive things, new eras, for it is easy only to remember that they have for father the ingenuity of man and what he desires to possess, and to forget that their nursing mother must be the past and what man already possesses. The Bill was supposed to start a new era of Reform. Men knew that the eighteenth century must be cleared away to make room for the nineteenth. Great changes were going to be made, and how could

63

such be reconciled to the surviving power of the King, and of the Peers? Perhaps, as many said, it was impossible.

§ 2

In 1832 Lord Grey's Whig Government successfully passed their great measure and they remained in office to face, among other things, its consequences. While they started their task with other men's hopes sticking on to them like burrs, some of them had their own fears pricking them like thorns; for the last two years had given birth to many fears of civil disturbance and revolution. They had to confront new principles, they had to ward off old chaos, and the two seemed sometimes to get blurred into one another. They had to consider, as no Government yet had ever considered, a real alliance with a real demagogue; they had to decide whether such a friend of the people was necessarily an enemy of the state, and the burden of this decision rested upon an administration which Lord Grey had gathered together from the diverse groups opposed to the Duke of Wellington's administration. It was a Cabinet not coherent and possibly not effective, without the consistency of an ordinary party Government. For a party cannot be made from a mere collection of oppositions.

It is true that its members had weathered the Reform Bill together, but the case of that measure had been peculiar. In 1830 there had been a strong and general feeling that some Reform was necessary, and under the obliterating shadow of that necessity their government had been formed. With some of them the Bill had been like the legitimate heir of a loveless marriage, the child rather of necessity than of desire.[1] It had been of a nature to exhaust some men's Liberalism, while some had been frightened by the incidents and dangers of its passing. Altogether the Reform Bill was too much of an incident of itself, and by itself, to offer a good first measure for a party's programme.

[1] See Grev., *Geo. IV and Wm. III*, Vol. II, p. 277.

The Reform Bill had largely monopolized attention during the last two years, but it had not been the Ministry's only problem. With their entry into office had begun their difficulties with Ireland. In 1830 Roman Catholic Emancipation had just been passed. If it was to be an effective measure Roman Catholics must be promoted into positions of trust, and the old system of depression and exclusion must be abandoned. There was increasing agitation against the large endowments and small numbers of the English Church in Ireland, culminating in violent and effective opposition to the payment of her tithes, and the tide of outrage was beginning to rise. The destinies and constituencies of Ireland were largely in the hands of an aggressive and excitable democratic party, distrustful of the Whigs, openly working for Repeal of the Union which every respectable Whig must resist, and whose language and actions the most liberalized Ministers could not condone. The master of Ireland was Daniel O'Connell.

Lord Grey's first appointments to Ireland were uniformly unfortunate. The legal appointments were obviously and exclusively Protestant, honour even being shown to those who had served under the old régime. The Lord-Lieutenant was Lord Anglesey. He had served as Lord-Lieutenant under the Duke of Wellington and at that time his constant pleading had probably hurried Emancipation. But he was a little inclined to self-sufficiency and was set against agitation, and before he had reached Ireland in 1830 he had quarrelled with O'Connell.[1] Soon the usual war between the Lord-Lieutenant and the agitator was being fought out with the usual moves. Processions were made and forbidden, a succession of societies was destroyed, and at last O'Connell was arrested, though his trial came to nothing, owing to pressure in the Cabinet. At the end of 1830 Lord Grey wrote that he hoped that Anglesey's resolution and rigour would teach O'Connell that he had to deal with a Government that would not

[1] *Corresp. of Daniel O'Connell*, W. J. Fitzpatrick, Vol. I, 233–7.

shrink from its duty;[1] and indeed O'Connell might learn much about the Reform Government from that vigour and resolution.

The Secretary was young Stanley, afterwards Lord Derby and a Conservative Prime Minister. He was brilliant, unreliable, high-spirited, a good orator and terrible in invective. He was not the man to be driven by O'Connell, and his predisposition and nature forbade him any sympathy with O'Connellism. He was ecclesiastically-minded and a loyal son of the English Church, yet the diminution of the Revenues of the Church in Ireland was the most outstanding problem. Anglesey was convinced, so he told Graham in 1832, that Stanley's views on Church matters were not sound.[2] "They will not be tolerated now," he said. They were not going to be tolerated, at least not by Stanley's present party.

Such actions and such men were unlikely to attract O'Connell. He had early conceived suspicions of the amount of good that the Whigs could bring to Ireland. Yet there might have been some sort of approximation. He had friends in the Whig councils, and he had sometimes some hope of their intentions. In the Ministry itself he had a correspondent and ally in Lord Duncannon, and he had been willing to assist them over the Reform Bill. But there were always Anglesey and Stanley equipped and equipping themselves, so it seemed, with all the apparatus of Orange Tyranny. The Ministry had done nothing for Ireland and these men were their representatives. There was much to dislike and nothing to thank them for. Their prosecutions led him to have Duncannon himself opposed at a Kilkenny election.[3] O'Connell declared that Anglesey had deluged Ireland with blood. He detested Stanley. There was agitation in Ireland, violent scenes between Irish mem-

---

[1] *Corresp. of Earl Grey and Princess Lieven*, Vol. II, 129 (Grey to Lieven, Dec. 29, 1830).

[2] Parker's *Graham*, Vol. II, p. 174.

[3] *Corresp. of Daniel O'Connell*, Vol. I, pp. 235, 239, 243, 254.

bers and the Ministry in the Commons. O'Connell disliked the Irish Reform Bill, and he naturally opposed a Bill of Stanley's which would modify but secure the tithes of the Church of Ireland; so the Ministry was at open war with O'Connell, and consequently with what was most powerful and articulate in Ireland. Yet Ireland was the country that would cry most imperiously for Reform. Crime, disorder, agitation and very real grievances would call attention to her. Justice, force of circumstances, uneasy Whig consciences and the voice of O'Connell would demand that something must be done; and of all the Ministry Stanley was the man who must be called upon to do it.

At the end of 1832 Brougham, the Lord Chancellor, and Althorp, the Chancellor of the Exchequer, wanted Anglesey removed and Stanley promoted from his troublesome position. Indeed Brougham went so far as to say that he would rather resign than face a Session that was like the time which succeeded the Reform Bill in 1832. But Grey held back. Stanley wished to resign from his position, but Grey prevented this; he would not disturb those members of the Government who must be disturbed in order to promote Stanley. He refused to move men from their posts for no better reason than that they had earned the opposition of those who were in reality opposed to the authority of the British Government itself. Meanwhile he enabled Stanley to force through the Cabinet a Bill for Irish Church Reform for the next Parliament.[1] Grey had the helm and he held the Government on its present tack; he did not think that this took them dangerously near the rocks or the shallows. His mind and attention were much taken up by the intricacies and difficulties of the questions then in discussion in the Cabinet. If only they were solved, he thought, the Government would have such strength as they never had before to prosecute "the measures of Reform which the times require," and to make, some

[1] *Life and Times of Lord Brougham*, Vol. II, 235. Parker's *Graham*, II, 174.

time, the arrangements necessary for "conducting comfortably the affairs of the administration." [1]

Grey had done his work. Though he was still a
reformer he was likely to be a strong friend of order, and
no friend to the Radicals. His great virtue had been a
loyal and steadfast adherence, through great difficulties
and despairs, to a belief in the necessity of certain measures,
such as the Emancipation of the Roman Catholics and
an extensive Reform Bill. These measures were passed
now, and he was old and had for some time been a little
aloof. In fact, as these troubles were beginning the
Prime Minister was drawing to the end of his career.

Earl Grey's satisfaction was not shared by all his
colleagues. Stanley's close friend, Sir James Graham,
was appalled by the task of the Whigs and the prospect
of the elections, and was much afflicted by fears and by
metaphors. If the Whigs failed to keep control, he said,
"the nation will be hurried into space and chaos is at
hand." [2] There was a strain of timidity in him, a strain
which made him lean rather heavily on other statesmen.
His mind was in some respects the mind of a Radical,
but his fears were often the fears of a Conservative, that
is, of a kind of Conservative.

Melbourne was alarmed. Melbourne was above all
things a moderate; together with Palmerston he had
tried to avoid extreme courses during the crisis of the
Reform Bill, at a time when Graham, for instance,
was urging an early creation of Peers. He was also
Home Secretary and had been a surprisingly vigorous
Home Secretary. An anxious servant of order, he had
been in favour of a firm policy in Ireland, and whatever
he was in his private relationships, as Home Secretary
Melbourne was instructed more by intellect than by
sympathy. There were those who were yet to learn that
the hand of this trifler was of iron. The reports of
election violence and of the meetings of constituents

---

[1] *Corresp. Princess Lieven and Earl Grey*, Vol. II, 400 and 428. *Life and Times of Brougham*, Vol. II, 249 (Grey to Brougham, Dec. 5, 1832).
[2] *Early Corresp. of Lord John Russell*, Vol. II, p. 36.

disturbed him, and he feared extensive election pledges
and an increase of the blackguard interest in Parliament.
He did not want to change the Government of Ireland
because it was unpopular, while he felt sure that Ministers
would be pressed to go further in Reform, certainly in
the Commons, probably in the Cabinet, and he was determined to resist.   "There is no knowing to what one may
be led by circumstances," he said, "but at present I am
determined to make my stand here, and not to advance
further." [1]

There was no telling to what Lord Melbourne might
be led by circumstances, for he had not many very
obstructive principles.   He was pleasant ballast, active
minded, unprejudiced, paradoxical, affectionate, charming and intelligent.   He was convenient, so convenient
that he was to become the Prime Minister of Great
Britain.   There was no telling to what he might be led
by circumstances, but it was pretty sure that he was
going to be led nowhere by a strong Liberal spirit or
by a great desire to lead the people.

But the Whigs had other leaders.   There was Lord
Durham, who was Grey's son-in-law and in the Cabinet.
He was a Radical, and of the stuff of which Radicals are
made, vigorous, merciless, proud and uncompromising.
He had vision, conceit, and recklessness.   Lord Althorp
was the mainstay of the whole concern.   He was leader
of the House of Commons, and of all men was most likely
to make a good leader of an English House of Commons,
for, open and honest—indeed strangely naïve—slow-
minded and sweet-tempered, short, strong and clumsily
built, he excited in men a very unusual confidence.
Yet though his conscience was sensitive and his opinions
Liberal and advanced, he was obviously, almost criminally, anxious to retire, and his mind and temper were
not so commanding as to make it likely that he would
force Liberal measures on his party.   He had always
been uneasy about Stanley's policy in Ireland, and in
October 1832, when he saw the Church Temporalities

[1] *Melbourne Papers*, 140, 145, 163.   Grev., II, 322 (Sept. 28).

Bill and the Irish Coercion Bill Stanley was preparing, he was apparently only dissuaded by Lord Grey from resigning.[1]

Besides these there were younger Whigs who had less gentleness towards old institutions than some of their elders. Howick, Grey's son, was an odd mixture of Radicalism, wrong-headedness and Conservatism. Something in the odd Fox blood gave Lord Holland, Charles Fox's nephew, though old and gouty, a Liberalism more capable of expansion than was that of Grey and Melbourne. Lord Duncannon was more in touch with O'Connell and the Irish, and Poulett Thomson with the middle class, than was consonant with the line Lord Grey was likely to take; and then there was Lord John Russell.

Lord John was in many ways a human embodiment of party principle. His father was the Duke of Bedford, his education had been under Professor Playfair at Edinburgh University, his relations and associates were mainly Whigs, and all these things, combined with his type of intellect, seem to have made the fabric of his mind as deeply Whig as was the Russell blood in his small body. In fact, at the age of 18 he was so sure of his own Whig principles that he felt qualified to criticize the Whiggism of Lord Grey, and to say in his haste and to his father's dismay that Lord Holland was the only remaining true Whig in England.[2]

It was not the last thing in his life that Lord John said in his haste; there was more than one crisis afterwards which he precipitated. Perhaps the resemblance of these events is a coincidence, and they are unconnected by any strand of character. There is much to show that he was useful and amiable. His friends liked him, he was certainly able, he was not unwilling to laugh and make jokes, and he had done good service by his early work on Reform. Yet there were moments when his impulses

---

[1] Le Marchant's *Spencer*, 288, 445.

[2] Spencer Walpole, *Life of Lord John Russell*, Vol. I, p. 50. *Early Corresp. of L. J. R.*, Vol. I, 156 and 131.

were sudden, not a little rash, springing from a nature sometimes determined, self-sufficing, perhaps a little suspicious even of friends. At those moments he seemed eager to demonstrate his own principles, eager to join profitably in other people's opinions when they seemed to resemble his own, a little eager to win a trick. It might be said that his actions sometimes resemble the dart and peck of a small eager bird with something of its self-centred aloofness. Only birds do not dig up explosive worms such as were sometimes the dangerous prey of John Russell.

In 1831 he became a member of the Cabinet, and he was one of its more Liberal members, although his Liberalism was that of a Minister and a Whig. He was to show in 1833 that he was prepared to resist further changes in the constitution, speaking caustically about not having a revolution each year, and he heartily disapproved of the conduct of O'Connell. He disliked O'Connell's extreme language and policy, his intractability and his having Duncannon opposed at Kilkenny. But Lord John Russell also disapproved of the Irish Church Bill that Stanley was preparing. In fact, in October 1832 he wrote to Lord Grey to tell him that he wished to resign over it. He did not resign, for he found that Althorp was also discontented about the same matter and he knew that he would endanger the life of the Ministry if he endangered Althorp's continuance in it.[1] But the fact remained that in the very year of its great victory the Ministry was already affected by restless consciences, unquiet fears, inherent divisions and proffered resignations.

Such fears, such consciences, such uneasiness in their Ministry at such a time were ill symptoms for the Whigs. They had gone beyond their chief points of union, and were in a new world whose demands they were not altogether in a condition to meet with consistency and decision. Their past had been unfortunate, the scales had been weighted too heavily against them, their success

[1] Spencer Walpole, *Life of Lord John Russell*, Vol. I, p. 182, 188.

and possibly their development had been held up, and, while the measures they had advocated such as Roman Catholic Emancipation and the Reform of the electorate, were being delayed, the tide was drawing to the flood. The past had not given these Whigs enough of the close and organized association of ordinary party life.   War and revolution had divided the party; despair and Canning had disintegrated it, and until 1830 it had remained highly disorganized.   At the end of 1832 Lord Grey, their leader, was likely to be too cautious for his position, and they lacked as yet the consistencies or the complaisances of an ordinary party government.   They were not yet a party.   They wanted leading and they wanted weeding.   Yet they were in office, and were faced with a time that was certainly difficult and possibly perilous. There were, indeed, powerful considerations that would disturb the efficient refashioning of the Whig party now that they had passed their Reform Bill.

§3

Still the Reform Bill was passed; it received the Royal Assent by Commission on the 7th June 1832.   "In Society," wrote Greville, "the excitement has gone, but the bitterness remains."   The battle was won and lost; and as with the Whigs so with the Tories, or rather Conservatives if that is what they should now be called, it might be hard to decide how they should conduct themselves after the end of the play.   It is comparatively easy to determine the fine pugnacious attitude that you are to take up in the catastrophe that brings the world to an end.   It is not the most difficult thing in experience to be "firm and faithful to the last."   It is after the last, and when the world has come to an end that your attitude needs a good deal of thinking out, and that your position becomes a little strained.   Since the simple opposition to the Bill was over there must be numerous questions to answer about the feelings and future of the Conservatives.

Would they be able to forget and accept the Reform Bill?   Would they even be able to help to arrange the conventions by which it would work? If not, the Reform Bill would probably have failed; great political changes have usually failed, if they cannot be forgotten. How would the Conservative party develop after the Reform Bill? What principles would they adopt and promote? They had had principles, but old principles in a new world may as easily be dead weights as living roots. If there were a change, in what direction would it be, and how would they preserve their unity, identity, and vitality? Perhaps they would never have it in them to rally at all, but would remain nothing more than a memory and a remnant, ineffective, dwindling, divided. They might possibly despair, perhaps large numbers of them might abstain from politics. The policy of secession, usually futile and harmful, naturally occurs to a faction that feels weak and disgusted; but against it there always would act in men's minds their unquenchable hopes and, still more, their unalterable habits.

Secession appealed to one eminent Conservative. Croker, who had for some time shown signs of retirement and disappointment, now determined that he would not re-enter Parliament under the new system. He would not, he said, be a member of that Parliament which would only consummate the Revolution. He would not "spontaneously take an active share in a system which must, in my matured judgment, subvert the Church, the Peerage, and the Throne," and he wrote long explanations of his retirement to Fitzgerald, to Peel and to the Duke of Wellington. But his feelings do not seem to have excited very wide or at least very eloquent sympathy. Apparently Peel made no comment at all, and the rest of Croker's political friends all disapproved. The Duke replied to Croker's letter to him, which was both long and explicit, in the shortest of short notes. He said he was sorry that Croker did not intend to stand for Parliament again, "I cannot conceive for what reason," and that was all.[1] For the Duke of Wellington had no thought of leaving his post.

[1] Croker, II, 183, 184.

Yet for all his steadfastness the Duke was neither hopeful nor content. His immediate past had displeased him. He had been annoyed at what he thought was the weakness of those who had allowed the Bill to pass the second reading in the Lords, a weakness which he thought had gone very far to ensure its final success, and he had disliked having to play the part of a leader in the final surrender.[1] In June his despair, if anything, increased. The Government of England was destroyed. He had heard bad accounts of the elections. He did not believe that gentlemen would be prevailed upon to offer themselves as candidates. The House would be filled by the classes that he feared, and, in consequence, "a Parliament will be returned by means of which no set of men whatever will be able to conduct the administration, or to protect the lives and property of the King's subjects." "There is no chance," he said, "excepting our keeping the House of Lords untouched in case of an emergency. This resource has failed us lately. But it may be hoped that the melancholy weakness which deprived us of it on this occasion may not occur hereafter."[2] The Duke, above all men, would have the decision in his hands, as to whether the Peers would in the future show melancholy weakness or perilous strength.

The first test of the Bill must be the elections. The old Parliament was soon to be dissolved and the first Reformed Parliament to be elected. Then would be the beginning of the end or of the era; at all events a new experiment would then be tried. By July the elections had become the most general topic of political speculation.

Even before the Reform Bill had passed Herries declared that their opponents were already in the field. He pressed the need of concerted effort on the part of Conservatives, that the party might invite and encourage

---

[1] Croker, II, 171. Herries, Vol. I, 159.
[2] *Courts and Cabinets*, Vol. II (Duke of Wellington to Duke of Bucks, June 23, 1832). *Desp.*, VIII, 357.

candidates and in some cases assist them financially.
He declared that they were anxious to know their leaders'
thoughts and intentions.   The organization and energy
of the Conservatives seemed to him to fall far short of his
desires.[1] Nevertheless, as the elections approached, many
Conservatives found themselves able to hope.   Indeed
in October their hopes were remarkably high; and light
even leaked into the darkness of the Duke of Wellington's
night.   He noticed a general change of opinion, he heard
of bright prospects in the elections, and he thought the
country would be nearly equally divided between Tories
on the one hand and on the other the Whigs, Radicals,
Unitarians, Quakers and Jews.   But he still feared the
preponderance of the latter party, and was disturbed
as to how the country should be governed.   There
was activity at headquarters; the Duke and his friend
Arbuthnot and two Whips, Holmes and Bonham, were
busy spreading over the Lords and landowners that
network of influences by which in those days party
authorities were used to catch votes.   Peel was exceptionally hopeful about the future of the party.   Goulburn thought that their friends were working well;
Bonham, the Whip, had sanguine reports from his
candidates and sent in sanguine reports to the Duke,
and the Duke said that with so many in the field they
would do even better.[2]

These hopes were not utterly futile.   If it was natural
for the Tories to expect succour from the country districts, they had reasons to hope for success in the towns
as well.   Chief of these was the crisis in Belgium, where
the tortuous international complications following the
Belgian Revolution of 1830 were developing into a
semblance of war between the Dutch on the one side and
France on the other, allied with Great Britain.   With war
possible, our Dutch trade endangered, the mischievous
tendencies of the French encouraged, the Tri-colour and

[1] Herries, II, 161 ff.
[2] *Desp.*, VIII, 423. Add. MSS. 40,616; 2 ff.   40,332; 129.   40,403; 71.
Raikes' *Journal*, Vol. I, p. 110 (under Nov. 28).

Jack in unnatural alliance on the seas and the elections coming on, it was thought that the Ministry must be damaged. There were meetings of protest in various parts of the country, the Dutch war was a constant topic of conversation in society, and the thoughts of it filled out Conservative expectations.[1]

The Conservatives refused to recognize how great was the power that was stirred against them. There seemed to be signs of reaction. They marched hopefully and confidently towards the elections, and they annoyed one who sat in his retirement and saw, as he said, "the appalling visions of a bloody anarchy striding towards us." In October Croker wrote to Peel, "One of the most, to me, appalling signs of the approaching ruin is the silly security in which, even more than the Whigs, the Tories seem to cradle themselves." "They dream of successes in the elections and fancy that the serving 100 or 150 Tories will save the Country!" and he added "for my own part I believe that by this day twelvemonth I shall be either in my grave or the workhouse, and hope it may be the former." Poor Croker! When the time came he was in neither.[2]

The elections came and the Tories were bitterly disappointed. Men found to their surprise that the Dutch War had made little difference.[3] Instead of about 250 members they had about 150. Half of Croker's prophecy had come true; what about the other half? Would some workhouse soon receive a cocksure, clever and extremely argumentative pauper, or Hades a most disputatious ghost? Nor was Croker the only man who had lately talked of the French Revolution, or remembered the time of Charles I. Perhaps this was a work which only one fitting end could crown.

It was not only that the Conservatives were defeated. There were other things to point the moral of the elections for men already alarmed or prejudiced against the

---

[1] E.g. Add. MSS. 40,403; 105.
[2] Croker, II, 185. Add. MSS. 40,320; 225. 40,320; 217.
[3] Add. MSS. 40,403; 142.

Reform Bill.   There had not really been as much violence
as might have been expected.   New arrangements for
taking the poll had hindered this, while the victories of
candidates who were for the moment popular had been
usually too easy to excite it.   But there had been quite
enough to arouse the fears of timid or doubtful Whigs
and beaten Conservatives.   Definite pledges had been
demanded by the Radicals and sometimes given by
candidates, and in those days definite pledges were
regarded as the extreme of democracy and as ominous
signs of the times.   Though prominent Radicals were
defeated, such as Orator Hunt and Duncombe, men could
point to such members as Cobbett and Gully, an ex-prize
fighter, who were returned, and men will always make use
of picturesque material for despair.   Conservative gloom
was natural and in some cases profound.   "I believe I
ought to go and shut myself up," wrote Arbuthnot to
Bonham, in January 1833.   "I can't bear to hear from
morning to night the dreary foreboding of every person
I meet."   He agreed with Bonham that the present
Government was not immortal.   "I am not sure that
I ought not to wish it was—when scattered to the winds
as it may be, it will not be to the advantage of our party,
but it will be to replace Lord Althorp by Joseph Hume,"
and he began to speculate doubtfully as to whether the
Government would now be Conservative.[1]

And yet in reality there was much about the election
that should have satisfied the Conservatives.   The
majority in Parliament was Whig, or Whig-Liberal.
Although in Ireland the followers of O'Connell had
defeated the Whigs, yet in England and Scotland, as was
said at the time, the new electors had remembered their
creators in the time of their youth.   There were said
to be in Parliament about 320 Ministerialists to 190
Radicals and Repealers.   Conservatives declared that
the majority would not be under the influence of the
Government,[2] yet when the Session came the new Parlia-

[1] Add. MSS. 40,616; 9.   E.g. *Desp.*, VIII, 423 (Aberdeen to Duke).
[2] Raikes' *Journal*, Vol. I, p. 121, under Dec. 14, and p. 123 under Dec. 19.

ment was to show itself ready to do its duty and to vote
against Radical motions and to pass, under oratorical
pressure, coercion laws for Ireland.

The constituency which had elected this Parliament
was one which might well in time prove amenable to the
Conservatives. It was mainly middle class. A large
proportion of it was still agricultural, and even the Duke
of Wellington wrote that "the gentry have as many
followers and influence as many voters at elections as ever
they did," although he thought they had been generally
overborne by intimidation and audacity and by Radical
elements in the towns and villages.[1] Nevertheless Lord
Chandos, a Conservative and the son of the Duke of
Buckingham, had introduced a clause in the Reform
Bill which had spread the franchise among lease-holders
farther than had originally been intended by the Ministry, and there were therefore in the counties a large
class of new voters, who at the same time owed their
votes to a Conservative and were peculiarly dependent on
property. Members were still returned by many towns
whose electorate was comparatively small and likely to be
easily permeated by Conservative influence. The future
might hold possibilities for the party, and the party
might be ready to use them. It was purged and healthily
frightened. At these elections they had lost Wetherell,
and at the next they were to show that many of them
had learnt not to rely solely on old-fashioned Toryism.
Disaster had come, but hope, real hope, was at the door.

But these are the useless consolations of history.
What is the importance of reality or of the future when
compared to the appearance of the present? Conservatives were likely to find the end of 1832 full of interest,
excitement and menace. There were the conditions and
problems of Ireland, the cry for Repeal, the bloody war
against tithe, the danger to the Church. Established
Churches everywhere seemed to be threatened, and the
Church of England seemed to be in danger of Reform
and possibly pillage.[2] Abroad there were troubles, and

[1] Croker, II, 203.   [2] Add. MSS. 40,403; 69.

the main train of events on the Continent had been such as to excite the fears of those who were ready to suspect the policy of France.   At home there was the threat of further Radical aggression, and it was not clear whether the Government was going to side with the Radicals or against them.   It was thought that some, at least, of the Government might wish to stand firm for order.   There seemed to be signs that it was already quarrelling with the Radicals.   But it was the same Government that had passed the Reform Bill.   The Conservatives naturally credited it with most unlikely wickedness or cowardice.   Possibly it was impotent and divided.   Many of the younger Whigs had been using Radical expressions which frightened Conservatives.[1] Many of the Radicals had called themselves Ministerialists during the last struggle.   The future was dark and the issues important and the Conservatives must decide what they must do in the struggle at hand.

The Duke of Wellington was resolute.   He would resist the spoliation of the Church in Ireland.   Tithe was a form of property and if tithes were abolished, rents might be endangered.   Repeal of the Union meant ultimately the complete separation of England and Ireland, and he thought that even now Britain was not so far gone as to look at separation quietly.   He was resolute on the question of reforming the Church of England; he recommended the Bishops to stand by their friends.   "Let no man say that the Bishops as a body ever gave their consent or countenace to a principle manifestly unjust, or to one inconsistent with the doctrine or discipline of the Church committed to their charge."   He nurtured doubts and apprehensions, and likened the times to those of Charles I.   The revolution was effected, the influence of the gentlemen of England was annihilated, and its government rendered doubtful. There would be a general attack on Establishments and institutions; the Church of Ireland would be the first

[1] Raikes' *Journal*, Vol. I, p. 134, under Jan. 2, 1833.   Add. MSS. 40,406; 16.   *Memoir of Lord Sydenham*, 56 ff.

to suffer from it. He thought that the United Church would, as probabilities went, suffer much spoliation; but he did not intend to give up the battle for his principles.[1]

Principle is the usual consolation prize in politics, and its retention may be but a harmless delight in those who are utterly defeated. It was not so with the Duke. He belonged to a faction which was weak, broken and discredited; but he also belonged to, indeed he commanded, a House of Lords whose constitutional power was as yet unbroken. He and his policy could still decisively affect the affairs of the country. In December he threw some light on what his policy was to be. He said that as far as he could form an opinion, "our course in the House of the Lords ought to be very firm and uncompromising, but very moderate, that we should attend constantly, discuss everything, but avoid dividing excepting upon occasions of great importance." He intended them to be moderate but uncompromising. He showed commendable self-restraint, which could all be entirely vitiated by the constant recurrence of "occasions of great importance."

But the decisions of the future were not to be entirely in the hands of the Duke of Wellington. It is important to consider the opinions of the men who must face and fight the battle not in the Lords but in the Commons. When the Duke had resigned in May and it was decided that he should let the Reform Bill pass the House of Lords, Peel was still afflicted by his inappropriate good spirits.[2] He had thanked God that he had not engaged in the struggles of Ministry making. He was very pleased that there was a way out of the crisis which did not entail the Duke's passing the Reform Bill himself. He thought it a most fortunate result for the Duke's character for honour. He had been most earnest in his view that it was impolitic and inconsistent for the opponents of the Bill to be responsible for its passing. At the end of May, typically and unwisely, he talked "with great complacency of its being

1 *Desp.*, VII, 496 and 486.   2 Add. MSS. 40,403; 31.

very well as it is, and that the salvation of character is everything," and with great injustice his cheerfulness was put down to pleasure at seeing the Duke of Wellington in difficulties.[1]

He left town about the end of July. At any rate about that time the Duke of Cumberland asked him to a political dinner party, and Peel apparently said that he must go to his constituency. He spent August building a new house at Drayton Manor, and buying busts and portraits. He boasted to Croker how little he heard about elections and politics, and engaged in controversy with him about whether he should have battlements instead of a balustrade in his house, and labels above the windows. Croker interspersed his instructions to Peel in matters of taste in architecture and his criticisms of the design of Peel's new house, with explanations of his retirement from politics, with accounts of the constituencies which had offered themselves to him and with despairing prophecies. But Peel was happy and did not despair. To Croker's wonder he did not intend to leave politics. In the summer he was exceptionally cheerful about the party's prospects. Croker went to stay at Drayton at the end of October and found Goulburn and Herries and Holmes, the Whip, there. He found Peel in "high force" and cheerful temper, believing more firmly than anyone Croker had yet met in the possibilities of salvation, and believing that the Dutch War would bring people to their senses. Peel was elected for Tamworth, apparently without much difficulty. He arranged, after consultation, whether Wynn or Goulburn was to stand for the Speakership, supposing there was an election at the beginning of the new Parliament; thus demonstrating that he kept the reins of his party in his hands.[2]

But the important questions remained as to what attention he would give to his driving, whether he intended to drive the whole team and whither he was to drive them. In the answers to those questions would

---

[1] Croker, II, 167. Grev., II, 301.
[2] Add. MSS. 40,403; 33. 40,406; 9. 40,320; 210. Croker, II, 188, 192.

lie much of the future of the Conservative party, and consequently of more than that party. Some of the answer was to be extracted soon by two of the men that Croker met at Drayton Manor in October.

§4

During the crisis in the Reform Bill Herries and Goulburn had shown a strong desire, possibly an almost instinctive desire, for the unity and order of the Party. This had not been exorcized by the final defeat, as Herries had showed. In November Goulburn was imbued with the feeling that the only way of stopping "the frantic career of the Government" was to keep together a party opposed to them. He was glad to hear that Peel was to come to London for even a few days before the dissolution of Parliament, for he thought it would give "a great confidence to our friends." [1] As the old year ended and the new year began both Goulburn and Herries wrote to Peel about the future which was swiftly approaching in the shape of the first session of the new Parliament.

Peel answered them both, giving his ideas on Conservative objects, Conservative policy and the Conservative party. He wrote a long and explicit letter to Goulburn on January 3rd, and also a less important answer to Herries. [2] His answer to Goulburn is indeed a confession of intention. He started it by saying that he presumes that the chief object of "that party which is called Conservative" would be to resist Radicals, and those further encroachments of democratic influence which were going to be attempted, and probably with success. At the end of what remains of the letter he further developed the party's objects. "I suppose," he said, "that the 140 members of whom you speak will agree as to the strict appropriation of Church property to purposes *bona fide* connected with the interests of the Established Religion, and to purposes for which in principle it was originally designed; as to the resistance

---

[1] Add. MSS. 40,332; 126; 129.
[2] Parker, Vol. II, 212. Herries, II, 165 (undated).

of all such schemes as excluding the Church from the
House of Lords; as to the protection of agriculture, the
maintenance of public faith to the public creditor, etc."
The rest of the letter is missing. It is just possible
Peel mentioned more principles, but if so they were
probably of like nature to those already described, and
he seems already to have given his party an ample
equipment.

They were principles he was not prepared to abandon.
He said in his letter to Herries that if he was challenged
he would defend them, even to an amendment of the
Address.   But he felt that an amendment would expose
his party's weakness, and it was far from the policy that
he had outlined to Goulburn for the beginning of the
next session.   Excepting only as regarded foreign politics
he wanted to play a waiting game.   He recommended a
system of caution and observation, for he thought that
the Radicals must move and must attack, and that the
Conservatives could act with greater effect after that
attack had started than before it.   Besides, he did not
want to attack the Government.   The party, he said,
was comparatively weak.   It could not replace this
Government with a better one if this Government was
destroyed.   Any victories that it won by the aid of the
Radicals would mainly promote the views of the Radicals;
and so Peel thought that Conservative policy ought
rather to be to "conciliate the sober-minded and well-
disposed portion of the Community," than to oppose the
Government, "on mere party grounds and for the purpose
of mere temporary triumph."

Indeed so far from attacking, he would like on occasion
to defend the Government.   He thought that that party
would have the greatest advantage which should inter-
pose itself between the two others.   The best position
that the Government could assume would be that of
moderation between ultra-Toryism and Radicalism, and
the Conservatives would appear to the greatest advantage
defending the Government whenever they espoused
Conservative principles, "as I apprehend they must do if

they mean to maintain the cause of authority and order."
But possibly they might be afraid to break with the
Radicals, and indifferent to the cause of authority and
order. In that case Peel said that the Conservatives
must do what they could to oppose both Radicals and the
Government; and he felt that their power to do this
would be greater if they did not appear to have forced
the Government into hostility by unreasonable opposition.[1]

"Unreasonable opposition," opposition on "mere
party grounds," opposition with the tainted assistance of
Radicals—these were not temptations well suited to
Peel's sensitive and peculiar conscience; and this was a
time when the case was most strong against such adventures, when the Government seemed possibly the last
breastwork for the cause of order, when to attack the
Government and to justify the ministers of the Crown in
joining the Radicals seemed to Peel "tantamount to
positive destruction," when the hopes or attempts of other
Conservatives were running on the chance that the
Government might resist the Radicals. This defensive
policy was one that Peel might have been expected to
suggest, and one that he had at various times already
put into action.

For in 1832 there had been some approximation between Peel and the Government, or at least between Peel
and one member of the Government. In April Stanley
had sent to Peel a confidential memorandum on which
he intended to found a report of a committee on Tithes,
in Ireland. He said in his covering letter that he believed that "you are not less anxious than myself to bring
to a satisfactory termination the important question of
Irish Tithes, and that there is no very great difference
in the view which we entertain of the principles upon
which the arrangement ought to be effected," and he said
"I feel assured that you will consider this as far too serious
for a party question."[2]

[1] Cf. with these views Princess Lieven's report of Peel's views, Jan. 25, 1833.
Corresp. of Princess Lieven and Grey, Vol. II, 438.
[2] Add. MSS. 40,403; 25.

These were words which were not likely to be without their effect on Peel.   In July Peel and Goulburn supported the measure which Stanley brought forward, against O'Connell's opposition, to ensure the payment of Irish Tithes.   In the debate on the Bill there was some show of Tory opposition, and Peel intervened a second time in the Government's defence, and in anger, or so it is said,[1] he declared "that he looked upon it as the paramount duty of that House without reference to divisions of opinion to support the Government in their efforts to put down the conspiracy against the laws now existing in Ireland."   Peel may have already begun to think of Stanley as a powerful and potential ally whom he did not wish to alienate, but such a theory is not necessary to explain why Peel did not propose to shock his conscience, reverse his policy, endanger the cause of order and attack the Government, in order to follow a course of uncongenial folly.

But though the Conservative party was to defend, it was not to become defunct.   Peel intended to keep his course and his party separate from the Government. He intended to offer them battle rather than compromise Conservative principles.   He said in his letter to Herries that he thought disunion among the Conservatives on any ground would be bad enough, "but disunion on the ground of individual accessions to a Government constituted like the present would be an intolerable evil." By his policy he intended nothing against the active, continued, individual existence of the Conservative party, and this letter shows that he believed that in the work and principles of that party he would have his share.

It will be remembered with what thoughts Peel had approached the Reform Bill crisis.   What doubts, what fears, what resolves he had treasured, how tired he had been and, during the crisis itself, with what obstinate hesitation he had guarded his freedom.   He had declared that he had not felt impelled to lead a party, since

[1] Hansard, 3rd Series, Vol. XIV, 131, 239 and 419.   Greville (G. and W.), Vol. II, 309.

H

he did not "feel real pleasure in the pursuit of the game";
that he regarded his return to office under any circumstances "with feelings of growing aversion," that
he had said he was sick of eating pledges, that he would
not abandon any opinion he had to conciliate ultra-Tory
support; that many powerful reasons operated with
him to make him exceedingly cautious about forming new
party associations, and that he would have to think very
maturely indeed before he formed a party connection
with the ultra-Tories.   In fact, in the last two or three
years he had shown a great desire to avoid the trouble
that had gone before.

Desires are often only formed to become anachronisms.
All these feelings seem to have had very little effect on
his position.   Peel was still in politics and, more than
that, he was still leading his party, or at least making plans
for it, and ready to engage in a new chapter in politics.
His weariness seems to have gone, to have only been
roadside weariness, and to have been dispelled by his
periods of rest and refreshment at Drayton.   The interest and danger of the issues raised by the Reform Bill
had carried him over from the bottom of one page to the
top of the next.   But the last page was turned over, not
torn out; it still remained in Peel's memory and fate,
and the past had left traces in this letter to Goulburn.

Goulburn had pressed him on the question of the
necessity of union and concert, and Peel would not say
that they could do anything without union and concert
as a party.   He did not want a general preliminary
meeting of the party to discuss the general outline of the
campaign, for various intelligible reasons, among them
that he did not think it would do any good.   He thought
that if "a common sense of danger and common views
on public affairs" did not unite them when the time for
action came, it could not be done by any preliminary
meetings.   He had spoken, earlier in the letter, of concessions of opinion for the sake of unity of action.   Perhaps on this point he was more conciliatory than he had
been before the Reform Bill had passed.   He did not

refuse all idea of concession; he merely said that it was hard to speak of such concessions without knowing the subject and extent of what might be required. But he added, "I must own I cannot think beforehand of any point on which I am prepared to concede much or indeed anything. Take the currency question, for instance."

It was not the first time in such matters that he had taken for his instance the currency question. Before the Reform Bill he had told Goulburn that on the currency question for instance, so far as abandonment of opinions went, he would not advance one single yard to gain a whole party. Indeed, the currency question seems to bulk very large in Peel's calculations. It was, of course, important and delicate, and as Peel went on to say, he thought it a question on which, now that it was settled, all wavering was an evil in itself, and on which in consequence no play and pretence at compromise could be considered. It was also a question on which ultra-Tories, at least agricultural ultra-Tories, were probably unsound; so perhaps it was right to give it so prominent a position.

Perhaps it was right; it was certainly ominous. Sometimes when Peel had worked at a thing, he saw it extremely plainly and extremely fixedly. Much of his best work he did by a clean intellectual process, relying on knowledge and statistics rather than impressions, on laborious calculations rather than great leaps of intuition. As he had said at the time of his labours on the Currency Commission, he had tried to work at that problem as if it were a problem in mathematics. When he had once settled a result in this way it would not be necessarily connected with his party position, or part of his general opinions. But he would not be likely to modify or abandon it. Since it would seem very obviously a portion of truth, and since he was both conscientious and self-conscious he would tend to become very sensitive about it. An opinion thus formed would become clear, impenetrable, and probably intrusive. On the subject he would have unflinching courage. It would become a fixed point; and whatever else decided his ultimate party position it was going to be plotted out so that such fixed points were included.

Insoluble truth and lingering memories may be almost equally inconvenient, and it is possible that Peel may have tended to minimize any shrinking from unity that he felt, when he was writing to Goulburn and Herries whose desires he knew. He had said enough to take Goulburn's attention on this point, who said to Herries about this letter, "I am sorry to see (what perhaps others would not observe) still an unwillingness to unite cordially with the Ultras, but this may easily be softened by our joint management."[1] They might find Peel an uneasy subject to manage. Still on the whole in this letter he had shown a sincere and satisfactory desire to engage in active endeavours for the Conservative cause, and in concert with the Conservative party. He might shrink, but he was by no means going to shirk. He was going to be active and willing enough to be able to work out his fate. But there were other difficulties about Peel's party position, difficulties which no one as yet could be expected to notice, for they could only be discovered by the illuminating passage of time.

The enemy of the party, as Peel described it, was Radicalism. Its main object in politics was to defend the constitution against further inroads; indeed, it was the desire to do this which had reanimated Peel's political life. But Peel was to see the Radical attack on the constitution itself diminish in force and fervour and in likelihood of success. There are few things so embarrassing in a battle as losing your opponents. Both Peel and the Conservatives were to continue till the end to resist the Radicals, but might not some of their unity, not of purpose but practice, come to be lacking when this specific danger had slipped to the background? Peel and the Conservatives no doubt had other objects in common, but this is the one which Peel puts first in his

[1] Herries, Vol. II, p. 163.

letter to Goulburn, and which seems to colour and temper the whole.

As it happened, in ten years' time, all, except one, of the specific points of union which Peel enumerates at the end of what remains of his letter had gone into momentary and comparative abeyance. Perhaps they might be supplanted. There might be a Tory or Conservative spirit germinating in Peel which would produce fruits agreeable to a Conservative party. Perhaps he and his party would have in common enough beliefs, prejudices, needs and experiences to colour and control his desires. There might be a treasury of Conservative traditions from which could be brought out practicable measures on which the party would be both interested and unanimous. Still the only question in Peel's list which would in ten years' time be of first importance was the protection of agriculture.

There was another complication in Peel's party position. Peel wished to resist any further encroachment of democratic influence. The part of the Constitution that was most likely to suffer from encroachment was the House of Lords. Peel had recently and desperately struggled for the independence of that House; he was still to defend it in his speeches. But could the Lords' independence ever again be exercised against what was popular and powerful? The Duke wished to be not factious but moderate, yet also firm and uncompromising. Would not that imply the constant rejection of the Government's important measures, the conscientious damming of the stream of reasonable Reform until the Lords had at last excited the dangerous impatience of moderate men? A firm and uncompromising policy on the part of the House of Lords might very easily lead to another contest with the Government and the country, and to another defeat. If that was to happen Peel would have to stand by the Lords, to expose his small party to the full weight of the attack of Government and Radicals combined, and to fail in any way to affect the issue. His choice would be easy, his task desperate; for when once the Lords and the Government were fairly embroiled over a Conservative principle Peel would only be able to follow a useless and unyielding consistency.

But the choice before him might be less fatal, and more embarrassing. The Government might be mild and unwilling to challenge the Lords to assert their independence. The Lords might be exposed to the possibility of self-restraint. There might be a way out. If such were the case the Lords' independence might be defended by being surrendered. Peel might defend it in his speeches, and yet be able to moderate its practice. He might be able to play for caution and peace, and to avoid the risks and results of exercising what he wished to maintain. The policy would be patriotic and tempting, but it would not keep alive the important constitutional questions on which his great party was formed. It would hardly be a resounding adherence to principle. Indeed, for the sake of caution and safety and peace Peel might be tempted to a gradual slurring of all his party's principles, to a course of unprincipled moderation. Would his party be then without principle? The question immediately arises as to what is party without principle? But on the 29th January 1833 the curtain was rung up on the First Reformed Parliament.

CHAPTER III

THE FIRST REFORMED PARLIAMENT, 1833

The first night of a new play was never awaited with more anxiety than was the meeting of the First Reformed Parliament. The new system, the new Parliament and about 300 new members were to be tried. The old game was to be played with new players and they might not know the rules; they might not even care for them.

They were strange, but not afraid. They were not to prove themselves as modest and malleable as new members should be. Soon Greville complained of their presumption and self-sufficiency; they behaved, he said, as if they had taken the House by storm and might riot in all the insolence of victory. Many were filled with great expectations, so that at the opening of the Session motions were tabled on all manner of subjects, and during its course the public business was liable to be tripped up and hindered by the ramifications of inconvenient hope. The bonds and discipline of party were loosed, and instead of the regular succession of party speakers sometimes fifty members would rise at the same time, impatient to be heard, and Conservatives complained of a general ignorance of the rules of procedure, of a tendency to sterile debate and a passion for appointing Commissions of inquiry. Meanwhile the noises and uproar of the House were more disorderly, tumultuous and brutish than before. This fact had probably little significance. The disorder may have been caused by ill-bred Irishmen, pertinacious and exultant Radicals, or the "young fry of Tory nominees," but it seemed to onlookers as if the hordes had already broken in. Peel told Croker that the first few nights of the debate on the address were "frightful, appalling," and Croker too began to call this Parliament the "national Convention." [1]

It must be remembered that Parliamentary life had

[1] Grev. II, 360. *Life of Roebuck*, p. 52. Croker II, 201.

always a background of noise, restlessness and bad manners. When an unimportant or dull speaker was trying to address them many members spent their time in talking, laughing, hooting and sleeping—at full length on the benches if the House were empty enough. At about seven o'clock members started to dribble out to dine. Between ten and eleven they came back, not always sober. A little later in this period there was one Tory Colonel who seldom, if ever, spoke. But returning from dinner he usually made the attempt, and sometimes he was able to twine his arms round one of the pillars of the House and thus, resisting all attempts to pull or put him down, he would declare vehemently that he would lay down his life if necessary for the Constitution in Church and State.[1] Sometimes the noise of laughter and conversation swelled so high that neither the Speaker's voice could be heard nor the voice of the member who in ironical phrase "had possession of the House." During personal collisions, when members had said exceptionally unpopular things, whenever certain members addressed the House or when the House wished to adjourn, there were passages of special disorder. The uproar grew considerable, and the cries of most of the ordinary animals, dogs, cats, sheep, cocks, and owls were imitated, sometimes with great ability.

Some men were daunted from speaking, others were put down, and others had to fight a long and stubborn battle to get out part of what they had to say. There may have been something in the tone and easy assured manners of the House that resembled the free, confident manners of assemblies of boys of the same standing at a public school; but sometimes the tone of the House must have seemed like the tone of a school where the public opinion happens to have been formed by louts and hobbledehoys. To make matters worse there brooded, over all, that time-soiled spirit of perverted chivalry which enforced the code of honour. Even if they were Members of Parliament, gentlemen felt that

[1] *Random Recollections*, 2nd Series, Vol I., 228.

they ought to resent insults and ask for that satisfaction
which no gentleman would ever refuse another; the
difficulty was intensified by the encouraging feeling that
however much members passed or resented insults in
the course of debate, the House would always prevent
any duel ever taking place.   The House was therefore
often tiresome and not always dignified.   An increase
of this disorder after the Reform Bill was no doubt well
fitted to chime with Conservative fears but, as a matter
of fact, the restlessness and hastiness of the House was
even better fitted to excite the ready disillusionment of
serious Radicals.[1]

At the moment, however, there were Radicals who
were not yet disillusioned.   There were active figures
among them who caught public attention.   On the first
night of the Session violent old Cobbett plumped himself down among the ministers on the Treasury Bench,
a place which he forsook on later nights for the front
Opposition bench next to Peel, to Peel's obvious distaste.
He spoke often and with violence, but he was very
ineffective, so that his Parliamentary service is only a
kind of postscript to his real career.   Equally obvious
and much more important was a Radical, not a new
member, who was in the full tide of his power.
O'Connell was a fine upstanding figure with a large
body, mouth and face both large and expressive, a
slightly turned up nose, unruly dark brown hair or
rather wig, and "dark laughing eyes."   He had come
back to the House of Commons from Ireland with a tail
or personal following of over thirty members, and he
walked incessantly about the House with something of
a swagger, talking and signing to his followers in various
quarters.   Here was an actor full of bonhomie and
violence, who must play a great part in the first Reformed
Parliament.[2]

[1] Warren, £10,000 a year, Book the Seventh, Chap. V.   Life of Roebuck,
p. 52.   (Description from Roebuck's extract from the diary of an M.P., Tait's
Edinboro' Mag., July, 1833.)   Grant, Random Recollections, 1st and 2nd Series.
[2] Grev., Geo. IV and Wm. IV, Vol. II, 353 (under Feb. 10, 1833).   Random
Recollections, 1st Series, 301 ; 2nd Series, Vol. II, 165.

§ 2

On January 29th the Parliament met and proceeded to elect a Speaker, for at the end of the last Parliament the old Speaker, Manners Sutton, had bidden farewell to the House. He had been voted a pension, but had not been given a peerage, and there had been continued speculation as to why the Government had omitted this customary honour and whom they would put up for the post. At length it became known that the Government intended to save a pension and retain experience for this inexperienced Parliament by asking the old Speaker to stand again. Joseph Hume, O'Connell and Cobbett opposed Manners Sutton and nominated the Whig Littleton, against his wish. The objection to Manners Sutton was that, as a Tory, and of a "tax-eating" family, he was unsuitable to rule or represent the first Reformed Parliament. The people would say, declared Cobbett, like sample like sack, in the language of the farmers.

The debate was prophetic and disturbing, with passages that pointed to present suspicions and to troubles to come. Hume and O'Connell declared that the proposal would seem to spring from a compromise between the Government and the Conservatives. O'Connell declared that they were throwing away the great advantage of the Reform Bill which was to put down Toryism. He taunted Althorp and Stanley with having said at the elections that the Reform Bill was final, to which Althorp declared that he had only meant final as regards the Constitution of the House of Commons. Much of the debate was occupied by futile but eager attempts on the part of the Radicals to prove that Sutton would enjoy at the same time both the pension voted to him and his salary as Speaker. Such a result was impossible, but the Radicals were driven on by the fierce all-interfering desire to destroy pensions and remit taxes, a desire which above all others had buoyed up the Reform movement; much, therefore, in the debate was significant, and the opposition to Sutton and the Government was at the same time a protest and a prophecy. But as opposition it was entirely unavailing, for Hume and O'Connell were beaten by 31 votes to 241, and Manners Sutton was elected into the Chair.

On February 5th the Commons started to debate on the Address in answer to the speech from the Throne. The speech mentioned various important topics, but the debate became focussed on what it said about Ireland. It spoke of Church Reform in Ireland, but it also deplored the disorder there, intimated the possibility of coercive measures and declared at the end a determination to maintain the legislative union between Ireland and Great Britain. All things, then, were not made new. Some old ill things had crept out of the grave of the old world to do more than sit in idleness upon it; like many another political grave it had never been securely sealed up. The mover of the address desired O'Connell's co-operation with the Whigs, after he had first called him a bird of prey. But O'Connell was stirred to something near frenzy. He followed the seconder of the Address and poured out his indignation, wrath, and contempt with a description of the grievances of Ireland, finding the words "base, bloody and brutal" nearest to hand when he dealt with the Whigs or their Government. He excited a passionate answer from Stanley.[1] Through four nights the debate went on, mainly about Ireland, and on the third night Peel rose and started upon his new task, a task whose possibilities and difficulties he did not entirely foresee, a task whose end was as yet very far away.

He was 45 at the time, and at the summit of those last broad steps of strength and gravity which bring a man to what is called maturity. He had been in office since his early youth, and had filled the highest posts in the country with great ability and integrity. Yet it was possible to think that he should be set aside like an old

---

[1] Hansard, 3rd Series, Vol. XV, 139.   O'Connell's Correspondence, Vol. II 320 (O'C. to Dwyer, Feb. 10, 1833): "I feel the vigour of youth in the elastic spring of my hate of ministerial tyranny."

coat, hung up in a cupboard to be left and forgotten. His past had not been dishonourable. The needs of his country had certainly ranked with him above the needs of himself and his party. He was self-centred rather than selfish, and his chief defect was a certain failure to understand what was going to be demanded of him. Yet he was considered to be deep and subtle, selfish and ambitious. He had gained that reputation which seems the easiest to get and the hardest to lose, the reputation of being insincere and shifty.

It was the old House of Commons in which he was speaking, a small dark room, gloomy and badly ventilated, a sordid unhealthy box in which had been brought to birth the eloquence and destinies of the past. On either side of the Speaker's Chair the benches rose sharply, straight-backed, but well cushioned, and covered with leather. The front benches were about three feet from the table of the House. On either side were galleries in which members sat; opposite was the Strangers' Gallery, the back row of which was occupied by reporters. There was a hole in the roof, called the ventilator, where women were allowed to go, and under which hung the principal chandelier. Beneath the Strangers' Gallery was the door and passage by which members entered the House, and several rows of seats where they could put friends. The atmosphere was often too hot and usually disagreeable, and the whole was utterly gloomy and ill-conditioned.

The House seems to have disappointed even those who were prepared to be disappointed. It was 33 feet broad and 47 feet long, certainly too small to accommodate all its members with comfort, or even with standing room. It was said that only 366 members could have anything like accommodation, and that members would often vote on the side opposed to their desires rather than go out into the lobby and lose their place, as they certainly sometimes voted on the wrong side through being asleep. In an important debate they seem to have been most uncomfortably packed, and they had to torture themselves into what positions they best could if they wanted to sleep. The pictures of statesmen trying to sleep in a full House look most like the distorted figures on the opposite seats of a crowded third-class railway carriage at midnight; in this winter Session they would be mainly dark-coated figures, with their great top-hats riding at all angles over their heads. Darkness and inconvenience and the grotesque manners and noises of the members must have made this a strange home for debate and destiny. Perhaps it was more fitting for disillusionment and disappointment.[1]

There was probably not much sleeping while Peel was speaking. He was one of the best debaters in the House and one of the most important. Inside and outside the House his speech was regarded with the greatest interest. He sat at this time on the front opposition bench, nearer the Speaker than he had been before the Reform Bill, owing to the invasion of the Radicals. Of the excellence of his manner of speaking there was some difference of opinion. Some found it heavy, monotonous and too obviously acquired, some found his jokes silly and self-conscious, especially when made against their party, and some still detected the awkwardness and provincialism of the North Country manufacturer of the "spinning jenny."[2] It is admitted that he did not produce what that age panted to hear, what they would call phrases of great philosophical truth or sublime conception. He spoke in the grand manner, but not in the inspired grand manner. Yet his speeches were very able and very competently produced. They interested, moved, and sometimes amused his hearers, and he was said to excel in the tones of deep tragedy. In that dark House he would rise slowly, sumptuously dressed, and wearing a watch chain and bunch of seals of unusually large dimensions and great splendour. He would arrange his

[1] *Random Recollections*, 1st Series, Chap. I. *Sketches by Boz*, Chap. XVIII. Roebuck, p. 52. Hansard, XVI, 371.
[2] Campbell's *Lives of the Chancellors*. Creevey Papers. Broughton's *Recollections*, etc.

coat tails carefully—at least Disraeli hinted in after years that this was almost as important with him as the arrangement of his periods.[1]   At the beginning of an important speech he would rest his left hand on his hip, his right he would use to strike the box on the table in front of him.   His voice was clear, pleasant and well controlled, and he would start slowly and solemnly and then become more excited and swift, always remaining distinct. Sometimes he used to turn right round and speak to his party behind him when he thought to catch their applause. He could turn to no solid phalanx of Conservatives in this Parliament.   They were scattered and few, and were mixed up with Radicals.   Cobbett and O'Connell used that side of the House, and Hume and others like him always sat there in perpetual opposition to all Governments, and thus it was that Peel rose to make the last speech on the third night of this debate, with a shrunken following and an uncertain future.[2]

He knew how he stood; indeed, early in his speech he mentioned the change in his position from the times when he had been used to speak with a large party behind him.   He knew how he stood, and he described to the Commons, as he had described in his letter to Goulburn, a policy both sensible, resolute and expressive both of party integrity and personal independence.   He declared provisional support of the Government, war on the Radicals, and the antitheses of moderation.   He could not refuse to consider Church Reform, yet he was resolved to defend the integrity of the Church's interests, privileges and rights.   With their safety was bound up not only the safety of other rights and other privileges, but also the much higher interests of truth, morality and pure religion.   From the language in the speech from the Throne he thought this might be the Government's view.   But it had spoken of treating the Church of

[1] *Tancred*, Chap. V, Book 1.
[2] Hansard, 3rd Series, Vol. XV, 366 (Peel's speech on Feb. 7).   For Peel and his manner of speaking, *Random Recollections*, 1st Series, 105–22 (Sir Robt. Peel).   *Life of Sir R. Peel*, by Sir L. Peel.   Bulwer Lytton (*England and the English*).

Ireland separately. Some difference of detail might be legitimate, but Peel would view with horror any difference of principle. Any alienation of Church Property in Ireland would strike at the rights of the Church of England to its property; indeed, it would strike at the roots of all property, public or private, if 300 years' prescription was not considered enough.

And here in his speech he praised and congratulated Stanley, and added that he had understood Stanley to say that he would never consent to the appropriation of Church property to other than Church purposes. He went on to speak with effect on a question, old with him but never exhausted, the outrages in Ireland and the proposed laws for coercion; and again he commended the Government. He spoke at some length against the Repeal of the Union, while expressing his friendship for Ireland. He dealt with foreign affairs, and then towards his close described his general intentions in politics.

He would support the Address. It was his duty to support the Crown in its measures for Ireland. And the course he was following now was the course he would follow hereafter. He would defend the Government when it opposed subversive principles, and attack it when it encouraged them. These intentions which he announced to the House were what he had outlined to Goulburn, but Goulburn was a friend who entirely believed in Peel's single-mindedness. Peel was now continually and painfully conscious that he might be confronting other opinions. He declared, indeed he repeated, and that more than once, that his support was dictated by principles perfectly independent and disinterested. His course was not one adopted, as some might imagine, to recover office. Between himself and office a wide gulf existed. He had no desire to return. He did not follow his course because he now reposed a greater confidence in Ministers. But the late great change had caused demands to be made on public men different from the demands of the past. Hitherto there had been two parties, each convinced of the rightness of their own views and each able to take the Government. Then all party tactics were justifiably resorted to for the acknowledged purpose of turning out a Ministry. Now it seemed doubtful whether the old system of party tactics was applicable, and whether it was not men's duty rather to give their attention to protecting property and law and order, than to considering what was the best way of harassing those in power. And yet, for all that he said, party politics had still a considerable rôle to play in British political life, and Peel was utterly wrong if he thought or feared or possibly hoped that the path of duty would not lead to the glory of the Treasury Bench.

At the very end of his speech he spoke of Reform. Certainly he had been against Parliamentary Reform, but he denied that he had been an enemy of gradual and temperate Reform. And he denied that up to now the country had been a mass of abuse, that everything had been wrong, and that a reformed House of Commons could set it all right. He feared the tendency, already manifested, to change everything radically and simultaneously. As to the Reform Bill, the Ministers had abstained from triumph over it, and he would not mention it. He would consider it as disposed of. He would look to the future alone, take his stand on main and essential matters, and join in resisting all attempts at such new measures as could not be stirred without unsettling the country, endangering prosperity, and disturbing that public tranquillity and those habits of obedience which were essential for the employment and welfare of the labouring classes.

He knew that there was no means of governing this country except through the House of Commons, and therefore he would take his stand in defence of law, order, the King's throne, and the security of the Empire, from motives as independent as those of the most Liberal member from the largest constituency. And on that note he ended.

§3

Peel had struck his first blow, and he had struck with success. The Government were loud in his praise.[1] Stanley "could not debar himself" from writing a note to offer his thanks for Peel's compliments; yet compliments from the Opposition may be unhealthy delicacies for a Minister.[2] Peel had roused men's interest and expectation; his waning had ceased and his waxing had begun. Both Greville and Raikes, in their diaries, declared that he had started in a bad position with opinion against him and had ended very well placed and popular, even with the ministerialists. But the agreement of the two diarists ran further than that. Both took him to mean that he was now of no party, both considered it likely that the country might come in the end to be ruled by him, and both spoke of his ambition.[3] And there they were wrong. He was certainly not scheming for office, at least not in the simple cynical way which men envisaged. Within the last year or two he had thought of office with distaste; in this very speech he had said he did not want to return to it. He was not insincere, but he may have been mistaken.

Peel scored a success, and so did the Ministry. The various amendments to the Address suffered sweeping defeats; all that were found to vote for them were O'Connell's tail and a handful of ordinary Radicals;[4] and the Ministry went on with confidence to their double and difficult task of Reform and Government. As an earnest of their good intentions on the side of Reform they introduced their Irish Church Bill into the Commons and proposed commissions of inquiry to furnish them with information for Corporation Reform. But the first great measure to be passed by the First Reformed Parliament was to be a coercion Bill, and on February 15th Lord

[1] Grev., Vol. II, 353 (under Feb. 10).   [2] Add. MSS. 40,403; 177.

[3] Greville, II, 354 (under Feb. 14, 1833). Raikes' *Journal*, Vol. I, 159 (under Feb. 14, 1833).

[4] Hansard, 3rd Series, Vol. XV, 455 and 458. *Corresp. Princess Lieven to Earl Grey*, Vol. II, 433 (Grey to Lieven, Feb. 9, 1833).

Grey introduced into the Lords a Bill for the suppression of disturbances in Ireland.   It was very severe; its most drastic clause was perhaps that which enabled Courts Martial to try offences under it.   Even the Whigs in the Commons were filled with uneasiness, while O'Connell caught fire with passionate resentment.   He used violent words out of doors, and he began to have hopes that the Bill would stir up a stronger opposition in the Commons than the Address had done.   It was O'Connell's nature to be unbridled and sanguine.[1]

The Bill was not the type of Government measure that the Lords were likely to obstruct, and it passed them with ease and celerity.   But when you are walking on a tight rope you can fall off on either side.   On February 27th Althorp introduced the Bill into the Commons.[2]   Althorp was troubled in mind.   This measure was painful to him, and he did not like the policy they were pursuing in Ireland, though he still led the Commons for the Government that pursued it. His speech was halting, unconvinced and unconvincing, showing only too plainly how stringent he felt were some of the clauses of the Bill.   He left the House bewildered and doubtful.   The prospects looked bad when, near midnight, Stanley rose, fiery, excited, the picture of a young fighting Lord.   He spoke with thrilling effect, giving the details of outrages, and pouring invective on O'Connell.   For once oratory had an immediate effect. When Sheil tried to speak at the end of the debate there were cries for O'Connell, and they were cries not for an orator but for an accused person, and one more than accused.   It is said that he looked like a condemned felon.[3]   Peel spoke on a later night again with success, dwelling on the details of outrages, in the rôle of high tragedy.   O'Connell's speech was a failure, and the Ministry carried the second reading by 466 votes to 89. The Ministry had been successful, but they had begun

---

[1] *Corresp. of O'Connell*, Vol. I, 334 (O'C. to Fitzpatrick, undated), 321 (O'C. to Fitzpatrick, Feb. 17).

[2] Hansard, 3rd Series, Vol. XV, 1210.   [3] Spencer, 456.

by showing their weakness. They would carry their measure, gaining thereby a fecund source of future embarrassment, and they were not cementing the alliance of Whig Liberal and Radical.

There must have been grave misgivings abroad on the subject of the Bill, for the Ministry thought that it was necessary to emasculate many of the clauses while it was in Committee. They made the Courts Martial clause so much milder than it had been that various Conservatives were encouraged to withdraw their support from it on the ground that it had now become a useless encumbrance. But the defection only proved that without Conservative assistance the Government still had a satisfactory margin between them and defeat.[1] Their majorities did not desert them, the Bill passed into law, and the Government felt that they had a majority, useful, faithful, obedient. And yet all was not well in the Commons.

No doubt there was in the Commons a large Whig majority, but the House contained much uninstructed and undisciplined expectation and desire. There was hope for reform, and a widespread exciting belief in the distress of the country. There was likely to be a strong desire for retrenchment, and savage war on sinecures and pensions. To increase the confusion the House was filled with members not bound very closely by party, and the lack of discipline emphasized a political derangement of the time.[2]

Each Ministry, as it takes up the paraphernalia of office, must take up with it the burden of the support of those things which seem to men at the time essential to the continuance of government. There must be a large body of action handed down unaltered from Government to Government, and yet men will not always see that

[1] Lieven, II, 447 (Grey to Princess Lieven, March 20, 1833). Bulwer, *Life of Palmerston*, Vol. II, 148 (Palmerston to Hon. Wm. Temple, March 21, 1833).

[2] Earl Spencer, 451. *Corresp. of O'Connell*, Vol. I, 332 (O'C. to Fitzpatrick, March 6, 1833).

there is a strict limit to the number of changes that can be made by any new Government, especially of those they can make at once.   It was not understood how much the Whigs would have to take over from the Tories.   They may have taken over too much, but it is improbable that they should have taken over little enough to satisfy the Radicals.

This was largely because the Party system was undeveloped or had been in abeyance.   A simple, well-developed party system may perhaps educate all shades of opinion for a period in the unavoidable needs of government; no light task and no inconsiderable service. Of course, there is always a danger that men should learn too much.   The necessities of government can become exaggerated and diminish still more the tiny circle of what is practicable in politics, for there is no experience which cannot be used as a cloak to hide folly, to guard indolence and to smother hope.   The extent of the necessities of government must be tested.   What each age takes for granted in that line is often one of the most interesting points of study in it, and often one of the most pregnant criticisms against it.   But it would be as well, perhaps, if they were tested with some sort of knowledge and sympathy; and there are often politicians or groups of politicians, who have not been enlightened by the discipline and disillusionment of power.   Perhaps they do not hope ever to form Governments themselves, or perhaps they will not listen to leaders who know what it is to be Ministers.   In any case, such men are likely to be factious and dangerous, and for their own purposes divided and sterile; to become more useful they must learn in the travails of office to prune their desires, and to fructify hope with a drop of despair.

In this Parliament the agriculturists might be held to come under this head.   They were a cross-section of the House, confined to neither side of it and infected by Currency heresies.   There were also the Radicals who were inclined to work by personal pertinacity rather than by organized party action.   Among these perhaps the

most notable man was Joseph Hume, who was a useful
but rather indiscriminate critic of Government expenditure, a placid and obstinate man of great pertinacity,
full of ingrained suspicions, and enlightened by the blind
reason of Benthamite politics.   Moreover as well as
those who were definitely Radicals there were many
loose and unattached members, fired by the hope and
forgetfulness of a new régime.

There was trouble in February over pensions and sinecures.   Hume, for instance, frightened some members
of the Ministry by a resolution on Naval and Military
sinecures.[1]   Soon the time of the House was much taken
up by the Irish Coercion Bill.   However, on March
21st Thomas Attwood broke in upon it in Committee
with a motion, which, Althorp opposed, to appoint an
enquiry into the conditions of the labouring classes.[2]
Attwood was the grand organizer and hero of the Birmingham Political Unions and a commonplace man in an
uncommon position.   All his politics centred round his
belief that a vast amount of evil had been done by Peel's
Currency Act in 1819, and that the cure must be sought
in some method of going back on the policy of that Act
and the standard of value which it imposed.   His motion
might be recommended to the House by a vague philanthropy and a general show of care for the distress of
the people.   But on the other hand it was brought
forward in a precipitate manner and at an unfortunate
time, while to some who might have voted in its favour it
seemed impracticable to appoint one Committee to consider the distress in all trades and in all districts.   Moreover, Attwood's own speech was long, rambling and bad,
while his well-known preoccupation with the Currency
deeply coloured his motion in other men's eyes.   Yet
the numbers on the division were 158 to 192.   A
majority of 34 was all the margin there was for the
Government and all the margin, as it seemed to some, for
the integrity of the Currency system.

[1] Hansard, 3rd Series, Vol. XV, 659.   Broughton, II, 285.
[2] Hansard, XVI, 918.

It may be guessed that one man, at any rate, was disturbed and excited by this. The events in the early weeks of the Session had made Peel proud of himself and his party. The Ministry had shown neither strength, constancy nor ability. The Parliament was light, changeable and dangerous. Peel felt that the Reform Bill only worked for the first three weeks of the Session through the self-restraint of the Tories, whom the Reform Bill had been designed to destroy. Many times they might have united with the Radicals, sacrificing no principle, and they had refrained. Peel thought that he himself could have moved the House on the doubtful first night of the Irish Coercion Bill just the other way to the one in which it ultimately voted, if the great question had been not how to turn the Government out, but how to keep any Government in, and avoid confusion.[1]

Those feelings of interest, importance and self-restraint were exhilarating, and it was the kind of exhilaration that might be the mother of hope. If Peel had no specific hopes, he felt competent and effective. It was not that his mind was always inflamed, as the vulgar imagined, by definite yearnings for office, but the whole man was filled with diffuse ambition and sense of power. He was ready to break out in exalted moments of sanguine, almost reckless endeavour. It might not be a question with him of far-seeing expectations, but he might become suddenly and enthusiastically engaged on a forlorn hope. Without schemes, without visions, the early part of this Session does not seem to have been always unpleasant to Peel, for his course was clear and his pride gratified.

But all was not clear and all men were not gratified in Peel's party. Public necessities are possibly clearest to those who are troubled with the fewest private ones. Such aids to clarity of mind as a satisfied ambition and a satisfactory income were enjoyed both by Peel and the Duke, but were not shared by every Conservative. At the beginning of the Session Raikes noticed that although

---

[1] Croker, II, 205 (Peel to Croker, March 5, 1833). Add. MSS. 40,320; 207.

Peel and the Duke were pacific in policy, some of their subordinates were not. They were likely to keep but one object in view; they would obtain on any terms a majority against the Government. Many of them were straitened in circumstances by losing their places when the Tories went out, and it seemed to Raikes that they were well aware that the troubles which might be caused by their actions would embarrass the leaders and not the subordinates.[1] Nor was the policy that Peel recommended one particularly acceptable or inspiring for a party man. It seemed mainly to consist in keeping, with difficulty, a rival party in office. There were the indigent and the ambitious, and there were also the Tory Agriculturists who would certainly complain of distress and try to get taxation remitted, and would probably confess unsound views on the Currency question.

The Duke seems to have complained that the party did not always support Peel. The Government complained that on occasion when principle demanded it, the Conservatives did not always support the Government; notably when the emasculated Courts Martial clause of the Irish Coercion Bill was proposed in Committee. The Division lists seem to show that on that occasion some Conservatives did vote against the Government, but that more voted in its favour, and that if the main body of the Conservatives were guilty of anything they were guilty of staying away. However, on March 21st the matter came nearer the surface with this motion of Attwood's, involving as it did a complaint of distress and an attack on the Currency system.[2]

The two leading agricultural Conservatives, Sir Edward Knatchbull and Lord Chandos, voted with Attwood. Knatchbull, one of the members for Kent, was to be a member of both of Peel's Governments. Chandos was to be invited to one and be a member of the other. He was the son of the stout Duke of Buckingham. The

[1] Raikes' *Journal*, Vol. I, 159. Disraeli's *Endymion* (Mr. Ferrars).
[2] Grev., II, 363. Spencer, 458. Grey and Lieven, II, 447. Palmerston, II, 148. Hansard, XVI, 872.

father was mainly a worthless intriguer who had, in times
past, been a greedy leader of an expensive faction, and
was now connected with the silliest and most dangerous
group in the Lords. The son was a better man. He
was sometimes foolish, he was not without foibles but he
was honest in purpose, proud of his position as the
farmers' friend, and prepared to make sacrifices in the
cause of agriculture—sacrifices which were not always
convenient to Peel. The motion may have attracted
an unnaturally high proportion of agriculturists, especially as it was preceded by some discussion on the malt
tax, while only a moderate number of Conservatives
voted at all. Still it must be significant that more than
half of them, and much more than half of the Conservative County Members, seem to have voted for
Attwood. A section of Peel's party, mainly an agricultural section, differed from him on a matter that he
was to prove near to his heart.

The division in itself is interesting; its effect upon
Peel was very remarkable. A few days afterwards
Croker called upon Peel at his house in London. He
found him giving great importance to Attwood's motion,
apparently taking it as a division on the Currency question. But to Croker's surprise he was prepared to
accept office himself, and to make battle. He spoke with
great firmness and spirit of an administration that would
be unyielding, if it only lasted a fortnight. "He seemed
to think there would be an entirely new combination of
which the Currency question would be the basis. On
that he was firm, but foresaw the Radicals and Ultra
Tories would unite aganst him."[1] So he was already
prepared to risk a Government, for all that his party
was so recently and so crushingly defeated. The broken
statesman of 1830 was now prepared for the spirited and
exhausting pleasures of a desperate struggle for principle
in power; he meant apparently to enter a coalition with
the Whigs and face opposition, not only by Radicals but
also by men of his own party.

[1] Croker, II, 205 (Croker to Lord Hertford).

For the agricultural Ultra Tories were really of the same party as Peel. They joined with him on other divisions, shared many principles with him, and provided members and supporters for his Governments. Yet here he was led to stand by the Whigs, and they to coalesce for a moment with the Radicals. No doubt one reason for their difference lay in the Currency question, but the matter went deeper than that. A phrase might be hazarded about the politics of intellect and of Government experience opposed to the politics possibly of class, and certainly of particularist sympathies. But perhaps it would be wise to leave it that Peel's first thoughts were of the needs of Government, of the stability of Currency, and of essential taxation, while some of his party's first thoughts were with their constituents. He thought as from the Treasury Bench, and they as from the country house. The sympathies of the Conservative Leader were likely to be with those whose misfortune it was to have to frame Budgets, but the sympathies of some of the Conservative party were quite as likely to be with those whose misfortune it was to have to pay taxes or to sell corn. But the difference was not brought to its climax. Peel was not asked to form a Government, and the Conservative party remained, for a time, undivided.

In the middle of April Althorp introduced his Budget and he was able to announce that he intended to reduce taxation by over a million. Peel thought the reduction too great,[1] but it was by no means enough to satisfy all men. Althorp had still retained various unpopular taxes. For instance he retained the taxes on knowledge, which was the strange name by which taxes which bore upon newspapers were known to the Radicals. The malt tax was untouched, which formed the outstanding grievance of the agriculturists. Worst of all, he kept the house tax and much of the window tax, both of which were bitterly hated in the great towns and in London, and not without reason, for their burden was

[1] Hansard, XVII, 326 (Budget), 342 (Peel's speech).

distributed with great absurdity and injustice. There
had already been plentiful signs of the depth and passion
of men's desires for the remission of the burden of taxation, and when the Budget appeared a hubbub immediately rose in the country.

There were troubles in Parliament. The debate on
the Budget was immediately followed by another Attwood motion.[1] It was proposed that they should
appoint a commission on the distress in the country with
a special direction to consider the monetary system.
The motion had been very much dreaded, for the tide of
opinion in favour of Currency reform was held to be
rising, while the prestige of the Ministry had noticeably
ebbed.[2] Althorp was afraid that men would vote for
an enquiry into distress, even if they did not really
desire to interfere with the Currency. He resolved to
propose an amendment guarding the Currency and
leaving the question of an enquiry open. He did not
wish for an enquiry; he believed that the amount of the
distress had been greatly exaggerated, and he believed
from experience that however well the Committee might
be fenced round, it would manage to break through into
Currency matters. But he felt that if they tried to reject
the enquiry they might lose their amendment to safeguard
the Currency. It was the old standing difficulty of a
definite policy having been tied to the tail of vague, widespread and generous sympathy.

On April 19th Althorp wrote a letter to Peel giving his
plan and these views, in the hopes that he might have
Peel's opinion if Peel thought his intention impolitic.[3]
His letter witnesses to his opinion of Peel's importance
and his trust in Peel's sympathy. During the debate
Peel made a long and elaborate speech against Attwood's
motion ending with an appeal to the members not to
yield their opinions to their constituents.[4] But from
the division lists it would seem that a fair number of

[1] Hansard, XVII, 384.
[2] Raikes, I, 171. Broughton, IV, 300 (Diary, April 22 to 24).
[3] Add. MSS. 40,403; 231.   [4] Hansard, XVII, 506.

Conservatives had remembered their constituents and forgotten their economics, and voted against the Government. Again, among these were many members for counties, including Chandos and Knatchbull.[1]

Nevertheless the Government obtained a large majority and saw with relief that this Currency difficulty was over. Not so were all their troubles. Althorp had not the swift strength and decision or the other instincts necessary for a Chancellor of the Exchequer passing a Budget through Parliament, and he led the House like a friend and not like a master. Very soon he made a bad blunder. On April 26th, Ingilby, a Liberal member for Lincolnshire, moved for a reduction of the duty on malt. His motion was treated by the Government as of little importance, on the ground that it was a motion that had originated "in a coalition of parties and unsanctioned by Sir Robert Peel." The Government whipping was bad, agricultural members showed a readiness to escape before the division, Knatchbull and Chandos and other Conservatives voted against the Government and the Ministry was beaten by 162 votes to 152. Althorp was unwise enough to say that he bowed to the decision of the House.[2]

The King was troubled, Lord Grey was angry and talked of resigning.[3] There was much talk of a property tax. Greville came back to town to find all in confusion, considerable penitence among ministerialists and "everybody gaping for what next." He had an answer to that question, for he was affected as were others of that time by a desire which, like a disease, haunts times of political trouble. He wished for a moderate and non-party Government. He thought it must end in Peel and Stanley, unless the country came to the reign of the Radicals.[4] Even the Whigs agreed that the breaking up of their administration would probably be followed by a patchwork administration of which Peel would be a part, and

---

[1] Hansard, XVII, 586.   [2] Spencer, 462.   Hansard, XVII, 689.
[3] Brougham's *Memoirs*, Vol. III, 264.
[4] Grev., II, 368.   O'Connell's *Corresp.*, I, 347.

Althorp thought that Peel might come in with some of the present set.[1]   Peel's sun was undoubtedly rising, but it was not yet high noon.

Through the medium of a Whig and a Conservative Whip Peel offered to help Althorp rescind the malt tax resolution, and again Althorp told him his plans.[2]   He meant to amend a resolution against the window and house taxes, which was announced for April 30th, by moving that they could not be repealed, and the malt tax reduced, without employing an income and property tax, and that such a change was inexpedient.   The window and house taxes were disliked by the towns, the malt tax by the country, and Althorp intended to drive both parties into the same corner.   Peel agreed to this manœuvre.   He agreed to it first of all in private and then again, quite unnecessarily, in a loud voice as he passed Althorp on the Treasury Bench in the Commons.[3]

Another mistake on the part of the Whigs was unlikely.   Many men wished to get rid of the Malt Tax but not of the Government; and though even on this division Chandos and a few others of the Conservatives still seem to have voted against them, the Government were able to carry their amendment by very considerable majorities.   The incident had been humiliating.   Meanwhile the storm over the assessed taxes rose in the country, and the Government laboured heavily.   There were angry meetings in London and in other great towns. Hobhouse, a Minister with a Radical past, who had just succeeded Stanley as Irish Secretary, felt that he was pledged on the subject, and resigned his place and his seat as one of the members for Westminster.   He was persuaded to stand again and not re-elected.   The police had to disperse an open air meeting in London, one of the policemen was stabbed, and the Coroner's jury brought in a verdict of justifiable homicide.   About the end of April and the beginning of May much of the popularity and prestige of the Government had deserted

[1] Broughton, IV, 302, 304.
[2] Parker, II, 216.   Add MSS. 40,403; 239.   [3] Broughton, IV, 305.

it, even its survival seemed to be menaced. O'Connell grew confident of its early discomfiture and Brougham confessed that it was seriously damaged.[1]

The people had not been long in losing faith in their first Reforming Government. Disappointment comes very easily in politics and some Radicals were not even disappointed. Some had never been satisfied with the Reform Bill, while others, who accepted the Bill, had always been suspicious of its authors. The Radical members of the Government had remained uneasily in office, but in March, discontented with Whig policy and tortured by ill-health and bitter bereavement, Lord Durham had resigned, never again to take his place in a Whig ministry.[2]

No doubt the Ministry was still much stronger than many believed, but it had certainly lost the great and peculiar power it had had at the time of the Reform Bill. Brougham attributed its plight partly to the immoderate hopes that men had formed about it, partly to the silence and uselessness in debate of some of the Ministers there, and partly to indolent and haphazard leading in the Commons.[3] The House of Commons was faithfully Whig, but it was turbulent and loquacious and difficult to discipline, and probably not enough had been done to lead or control it. Meanwhile, as was natural, the hopes of some Conservatives increased. But Peel's spring had come too early.

Peel had been defending the Government so closely that at times he stood almost in their ranks. He had been spoken of lately by men of different parties as a possible Prime Minister, but that possibility had depended on one thing alone. The question at issue must be the essentials of government. He must be asked to come in not as a party leader but as a strong man to

---

[1] O'Connell's *Corresp.*, I, 347 (April 27), 350 (May 10), etc. Brougham's *Memoirs*, III, 265 (Brougham to Grey, Whitsunday, 1833).

[2] Graham Wallas' *Life of Francis Place*, 324. Broughton, IV, *passim*. *Life and Letters of Lord Durham*, Vol. I, 321 (Durham to Grey, March 12, 1833).

[3] Brougham's *Memoirs*, III, 265 (see above).

set straight confusion. A strong man is chosen for his strength alone, a party leader is chosen for his principles. Peel may have been better fitted for strength than for principles—many statesmen must be—but principles cannot be escaped, and Peel was too honourable to try to elude them. Peel might yet be destroyed by his principles. If his Party principles became the chief subject of Parliamentary discussion, his position would make him politically desperate and perhaps personally ineffective. He must leave his thoughts of the first office and seek again the last ditch; and Peel in the last ditch was indeed a god in the gutter, something very ill placed for usefulness. He would have to fight it all out, and with but little to help him. In the Commons his party was miserably small, and he knew well enough that there was no hope as yet of succour from the country.[1] He would have to expose all his weakness, and then be defeated; and after his defeat in the Commons would arise the question of the House of Lords.

§ 4

At the very beginning of the Session the Government had introduced their Irish Church Bill. It was sweeping enough to please if not to satisfy O'Connell, and it certainly contained provisions that Conservatives might well consider objectionable. The most startling of these was the abolition of ten Irish Bishoprics; also the estates of the Bishops of Ireland were to be managed by a body of Commissioners to be appointed under the Act, and it was intended to appropriate to any purposes to which Parliament might think fit the increase in their value which would be obtained by this change of management. Such purposes would not be necessarily connected with the Church. There were other objectionable points in the Bill, such as the abolition of Church cess, a graduated tax upon livings, and arrangements to prevent reappointment to livings where no duty was performed. Here was certainly enough to set Conservatives voting, and

[1] Parker, II, 223.

Churchmen preaching and writing, praying and resolving, up and down the country.

The most dangerous provision of the Bill was probably that which in the eyes of Conservatives raised the question of Parliament's right to appropriate to other than Church use the property of the Irish Church. The Government denied that this was involved in the Bill. The Church still kept what belonged to it, the State taking only such increase in value as its own action had created. But the argument did not convince either Radicals or Conservatives, who applauded or opposed the clause on the ground that it established the right of Parliament to re-appropriate Church property.

The Church members of the House of Commons joined issue immediately. They dragged into the fight all their old accustomed artillery, the King's Coronation Oath, the Act of Union and the oath required of Roman Catholic members under Catholic Emancipation. The effects of the Bill and all its objectionable points were debated at length and with fervour. Of Church members by far the most interesting and exalted in doctrine was Sir Robert Inglis, now a member for the University of Oxford. At the second reading he said that from the crown of its head to the sole of its feet, from its preamble to its last schedule, the Bill was bad. It began with a lie, calling itself the Church Temporalities Bill, whereas by tampering with the number of Bishops it was meddling with the spiritual succession, which certainly ought to be outside Parliament's sphere. The Church's temporalities, he said, had not been given to her by Parliament. What had been done at the Reformation had been done by Convocation pari passu with Parliament. Parliament could not touch what the Church had not first permitted it to touch. He did not deny the power of Parliament to pass such a Bill, but he denied its right.[1]

Peel was in difficulties. His principles had become involved, and there were parts of the Bill of which he

[1] Hansard, 3rd Series, XV, 561 ; Vol. XVII, 966 (Inglis' speech), 986 (cf. with Peel, 994).

most obviously and sincerely disapproved. He could
not but oppose what he regarded as the misappropriation
of Church property. He expressed great disappointment that Stanley had been able to persuade himself
differently on that matter, for it was Stanley's views
on the Church that had enabled Peel to hope that he
could work in some sort of an alliance with the Government. He heartily disliked the tax upon benefices.
He had objections to the reduction of Bishoprics in
Ireland, and he was afraid that the Bill would control the
"expansive force of the Protestant faith" in Ireland.
Yet he was anxious to show himself ready to agree to
reasonable Church Reform. And he could not share all
the doctrines of Inglis and others. Parliament, he
declared, had united Bishoprics before and could do it
again. On the question of Emancipation he had always
refused to use the Coronation oath argument, and he
would not use it now. His common sense and his
reading of History kept him from believing in a state
of affairs largely ideal, and he remained, as he was to the
end, a faithful, cautious, sensible Erastian. But what
one man takes for good sense is often taken for bad
faith by others.

Through blunders, hesitations and a little improvident
haste on the part of the Government the Bill was delayed,
altered, and reintroduced, so that the real second reading
was not taken till May 6th.[1] The Conservatives divided
against the second reading and were defeated by 317
votes to 78. On May 20th the Bill went into Committee.
The position was hopeless for the Conservatives, with
their principles violated, their passions raised and their
prospects bad; and over all the scene began to loom
the shadow of the Lords. The Government grew
anxious, for they were pledged to pass this Irish Church
Bill. The Conservatives seemed to be marching on to
a serious crisis, preoccupied with their principles.

Peel lagged behind. He was not always, it would
seem, so intent on his principles that he had no time to

[1] Hansard, XVII, 966.

regret his position and remember the hopelessness of action without allies.   On May 25th he wrote to Goulburn a letter in places difficult to understand, for it lacks other documents to elucidate it.   He declared that it was obviously of utmost importance for those to unite who wished to preserve the Irish Church from spoliation, and that his was the ungracious task of securing concessions from all parties.   One of the parties to be thus united seems to have been Stanley.   Peel had received a letter from Stanley and found it very different to the views Goulburn had expressed.   He speaks obscurely of putting various groups, comprising it would seem both Lords and Commons, into direct communication with one another, in the hopes apparently that the Church might not risk the consequences of disunion among its friends.   The clash of principle had come, the Government were openly at war with the Conservatives and with Peel; but Peel could still work and hope for assistance from one member of the Government.[1]

But what a difference was here from his earlier position. A short time ago he had been in communication not with one individual Minister but with the Government's representative in the House of Commons.   Then it had been merely a question of defeating the Radicals, a task both congenial and effective.   Now he must engage in the dreary and doubtful labours of compromise and surrender.   He had fallen, but he had reached the ground.   His present position gave more nearly the measure of his real task and his real resources. His earlier alliance with the Government came to nothing, since the conditions that had brought it about passed away, while unfortunately the divisions of principle remained.   The alliance between Stanley and Peel played a large part in the foundation of the new great Conservative party as also, perforce, did the policy of compromise and surrender.

If there were any communications such as Peel had suggested between Stanley and other Conservatives, they

[1] Parker, II, 220.

K

did not serve to allay the fears of the Government. These remained unabated. In the middle of June the Government made an expensive bid for the safe passage of their Bill through the Lords. At the suggestion of Lord Grey the Cabinet decided to drop the Clause which had been held to involve Appropriation. The Bill was still in Committee in the Commons, and it was there that they announced their decision.[1] The Government had very possibly some intimation from some one that this would help the Bill in the Lords, but there is too little evidence to prove that their action was the result of any definite agreement between Stanley and the Conservatives.[2] In the course of the debate on the Clause Peel declared that, though he heartily welcomed the decision, he knew of no compromise and had not heard of what the Government intended until he entered the House. The concession could not, he said, affect his views on other parts of the Bill, and he would still continue to criticize the Bill in Committee. The Government might have rendered more likely the passing of the Bill, but they had not ensured it, and they had certainly aroused the anger of the Radicals. The House divided on the question, and the Government had a large majority, but it was observed with fear how many important members voted against them. And O'Connell declared war on the Bill.

The Radicals would vote against the third reading of the Bill; the question remained, should the Conservatives join them? Peel again wrote to Goulburn and asked his advice. His letter was written in a manner habitual to him. He often wrote down the arguments on both sides of a question as they occurred to him, not to state an opinion but to give food for thought. Only the arguments on one side usually grew with more vigour and speed than the arguments on the other. It was like a

[1] Hansard, 3rd Series, Vol. XVIII, 1073 (June 21).

[2] Creevey, Vol. II, 255, and Spencer, 473, seem to point to an understanding. But the correspondence of Peel and Goulburn shows no sign of one, while Peel puts the concession down "to a positive order from the King" (Parker, II, 222, Peel to Goulburn, June 24, 1833).

man stepping sideways with great rapidity, and yet announcing meanwhile that he was still open to conviction as to whether to turn and walk to the right or the left. Perhaps his strong mind, which knew reverses and changes well enough, too seldom knew real indecision, and that may be a loss as well as a gain in a leader of men.

He seems in this letter to lean to the opinion that it would be better not to vote with the Radicals against the third reading, and better to be content with this Bill than to hope for another. He could have no confidence in the future temper of the House of Commons. The Dissenters were firmly entrenched in the power given them by the Reform Act, and it was admitted that half the Cabinet were in favour of alienating the property of the Church. His hopes for the re-establishment of Church principles were few, and his instincts were for the settlement of problems lest worse should befall. It was an instinct that was to play a great part in the building up of Conservativism.[1]

Goulburn's instincts were different. He had disliked this Bill from the start, and had been ready and profuse in opposition.[2] He felt that the measure still embodied principles that made it impossible for him to give his support. He was engrossed much more than was Peel by his principles, yet he gave weight to Peel's arguments, but pointed out that with half of the Cabinet in favour of spoliation he could have no assurance that this measure would be final. He spoke also of other considerations, which Peel had not mentioned, for perhaps they occurred earlier in the process of reasoning to Goulburn than to Peel, his leader. He thought that they ought to discover the views of the Church and of the Lords on the subject. If the Church and the Lords meant to fight the Bill, and the Lords to reject it, their difficulties would be increased were the Conservatives in the Commons to forbear opposition on the third reading. And there

[1] Parker's *Peel*, II, 222 (Peel to Goulburn, June 24, 1833).
[2] Add. MSS. 40,333; 158.

was something else to be taken into account.   If their course was to be governed by prudential motives it might be desirable to find out how many of their friends, even in the Commons, would go along with them.[1]

How the discussion proceeded is not clear, nor what it was in the end that decided Peel.   Later on in the crisis he advised the Duke not to throw out the Bill, but at this moment his instincts did not prevail, for to the Government's surprise and dismay he did vote against the third reading.   The Bill went up to the Lords with a disturbing burden of hopes and fears.   The Radicals were openly counting on a breach between the Lords and the Commons.   Charles Buller, for instance, said in Committee that he would support a certain clause in order that the Bill might be as popular as possible in character, so that they might appeal to the people if it was rejected in another place.[2]   It seemed as if one of the great questions left unsolved by the Reform Bill was now to be fought out, for if Peel opposed the Bill in the Commons, would the Duke in the Lords be more merciful? He could certainly be more effective.

§ 5

The Duke was not, any more than was Peel, a man to delight in the heedless destruction of Governments.   He too had wished to keep the Government in power.   He was far more despondent than Peel;   he had not even the symptoms of hope.   The revolution was made, the electorate democratized, the Government would stay in for a little and then go out, to be succeeded by chaos; and so whatever men thought of these Ministers he held that it was a duty to keep them in office as long as might be, to ward off confusion.[3]   His policy was rather like asking a burglar to stay in the house to keep out an assassin, for he had no sort of liking for the Government. At the best they were an evil necessity, and by the opening

[1] Add. MSS. 40,333; 162.   [2] Hansard, XVIII, 919.
[3] Croker, II, 207 (Memorandum by Croker, March 13).   Grev., *Geo. IV and Wm. IV*, 362 (under Feb. 27, 1833).

of the session the Duke had brooded too much over his dislike of this Government which he did not wish to destroy.

The dictates of patriotism and prudence might save the Government from defeat, but not from criticism. The Duke might feel called to put down the axe, but not to abandon the rod; and he might not realize how dangerous a weapon he still held in his hand. He might be like that merciful magistrate who commuted a hanging to a beating of which the culprit happened to die. The Duke and his past foreign minister, Aberdeen, had long been troubled by the state of the continent and of British foreign policy. The affairs of Portugal and Belgium, and the intrusion of French armies into both of those countries, were all in various ways peculiarly fitted to excite their susceptibilities, while they naturally felt aggrieved at the doings of the inheritors of their problems and places. So they devoted a large part of the debate on the address to foreign affairs and were to return to the subject.

There were others in the House anxiously interested in other subjects, and much that the Government did came up for criticism in a hostile debate. The amendments made in the Commons in the Irish Coercion Bill excited opposition, and caused a division in which the Duke voted against the Government, but the Government were victorious.[1] Feelings were warm in the Lords, and even ineffective debate might make them warmer. To make matters worse, the Duke was most assiduous and conscientious at his duties as leader of the opposition. He prepared himself carefully, came down to the House often, and spoke on all conceivable questions.

This intensified matters. Grey and the Duke viewed each other with a certain distaste. They started the Session upon a balance of dislike, for they had behind them three exciting years of strenuous disagreement, and there are rumours of an earlier quarrel. As the

[1] Hansard, XVI, 1294.

Session proceeded affairs did not improve. The Duke did not modify his opinions of Lord Grey's work and words and Government. Grey felt that the Duke was a mischievous nuisance, who made a great many speeches that were very bad and nonsensical, and the debates gained an edge that was unnecessary for the ordinary uses of political warfare.[1]

From the personalities of Lord Grey and the Duke, from their prestige and dignity and from their high positions in the nation, this dislike might be touched up into tragedy. There was a second important rivalry in the Lords which might easily be broadened into farce. For one thing there was no real enmity between the principals at all. For another thing one of them was Brougham, the Lord Chancellor. He was a curiously untrustworthy man for the high place he held. He was undoubtedly brilliant, exceedingly vain, and very erratic and absurd. It is only necessary to look at his picture in order to laugh at his strange features and foibles and to forget, rather unkindly, his power and genius and the great part he had played. It was nearly played out now, for he had left most of his power behind him in the Commons, while he had taken his foibles up with him to the Lords. The poor eagle was now shut up in that coroneted cage where so many eagles have moulted. There lay ahead of it long years of busy but heart-sickened impotence; it was to lose all its feathers and become a very strange and disreputable object; it would be easy to forget that it had been an eagle and not just a crow.

The other principal to this quarrel was Lyndhurst. He had been Lord Chancellor in the Duke's Government, and was a friend of Brougham, who had given him a judgeship. With great zest and enjoyment, making magnificent speeches, he fought Brougham's local Courts Bill. Greville has a pleasant picture of him happy and

---

[1] *Corresp. of Earl Grey and Princess Lieven*, Vol. II, 441 (Grey to Lieven, Feb. 6, 1833). Lieven, II, 452 (Grey to Lieven, June 26, 1833). Grev., *Geo. IV and Wm. IV*, 20 (under Aug. 7, 1833).

self-satisfied, drinking tea after a speech, and in a hurry
to get back to the House to hear what the Chancellor
had to say and what lies he would tell.[1]   For Lyndhurst
was one of those fortunate statesmen who enjoy the
struggles of politics and do not take their issues too
deeply to heart.

If there were to be any indulgence in criticism or
personal annoyance, or even light-hearted rivalry, something dangerous might be done with the large Conservative majority in the House of Lords.   Up to June, however, the Government suffered from but few divisions
and no defeats.   Loyal to his resolution of the year
before, to debate often and freely but to divide seldom,
the Duke held his hand.   He often spoke strongly
against the Government without pressing the matter to
a division.   He did not try to use the engine of party
against the Government.   In the division in the Lords
on one of the amendments made by the Commons in
the Irish Coercion Bill, 46 peers voted for the Government and 40 for the Conservatives, in addition to which
the Government used 39 proxies and the Conservatives only 5.[2]   If the Duke had wanted to win the
division, he must have had more than five proxies
available.   So the Session went on, and he did not
organize any general attack on the Government, or
encourage his followers to believe that a vigorous stand
was going to be made;   indeed the intentions of the
Conservative leaders in many directions do not seem to
have been made very clear to their followers in the
Lords.[3]   Others might talk, but the Duke remained
angry, persistent, restrained, and the Government rested
immune.

Other Peers of his party may have been frightened
and sympathetic, but the Duke had to reckon with not
a few whose feelings were different, and who might bring
about difficulties and perhaps disasters.   The Conserva-

[1] Grev., III, 7 (under July 12, 1833).   [2] Hansard, XVI, 1317.
[3] E.g. Parker, II, 217.   Add. MSS. 40,403; 266 (Lord Talbot to Peel,
July 14, 1833).

tives had among them men of principle and men of
ambition, and the Duke's policy specially annoyed one
foolish and violent group. This was not the party of
the old, honest, unbending Tories such as Eldon and
Newcastle, whose impracticability was dictated by
principle, and who when they were least convenient were
also least self-seeking. It was the small group represented by the Marquis of Londonderry and the Duke of
Buckingham and the Duke of Cumberland.

Londonderry was the rather unworthy brother of the
great Castlereagh. He had distinguished himself as a
dashing cavalry officer in the wars, and as a diplomatist
at the subsequent conferences. He was a man of an
independent, indeed uncontrolled mind, vigorous and
rash. He was selfish, inconsiderate and very ambitious;
very covetous, that is, of what he considered his due of
the honours and prizes of politics. He was probably
an able man who misused himself in politics. The Duke
did not like him, he had found him troublesome in the
Peninsula, where Londonderry had served on his Staff.
As the upshot of this and other experiences the Duke
had apparently come to the conclusion that he would
trust him to do well enough in specialized tasks, but that
this was as far as his confidence went; and it was not
far enough for Lord Londonderry.[1] They corresponded
with a show of intimate friendship, but Londonderry
was not quite sure of his old comrade the Duke.

The fat Duke of Buckingham, father of Chandos, was
a less interesting character. Cumberland is notorious,
the most notorious of all the sons of George III. He
made a show of being bluff and jovial, frank and reasonable, but men said that his chief delight and most constant
motive was to cause mischief and pain. There is probably some good to be said about him; it is certainly
untrue that he murdered his valet. Besides he probably
had courage, for he had to face great misfortune and the
most horrible calumnies. He was certainly persistent.
He may have had some hasty idea that he was doing

[1] Grev., *Geo. IV and Wm. IV*, Vol. III, 227.

good in his politics, for he cannot have been, as the
Duke of Wellington describes him, simply a malicious
busybody.   He was extraordinarily unpopular and, to
darken the future, there stood between him and the
Throne only a delicate girl, the Princess Victoria.   To
trouble the present there stood very often nothing at all
between Cumberland and the Closet and the ear of the
King.

These men soon received most unfavourable impressions of the Duke of Wellington's policy.   On
March 25th Londonderry deplored to Buckingham the
Duke's total secession.   The Duke, he said, was making
the House of Lords of no use in the Country.   He had
heard the Duke would not oppose to a division by proxies
either the Irish Grand Jury Bill or the Irish Church and
Corporation Bills, in spite of the fact that the two last
struck at all property in Ireland.   Nor, so it seemed to
him, was there any hope of a division in the Lords on
the Irish Coercion Bill when it returned there, however
mutilated it might be.   It would seem from this letter
that the Duke was not hounding his followers on to
attack the Government.

Unfortunately, though unhounded, they still hoped.
If the Duke seemed neglectful and undesirous of victory,
the Government were not secure.   The 25th of March
was only four days after Thomas Attwood's motion.
About that time Peel was considering the chance of his
being called into office to fight a last battle for King and
Currency, and hope seems to have stirred in the large
breast of the Duke of Buckingham.   He had apparently
written to Londonderry of a more immediate working of
the Peel party in the Commons, probably meaning by that
the early promotion of a Conservative Government or a
Government containing Conservatives.   But Londonderry
could not understand where they could look for the support of numbers, and saw difficulties in coalition with the
Whigs, at least on the first break up of the Government.
He was not hopeful, though he was interested.   Meanwhile, since there seemed no chance of any division in

the House of Lords, he decided to carry his despairs to Paris. Buckingham stayed at home, writing to the Duke now and again letters referring to the future conduct of affairs in the Lords, which the Duke answered with brevity, courtesy and very little encouragement. The Duke would reserve his own intentions, and be obliged without comment, when he heard those of Buckingham.[1]

Matters developed, the Malt Tax motion was passed and rescinded, and Peel was found to be as unsatisfactory as the Duke had proved himself. He seemed, both to Londonderry and Buckingham, determined to prop up and carry the Cabinet, now humiliated every day by circumstances and their own blunders. The difficulty, or so Londonderry thought, was that Peel had no courage. Peel would not take office until the Reformers had so much disgraced themselves that they wished Peel to take their places. It was a miserable state of affairs; it drove Londonderry out of all patience, as it had driven him out of the country. Indeed he confessed that the reason why he had absented himself from the Lords was because his nature was "too open" for him not to say what he thought.[2] So Londonderry lost his patience, and the country and Government gained a breathing space.

But it was only a breathing space. With June there came difficulties. Foreign affairs had continued to interest and annoy the Duke. In June he thought that circumstances forced him to bring the affairs of Portugal before the House of Lords, and so he proposed an address to the Crown on the Portuguese policy of the Government. He pressed it to a division and won it by 79 votes to 69.

The action was startling and seemed to be menacing. It betrayed in the Duke a most dangerous state of opinion. In the course of the debate he denied that it was a vote of censure on the Government, but he declared

---

[1] *Courts and Cabinets*, Vol. II, 39, 41.
[2] *Ibid.*, Vol. II, 48 (Londonderry to Buckingham, May 5, 1833).

that he would not have the slightest hesitation in moving
a vote of censure if he thought the case justified it.   He
told Greville afterwards that he was not by any means
dissatisfied at what he had done.   If the Government
turned their defeat to account in the Commons, it would
be of great use to them.   They could show their followers
that the House of Lords could be depended on for good
purposes, and thus persuade them to pass good measures
in the House of Commons.   The Government could
not make Peers, the Conservatives were not frightened
or disheartened, and he could not restrain them from
attacking the Government; and, so said the Duke, if
the Lords had to give up their freedom of action, the
sooner they were swamped the better.[1]

A little immunity had done its work.   The Duke
had, unfortunately, recovered from the depression
occasioned by the Reform Bill.   He had been made
amenable by political caution, not by constitutional
theory.   The constitutional theory of practically all
Conservatives remained unimpaired and impossible.
Like all unreal or doubtful constitutional theories, it
was an arsenal well filled with specious arguments for
unwise actions.   The Duke had always proposed limits
to his self-restraint in the Lords, and now the state of
mind that had helped to whet his caution was passing
away, while the party behind him became courageous and
unmanageable.   Also he showed the limits of his
knowledge of his position, for he showed that he did not
understand how little a modern Government can stand
independence in Parliament.   He seems to have thought
that a Government could remain in power and allow one
House to do independently what it thought was right,
and that this impossible position was the only tolerable
one for the House of Lords to occupy.   The Duke's
political education was dangerously incomplete.

His motion had been already vigorously countered.
On June 6th the Commons, in avowed contradiction to
the Lords, passed by a very large majority a resolution

[1] Grev., II, 380.

of confidence in the Government's Portuguese policy. The King's answer to the Lords' address was short and sharp, and decisively in favour of the Government.[1]   It was held by the Whigs that the only effect of this incident was to demonstrate clearly that a vote by the Lords, of no confidence, had no effect at all on the Government. "Nobody seems to care a straw," said Macaulay, "for what the Peers say about any public matter."   "The institution of the Peerage," he said, "is evidently dying a natural death."[2]   And there even young Macaulay was probably wrong, or if the Peerage was dying it was to outlive many that watched in contempt at the bedside. Besides they should have mixed their contempt with fear; the Lords could die dangerously.

The King and the Cabinet were afraid.   What the Lords had just done was held to be a warning.   There were disquieting rumours that hopes for a Conservative Government were treasured among them; perhaps the Government may have got wind of such plans and desires as were exchanged between Buckingham and Londonderry.   Brougham says that he noticed, as an alarming symptom, the position which the Duke of Cumberland seemed to have been able to assume among the Tories. It appeared that he had put himself at the head of the most extreme faction of Tory peers, and that since he spoke often and on important subjects, he was flying at high game; and Brougham says that he seemed at this time to be in close alliance with the Duke of Wellington.[3] The King was afraid of a repetition of the crisis of the year before.   His alarm was so great that he took what was perhaps an unconstitutional step.   On the last division one Bishop only had supported the Government, while eight had earned abuse by voting on the other side, and the King wrote to the Archbishop of

---

[1] Hansard, 3rd Series, Vol. XVIII, 391, 379.

[2] *Corresp. of Earl Grey and Princess Lieven*, Vol. II, 448 (Grey to Princess Lieven, June 6, 1833).   *Life of Lord Palmerston* (Bulwer), Vol. II, 161 (Palmerston to Hon. Wm. Temple, June 25, 1833).   *Life and Letters of Lord Macaulay* (to H. M. Macaulay, June 6, 1833), cf. O'Connell's *Corresp.*, Vol. II, 354 ff.

[3] Brougham's *Memoirs*, III, 273.

Canterbury urging him to restrain them from engaging in purely party matters. The advice was good, but the document was embarrassing, and the Archbishop was probably right in not communicating it to his brethren. Meanwhile Brougham's Local Courts Bill was experiencing rough treatment at the hands of Lyndhurst. The Lords might very soon show that they were not afraid of throwing out a Government measure.[1]

The Government had to consider what they must do if the Lords threw out the Irish Church Bill. They might of course advise the creation of enough Peers to counterbalance the majority against them. But there were grave objections to this. Both Brougham and Grey, and probably others, were apparently averse to the revolutionary measure of swamping the House of Lords with the new creations that would be necessary. Their objections were shared in a much stronger degree by the King, whom Grey found to be very nervous and apprehensive lest such advice should be offered to him. Probably as a consequence of this situation the Cabinet came to the conclusion that the question of Peers in large enough numbers to put them in a majority "was out of the question on the present occasion," a decision which Grey communicated to the King in order to relieve his anxieties. But Grey reserved to himself the right to advise the creation of four or five peers in order to prove the King's confidence in the Ministry, and Brougham took upon himself to throw out to the King more or less the same suggestion. The King's reply to Brougham was in terms which showed his great objection to any creation of Peers, making it seem unlikely that he would have acceded to the request, however recommended.

About the middle of July the Cabinet came to their determination to drop Clause 147 of the Irish Church Bill, the Clause that had been held to imply the Lay appropriation of Church property. Le Marchant, Althorp's biographer, who was at the time Brougham's private secretary and seems generally well informed,

[1] Brougham, III, 275. Grev., II, 383.

gives an interesting account of the transaction. It is not a description of deep, calm, and far-sighted consideration. Indeed if his account be correct or at all complete, gout, haste and personal preferences seem to have played almost too large a part in the taking of this important decision. However other Cabinets have perhaps suffered from the intrusion of these factors, and even without them a knowledge of their own divisions on the question at issue was enough to decide the Government.

At any rate, Lord Grey and those who controlled Government policy had shown themselves to be moderate, but their moderation was limited. Lord Grey had told the King that he might advise the creation of four or five peers. If the Bill was thrown out the Ministry let the King know that they would resign.[1] Their resignation would obviously be an act of great consequence. It was exceedingly improbable that a Conservative Government would be able to replace them for long. It must have seemed likely that the King would have had soon to appoint a Government pledged to the Church Bill, and this time empowered to force its passage through the Lords. Their resignation would start a train of events that must in all probability lead through confusion to the humbling of the Lords. Yet they still contemplated resignation.

It is possible that Grey conceived that his public duties were at an end when he left office. It is probable that both Grey and Althorp thought too readily of resignation, and became a little too fatalistic when resignation might become a possible duty. Such an attitude in Ministers is perhaps a disadvantage inherent in the employment not of professional statesmen to whom politics are life, but of gentlemen amateurs to whom politics, at least in office, are not life at all. But Grey must have known what would be the result of his resignation over the Bill, and was not prepared to avoid it. He was calm, however, and not much afraid

[1] Brougham, III, 292. But Creevey, II, 254, under June 18.

of a crisis. He may have felt sure that he could ultimately get power to control the Lords; after all, in 1832
he had played such a hand coolly, and had won.[1]

The first weeks of July 1833 were weeks of conflicting hopes and fears, and of various reports of the temper
of the opposition.[2]   Before the end of June, Macaulay
saw revolution ahead, if Peers were refused, and admitted
that he had never seen political circles so excited, even
during the Reform Bill. As time went on various incidents combined to make matters look grave. On July
8th, Peel voted against the third reading of the Church
Bill in the Commons. On July 9th, on the first reading
in the Lords, Eldon, Cumberland and the Bishop of
Exeter made trouble, and dragged the Coronation Oath
into debate. The same evening Lyndhurst with the
aid of his party managed to throw out Brougham's
Local Courts Bill. On July 11th, on a petition, the
Duke spoke violently against the whole Bill, again
bringing in the Act of Union and the King's Coronation Oath. He stirred up Lord Grey to declare in the
House that the Duke apparently meant to oppose altogether the second reading, to which the Duke merely
replied by repeating his opinion that the Irish Church
Bill was contrary to the policy of the country and to
the King's Coronation Oath.[3]

It looked as if he had agreed to the accuracy of Grey's
supposition. There was some restlessness in the Commons. On July 15th, Sir John Wrottesley proposed a
call of the House for July 18th to ensure good attendance in case there should be a collision between the
two Houses. His motion was defeated, but it showed
that there were eager allies to hand, if the Ministry
wished to face it out with the Lords.

And by this time some of the Ministry did wish to
face it out with the Lords, and to settle the matter.

---

[1] *Corresp. of Princess Lieven and Earl Grey*, Vol. II, 452. Brougham,
III, 294.

[2] Brougham, III, 295 ff. (Sir Herbert Taylor to Brougham, July 14, 23, 24).

[3] Hansard, XIX, 303, 550.

Their position with regard to the Lords had become, obviously, intolerable. Duncannon owned to Greville that he was almost glad of the crisis.[1]   On July 12th, Althorp wrote to his father that "the attempt to carry on the Government of this country with a dead majority against us in the House of Lords must lead to disgrace to us and detriment to the country." He said that on July 11th he had proposed that they should resign, but that his colleagues had thought that they ought first to go into action on the second reading of the Irish Church Bill. Althorp told his father that he was satisfied on the whole with this decision, because from what the Duke had said in the Lords, and from what the Conservatives' Whips reported, it seemed to be certain that the Lords would throw out the Bill. The King seemed to have made up his mind and the Conservatives to have determined to take the Government.

Althorp was not hopeless about the future. There would be storm, he thought, but no revolution. A storm was necessary to set the country on its legs; it had been made necessary by the lack of common honesty among the Tories. As he foresaw the sequence of affairs, there would be a Conservative Government and, of necessity, a dissolution. Then the new Government would fail in the new House of Commons and the King would have to turn again to the Whigs. No Whig in his senses, said he, would return to power without first exacting a promise from the King to secure a majority in the Lords, and after that things would go on more prosperously than ever before. One Whig, however, would never return. Althorp declared that he would take the opportunity to resign entirely from political life.[2]

It was an interesting prognostication, right in some of its details, wrong in all its essentials. It is true that a year hence the Whigs were to be driven out, but by the King and not by the Lords. There was to be a dissolution in which their opponents would fail to obtain

[1] Grev., III, 9.
[2] Spencer, 473 (Althorp to his father, July 12, 1833).

a majority but not to improve their position. Finally,
the Whigs were to return, presumably in their senses,
but without any promise of Peers.   The explosion was
to come when the powder was damp.

Perhaps this year the powder was dry, but it was not
to be exploded.   The Whig leaders had not schemed
to deal with the Lords; they had drifted into their present position.   Even Althorp's determination seems to
have been due to recent exasperation, for he told his
father that this storm had only been rendered necessary
through the lack of common honesty among the Conservatives. The Cabinet had been carried to their
present position by the current of events, and the current of events could carry them away again.

Althorp had hoped, indeed he had confidently expected, that the Government would be beaten by the
Lords on the second reading of the Irish Church Bill.
But it is not in mortals even to command failure.   Their
fate depended on the Duke, in whom anger had masked
some wisdom, so that it was not even possible to rely
on the man's folly.   There were Conservatives who
were probably ready to go to any extreme, some to
throw out the Bill merely because they thought it was
bad, some to risk forming a Government and facing a
dissolution, heartened by the Government's tempting
unpopularity and by the talk of reaction.   The Duke
had seemed of late to have given his countenance to
this violent party, but all their hopes and most of their
desires were far from him.

No doubt his feelings of defeat and depression had
worn off, and with them some of his caution.   The
eagerness of his followers had driven him forward.   He
had not understood the danger of criticizing the Government too successfully, and his dislike for Lord Grey
had spurred him to go much too far in debate.   But
that was all.   He was not scheming for government; he
expected, indeed, never to be in office again.   He had
no delusions about reaction.   He was still in reality
acting on his earlier policy of not expelling the Govern-

ment.[1]   The Duke's caution and sanity had not entirely disappeared.

In the few days before the second reading it began to be known that the Duke would not oppose it.   On July 13th, Wharncliffe told Greville that the Duke would be able to prevent any attempt to throw out the Bill on the second reading, though he might not prevent a division.   On July 15th, the Duke apparently called a meeting of peers at Apsley House, and told them that some such measure as this Bill must pass in order to save the Irish Church, and that though he did not approve of it he would not prevent it going into Committee.   On the same day Harrowby sent in his adhesion to the Government.   The news must have become general, and got into the Press.   It was not grateful to all. On July 16th, Eldon heard of it to his distress and surprise, and determined that he at least would fight for his old principle to the last.   Luckily he was not likely to be very effectual, or else this last which he confronted so manfully might not have been the last of Eldon alone.[2]

On July 17th Lord Grey moved the Bill's second reading.   It was opposed.   Strong speeches were made against it, and the debate went on for three nights and only came to a division on July 19th.   On that night Wellington spoke.[3]   He was still angry; he made his surrender without grace.   He attacked Grey and he attacked Anglesey, quite unnecessarily.   But he went on to use the same arguments that he had used to his followers.   The Church needed this Bill, and they ought to let it pass into Committee, perhaps to amend it there. His arguments did not refer to the dangerous position of the Lords, though he was at least partially aware of that position, but it was lucky that he had other arguments to hand, otherwise he might still have been led

---

[1] *Corresp. of Grey and Lieven*, II, 450 (Lieven to Grey, June 22, 1833).

[2] Grev., III, 8, 10 (under July 14 and 15).   O'Connell's *Corresp.*, I, 372. Twiss' *Eldon*, III, 207.

[3] Hansard, XIX, 948.

away by the phantasm of the independence of the House
of Lords. Even the arguments that he used really
admitted the dependence of the Lords on the will of
the Executive, since he admitted that in order to get
necessary legislation passed they must take it in the
form provided for them by the Cabinet. Still it was
easier for the Peers to pass legislation to save the Church
than to save themselves, and it did not matter if so be
they saved themselves also.

The Duke did not manage to go so far as to vote for
the Government. He had only said at the meeting
that he would do it, if necessary. In the event, as Hansard reports, he and Aberdeen and other peers went
away without voting. But it was enough. The Duke's
attitude must have done its work. The Government
obtained 157 votes against 98, and before the division
most people seem to have taken it for granted that the
Tories in the Lords could throw the Bill out.

Many of the peers were not pleased. Here was more
cowardice. First it had been Peel and now it was the
Duke who showed want of pluck, and as a result principles were abandoned and ambitions frustrated, for the
Session at least. Many peers no doubt were willing,
many perhaps were anxious to follow the Duke, but
many others were hot against the Bill. Eldon spoke
and voted against it, as did most of the ultra-Tories.
Cumberland, Buckingham and Londonderry all voted
against it. More important than all these, the Archbishop of Canterbury, the head of the Church, whom
Cumberland had called "wishy-washy," definitely opposed it. There was likely to be much disappointment
when a Bill, so opposed, was enabled to pass its second
reading.

It had only passed its second reading. There was the
Committee stage to come, and even the Duke had
threatened amendments.[1] There was danger abroad,
and there were destructive desires. A letter to Peel,
which the Duke wrote on July 23rd, shows him in his

[1] *Life and Letters of Lord Macaulay* (to his father, July 22, 1833).

difficulties.[1] It would be hard, he said, to make the Bill better, and if there was a division it should only be on some point of importance on which the Government was manifestly wrong. It was hard to restrain the Lords from destroying the Bill. They were very much displeased. "But it is better to displease them than to increase and aggravate the confusion of the times."

But there is more in the letter. It shows the Duke involved in his difficulties, but it shows much more than that. He declared in it that he concurred in Peel's opinion "of the State of the House of Commons, of the consequences of breaking down the Government by a vote of the House of Lords, and of the prospects from a new election." So it was not only the state of the Church that had made the Duke hold his hand. He had been deterred by the state of the country, the state of the House of Commons, and the will of the Ministry. If he acknowledged those things it would seem that the independence of the House of Lords was gone, almost as if it had never been. This was a hard lesson to learn, and a harder to teach, and he told Peel in this letter, that he found it was difficult to make men who were lately of such great weight, and were still possessed of peerage and property, understand that they were of no importance in the country. However, "the true sense of their position will be inspired at last, when they will become more manageable."

The schoolmaster himself had much to learn. His letter seems to show that he was still thinking of making a Government Bill better, of amending it on some important point on which the Government were manifestly in the wrong. His task was a difficult one for an old, prejudiced, and irascible man; and it speaks very highly for his good sense and his sense of public service that he should have undertaken it rather than yield himself up to the easy fatalism of passion. But the letter shows one more thing. Peel was at the Duke's side, Peel had communicated to him his fears about the state of the

[1] Parker, II, 218. Add. MSS. 40,309; 264.

Commons and the country, Peel was in a position strong enough to bring into effect in his party all the good and some of the ill results which are caused by men having a sense of their position. The connection between Peel and the Duke was almost the most important factor of all in the solution of the House of Lords' question.

As a matter of fact the Committee produced nothing serious. The Duke proposed without much success various amendments that were obviously, from their nature and his speeches, intended to improve the Bill. His amendment on the Bishops' question may have been too much like the clause it was intended to supplant to cause much enthusiasm. It is said that he wished to withdraw it.[1] At any rate it was defeated by 90 votes to 76. One amendment was carried by two votes, largely under the impulse of the Archbishop of Canterbury. After the division Lord Grey delayed the Bill in order that he might consider the matter. There was strong talk among the Whigs at Brooks'. But Grey was able to consider the clause as of little importance, and to continue the Bill after lecturing and warning the Lords.[2] The Bill easily passed its third reading, the amendments made in it were not enough to cause opposition in the Commons, and the Bill became law. The Crisis was over for the year.

The first Session of the First Reformed Parliament was drawing to its end. It was said that it was the longest Session with the largest number of hours of labour in the House of Commons that there had yet been in any Parliament.[3] The Ministry's troubles in the Lords were over for the time; they had to bear further criticism there, but no further menace to their existence. No doubt a lengthened Session and shrunken hopes kept many Peers away from the House. Lyndhurst was reported to have said that he saw no use in

[1] Grev., III, 15.
[2] Hansard, XIX, 1220. Grev., II, 20. *Life and Letters of Macaulay* (to H. M. Macaulay, July 27, 1833).
[3] Hansard, XX, 907.

his attending any more. "The Duke comes down every day and tries to make the Bills better; if I could make them *worse* I would come too."[1] Lyndhurst was to have his chance in the future, but at the present the House of Lords had merely become a very mildly ameliorative body. It seemed to have abrogated its real functions.

It seemed even to Peel that the House of Lords had had to abrogate its functions. After the end of the session he told Croker that the business of the Session had only been got through because the popular assembly exercised supreme power, and the House of Lords, to avoid collision, had declined acting upon what was notoriously the judgment and conviction of the majority. In particular, the course in respect of the Irish Church Bill was taken in spite of the opinion of two out of the three branches of the legislature. Peel speaks of this state of affairs as if it were a change in the Constitution.[2]

Yet if it had been changed at all, the Constitution had not been effectively changed. The problem of the House of Lords was still unsolved, the members of the House of Lords were still unsubdued. The Duke was not altogether enlightened. The unbending Tories were still unbent. No one had robbed Lyndhurst of his tongue of gold and his heart of quicksilver; while Londonderry, Buckingham and Cumberland still dreamed dangerously. In September, Cumberland wrote to Buckingham, begging him by all that was dear to him to be in London for the next Session, and to write to his friends that they might all act in unison. "If," said he, "we go seriously to work this Session we may do what we ought to have done in the last."[3] Cumberland's hopes were probably ill founded, but if Cumberland hoped at all the country's troubles were not over.

The problem of the House of Lords was still unsolved. The King had been unwilling, the occasion had not occurred, and the Whigs had not gone out of their way

[1] Grev., III, 23.   [2] Croker, II, 214 (Peel to Croker, Sept. 29, 1833).
[3] *Courts and Cabinets*, Vol. II, 64 (Sept. 20, 1833).

to solve it. The Constitution was still embarrassed by a popular House of Commons and an unrestrained and hostile House of Lords, perhaps an irresistible force, certainly an immovable body. It may seem strange and unwise that the Whigs had not made a point of settling with their adversary while they were in the way with him. Althorp thought that the matter might have been settled with storm but without revolution. But the Whigs had not planned or desired to go further in Constitutional Reform. They were moderate Reformers, and though the step appears logical to us, it had not appeared necessary to them. Even Althorp had thought that no change would have been necessary if it had not been for the dishonesty of the Tories. The Whigs would have preferred to treat this problem as settled. As is the tendency with most Ministries—indeed it is possibly a necessity of government—they took things as they came and, as is usual, things did not come at the right time. They paid their price in the end. But in politics even the lovers of logic and foresight have sometimes to pay for their pleasures.

§6

But whatever had not been done to the Lords, it could not be said with justice that the Session had been sterile. The Ministry had done important and valuable work. In March, Stanley had been moved from Ireland, to be Secretary of State to the Colonies. There he had replaced poor goody Goderich who became Earl of Ripon as compensation amid many sneers.[1] Goderich had been dallying with the problem of slavery, and Stanley took over his labours, and crowned the long battle of the Evangelicals and other pious Abolitionists with success. Stanley's measure was not at first entirely approved by the Abolitionists, who forced him to submit to an important amendment. Hume and others objected to the large compensation that was voted to slave proprietors. But so important a measure could

[1] Croker, II, 208.

not fail to bring prestige, even if the settlement of the question robbed the Whigs of a bond of union with the Saints that they might sadly need hereafter. There were other reforms to their credit. They had settled for a period the Charters of the East India Company and the Bank of England—the Bank measure exciting some opposition from Peel, who feared that part of it endangered the gold standard. They had effected various legal reforms, and they were able to make a very good showing in a joint pamphlet which they published on the work that had been done, entitled "the Reform Ministry and the Reformed Parliament."

However, the Reformed Parliament had passed one Reform that had not sprung entirely from the impulsive force of the Reformed Ministry. There had already been some attempts at reforming the evil conditions under which children worked in factories. The opinion behind the call for Factory Reform was very various in nature. Some of it was Radical, a very large part of it was Evangelical, some of it was Tory or, to speak more accurately of the state of affairs at the very beginning of things, some of it was Evangelical and happened to be Tory. The prime mover in Factory Reform in the last Parliament had been Sadler, an Evangelical Tory. He had had a Bill in hand for the protection of children, but confronted by Macaulay at the last election he was defeated at Leeds and was unable to get into Parliament. Those who were interested in his endeavours managed to get another Evangelical Tory, Lord Ashley, later Lord Shaftesbury, to take the matter up. At the beginning of the Session Ashley announced his intention of proposing what was in effect Sadler's old Bill, forestalling a Whig, Lord Morpeth, who had wished to propose a Bill on the subject.

There seems to have been very general agreement in the House that more effective action ought to be taken to protect the children, but Ashley's Bill seemed too drastic, and it was thought that it might interfere with the hours of labour of adults. It raised considerable

opposition from the usual opponents of factory legislation, from men who dreaded the effect on trade or on
the working classes themselves, who disliked restrictions on trade or were willing to put all evil down to
existing restrictions, such as the duties on corn and
raw cotton. The Government itself was affected by
the current theories in economics, and disliked Ashley's
Bill. Altogether the opposition was much too strong
for him; he was forced to submit to another Commission
on the subject, and when his Bill came into Committee
it was drastically amended, so drastically that Ashley
resigned it into the hands of the Government to be
carried into law.

Something had been done for factory reform and,
what is more to the present purpose, something had
been done for Ashley. He had been put in touch with
a subject, and with a group of men who were strongly
to affect his future and his relations with his party. It
was a group not only of enthusiastic reformers but also
of working men, and they gave to Ashley, by instinct
an aristocrat, a connection with men of the people.
In the House of Commons his supporters were strangely
heterogeneous. He had Radicals both among his opponents and his supporters. Sheil and O'Connell had
given him steadfast and eloquent support. The Att-
woods, greatly to their credit, had not taken refuge behind
the Currency question, which then, as always, could
have served to protect its devotees from having to make
troublesome and responsible decisions on any other
important question. Sir Robert Inglis and others of
the pious supported Ashley, while the lists printed in
Hansard of those who voted with him in the various
divisions show a fair number of other Tories, often
agricultural Tories, who no doubt could feel an easy
indignation at the wrongs done by manufacturers.
But Goulburn is not there, nor Herries, nor Sir Robert
Peel.[1]

[1] Hansard, XVII, 79; XIX, 219 and 883 (the debates with important
divisions).

There is nothing to show Peel's attitude on this particular Bill, and it is possible that he did not attend the House. Nevertheless he was often affected by the dictates of political economy, and perhaps the factory question divided the party in much the same kind of way that the currency question divided it, and for the same kind of reason. On the currency question Peel would not alter a jot, whatever the party thought, and perhaps the cry of the children might reach the heart of the party and yet not find so easy a way to its headquarters. Yet the cause of Factory Reform must appeal to the feelings, and Peel was by no means insensible. It was a cause that was furthered by good men of his own party, stirred on by religion, and Peel cared for religion and the estimation of the religious. But the situation had yet to develop; much was to happen to make it more clear and more poignant. Factory Reform would play its part in the future in the trial of Peel and of Conservatism.

The future was to be tried by the future. It was the Whigs and the Reform Ministry and the Reformed Parliament that had just been on their trial, and in spite of all they had done and claimed credit for, a good deal could be held to the Government's detriment in various quarters. Their retention of unpopular taxes still rankled in Radical hearts. They had not satisfied the Radicals in the amount or the nature of their Church Reform. They were unpopular in Radical circles, and had been disappointing. Their defects in the House of Commons were remembered against them. They had been forced to make very important alterations in several of their Bills after they had introduced them. It was said that they could no longer depend on the spirit of party in the House of Commons. They were known to be divided, and some of them had notoriously deserted on specific occasions. Worst of all it was thought that Althorp was not likely to remain with them long, and Greville was told that Stanley, his obvious successor, was not generally trusted. The immediate

past of the great Reformed Ministry was confused; in
their immediate future they might be confounded.

All these things could be studiously recounted by the
Government's enemies and bewailed by its friends.   Yet
in spite of all there was much to make the Government
pluck up courage.   They had done much good work,
Ireland was quieter and manufactures were improving,
if the depression in agriculture had not passed away.
Parliament, if at times it had been difficult, had usually
shown itself ready to pass Bills and vote money at the
Ministry's wishes.   Above all there seemed to be no
possible alternative to the Whigs.   The reckless might
not recognize this fact, but it gave the Government
the whip-hand over any that did not deal in absurdities.

Against the new Parliament much contemptuous
criticism could be levelled.   It had been talkative.   It
had wasted time in sterile debate.   It had disappointed
those who had deserved disappointment.   It had been
variable and at times violent.   It had not been more
than ordinarily equipped with talent.   Such were the
accusations levelled at it.[1]   Yet though the Conservatives might sneer and the Radicals perhaps despair of
its ever doing its duty, there was one real lesson that
the Session might have taught, an important political
lesson from which, if it were necessary, generalizations
might be spun.   Some people recognized that this first
Reformed Parliament was remarkably like those that had
gone before.[2]

---

[1] E.g. *Ann. Reg.*, 1833, *History*, pp. 122.   *Quarterly Review*, Vol. XCVII,
Art. XIV.   Blackwood's *Edinburgh Magazine*, Vol. XXXIV, No. CCXV.

[2] Grev., III, 27 (under Sept. 3); cf. with Grev., III, 17 (under July 25).

CHAPTER IV

1834—THE END OF THE GREAT REFORM MINISTRY

Complete and sudden changes are what men cannot always succeed in commanding or refrain from discerning. 1833 had seen no entire change of nature in the House of Commons, and it had not seen much change of nature, or even of opinion, in Peel.

It is sometimes said that there are two Robert Peels, one before and one after the Reform Bill, but no Peel of darkness had really vanished mysteriously before a Peel of light. Much the same Robert Peel had emerged from the years 1831 and 1832 as went into them. The same conscience was there, and the same necessities, only the conscience had possibly been stimulated and the necessities had certainly increased. Before the Reform Bill he had been a Reformer, and before the Tory collapse he was one who believed in the necessity of comprehension and reason as a foundation upon which his party should be based. The Reform Bill was completed, and like a wise man he had accepted the fact. But he still felt that the Constitution had been outraged, and that it remained tacitly altered in order that the Reform Bill might work.[1] He could still fear the fears by which of late statesmen had been haunted, fears which still persisted in politics to darken imaginations and to confuse issues.[2] In July 1835, for instance, Peel was alarmed at the evidence which he heard at a Parliamentary Committee on the arming of the Political Unions, and it seemed to him that the Radical members endeavoured to prevent it coming out. Both in 1833 and in March 1834 Croker reported that Peel had come round to his point of view, and, as he said in 1833, he thought ill of everything.

---

[1] E.g. Hansard, XXIII, 71 (April 25, 1834) (Peel's remarks on the passing of the Reform Bill through the Lords). Croker, II, 214 (on first session after the Reform Bill).

[2] E.g. Privately printed Aberdeen Correspondence (May 23, 1834).

But when Peel thought ill of everything he had usually habits of mind which gave an edge to his thoughts. He had still his old ready resources of contempt and of practical acumen, to help him to powerful criticism of the Government's methods of proceeding. He could not see that they had much cause for pride in the results of the Session, which had been got through by means of violence to the Constitution and the restraint of the Conservatives. The praise that they got rather sickened his palate and he was unwilling to read their pamphlet on their successes; while there were mistakes and shufflings under the Reform régime which he could describe to Croker with scorn and effect.[1]   He had indeed enough and more than enough critical sense fully to equip an opposition leader.

It was not only the Government that Peel had criticized. He had had his moments of satisfaction with his party, but his work as a party leader had not always been comfortable and gratifying. During the troubles over the Irish Church Bill he had spoken to Goulburn of his task of recommending concession as "difficult and ungracious."[2]   There had been the great difficulty of those who wished to attack the Ministry on all occasions and with any possible allies, and about the end of May, when Peel was in correspondence with Lord Melville on that problem, Melville had had to comfort Peel with the assurance that the course he was taking was not so unpopular as he had supposed.[3]   Here, like a weed returning into a lately cleaned garden, was the sense of loneliness and of unpopularity, the bitter strangling growth of 1830.

All had not been altered by the Reform Bill. It was the same Robert Peel, sensible, sensitive and censorious. He still kept one foot in his home, where there was a well-beloved family and no critics, so that for an opposition leader he seems to have spent too much time at Drayton. He still naturally and honestly agreed with his party's

---

[1] Croker, II, 214 (Peel to Croker, Sept. 29, 1834).
[2] Parker, II, 221.   [3] Add. MSS. 40,403; 249, 259.

principles and common opinions—indeed even with their unwise and commonplace opinions—sometimes seeming to concern himself too exclusively with the arguments whereby to defend them. Yet he was a man who often suffered both his policy and his way of regarding his followers to lie open to the ravages of good sense. He was playing a difficult game with skill and perseverance. Others wished to play it otherwise, and were violent and unruly. They had hurt him already, and were to hurt him more. He was right or nearly right in his policy and they were entirely wrong; and his work was to be crowned with success, if only partial success. The Session of 1833 had opened a great career for him; but, as was to be expected, it had not opened his heart.

§ 2

With the same continuity, at the beginning of 1834 much reappeared in politics that had been familiar to 1833.   In January the Duke of Wellington wrote in a letter to the Duke of Buckingham that the government of England was impossible under existing circumstances.[1] The Ministry had trouble over pensions, and there were again complaints that Conservatives did not come down to succour the Government on such occasions.[2]   There was complaint and distress among the Agriculturists, who had not shared in the improvement in trade in 1833. Chandos had already been to the Duke to gain his assistance against the Malt Tax.   But, like Peel, the Duke was a Government man, and he told Chandos that he would not help; that the Revenue of the country ought to be supported, for if it failed recourse must be had to a property tax which would fall on the aristocracy.[3]

Sympathy is the small change of Government men, and even Ministers and ex-Ministers were able to sympathize with the Agriculturists.   In the Speech from the Throne

[1] *Courts and Cabinets*, II, 36 (Well. to Buck., Jan. 31, 1834).
[2] Hansard, 3rd Series, XXI, 480.   Grev., III, 60 (under Feb. 19, 1834).
[3] Grev., III, 60 (under Jan. 8).

the Ministry acknowledged the existence of agricultural distress and thus, till the end of the year, strongly reinforced agricultural complaints. Peel also sympathized. In his speech in the debate on the Address, and at other times during the Session, he showed himself friendly to agriculture, as was fitting for the head of a party so largely agricultural. But some friendships are fated and some fates are foretold, even in expressions of friendship.

Althorp made his financial statement fairly early in the Session. With strange, improper but attractive frankness, he announced that he meant to repeal the House Tax, not because it was a bad tax economically, but because it was unpopular. Peel did not approve. He dealt with the matter in no less than five speeches in the course of the Session. He declared that the remission, explained as it was by Althorp, was merely an invitation to ravishment. It was relief in response to agitation. The remission helped neither agriculture nor the poor. He thought that the local burdens on agriculture, such as the upkeep of roads and the expense of criminal prosecutions, might be enquired into, and that the tax on horses and agricultural servants might be reduced.

So far he was safe, but he had further opinions. He held that agriculture was so intimately connected with commerce that the best way of helping it was to extend commerce and to remove any fiscal or political regulations that impeded its growth. The repeal of the House Tax did none of these things, indeed it seemed to Peel that few taxes were so good as the House Tax, for it partook of the nature of a property tax without its inquisitorial character, and, in a speech at the end of the Session, when Althorp had dealt to some extent with the taxes on farm horses and on farm servants, Peel said that instead of repealing the House Tax, Althorp ought to relieve the taxes on glass and raw cotton. Among the words and ideas of this series of speeches, with their desire to keep direct taxation and to relieve that which pressed immediately on trade, the future seems to stir, and to beckon menacingly. Peel was sincerely willing to help the agriculturists, yet they might find that their rose was not without a thorn.[1]

Though Peel supported Chandos' motion of February 21st, he opposed the reduction of the Malt Tax.   But there were other occasions on which he could prove himself an active friend of agriculture.   There were various attacks on the Corn Laws in the House of Commons. Peel thought their defence was left by others to rest on unsatisfactory grounds; on a kind of appeal ad misericordiam, grounded on the distressed state of agriculture, and—which seemed to Peel even worse—on the plea that the landed interest was the most important one.   But he had himself made a most able speech on the matter and he felt that he had based their defence much more securely.[2]   He had founded his case partly on the special burdens the land had to bear.   He had also described with great spirit and verve the protection that was afforded by the country to other interests than agriculture. He supposed himself to go for a walk with a farmer, and detailed the number of things his companion used which had had to pay duty, even down to the cane that he walked with if it were painted or ornamented, bamboo, rattan, dragon's blood, whangee or jumboo.   He then asked with considerable force why the farmer should submit to all these protections and yet be himself stripped bare to free competition.

The speech had an immediate success; Peel had indeed found a way to build up a strong foundation for the Corn Laws.   It was a good thing to be defended by intellect instead of old inarticulate, unreasoned prejudice.   But intellect can sometimes be too active, and reason can be unravelled, while honest unreasonable prejudice may never pass away.   This was a foundation that could gradually stone by stone be removed   Even this Session Peel had shown how he himself might be ready to remove

[1] Hansard, XXI, 33 (address), 360 (Althorp's first financial statement), 649 (Chandos, Motion, Feb. 21, on agric. distress), 877 (Malt Tax); Vol. XXV (Althorp's last financial statement).

[2] Ibid., XXII, 442 (March 19).   Peel's comments on it, Croker, II, 221 (Peel to Croker, March 24).   A previous debate, Hansard, XXI, 1195.

that other protection which was the useful complaint of the landed interest. It might be that the corn laws would not always be able to be defended by canes that were dragon's blood, whangee or jumboo.

In this Session, too, much was done and more was hoped to be done by the Government in removing the burdens on the land. Among other things they hoped to reform the method in which tithes were collected in England, but the support that the English Tithe Bill received was not considered sufficient, and it had to stand aside for what was almost the last and almost the greatest, and certainly the most widely and bitterly hated work that was effected by the great Reform Ministry.[1]

It was the new Poor Law. It is well known what scandals it was framed to meet, and how heavily they were held to press in various parts of the country, especially on agriculture. It is also known with what ruthless and Benthamite efficiency the Commissioners were accused of going to their task; how they denied out-door relief, how they joined different parishes into unions to make workhouses or, as some learnt to call them, bastilles. How they framed bastardy regulations which seemed to lay all the burden on the woman and how they overrode the old local authorities such as the magistrates, granting almost tyrannical power to new, ruthless, cold-hearted and centralized Commissioners. There is no need to paint dark pictures of what was being exorcised or of what was being conjured up. It is enough to say that the new Poor Law was to play a great part in political history.

Peel was held to be in favour of the Bill, though he made no speech in its support, contenting himself with a few words on procedure.[2] The opposition in the Commons was mixed in its nature and not very large in its numbers. It was mainly Radical, but the Bill in one respect at least was peculiarly likely to offend the Conservatives. It overrode the powers of the magistrates to grant relief, and instituted a centralized authority such as was held to be

---

[1] Spencer, 482.　　　　[2] Hansard, XXIII, 961.

M

foreign to old English principles. The debates gave signs of the feelings to which this change might give rise among Conservatives, and that ultra-Tory paper, the *Standard*, grew hysterical against it. But the Bill was a notable relief to agriculture, and not yet likely to excite much Conservative opposition. It passed the Commons with considerable majorities and went up to the Lords. The representatives of the people had passed what Cobbett called the Poor Man's Robbery Bill.

In the Lords it was the occasion for long and elaborate speeches by Brougham and for some whole-hearted opposition from the ultra-Tories. This may have been factious, but there is no real need to disbelieve in the integrity of a man's principles or in the sincerity of his religious feelings whenever these lead him to generosity towards the poor. However, the Duke admitted the value of the measure to agriculture and steadfastly supported it. Indeed it was a measure whose practical nature and obvious necessity had good right to make a strong appeal to honest and practical men like the Duke and Peel. It obtained even in the Lords easily adequate support, was but slightly amended, and passed into law to be a source of passion in politics and popularity for the Conservatives, if they could use to that end the hatred inspired by the work of their opponents.

The amendment of the Poor Law was unquestionably a measure of the greatest importance. It would affect the length and breadth of England. It was to probe the passions of men and the principles of administrators. It would play a great part in the fortunes of the Conservatives, as would in the more distant future the question of the Corn Laws. But these two things must be as yet matters for the future. From the narrative of 1834 itself they have had to be abstracted and taken as a kind of curtain-raiser before the main argument of the year is considered, which treats of the Church and the Dissenters, of Ireland and the tithes, and of fate and the Ministry.

§ 3

For some time the Church had been alarmed, and had had reason to be alarmed. Even before the Reform Bill there had been strong feeling against her in the country. She had many enemies, and there was much involved in her position to keep their hostility on edge. There were tithes, often taken in kind, to engage rustic hostility, there was the theoretical dislike of Church Establishments among liberalized intellectualists, and there were also the excited feelings of the great body of ordinary Dissenters.

The Dissenters still complained of definite existing grievances. They naturally complained of Church Rates, rates, that is, which were levied on people of all persuasions in a parish to provide for the fabric and for some of the necessaries for the services of the Church. They complained of the necessity under which most of them laboured of being married in Church, they complained that they were not allowed to use their own ministers or services if they buried their dead in the churchyards, and that they were not admitted to degrees at Oxford or Cambridge; and to such actual grievances they added the feelings for the Church proper to their calling and their past. It was a period in which there were many militant Dissenters, both in Scotland and England, and their object was often not only to secure the redress of grievances, but also to obtain the separation of Church and State.

There were also notorious Church abuses to contribute arrows to the quiver and to increase the anger and contempt in the hearts of any enemies the Church might have. There were too many stories of the fat slumbers of the Church, though sometimes they were wildly exaggerated. Men talked of pluralities and commendams, they pointed at overpaid bishops and luxurious deans, and contrasted them with starving curates and souls untended by any shepherd. The lukewarm despised and the hostile abused and a great many ingenious men filled the air with printed schemes for Church Reform. Even the best friends of the Church felt that something must be done to remedy the Church's defects

Politics of late had been disastrous. The Repeal of the Test Acts, the Emancipation of the Roman Catholics, had seemed to alter the old constitution of the country and to make the Church's position most dangerous and illogical. After Emancipation had come the Reform Bill. The Bishops had earned unpopularity by their votes upon it, and they had been taught by fire and riot what the mob felt about them. The old defences were undermined and new perils were imminent. The House of Lords had been considered the Church's great stand-by and defence, and now the House of Lords seemed no better than a tottering wall and a broken hedge. The Government was held to be hostile, Lord Grey was reported to have told the Bishops to set their house in order, and in 1833 the First Reformed Parliament had come as a last dangerous portent.

It seemed hostile in bias and clamorous for Church Reform, and even Peel believed that the Reform Bill had transferred power in the country to Dissenters.[1] The Ministry promised Church Reform in their speech from the Throne and they produced their Irish Church Bill, in which the State laid violent hands on ten Irish Bishop-rics. There were motions in the House of Commons to relieve the Bishops from their attendance in the House of Lords and to save the Church from the contamination of establishment by State. The waters had risen dangerously, and lapped round the buttresses.

The times were very evil and very exciting. Religious people put the most interesting and highly coloured meaning on all that was happening. An outbreak of cholera had occurred to make men suffer and see visions, and it was put down to direct divine interposition and as a sign of divine displeasure. Some of the clergy set it down to the wickedness and infidelity of the Ministers, though one, a chaplain of Brougham's, thought that the

[1] E.g. Parker, II, 223.

cause was the wickedness of the Tory opposition to the
Reform Bill.[1]   Dr. Whately, whom the Government had
appointed Archbishop of Dublin, sometimes thought that
the days of the Church were numbered,[2] while Arnold
at Rugby saw many signs of the destruction of the Church
and some of the end of the world, or of the era.[3]   Men
dabbled in the ideas of violence, and the eloquent had
strong colours to paint with.   In the first of the Tracts
for the Times Newman could not wish the Bishops a
more blessed termination of their course than the spoliation of their goods and martyrdom.   The termination
might be blessed indeed, but it might seem to us a little
inappropriate for those banded and bewigged gentlemen
whose portraits ornament so suitably the walls of so
many common or combination rooms at Oxford and
Cambridge.

In this thunderous and electric atmosphere it was not
to be expected that the Church would only cower in
impotent panic like a fat chicken under a hawk.   Already
in 1830 clergymen had thought of forming associations
to protect her.[4]   1833 produced greater activity.   In
that year, for instance, there came the sequence of events
that started the Oxford movement.   They are very well
known; Newman's impassioned return, on the morrow
of the Reform Bill, from Sicily and the gates of death;
Keble's sermon on National Apostasy, and the meeting
at Hadleigh of a few High Churchmen to consider what
might be done.   At Hadleigh they projected an association of the friends of the Church, and various local associations were formed in the country, though in the main the
project came to nothing.   A little later in the year they
started an address from clergymen to the Archbishop of
Canterbury, to express their confidence in him.   It was
successful, and it was followed by an address to the Archbishop from lay heads of families.   Meetings took place
in many parts of England in support of the Church, and

---

[1] Whately, I, 134.   [2] *Ibid.*, I, 159.
[3] *Life of Dr. Arnold*, pp. 240, 241, 242 (Aug. 2, Oct. 31).
[4] Blomfield, I, 162.

were studiously scored up each time by that ultra-Tory paper the *Standard*. Meanwhile, in September 1833, Newman and his friends had started the Tracts for the Times. Churchmen had begun to work together for the Church's need.

To work together meant to be divided. It was a question of one story getting mixed up with another. The History of the Oxford Movement and of the Conservative Party were to have very little in common. It is true that the origin of the Oxford Movement was largely political,[1] but the originators were not ordinary secular politicians. They had other interests most strictly ecclesiastical, they had another task to do, another play to act through. They were not on the whole natural Conservatives, they dreamed of Apostolical Christianity, while Conservatism means very often only the defence of yesterday against the day before that. They did not delight in ordinary secular politicians. Hurrell Froude, Newman's friend and spur, had the deepest contempt for Conservatism as he imagined it; he felt that it was something faint-hearted and compromising. They were shocked, as were many ordinary High Churchmen, at the State's interference with the Bishoprics, but they considered extreme measures, which would again shock ordinary High Churchmen. Keble and Newman toyed with ideas of disendowment and disestablishment which might leave the Church free. Newman spoke of basing the Church on the people, now that the aristocracy could no longer help it. In a moment of enthusiasm he called the old union of Church and State a "happy anomaly." [2] He did not remain in this position, but the thoughts had been there and the feelings remained. A Church, a real Church, of the sort which Newman imagined, could not suffer the changes put upon it by the State, and perhaps could not perform all the duties its unreal position de-

---

[1] Church's *History of the Oxford Movement*.

[2] Newman's *Anglican Correspondence*, Vol. I, 442, 447 ff., 454, 458, etc. (Newman, Aug. 31, 1833, to Bowden and Rogers; Newman to Wilson, Sept. 8, 1833; Newman to Froude, Sept. 18, 1833), etc., etc. Vol. II, 4 (Draft of Instructions, 1833).

manded of it.[1] He was looking away not only from the tumultuous present, but from old Church and State, and he was inclined to distrust the "establishment men" among his own party in the clergy.[2] Part of the forces of the reaction were to spend themselves far away from Peel's destiny and were to be, if anything, a hindrance to him. Newman's position was very far from that of Peel; but the two men had one similarity. In each were the seeds of disruption.

Even in 1833 the Tracts for the Times and their authors had begun to excite the suspicions of Churchmen. There were expressions in them that displeased. There were rumours that their authors contemplated the severing of the union of Church and State. The Evangelical party began to attack them.[3] But even the terms of the address from the laity did not escape criticism, although it was pressed forward by Churchmen who were in no way responsible for the tracts. It also was too ecclesiastical to be relevant. Its sponsors were clergymen or clerically-minded laymen such as Sir Robert Inglis, who were chiefly interested in their fears of an extremely unlikely attempt on the part of the Government to change the Liturgy of the Church. When Inglis first showed his address to him, Goulburn, as he told Peel, objected to it. He felt that the time was inexpedient, as it so often is in politics, and that the declaration was one that would sow dissensions and be only exclusively signed. It omitted all reference to the property and privileges of the Church, which seemed to Goulburn to be more in danger than its Liturgy. It appeared to exclude all those Reforms that would really advance the objects of the Establishment, and to be desirous of reviving obsolete claims of authority over the laity and, finally, it seemed to be a direct challenge to the Government. He admitted, however, that the desire to sign was very strong, and when it had been altered into

---

[1] E.g. T. Mozley's *Reminiscences of Oriel*, etc., Vol. I, 391.
[2] E.g. Newman's *Anglican Correspondence*, Vol. I, 478 (Nov. 13, 1833).
[3] *Ibid.*, Vol. II, 8 (Newman, Dec. 15, 1833).

a declaration more compatible with Goulburn's desire, in spite of many difficulties and inefficiencies, it was presented to the Archbishop of Canterbury with the signatures of 230,000 heads of families, among whom was Sir Robert Peel.[1]

Even in counter-attack the Church was divided. There were the young Apostolicals dreaming of a Church Catholic and free from Erastian taint, and there were those who had already begun to object to their doctrines. There were statesmen made more cautious and pedestrian by political life than men are made by youth and religion; and there were the devoted and ecclesiastically-minded lay members of Parliament. The Church was divided, but the Church was alive, and her activities had served to encourage her allies and defenders. Goulburn told Peel, in the December of 1833, that Lord Grey was reported to have declared that he had found the Dissenters weaker and the Church more strong than he had expected. This may not be very good evidence of what Lord Grey had said, but it probably shows what Conservatives were inclined to believe at the beginning of 1834.

The Church was rallying, but the storm was by no means abated. In 1834 the Dissenters raged furiously and also together; there was already a standing alliance, and at the end of 1833 it had been reinforced by increasing agitation. This was especially excited by a legislative coincidence which happened to fill the Law Courts at the beginning of 1834 with cases over unusual claims for tithe, and filled the hearts of many with anger. Men felt that the country was on the eve of a fierce religious struggle. Bishop Blomfield of London was afraid that a war was beginning between Church and Dissent.[2] The onslaught was so hot that it seemed as if the Church might go down without time to do more than mutter hastily the curse against sacrilege. On March 19th

---

[1] Palmer, *Narrative*, 110, 216–20 and 223–8. Add. MSS. 40,333; 168 and 170 (Goulb. to Peel, Dec. 29, 1833; Jan. 18, 1834); cf. with Blomfield, I, 190 (Bp. of London to Archdeacon Lyall, Nov. 21, 1833).

[2] Blomfield, I, 201; see also Grev., III, 94, etc.

Newman declared that the Dissenters seemed likely to carry everything, and on March 22nd O'Connell told the Roman Catholic Archbishop of Tuam that the Protestant Dissenters were storming the Established Church.[1] Meanwhile the rallying Church and the storming Dissenters could not but affect the parties engaged in the parliamentary field in more purely political contests.

§ 4

The Oxford people seem to have pictured the Ministry as a group of Liberal free-thinkers, bitter and hasty, ready at any moment to sacrifice the Church and its Liturgy. But Oxford was in those days very far from London, and their picture was wrong. The Ministers were most of them loyal members of the Establishment, if some were a little lax. Of all men the Whigs seem on the whole to have been furthest from the theological turmoil of those days; it might be said that their minds were sometimes like pleasant and cultivated gardens in valleys, very different from the uncomfortable beauties of the heights above. They did not encourage thoughts of Disestablishment or of any very serious Reform in the Church of England. They were inclined to preface their reforms with declarations that these were largely desirable as making the Church secure, and they were inclined to speak too scornfully of the folly of those who were making the country ring from end to end with the cry that the Church was in danger.

However, they were Whigs, pledged by their principles to remove civil disabilities, and dependent in many cases on the votes of Dissenters. In 1834 they set about their business. They produced a marriage bill for Dissenters, sponsored by Lord John Russell and a measure on Church Rates, sponsored by Althorp.[2] Neither of them were very good measures and neither of them satisfied the Dissenters, so that both came to nothing,

[1] Newman's *Correspondence*, Vol. II, 29. O'Connell's *Corresp.*, Vol. I, 44.
[2] Hansard, XXI, 776; XXII, 1012.

partly because the way had to be left clear for their great Poor Law Bill.[1]   Two other Bills of a Liberal nature on religious matters passed through the House of Commons, one to remove the disabilities of the Jews and the other to admit the Dissenters to degrees at the Universities.   Indeed, neither the House nor the Ministry had forgotten their Liberal origin.   But the Ministry was divided and in difficulties.   It was not ready to give a clear lead or to follow a clear policy.   It was like a ship going about clumsily, sails flapping, spars creaking, way sacrificed, at the end of a tack.

But they were at the end of a tack, and they were going about.   There was not much fear of the Cabinet's remaining united.   In January there had been a notorious division among them, over which Lord Grey had nearly resigned.[2]   He still sat loose in the saddle, and longed to get down.   There were uneasy stirrings of Liberalism in the Government.   Hobhouse noticed that Littleton, who was now Irish Secretary, was discontented, and that Poulet Thomson grumbled at his position and declared that the Tories must come in before they got a good Government.[3]   It must be remembered that good is the chameleon among adjectives.   It seems very probable that John Russell was nursing a bomb at his heart; and there remained in full an unavoidable activity which was for long the commonest solvent of English politics—the problem of Ireland.

The Government of Ireland had been changed. When Stanley retired from the Irish Secretaryship he was replaced first of all by Hobhouse for a very short time and then by Littleton, a Liberal Whig, whose character was at least accommodating and amiable. After the Session Anglesey came home and was succeeded by that splendid ruin and symbol—in more ways than one—of the vanity of human grandeur, Lord Wellesley, the Duke of Wellington's elder brother and, as it happened, Littleton's father-in-law.   The change from the Stanley and Anglesey régime was considerable.   Little-

---

[1] Spencer, 482.   [2] Brougham, III, 328.   [3] *Ibid.*, Vol. IV, 331.

ton was imbued with Liberal desires, and in September
1833 he told Graham that he wished to enlist O'Connell
on the side of the Government.   Indeed it seems probable
that in that month steps were taken to that end.[1]

But O'Connell was a difficult fish to land, and a
dangerous one for the fisherman.   It is true that he had
by no means given up hope of gaining something for
Ireland out of an English Ministry.   Indeed he had
welcomed Wellesley's appointment because it got rid of
Anglesey and implied, so he thought, that the power
would be in the hands of Littleton.[2]   His mind was not
so full of Repeal that he could not think of other Reforms,
especially of clearing the present executive Officers out
of the Castle in Dublin.   But he had not, at least at this
time, much trust in English Cabinets.   He was determined to remain out of office, for he knew he could best
put pressure on them from outside.   He was still inclined
to base his hopes not on the Government but on the
Radicals.[3]   Repeal was always there, to be taken up
with renewed belief in its necessity when the English
Cabinet disappointed him, and he had always at his
command the thunder and violence of his oratory.   As
things stood at the moment Littleton was not very likely
to draw leviathan with a hook.

As was not unusual, from the start of the Session of
1834 the affairs of Ireland were the subject of lengthened
debate and personal recriminations, with the grotesque
result that Althorp and Sheil were taken into custody
by the House to avoid the possibility of a duel.   There
was a vast debate on the Repeal of the Union in which
O'Connell and Spring-Rice, Secretary for the Colonies,
made great set speeches against one another.[4]   It went
on for six nights, and in the end O'Connell and his friends
were defeated by 38 votes to 523.   It was a sweeping
victory for the Union; there was even a majority against

---

[1] Parker's *Graham*, I, 183 (Littleton to Graham, Sept. 30, 1833).   O'Connell's
Correspondence, Vol. I, p. 387.
[2] O'Connell's *Correspondence*, Vol. I, 380 (Sept. 3, 1833).
[3] *Ibid.*, Vol. I, 396 (Nov. 1833).   [4] Hansard, XXII, 1092 ff.

Repeal among the representatives of Ireland. As for
the Ministry, they were of course all equally and whole-
heartedly opposed to Repeal; but they were not equally
and whole-heartedly opposed to Repealers.

In February there was an example of their divisions,
in the confusion and contradictory conduct which they
exhibited over a motion which O'Connell brought
forward against the proceedings of an Irish Judge,
Baron Smith.[1]   It was merely an incident, a premonitory
symptom, but the Cabinet's divisions remained so bad
that Brougham thought it necessary at the end of April
to send a strong memorandum round the Cabinet, urging
them to hold together;[2] and they had certainly never
healed their divisions concerning the Irish Church.

Owing to the cessation of tithes many of the clergy in
Ireland were in very great distress. For their sakes,
and for Ireland's, it was essential that the Irish Secretary should immediately make another attempt to settle
the tithe question. Humanity and Patriotism urged
Sisyphus to hard responsible work on his stone. By
way of immediate provision for the clergy, arrangements
had been made in Parliament towards the end of the
Session of 1833 for a million pounds to be advanced by
the Government. Littleton tried to prepare a Tithe
Bill which should gain the support of all sections of the
Cabinet.[3]   The plan was elaborate, conceived as it was
in the complicating spirit of compromise, and the question of appropriation was studiously avoided. The
measure was proposed to the Commons in February
1834, and was received with contempt and opposition
by O'Connell and his friends.[4]

The work of making it more palatable to Irishmen
immediately began. Some of the Irish members waited
on Althorp to propose its amendment in various particulars. Althorp obtained Stanley's unwilling assent to
a change being made, and the Bill as amended was pro-

[1] Hansard, XXI, 272. Parker's *Graham*, I, 184.
[2] Brougham, III, 387.   [3] Hatherton's *Memoir*, pp. 1–5.
[4] Hansard, XXI, 572.

duced in May.[1]   Again there was opposition, with long
debates on May the 2nd and 6th in which, however,
O'Connell spoke more mildly than usual, producing a
plan of his own.   Then suddenly came the first climax
of the Ministry's divisions.   Stanley spoke, and seemed
to Lord John to imply the continued appropriation of
the revenues of the Irish Church to none but Church
uses.[2]   Lord John felt that it would be held to be the
opinion of the Cabinet if no one denied it.   He rose
inspired, or so he said afterwards, by feelings which had
long been maturing in his mind, and inspired to one of
those sudden self-determined actions by which at times
he altered History.   He declared that it was his belief
that the revenues of the Church of Ireland were larger
than was necessary for the religious and moral instruction
of the persons belonging to it and for its own stability.
That when Parliament had vindicated the property as
to tithes he would assert his opinion with regard to their
appropriation, even if the assertion of that opinion should
lead him to differ and separate from those with whom he
was united by political connection.   He said that if ever
any nation had a grievance to complain of, the nation was
the Irish and the grievance was the Irish Church.[3]   His
terms were strong and unavoidable, his bomb was well
loaded and very effective.   The cheering was loud and
general, Liberal members effusively greeted his declaration, and Stanley passed to Graham a famous note.   After
what Lord John had said about the Irish Church, he
wrote, they could no longer remain in the Ministry.
"John Russell has upset the coach."   And it was a good
thing that it should be upset, if it were driving nowhere.[4]

From May the 6th to May the 27th the course of
events was obscure but decisive.   The Ministry was in
its throes, and all men were debating what would follow

[1] Hatherton, p. 6.   Hansard XXIII, 422, 622.
[2] Lord John later in life could not find the passage in Stanley's speech
(*Recollections and Suggestions*).
[3] Hansard, XXIII, 664.
[4] Parker's *Graham*, I, 186.   Earl Russell's *Recollections and Suggestions*,
118 ff.   Spencer Walpole's *Life of Lord John Russell*, Vol. I, 198 ff.

the declaration of Lord John Russell. It must be remembered as a key to these crises, and to more than these crises, that at that time in the minds of statesmen two instincts or opinions were at work. They might be labelled with the words, government and consistency, although it is not necessarily pretended that those are always incompatible ideas. But on the one hand a man might feel that it was his pre-eminent duty to provide the country with a Government, or on the other, that he ought to obey the interesting claims of principle and personal and party consistency, even at the cost of a Government of which he might be a member. Both views are honest and both are useful. Those who act when inspired by the second are grievously annoying to those who are possessed by the first. It is felt that what is necessary for the country has been destroyed by indefensible egotism and by an unrestrained indulgence in private integrity. Still principle and consistency have their uses in politics, and men may over-estimate the necessity and fruitfulness of the continuation of the Governments to which they belong. They may keep the dead on the throne for fear of lacking a King.

With the fears that haunted those days, this dilemma was particularly prevalent, and the reasons which supported the Government side of it were peculiarly strong. Especially did they appeal to the Whigs. In 1834 they felt that there was no safe alternative to themselves. They would be followed by a succession of ephemeral Ministries. The Conservatives would not be successful in maintaining a Government, their attempt would be dangerous, and might be followed by a disastrous dissolution which might produce a much more extreme House of Commons, while there would be a loss of such control as was now exercised by the Government over the more advanced Liberals.

These were Brougham's views, and his pen grew active in excited and sometimes undated memoranda and letters.[1] He was exceedingly anxious that the Ministry

[1] Brougham's *Memoirs*, III, 365–8. Parker's *Graham*, I, 187–9.

should not come to an end, and exerted all his nervous
and dangerous activity to strengthen it.   Lansdowne and
Palmerston were probably moved by much the same
feelings, and there was some anger in the Cabinet against
Lord John after his outburst.   But there were others in
the Cabinet, and many others in the party, who felt
differently.   Liberalism was coming more into its own,
and many were glad.   Althorp bore witness to the cheers
with which Lord John's announcement was received.
There seems to have been a strong feeling in the House
of Commons and in their party in favour of some form
of reappropriation of the Revenues of the Irish Church
to which Althorp and others were extremely sensitive.
The position was made worse by the fact that the Ministry
were to be confronted at the end of the month with a
motion in the Commons, proposed by a Liberal called
Ward.   He asserted that there was a surplus over what
was needed in the Revenues of the Church of Ireland,
and that Parliament had the right to reappropriate it.

This motion might very well bring matters to a
decision.   Yet it might be met by moving the previous
question, and thus avoiding a decision upon it.   This
was the desire of those who wished to retain Stanley and
Graham and to keep the Government on in its old course.
They did not wish it to be Liberalized; Palmerston
regarded Ward's motion as merely a plot of Durham's
to drive a wedge into the Ministry,[1] and there is a natural
tendency in all Governments to wish to keep even their
dangerous weapons.   But there were other opinions.   It
was said that the Government might not be able to carry
the previous question.   Some Whigs, like Lord John,
were set on their desires for appropriation, and no doubt
it was high time for the Government Liberals to embark
on a policy more consonant with views widely held in
the House, and more consonant with their own principles
and desires.   Apparently there were some who even went
to Stanley and Graham during May to suggest their
retiring in order that the Church question might be

---

[1] Bulwer's *Palmerston*, II, 195.

settled and the Government relieved.[1]   And both Stanley
and Graham wanted to go.   They too felt the call of their
principles; more than once Stanley pressed his resignation on his colleagues, but they demurred.[2]   The Cabinet
was torn between principle and moderation, with the
added complication that principle might be the safest
course after all.   Meanwhile, feeling old, tired and
harassed, Lord Grey again wished to be released.

The end came at last on the night of May 27th, while
Ward's motion was being actually debated in the House
of Commons.   It was hurried and confused.   Pressure
was suddenly applied by Holland and Ellice the Whip,
to hasten the resignations in view of the temper shown
that night by the House.   Ineffective annoyance was
shown by Lansdowne and Palmerston, but Stanley and
his friends probably already intended to resign.   Grey
seems to have been kept in office by the King's only
agreeing to accept the others' resignation on that condition, and Lansdowne by Grey's saying that he would
throw up the Government if Lansdowne retired.
Principle had won.   That night Stanley retired, with
him his friend Graham, Ripon who had been of their
counsels, and Richmond who was a Tory driven into the
Whig camp by Roman Catholic Emancipation.   Matters
were straightening out.   The Ministry might soon be
feeling the wind in its sails, and the Conservatives might
be finding Stanley in their ranks.[3]

The difficulties and divisions of their rivals naturally
interested the Conservatives.   In January they had
watched with attention the threatened split of the Government over sending troops to Portugal.[4]   When the
collapse of the Ministry drew near, hearts beat fast and
breath framed itself into rumours.   They foresaw the
division and they feared the radicalization of the Ministry.
The Ministers might throw themselves into the arms of
the Dissenters and the advanced or, as it was called, "the

---

[1] Brougham, III, 309 (Brougham to Grey, May 25, 1834).
[2] Grev., III, 91 (under June 2, 1834).
[3] Parker's *Graham*, I, 190.   [4] Add. MSS. 40,313; 176.

Mouvement party." [1]   The re-entry of Durham into the
Ministry seems to have played a large part in men's
thoughts. Yet there was another possible solution, and
even the most responsible believed that the Conservatives might succeed the Whigs. On May 2nd, even
before Lord John's outburst, Arbuthnot, the Duke's
confidant, believed that they might at any moment be
called upon to undertake office.[2]   On May 12th the Duke
was of opinion that Peel might have to make up his mind
at any moment, and that this time the Minister ought
to be in the House of Commons.[3] When Ward's
motion drew near, there were rumours of resignations,
and London was full of excitement and speculation. But
Sir Robert Peel was at Drayton.

Goulburn was in charge in the Commons, and he
begged Peel to come up to town, for he felt that matters
were getting beyond such dexterity of management as he
had at his command. He had heard that the Government
proposed to meet Ward's motion by moving the previous
question. It was a matter of principle, and he would
rather have met it with a simple negative and no evasion.
But he felt that it would be safer to support the Government on the previous question. He did not wish to
reunite the Government by opposition. He did not feel
sure of Stanley's adherence to his opinions; if the
previous question were negatived, Stanley might vote for
Ward's motion in a pet, and pledge himself for ever to
the Radicals. Goulburn would do nothing that might
heal the differences in the Cabinet, and he would avoid
if possible entering at all into the real subject of discussion.[4]   In fact the Conservative leaders were engaged
in the nervous and difficult task of waiting for opinion,
and waiting for Stanley must have seemed like waiting

---

[1] Add. MSS. 40,313; 191 (Hardinge to Peel, May 27).
[2] Arbuthnot to Aberdeen, May 2, 1834 (Add. MSS. 40,312; 178. Parker's
Peel, II, 232).
[3] Parker, II, 240 (Arbuthnot to Peel, May 12, 1834).
[4] Goulburn to Peel, May 24, 1834 (Parker's *Peel*, II, 243. Add. MSS.
40,333; 172). N.B.—All reference to Stanley or to the inadvisability of
reuniting the Government is left out in Parker.

N

for a highly bred and highly strung horse to come up to them, when the slightest unfortunate movement would send it off at a gallop to another end of the field.

Peel agreed with Goulburn. Of course he agreed with him, for Goulburn's policy was in effect the old policy that Peel had preferred in 1833. He told Goulburn he would much rather have given a direct negative to Ward's resolutions than have voted for the previous question, had he felt that he was sure of carrying whichever he wanted. But he felt that the effect of combining with the Church's enemies against the previous question would be to alienate from the Church many lukewarm supporters, and possibly to make the condition of the Irish Church even worse than it was at the moment.

So much for the course pursued over Ward's motion; but Peel was led in his letter to Goulburn to enter into a more comprehensive view of Conservative policy. He gave vent to those general opinions which were fixed in his mind so firmly, and were so near to his mouth and his pen. Again he spoke against those who wished to ally with the Radicals, or with anyone else, to put the Government in a minority. He spoke against all petty manœuvring, all coquetting with Radicals, all those "little devices and artifices by which perhaps in other days parties were strengthened." To the Conservatives' forbearance from such he attributed much of the present weakness of the Government and still more of their own present strength. Such forbearance was necessary if a more splendid reward were to be retained. For if the Conservatives were called into office they could only hope to maintain themselves by conciliating many of the more moderate and respectable supporters of the present Government, or at least by mitigating their hostility. The use of party tactics would have been the surest way to make this impossible. If the present Government broke up through its own misunderstanding, there would be a forcible appeal to the country on behalf of its successors, while it would be but a very short-lived triumph that had been won by the union between Radicals and Conservatives. This was

Peel's creed and, like a creed, was meant to be repeated, and the next day he repeated in a letter to Arbuthnot what he had said to Goulburn, all over again.[1]

These opinions which he so often and so forcibly expressed must have lain much to the front of Peel's mind. But their roots ran right down beyond the ephemeral needs of the moment to his mind's core. There lay, massive and immovable like the eternal bed-rock, his sense of integrity and his sense of distaste for much of the ordinary business of politics, for the ambitious desires and activities of many politicians. Plots to unite with the Radicals were not only unwise, they were also obviously unprincipled. The conditions he laid down for Conservative success—that they should adhere to principle, manifest no anxiety for power and eschew all party manœuvring—bear a family resemblance to his own earlier more personal resolutions to serve his principles and not-to seek intemperately for the prizes of politics. This must not be exaggerated. Peel was not only regarding in his considerations his own most inward feelings. His policy was undoubtedly founded on an appreciation of the necessities of the moment; indeed it was probably the only policy at that time which ought to seem possible to an intelligent statesman. But it owed some allegiance to an exterior power, whose recommendations might not always be so relevant. It might not, for instance, always be good for the Conservatives to manifest no anxiety for power; and above all the connection of the words "mere" and "party" might become a dangerous cliché.

Peel did not come up to London for Ward's motion on the night of May 27th, which was to decide the fortune and the fate of the Ministry. Goulburn watched the Ministry for him in the House. He watched the empty Treasury Bench, and watched Althorp come in all alone to take his seat upon it. Ward made a long meandering speech, a tissue of quotations, and men speculated as to

[1] Parker, II, 243 (Peel to Goulburn, May 25), 244 (Arbuthnot to Peel, May 26), 247 (Peel to Arbuthnot, May 27).

why the other Ministers were not there. Goulburn watched and wondered, while Althorp was summoned out by Lansdowne, and returned after a short absence. Possibly something was happening. After the speech of the mover and seconder Althorp rose and said that information had come to him, since the beginning of the debate, of a kind that made it necessary for the debates to be adjourned. Something had happened. That night the blow had fallen. The great Reform Ministry was drawing to its end.[1]

It drew to its end but it was not yet ended. Grey had been persuaded to stay in. The gaps were filled up, and not with Radicals, but rather with what men thought to be rubbish. Durham was not asked to join. The worst Conservative fears were disappointed, and so were the worst Conservative hopes. Peel had done nothing to make use of the crisis to drive out the Government, as some thought that he might have done. Peel's friend Sir Henry Hardinge reported that these voracious appetites were satisfied with Peel's course, although grievously disappointed. Some there were, at least among the Lords, who were disappointed and not satisfied. Hardinge added that he felt that the administration was a mere stop-gap till it contained O'Connell and Durham. He was talking wildly; but he had not invented the instability of the Government.[2]

§5

There was much yet to happen. The waves from the feelings of Chapel and Church kept up a swell in the waters of politics. On May 28th the King broke out in a speech to a deputation of Irish Bishops in which he declared his intention of defending the Church.[3] On June 2nd there came on the adjourned debate upon

---

[1] Add. MSS. 40,333; 174; 175. Hansard, XXIII, 1368.

[2] Grev., III, 88 (May 28). O'Connell's *Correspondence* (May 30, 1834). Add. MSS. 40,313; 192 (Hardinge to Peel, May 28). Cf. Disraeli's Corresp. with his Sister, p. 24 (June 4, 1834).

[3] *Standard* Newspaper, May 29, 1834. Grev., III, 92 (under June 2).

Ward's motion.[1]   The Ministry met it with the previous question and an assurance that they had issued a Commission on the revenues and needs of the Church in Ireland.   They admitted that by this they implied the right to reappropriate that Church's surplus Revenue. They merely wished to test the existence of a surplus before they resolved how to deal with it.   Peel and Stanley both adopted the previous question, but condemned the Commission.   Peel was so much impressed by his idea of his party not indulging in petty manœuvring to embarrass the Government that it crept into his speech. There seem to have been signs that some of his followers were less enamoured of the doctrine.[2]   However, the previous question was carried by 196 votes to 140. Ward's motion was successfully avoided after it had done its work.   Perhaps the war of principle had begun.

For Peel stood by the Church.   He was a man of principle, even if reasonableness would keep on breaking in.   Adherence to principle was to be the duty of his party, while it avoided those attacks on the Government which were only the misbegotten offspring of rashness and ambition, and had nothing to do with principle at all.   Peel did not wish to escape the defence of those things for which his party especially stood.   He had stood up and spoken out for the landed interest.   The defence of the Church was a much more integral part of his creed, and much less likely to suffer from the chilling considerations of economics; and Peel with unquestionable sincerity stood by the Church.

He had signed the address to the Archbishop.   He opposed with considerable debating ability the petitions and proposals to admit the Dissenters to the Universities; Greville says that some were surprised at this and had thought that Peel would have abstained, from prudential motives, from saying anything against the Dissenters. For Peel was still suspect, and his actions and motives were still liable to harsh judgments and unnecessarily

[1] Hansard, XXIV, 10.   [2] Spencer, 492.

complicated explanations.[1] But Peel watched the lumbering realignment of the ministry, he felt the hot breath of the Dissenters on their prey and he feared for the Church, even in England. He suspected, and was able to expose, the worst desires on the part of the Dissenters. On June 11th he called the attention of the House to a declaration by the United Committee of Dissenters in London that they desired the separation of Church and State and the partial reappropriation by the State of the Church Revenues, though they did not wish that these should be appropriated to the use of Dissenters. Peel drew Baines, a leading Dissenting member, to admit that this was more or less what the Dissenters desired. On June 20th, on the Bill for the admission of the Dissenters into the University, Peel admitted that he considered that Bill to be one of a series of measures which were aimed at the very existence of the Church of England, and he referred to the various measures of the Ministry. In fact he was astride of his principles, and had let loose the reins. On June 18th he seems to have made, at a Conservative dinner, a fighting speech on the necessity of a stand being made. Some held that this was an announcement that he was ready to undertake the Government.[2]

The Ministry had still their Tithe Bill to propose. Without it no tithes could be levied, the Church must go lacking, and the possibility of collecting tithes for that or any other purpose would fade quite away. They decided to amend their Tithe Bill in the Liberal direction. and the warlike attitude of the Conservatives did not promise well for its prospects. Peel's fighting speech frightened Littleton. He felt that it would be followed by action in the Lords. They would put the Bill back into its old shape and force Grey to choose between the Bill as they wished it and no Bill at all. Meanwhile O'Connell and his friends were enraged at the prospect

---

[1] E.g. Hansard, XXII, 702. Bathurst Papers, 665 (Bathurst to Apsley, June 21, 1834). Grev., III, 75 (under March 21, 1834).

[2] Hansard, XXIV., 354, 697. Grev., III, 96.

of the renewal of the Coercion Bill.[1] O'Connell had thought, so Littleton believed, that by procuring submission in Ireland to a Tithe Bill he would procure the abandonment of the Coercion Bill, or at least of those clauses in it which forbad public meetings. Littleton seems to have thought it important that the Government should not be divided from the majority of the Irish members now that it was threatened by the Lords; and Brougham, anxious, active, excited and unwise, desirous above all things of strengthening the Government, also wished to secure the support of the Irish members. Brougham and Littleton, stimulated by him, both wrote, without Lord Grey's knowledge, to Wellesley to ask him to advise the abandonment of the clauses in the Coercion Bill about public meetings. It was the opposite to the advice that Wellesley had hitherto given, but he acceded to their request. With the best faith and the worst folly a mine had been laid under the Cabinet.[2]

On June 23rd the change in the Tithe Bill was explained to the Commons. The position of the Ministers was neither clear, dignified nor satisfactory. They muddled the matter of Appropriation by speaking of the surplus revenues of the Irish Church going to objects connected with the moral, spiritual and Christian edification of the people. Their declarations did not tally, and Grey and Lansdowne in the Lords did not seem to fit in with Althorp and John Russell in the Commons. O'Connell tried to pin them to Appropriation, and announced that he intended to continue to oppose the Bill. Peel also spoke against them, taunted them with their indecision, and declared that men were quite justified in raising the cry of the Church in danger, when the Dissenters openly desired its separation from the State and when Lord John Russell had spoken as he had about the Irish Church.[3] The Tithe Bill continued

---

[1] O'Connell's *Correspondence*, I, 442 (June 17, 1834).

[2] Hatherton's *Memoir*, p. 29 (Littleton to Wellesley, June 18), p. 10 (Littleton to Wellesley, June 19), p. 30 (Littleton to Blackburn).

[3] Hansard, XXIV, 731.

its course, meandering with a mazy motion and becoming in its complicated way more favourable to Liberal views.

Graham and Stanley began to draw in with Peel, each in his peculiar fashion. Graham, active and busy, attended meetings with Peel on the subject, was pleased with the reception Peel gave him, and arranged what Stanley was to say in the House.[1] Stanley said it with eloquence and without wisdom, indulging in invective that was quite improper as towards colleagues whom he had just left. He was particularly picturesque and unwise in his comparison of the Government to men engaged in the popular racecourse fraud of thimble-rigging. Lord Grey was hurt, and men were ever after inclined to remember against Stanley the ungracious violence of his thimble-rigging speech.[2] Then, on July 1st, the Coercion Bill was introduced into the House of Lords, and the mine that had been laid under the Government went off with violence.

It would be tiresome to recount all the unpardonable actions in which well-intentioned men had been engaged to prepare this petard.[3] Littleton thought he had reason to believe that the public meetings clauses in the Coercion Bill would not be proposed, and with Althorp's modified concurrence he had told O'Connell in confidence that this would be the case. Grey, knowing nothing of what had been done except that he had received a letter from Wellesley giving advice in direct contradiction to all that he had before advised, had stood by his original opinion, and forced the clauses on the Cabinet. They were introduced with the measure in the House of Lords. O'Connell apparently thought that Littleton had betrayed him in order to gain his support in an election in Ireland, and he exposed in the House of Commons what Littleton had told him in confidence. There were

[1] Parker's *Graham*, IV, 206 (Graham to Stanley, July 3, 1834).
[2] Hansard, XXIV, 1146.
[3] See Hatherton's "Memoir and Correspondence relating to Political Occurrences in June 2, July, 1834," which is Littleton's *Apologia* with documents.

angry and exciting debates, personal explanations,
motions for papers and the like. Littleton offered to
resign, Althorp resigned, and then Grey declared that
his Ministry was at an end. The great Reform Ministry
was dead. Its manner of death was neither dignified
nor necessary, but it owed its departure to time and to
principle. It may be praised for its past, but it need
not be regretted.

It need not be regretted. It was a survival, an
inconvenience, something left over from the Reform
Bill into a political world which it had created but could
not serve. It was wrong that so much divergent opinion
should be tied together by the artificial bonds of the past.
Men merely hindered each other. It was good that
Stanley and Graham should go. Their presence had
complicated the problem of Ireland and had enforced a
series of mysterious expedients and the use of a muddled
silence, in the treatment of the matter of Appropriation.
Stanley's manner in itself unfitted him for a Liberal
Government. Though they might not have admitted
their true destination, Stanley and Graham were wanted
for and by the Conservatives. Peel wanted them. He
could not yet know of Stanley that a man by principle
most fitted for him as an ally, was by psychology most
unfitted for him as a companion; for that was merely one
of the unforeseen ironies of politics. Lord Grey was
needed for posthumous eulogy. He had finished his
work, he was old, and he wished to go into retirement and
end his political life. As the years went by in retirement he grew more and more Conservative, and it is
probable that he would have done so in office. He was
fairly Conservative now. He had just given rise at
Brooks's to many criticisms on the Conservative tone
of an open letter he had written. The Ministry would
be more flexible and adaptable without him. Yet his
retirement would be not all gain. In losing him the
Whigs lost steel, and there were very soon to be times
when the Whigs stood in sad need of the qualities of
steel.

It was a good thing that the Reform Ministry should be destroyed; it was right that the cards should be redealt in order that there might be two real parties, each capable of giving its appropriate service, instead of there only being a mixture and a morsel. Perhaps the Whigs might even induce O'Connell to trust them, and leave for a while his hopeless and violent advocacy of Repeal. Perhaps they might be better able to lead and unite their own party. The ministerialists seem on the whole to have been ready for a more Liberalized policy. There was, said Macaulay, a great party of the left centre which went farther in politics than the majority of the old Ministry, but not so far as Hume and the Radicals. It was, beyond all comparison, the strongest party in the Empire, but it had no head. Lord Althorp, equipped with Althorp's opinions and temper and with Stanley's abilities, might have led it.[1] The Whigs might now be able to supply what was wanting. If Liberalism was not at this time essentially divided or sterile, perhaps there were great things to be done for the country by the determined leading of a more Liberal administration.

But perhaps the country was not to get a very Liberal or a very determined administration. It would be mainly Whig, in whatever way that would affect the matter. There were impediments in the constitution which might cramp and stunt its free growth. It would have to fill a very difficult position, into which malleable stuff might fit more readily than what was stubborn and heavily principled; and the King must be a party to its formation. He had lately been very Conservative. It was supposed that the Conservative influence of his queen and his household had their effect on him. His speech to the Bishops announced what he considered to be his intention of preserving the Church. He was afraid of the introduction of men of dangerous opinions into the Cabinet. He had

---

[1] Macaulay to Spring-Rice from Ootacamund in India, Aug. 11 (he had no news of the splitting of the Government, for his news from England only went down to April 10) (McCullagh Torrens, *Memoirs of Lord Melbourne*, Vol. II, p. 15).

long desired the union of the respectable and steadying elements in the country.[1]   Brougham declared afterwards that the King was only frightened from proposing the formation of a Tory Government by a speech that he made in the House of Lords.   Brougham did make such a speech,[2] but Brougham's distant recollection of his own exploits is never considered the very best evidence.

On July 8th, the day of Grey's resignation, the King sent for Melbourne to advise him.   He wished Melbourne to communicate with Stanley, the Duke and Peel, in order to form a strong coalition.   Of course the project was impossible, and Melbourne wrote a long memorandum to the King to say that the Duke, Peel and Stanley had recently been in open disagreement with the administration generally, and in particular with their Irish Tithe Bill and Church Commission, both of which Melbourne believed were essential measures.[3]   The King was not satisfied, and under his instruction Melbourne sent to all three the document in which the King's views were embodied, and with it he included his own memorandum.   He added that they would see from his memorandum that he only wrote at the King's command.   Thus the negotiation was dead from its birth, and the Duke and Peel only wrote short notes to acknowledge Melbourne's letter.[4]   So short were they that the King made Melbourne write again to Peel and the Duke asking for a further explanation of their views. They answered in letters separately written but of the same tenor, on which in a personal memorandum written at the time Peel comments very significantly.

For there had been a significance in the shortness of

[1] Brougham, III, 281 (Sir H. Taylor to Brougham, June 6, 1833).

[2] Hansard, XXIV, 1323, July 9 (Brougham said neither he nor the other Ministers except Althorp and Grey had resigned).

[3] McCullagh Torrens, *Memoirs of Lord Melbourne*, p. 4 (extract in Melbourne Papers).

[4] Torrens, *Memoirs of Lord Melbourne*, p. 8 (Melbourne to the Duke, July 11, 1834, and Duke to Melbourne, July 11, 1834).   Martin's *Lyndhurst*, 216 (Peel to Lyndhurst, July 15, 1834, recounting and explaining his actions). Sir Robert Peel, *Memoirs*, Vol. II, pp. 1-13 (Melbourne to Peel, July 11 and 12. Peel to Melbourne, July 11 and 13, etc.).

their first answers and in the terms of their second ones. To avoid misrepresentation they would leave the dead child in the arms of him who had killed it, however much they agreed to its death. Peel declared to the King that he concurred in Melbourne's statement that a junction between himself and men of the late Ministry was impracticable, but he took care to guard against the King being led to believe that it was he who refused even to listen to his proposal.[1] As he said in his memorandum, both he and the Duke were ready to give the King every assistance in their power, should His Majesty require it without conditions as to union with others of different political principles and party connections, and giving them free liberty in respect to the Dissolution of Parliament and public measures generally. They did not wish to be invited to take office even upon these terms, but they were resolved, if invited, not to decline the responsibility, but to exhaust every Constitutional means of ascertaining whether the Constituent body would support an administration formed upon Conservative principles. "Those principles," added Peel in his memorandum, "I for one consider to be perfectly compatible with cautious and well-digested Reforms in every institution which really requires Reforms and with the redress of approved grievances." [2]

Conservation with Reform. Here is more of Peel's creed, clearly formularized in his mind and in direct continuity with another production of 1834, the Tamworth manifesto. The cat is out of the bag or, perhaps it would be kinder and truer to say, the device is on the shield. The words are obviously fitted to be the foundation of a party programme, they seem already to smell of the public platform and the public press, though they were produced in what was presumably a private memorandum; it is like a man who should wear a top hat in his bath. They are rather important than remarkable, but

[1] Martin's *Lyndhurst*, 216 (see above).
[2] Memorandum, July 23, 1834. Add MSS. 40,404; 222. Peel's *Memoirs*, Vol. II, p. 13.

after all, though the man who can invent a phrase may win fame the man who can launch a cliché will govern nations. The idea is not new to Peel. Most of the animal had been exposed before, or rather, Peel had already drawn his sword under this device. It was the logical extension of his pleas for concession over matters like the Irish Church in order not to alienate those who might be lukewarm supporters of it. Comprehension had always been necessary for survival. But there was more than that. It was self-justification. The moral defence of the Conservative creed was that it was compatible with all that was necessary in the way of reforms; the moral defence for Peel himself was that he was ready to be a safe Reformer. He was already a Reformer. He had claimed to be a Reformer in the first great debate of the first Reformed Parliament; he had since his youth been increasingly the conscious cautious Reformer of approved grievances. The creed is reasonable; his conscience had always urged it, his necessities often demanded it, and Heaven had made him for it. But the creed is dangerous. He would gain new votes for his party, not new life for his principles. His expedient was comprehension and concession, not fructification. There was a danger that living reforms might be yoked with dead Conservative principles: and the living partner in a concern is very often the dominant one.

These were problems for the future. But there was one other problem more clearly connected with the present. Peel had announced in his memorandum that he and the Duke would undertake office not from desire but from duty, should the King ask them unconditionally. This was a responsibility, but was it to be undertaken without reference to its probable outcome? It would have been interesting indeed for Peel to have explained the reasons and limits of this duty.

But this time the King did not send unconditionally for the Tories. When his absurd attempt had failed, he fell back on Lord Melbourne. Melbourne was a strange easy-going paradoxical fellow to whom to entrust the affairs of Empire and the destinies of the future.   Althorp would have seemed to be the man cast by fate for the part.   Indeed speculation, when it was not playing with the idea of the King summoning Peel, had put Althorp at the head of the Government.[1]   He was exceedingly popular; he was held to be the only man who could keep in check the present House of Commons and, as a testimonial, he had just received an address from 206 Liberal Members of Parliament, expressing confidence in him.[2]   He seemed cast for the part by fate, but not by nature.   He might have led and united the Liberal opinion of England, but nature made him want to be a farmer.   Anyhow it was Melbourne that had been chosen for Prime Minister.   Melbourne was clear-headed and very likeable.   Durham said his was the one name with which no one would disagree; the hope was that he would show unwonted energy; but it was rather like entrusting your life to a man who had charmed you at dinner.

If Althorp was not to be at the head of the Government, it was felt that he must be a member of it.   Melbourne called him the tortoise on which the world rested[3] and made his taking the Government conditional on Althorp's holding office.   It was a restive and refractory tortoise, that did not much like the weight of the world, but they managed to persuade it to come back to its task on the condition that Littleton should come back as well.   For the rest, although the new Government was much the same as the old, yet there were changes, and in a Liberal direction.   Duncannon, Melbourne's brother-in-law, was called up to the Lords and made Home Secretary.   He was a Liberal who had no great capacity for speaking, but he had what was far more important, the confidence and sometimes the confidences of O'Connell.   Hobhouse, who had been lost over the window taxes, returned to the Ministry and entered the

---

[1] Greville, *Geo. IV and Wm. IV*, III, 104 ff., etc.
[2] Spencer, 576.   [3] Hatherton, 96.

Cabinet. Stanley and his party were gone, and their places were filled by lesser but more Liberal men. Lord Grey was gone, and with his departure others must become more important. Lord John Russell, especially, was coming into his own. He had done much of late, and under the new régime he was often engaged in important and intimate correspondence with the Prime Minister. Perhaps that small man was to take up the destiny which Althorp was very soon to be fortunate enough to have to leave for the plough; perhaps Lord John was to direct and unite that great leaderless party of which Macaulay had spoken.

The Ministry was liberalized both in personnel and intention. The King made another and futile attempt to satisfy his Conservatism, by writing a memorandum to Melbourne with questions and comments on Melbourne and his administration. But Melbourne, in agreement with his colleagues, reserved the right to suggest anyone they liked for the Cabinet, to propose the Coercion Law without the public meeting clauses, and to offer to the King such measures of Church Reform as seemed advisable and as the Commission just issued on the Irish Church might recommend. When he received the paper containing these things, the King seemed a good deal agitated and annoyed.[1]

But the Session was not ended. The Irish Coercion Bill ran through its various stages in safety. The Tithe Bill continued its course. It was piloted through the Committee in the House of Commons, where O'Connell moved and carried an amendment against Althorp, who had however not asked his party men to oppose it. O'Connell began to talk of it as "my Tithe Bill" and to give it his support, while it emerged from the Committee in such a shape as to earn fierce Conservative opposition.[2] It seemed to them already in various ways

[1] Melbourne Papers, 204 (Melbourne to King, July 15). Torrens, *Melbourne*, Vol. II, 17 (Melbourne to Lansdowne, July 18); and cf. Torrens, *Melbourne*, II, 9 (Spring-Rice to Lansdowne, July 10, 1834).

[2] Hansard, XXV, 755 ff. O'Connell's *Correspondence*, I, 467 (July 31), 460 (Aug. 5 and 6).

to deprive the Church of a large part of its income, and yet not to settle the tithe question. Exciting such feelings as it did, it was like the wicked and wealthy whose present is assured, whose future is doubtful. On August 5th it was able to finish its course in the Commons without further mishap. It was sent up to try the dangerous passage of the House of Lords.

§6

It was indeed likely to be a dangerous passage. The Duke and the Lords, like death or the winter, waited for the Government's controversial legislation to come to them at the end of each Session: and in this Session the Duke was likely to be more courageously destructive than he had been in the last. It is true that at the beginning of the year he had not lost his old hopelessness. He never did lose it beyond recall, for it was part of himself as well as part of his view of the country. At the end of January he had repeated to Buckingham many of his old complaints. The Lords could do little. If they resolved anything, King, Ministry and Commons would combine against them as had happened last year. The Government would not split, and it would be of little use if they did, unless it was agreed that all that had been done in the last three years required revision. The government of England was impossible under existing circumstances, and with the House of Commons in its present privileged position.[1]

It was the old skeleton with the same grin and dance; but the Duke was to find a cupboard for his plaything. He was always liable to sanguine moods, and there were influences at work to encourage and invigorate him. There was, for instance, the rallying of the Church, and there was encouragement from Oxford. In 1833 there had been a subscription among residents at that University to have a bust made of him in token of their admiration of his late political struggles against the

[1] *Courts and Cabinets*, II, 76.

Government. The Duke answered this proposal in a letter which was very true to type, expressing manly resolution a little salted by self pity. Before this, he said, he had not an idea that anybody in the country had approved of what he had done in 1832. He had done what he considered his duty, others had thought differently and he had failed. He had thought that he had satisfied nobody but himself and those of his friends who understood his motives. He was satisfied to learn what Keble and others felt, and would attend their sculptor.[1] Poor Duke. He had probably been very lonely in the midst of his failure, and behind the mist of his moral and physical deafness. At the beginning of 1834 Oxford paid him a much greater compliment. Their Chancellor had just died. Newman and his friends, true to their clericalism, wanted the Archbishop of Canterbury to succeed him.[2] But most of Oxford thought otherwise, and after a little flirting with others, amongst whom was Peel, the Duke was elected.

His new position bound him more closely to the interests of the Church, and engaged him immediately in the struggle against the admission of the Dissenters to the Universities. In April the Duke opposed their plea at great length on a petition in the Lords, making a speech which Greville said was so bad that it might even have been delivered by the Duke of Gloucester, the Chancellor of Cambridge; and Lyndhurst told Greville that he thought that the Duke's new office might make him commit himself very inconveniently.[3] The Duke's new position was not to be a tithe as inconvenient as Lyndhurst's old nature.

However the Duke's position was commented on without much annoyance by others, to whom Lyndhurst was very soon to be an ally. But they may have been less clever, and a little more constant than that attractive man. Londonderry told Buckingham that the

[1] *Life of Lord Sidmouth*, III, 436 ff. (Duke to Sidmouth, April 2, 1833).
[2] Newman's *Correspondence*, e.g. II, 27 (Feb. 9).
[3] Grev., *Wm. IV and Geo. IV*, III, 73.

Duke of Wellington seemed much more active that
Session than he was in the last. "His appointment to
Oxford has been the cause of his being entirely armed
for the Church, and he seems more eager and determined."[1] It was true. The Duke was armed and
determined, and was becoming dangerous. He was
breaking his way out of Doubting Castle, where he had
been confined to his own undeserved misery and, it
must be confessed, for the convenience of the State.
At the end of April he declared that he thought that
the Church had gained strength by recent occurrences,
and he believed that the Bill which had been introduced
into the Commons for the admission of the Dissenters
to the Universities could be thrown out by the Lords
without mischief, because it was not a Government
measure but introduced by an individual.[2]

The House of Lords was going to be effective again
or, as some would say, useful; but there was still an
unsatisfactory side to this disappointing Duke, and something much worse than unsatisfactory in Peel, his colleague. With the end of April the Government's
troubles came upon it. The plot thickened, as Londonderry said rather often in his life. Some of the party
began to have great hopes for a Conservative Ministry,
and to believe that something might be done to dismiss the one at present in office. They must have been
thinking of those petty manœuvres and alliances with the
Radicals so often condemned by Peel, unless they meant
to do what they wished entirely through the House of
Lords. The vultures began to gather together, and
with them an eagle in bad company. Cumberland and
Buckingham and Londonderry had drawn Lyndhurst
into their councils. He was not by nature an ultra-
Tory, but he was exuberant, not, it may be, wildly ambitious, but surrounded by a little group that could prod
him into adventures, a little group into which young Disraeli was making his way. Lyndhurst was rash at times,

[1] *Courts and Cabinets*, II, 86 (Lond. to Buck., April 24).
[2] Ellesmere, *Personal Reminiscences of the Duke of Wellington*, p. 139.

rather a lover of cavalry politics, as have been others of his lawyer's trade, where the first essential is self-confidence and the next an unreal clarity of quickly formed opinion. He was one of the greatest speakers alive in England, a splendid ally for Londonderry and Cumberland. But he was not so valuable as he might seem to be. He was a very brilliant man, but he was also a weak one.

Just after Lord John Russell's outburst on May 6th, Cumberland and Londonderry apparently were engaged in trying to bring Lyndhurst to bear on the Duke of Wellington. Lyndhurst they thought saw everything as they did. How they saw everything is not clear, but at any rate Cumberland gives his own simple policy for the crisis. "My opinion is blow them up at once; when or how I care not."[1] Ward's motion came on. Hope swelled and blossomed in some Conservative bosoms, but it was hope of which the Duke of Wellington would not feel the influence, till it seemed to Londonderry "the *wish* of both—His Grace and Peel—that the Session should be got through by these men as most beneficial to the country."[2] June began to pass and the Government did not feel sure of its seat in the saddle. Buckingham's letters to Londonderry seem to have been stirring, and Londonderry determined to try to draw the Duke of Wellington out by saying that Buckingham resented these people remaining in, and did not seem to lean to any confidence in Sir Robert Peel's individual career.[3]

It might have been prophesied that Peel would not give satisfaction to the militant school. It was not that Londonderry disliked him. At least he always kept on good terms with him, and wrote to him in a friendly fashion. This very year he had written most warmly to compliment him on his speech on O'Connell's Repeal motion. He had declared among other things that he

[1] *Courts and Cabinets*, II, 94.
[2] *Ibid.*, II, 96 (Lond. to Buck., May 26), 98 (Lond. to Buck., May 21).
[3] *Ibid.*, II, 103 (Lond. to Buck., June 13, 1834).

never would forget it.[1]   Whatever was the truth of that, he and his friends would always be disappointed in Peel's cautious policy.   Peel was no tiger for the jackals to follow, no mere beast of prey heedlessly pulling down Governments.

And if Peel was essentially unsatisfactory, so was the Duke of Wellington.   His view was in reality the very opposite to that of the Duke of Buckingham.   So far from resenting the Whigs staying in, he resented it when they went out.   This feeling was so strong that it some-times had painful results.   When poor Grey went out in July, he made his speech about his dismissal with great chivalry and dignity and some emotion.   It would have been wise and kind to have spared him further debate that night, but the Duke bombarded and bullied him for leaving the King, in a way that many noticed and several condemned.[2]   He spoke in the same manner to Melbourne a little later.[3]   He was not dreaming of a possible Conservative Ministry, he was desiring with all his heart that the country should have, if indeed it were possible, a Government; and he felt, even with passion, that the Whigs, after what they had done, had a special duty to His Majesty to furnish one.

But, for all this, his policy might end by pleasing the Duke of Buckingham.   The Duke of Wellington's con-fidence must have been increasing.   It was always hard to tell how much the Duke was affected by applause, but other Conservatives felt very much encouraged by the brilliant reception he had at his installation at Oxford in June, and it provoked angry comments in the House of Commons.   The policy in the House of Lords became more militant.   They threw out the Bill for removing Jewish disabilities, and they dealt as they pleased with minor measures.   Perhaps the Lords were going to be made of some use, were to risk a resolute

---

[1] Add. MSS. 40,404; 126 (Lond. to Peel, April 26, 1834).
[2] Hansard, XXIV, 1319 (cf. Disraeli's Correspondence with his Sister, p. 27, July 11).
[3] *Ibid.*, XXV, 668.

policy and launch out into the glories and dangers of independence.

In later years the leaders of the Conservative party in the Commons were to modify that independence. Indeed sometimes it seemed that they were the cable which attached the Lords to the earth, and kept them from floating into the exalted altitudes of high Toryism, and altogether away. But the Conservative party in the Lords and the Conservative party in the Commons seem to have been strangely independent of one another; their leaders were different and their meetings separate. The personal connection between Peel and the Duke was therefore of the greatest importance, and in 1834 that connection was not as close as it might be.

There were various reasons. For one thing a careless or ironical fate had not prepared them to dovetail easily together. They were too different, and they were too much alike. Their habits of life and mind were very different, yet they were both strong, self-centred and masterful. They had habits which seemed especially calculated to wound one another. The Duke was liable to sudden and vehement outbursts, and Peel was strangely and unusually sensitive. Peel grew set and sure in his opinion and the Duke would manfully yield, but would not be so well able to control his sense of grievance. They were not meant to be comfortable together, although it is true there were some things that greatly assisted their union. Each respected the other and understood him in a way of which their common friends had no knowledge. It was like men in a constantly repeated partnership at cricket; they may not know each other's hearts but they can often run without calling.

Still they were both made to be difficult, and of late there had been some sort of estrangement between them. There had been their differences of opinion over the Duke's attempt at office in May 1832. Peel remembered how the Duke had seemed to reflect on him, in describing his sense of his own duty. Afterwards there had been no breach. They went on corresponding.

Peel even asked the Duke to stay with him,[1] yet in 1834 the Duke's vehement words came very readily out of Peel's memory.[2] Perhaps the Duke remembered Peel's refusal, which had stultified all his endeavours. Their communication became infrequent. Once at least the Duke would have it that Peel had taken a different course to his own, though at other times he would discover with pleasure that they had moved along the same road. Meanwhile memories festered, long silence provided unpleasant surprises, and matters became uncomfortable. The Duke felt that he made advances to Peel to which Peel did not respond, and it was said that the Duke had as much as Peel, and more, to answer for. Then, at the beginning of 1834 there came a new source of grievance. Peel felt aggrieved that the Duke did not refer to him when he accepted the Chancellorship of Oxford, although the Duke knew that Peel was named as a candidate.

Consequently there was a distinct misunderstanding between the Duke and Peel in the first half of 1834, and an explanation with Peel on the matter was entered into by Arbuthnot and Aberdeen.[3] It did not alter the men's natures nor much affect their relations. They still remained in dangerously bad communication. On May 23rd, after Arbuthnot's effort, the Duke asked Aberdeen to communicate with Peel on a point of foreign policy. He had had, he said, no communication with him for some time upon any subject excepting the mere forms of society "and I don't think that he would like either to advise a proceeding in the House of Lords, at least through me, or that I should advise one in the House of Commons."[4]

So the high command of the Conservatives was in no healthy condition. Peel went to hear the Lords debate the Irish Coercion Bill as sent up to them by the Mel-

[1] Add. MSS. 40,309; 260.
[2] Parker, II, 236. (See Add. MSS. 40,312; 173 ff.)
[3] Parker, II, 232 ff. (Add. MSS. 40,312 ; 1743 ff.)
[4] Privately printed Aberdeen Corresp., May 23, 1834 (Vol. 1832–34).

bourne Government. He received a horrible fright, for the Duke appeared to be moving the reintroduction of the public meeting clauses.[1] The opposition was strong in the House and the Ministry weak, and if the Duke had divided, he would have been successful. It would have caused, so Peel thought, a collision between the Houses and the disruption of the Ministry. Worst of all, it would have prevented Peel's going home to his family. The Duke did not divide, his speech was only meant as a protest, but Peel showed by his fright a most curious ignorance. He did not know whether at any moment the Duke might not start off the wheels of destiny and stop the wheels of the coach that would carry him back to Drayton.

Peel went home at the beginning of August, and it was during August that the Duke tasted the full glories of the Session. His knife was sharp, and fat geese came to be killed. On August the 1st the Lords threw out the Bill for the admission of Disserters into the Universities by 187 to 85.[2] Enlivened by this large majority, on August 2nd the Conservative peers met in the great gallery of Apsley House. The Duke declared, in strange but significant phrase, that they had shown what a large majority they were "in the country." Several pledged themselves to stay up till the end of the Session; and they considered the Government's Irish Tithe Bill. The prey was in view, and the pack soon in full cry. Cumberland and Kenyon pressed the Duke to have the Bill thrown out on the second reading. The Duke said he would be guided by the Bishops, an answer with which the ultras had reason to be satisfied. Londonderry read a letter from Buckingham in favour of defeating the Bill on the second reading, and apparently Lyndhurst backed him up. The Bishops at their meetings condemned the Bill. The Lords met again and decided unanimously to reject the Tithe Bill. Harrowby and Wharncliffe, the old waverers of the Reform

---

[1] *Private Letters*, p. 146 (Peel to his wife, July 30, 1826).
[2] Hansard, XXV, 815.

Bill time, tried to throw doubts, but they were not supported. The decision was taken and the die was cast. The Lords' spirits had risen so high that they were ready to throw out a Government Bill of the first importance. They did not even alter the Bill in Committee back to what it was before its various liberalizing modifications. On Monday, August 11th, they rejected it on its second reading by 189 votes to 122. They had used their strength to the utmost, they had interfered with the desires of the Ministry. The Lords were again to be of some use in the country, for they had dared to do what it might have been thought they would never do again without disaster.[1]

§ 7

And nothing happened. Comment was smothered in the Commons,[2] and in a few days the Session ended. Perhaps it was fortunate for the Lords that they were usually called on to do their heroical acts in August in a dying Session and on an emptying stage. The Ministry must have longed for the end of this harassing Session, especially since vanity, restlessness and ferocious newspaper attack seemed to be driving Brougham mad.[3] It was through his old most disastrous fault; he could seldom be cautious and never quiet. Perhaps the Ministry's desire for the end dulled the edge of their anger. At any rate, when Hobhouse attended his first Cabinet on August 12th, the day after the rejection of the Tithe Bill, he found them not at all dejected by what had just happened, but only anxious as to its probable consequences in Ireland.[4] The effects in Ireland were indeed likely to be serious, and Ellice and Spring-Rice, referring it would seem to these, called the Lords' decision the

---

[1] *Courts and Cabinets*, II, 115–22 (Lond. to Buck., Aug. 2, 1834; Cumb. to Buck., Aug. 7, 1834; Lond. to Buck., Aug. 8, 1834, and Aug. 12, 1834; Cumb. to Buck., Aug. 13, 1834).

[2] Grev., III, 120. Hansard, XXV, 1143, 1240 ff.

[3] E.g. Torrens, *Melbourne*, II, 18 (Campbell to Melbourne, but Campbell was very malicious against Brougham).

[4] Broughton, IV, 331.

most fatal and important that had occurred for years. The question that proposed itself to Ministers was what would happen in Ireland when the time came for the payment of the tithes. Perhaps the question should have been whether the time had not come for the repayment of the Lords.

One old statesman felt that he would have acted differently. Lord Grey told Madame Lieven that he had long looked to the possibility of such an event, and that he had been resolved that the moment any important measure should be defeated in this manner he would resign. "Nothing would have induced me to remain in office after being refused the means of acting in the manner that I thought necessary for the public interest; and this in such a case appears to be the natural course."[1] Maybe this is only the usual resolution of those who have retired, but it seems very probable that as he says he had long treasured some such intention. His cool dignified determination, when his Tithe Bill was threatened in 1833, seems to bear it out. Lord Grey was less complacent with Liberals than was Melbourne, but he was more finely tempered and had a sharper cutting edge. His Ministry was less advanced than Lord Melbourne's, but in certain circumstances it might have been more effective.

Lord Grey had retired, the Reform Ministry was gone, the first Reformed Parliament was drawing to its end. The immediate Reform Bill era was being cleared out of the way, as it was right that it should be. But was it to be succeeded by an age of hesitation and complacency, an age in which obstruction might be encouraged by immunity and politics become starved, dead and unreal, in which the Lords should be allowed to flourish and Liberalism to flag and fade? The end of that might be stagnation, which is unhealthy for all. The Reform Bill era might be followed by neither Heaven nor Hell but by Limbo, by empty routine politics, outside whose

[1] Grey to Princess Lieven, Aug. 15, 1834 (*Corresp. of Earl Grey and Princess Lieven*, III, 3).

ring should menace and gesticulate the pitiable shadows of dangerous hopes.

But it is unfair as yet to condemn the Ministry. Men's eyes could be legitimately fixed on next year. A Tithe Bill would have to be introduced next year. The Commission on the Irish Church would report next year. O'Connell was determined to press for better measures for Ireland next year. Lord John was even in favour of a November Session, to attempt something for tithes this year before there was time for trouble in Ireland. The Lords would reject a new Tithe Bill and, if so, theirs be the responsibility. It seems almost a weak ending to a strong suggestion.[1] Still weakness or strength cannot yet fairly be judged: and in the meantime there was enough to occupy men's minds in anxieties about Ireland. For a little while they could leave the Duke to rejoice in his immunity.

He did undoubtedly rejoice in his immunity. He was in a spirited mood, a happy statesman prepared for much further obstruction. He expounds himself in a correspondence with Aberdeen. The Government, he said, seemed to bear very tranquilly their majority on the Tithe Bill. They knew it must have been larger had he allowed the Bill to go to the third reading, so that upon the whole the Government must see clearly that in their legislation at least they must reckon with the House of Lords. "I consider," said he, "the destruction of the House of Lords to be now out of the question and that we have only now to follow a plain course with moderation and dignity to obtain a very great if not a preponderating influence in the country"; and he goes on to recount their grand record of obstruction. They had rejected three important measures supported by the Government, together with some of less importance, and they had altered others to prevent their mischief.[2]

There was probably still a sediment of restraint in him.

[1] O'Connell's *Correspondence*, Vol. I, 463 (Aug. 27, 1834), p. 333.
[2] Duke of Well. to Aberdeen, Aug. 23, 1834 (privately printed Aberdeen Corresp., 1832–44, p. 14).

He thought it necessary to explain why he defeated the Tithe Bill on the second reading; and one of his reasons was good.   The Bill was abominable, Committees in the House of Lords were always unmanageable, it would have been lost anyhow, and he might have lost command of his majority.   It would have meant additional mischief had the majority of the House of Lords not been under his direction.   In this last he was right; that would have meant additional mischief, but with so sanguine a Duke and such uncontrollable Lords there must be mischief enough in 1835.[1]

It was indeed a sanguine Duke.   He believed that it could be shown there were a great many more opposed to the destruction of old institutions than had dared to show face.   He believed that the people of England might possibly support the Irish Protestants, should they fight their battle on the basis of Protestantism, property and the Union, and put the Orange Society into the background.   At the least that would put them on their right basis, and of one resource he felt sure.   "But thank God!   We have a House of Lords, and if the Irish noblemen and gentlemen will only be true to themselves, I'll engage that we will carry them triumphantly through their difficulties."   The Duke felt in fact that the Lords might effectively stop mischief; that is, that an entirely irresponsible body might effectively cripple political development.   These are interesting words and seem to promise interesting events for the next Session.

There were to be plenty of interesting events in the next Session and before the next Session, events not all of them promised by any man's words.   But for the moment it was holiday time.   On October 16th Peel had gone abroad with his wife and daughter to engage in that foreign travel of which he had once dreamed.   No doubt he thought that he had escaped.   He travelled down through France into Italy, probably little dreaming with what speed he would have to return, and probably little

---

[4] Duke to Aberdeen, Sept. 4, 1834 (privately printed Aberdeen Corresp., 1832–44, p. 7).

caring that his hours of freedom were meted out to him by the enfeebled pulse of a dying nobleman.   But when that stopped the whole noisy show would start again into motion, and the puppets would be pulled back to their dance, even from Italy.

CHAPTER V

AN UNSUCCESSFUL EXPERIMENT, 1834-5

At a quarter to three in the afternoon of November 10th, 1834, Althorp's father, Lord Spencer, died, and thus altered the whole political situation, or rather gave the excuse for its alteration. During that period there were always three factors to be considered. There was not only the House of Commons, wayward and difficult; not only the House of Lords, vindictive and stubborn; there was also an old gentleman whose actions and sayings were so odd and eccentric that most people realized that he was a little mad. But "what," as someone said of His Majesty, "could you expect of a man with a head like a pineapple?"[1]

Even the Tories did not now expect very much. Yet long before that September the King had shown signs of alarm and of Conservatism, both privately to his Ministers and, on occasions, too publicly for a Constitutional King, as in the speech which he had made to the Bishops in May 1834, declaring his intention to support the Church in Ireland. But when all had been said privately or publicly, very little had been done. The King had remained saddled with the Whigs and he had given his assent to the introduction of their measures. His speech to the Bishops had been immediately followed by the formation of a Liberalized administration and the signature of the Commission on the Revenues of the Irish Church. In fact the Duke said that that speech had deceived the public, and he had strongly disapproved of its publication by the Irish Bishops, when they knew that the King had allowed a Government to be formed on opposite principles. Not but what the Duke allowed full importance to the subject of the speech, for in the same letter he had gone so far as to say that he believed "that there is nothing that people care so

[1] Greville, *Geo. IV and Wm. IV*, III, 32 (under Sept. 10, 1833).

much about as the Church, excepting always their own properties." [1]

Yet the King never meant to deceive anyone at all. He was merely an old sailor in a task that was too hard for him, and with an uncontrollable desire to make speeches. He was weak, troubled and well intentioned, unable to stem a current of events which he had learnt to fear. He had still some confidence in Grey and Melbourne and some sort of loyalty towards them, and he had had his foolish hopes, which had utterly miscarried, of using Melbourne in a coalition of all that was Conservative and respectable. But in most of his present Ministry he had not much confidence, and Duncannon had foolishly alarmed him by detailing their intentions towards Ireland. Moreover, he had been extremely annoyed by Brougham's fantastic behaviour, at the end of the Session and after it, when he had gone on tour in Scotland with the Great Seal and had made his colleagues dread the appearance of each newspaper report. The Ministry, therefore, was in bad odour with the King when the death of Lord Spencer reopened the whole question of its existence by withdrawing Althorp into the Lords. The fates had withdrawn the tortoise on which Melbourne had said the world rested.

It was in the House of Commons that Althorp's essential usefulness lay, and it was probable that his ancient desires, together with the financial position in which his father had left him, would make him leave the Government. Consequently it was to be expected that Melbourne should write in grave terms to the King, when he asked leave to visit him at Brighton in order to suggest new arrangements. He did in fact offer to continue as Prime Minister, but he begged the King not to be debarred by personal feeling from appointing anyone else.

There was no real reason for Melbourne's Government to be disturbed. No other set of men were likely to be able to fill their places. If the Whigs had lost in prestige

[1] Add. MSS. 40,309; 368 (Duke to Peel, July 5, 1834).

or had suffered from general abuse, especially from the newspapers, that is a very common and not a very decisive misfortune with Governments. They could have stood without Althorp, and Melbourne told the King that he had no doubt they could still retain the confidence and support of the House of Commons. But in his interview Melbourne said too much. He was probably not filled with enthusiasm for his prospects, he did not believe very heartily in the constancy of popular support in England, he spoke too freely of the future difficulties of the Government—apparently giving the King the erroneous impression that Lansdowne and Spring-Rice were likely to retire over the Irish Church ; and he too nearly offered his own resignation. He suggested that Lord John Russell should succeed Althorp as Leader of the House of Commons. To this the King had special objections. He disliked Lord John's opinions and did not consider that his powers were equal to coping with both Peel and Stanley in opposition. The King believed, as others did, in the increased strength of the Church and the Conservative party, and Melbourne's words had suggested that this Whig Ministry which he disliked were unable to continue in power. So he took a decisive step. He dispensed with Melbourne's further services, and summoned the Duke of Wellington.

The act was foolish, but Melbourne had invited it. He told Lord Grey afterwards that he was not surprised at the King's decision, and that he did not know that he could entirely condemn it; although it is true that he called sending for the Duke a "fearful expedient." He went up to London on November 14th, intending to tell his colleagues the next day. Unfortunately he was anticipated. Brougham called on him that night and was told under confidence what had happened, and next morning Melbourne's other colleagues learned of their dismissal from the newspaper. The Times had received a message from someone, recounting the news and with it the dangerous and untrue addition that the Queen had

done it all.   Men made little doubt that Brougham had
been at his old tricks again.[1]

§ 2

But was the Duke to be at his old tricks again?   Was
it to be restoration or rehearsal, prologue or epilogue?
The dismissal of the Ministry was not that collapse from
internal divisions to which Peel had looked forward, and
when he heard of it he doubted whether the causes for
it were sufficient.   The Duke thought that the King
would have done better to wait till the divisions which
had been foretold for the Ministry had taken effect.
The Conservative Leaders had not desired this dismissal,
and they certainly had not plotted it.[2]   But, unpleasant
and undesired, the chance was important.   It might
serve to show what goods the Conservatives had to offer
the country, to consolidate their position, to forecast the
future.

The King's message found the Duke going out hunt-
ing, and he came to Brighton so suddenly as to surprise
the Court, who did not yet know of his errand.   He
found the King's quarrel with his late Ministers a settled
affair, and consequently he told Peel that he did not
consider himself and Peel responsible for it.   In this,
from a Constitutional point of view he was mistaken,
for the assumption of office by the Conservatives would
imply the assumption of responsibility for the dismissal
of their predecessors.   But it is doubtful whether consciousness of this fact would have made much difference
to the Duke's actions.   On the way to Brighton he had
decided what to do.   When the King asked him to
undertake to form a Government, the Duke pointed out
that the chief difficulties would be in the House of
Commons, and earnestly recommended the King to
choose a member of that House as his Minister—in fact,
Sir Robert Peel.   It was the transference of power that
he had suggested as far back as 1830.   The King
assented.   Hudson, an officer of the Court, was sent out

---

[1] *Melbourne Papers*, 209 and 219 to 227.   [2] E.g. Grev., III, 131.

to fetch Peel home. Meanwhile the Duke determined to make a temporary arrangement and to do nothing that might fetter Peel's decisions when he came home, and for the next three weeks the country watched and waited for Peel to return and govern it.

The country was tranquil; all attempts to raise trouble failed. Melbourne was equable, the other Whigs apparently sullen and angry at their dismissal, and the least peaceful feature in the landscape was Brougham, who was in a wild state of resentment and excitement, so that men feared what he might do or refuse to do with the Great Seal. The Duke felt himself to be master of the event. "The Government," he told Aberdeen, "went out rather sulkily; Brougham is outrageous; but I was very cool and quiet, and I entertain no doubt that I shall keep matters very cool and quiet till Peel will return." [1]

But notwithstanding the doubts that the Duke of Wellington did not entertain, the country would watch but not wait, not even when he had directed that it should. He strove most honourably to keep all matters open for Peel, but the situation went on developing, and the Duke himself unwittingly assisted its development. He could always be honourable, but he found it much harder to be tactful. The King did not, as is usual, accept the services of his old Ministers till new were appointed, but dismissed them immediately. In this difficult situation the Duke acted avowedly on the doubtful and dangerous maxim that it is better to be uncivil than absurd. [2] He had assumed most of the important offices of the State and appeared at each in turn, without apparently communicating with the old Minister, to take over the current business. He settled down at length at the Home Office, making occasional raids on the others. His sudden appearances excited the amusement of some men, but

---

[1] Privately printed Aberdeen Corresp., 1832–44, p. 27 (Duke to Aberdeen, Nov. 18, 1834). Peel's *Memoirs*, II, 23 (Duke to Peel, Nov. 15, 1834). Ellesmere, *Personal Recollections of the Duke of Wellington*, 142 (Duke to Egerton, Nov. 29, 1834).

[2] Ellesmere, *Personal Recollections of the Duke of Wellington*. Grev., III, 155. Croker, II, 242 (Croker to Lord Hertford, Nov. 24, 1834).

unfortunately the annoyance of others, while his assumption of nearly all the great offices of state gave some, even of the older Whigs, grave alarm. He was not conciliating opinion for the new Ministry.

Even by being sent for the Duke had innocently done wrong. His name had been associated with the Ministry's formation, and had already seemed to colour its politics. It was a famous and a notable name which none could pass over and which many distrusted. In Berkshire it was said that the coming election was dominated by the cry "Duke or no Duke";[1] and the trouble was not only with the electorate. Soon after the Duke's appointment Graham wrote to Stanley that the King "has put up the wrong man to ride this second heat. Bob was the lad who had the best chance of winning."[2] Bob's chance had got worse if Stanley and Graham learnt to look on the Duke as the King's jockey.

Men would form opinions, and candidates would issue addresses. Many took it for granted that Parliament would be dissolved, and naturally prepared for their contests. Indeed, from the earliest days the Duke had assumed and prepared for a dissolution, and when Peel came back home he found, as he said later, that that decision had virtually passed out of his control.[3] Money had been expended and election warfare had started, he could not call in a pack in full cry. It is true that he would almost certainly have decided not to face the vast Reforming majority of the old Parliament. Still, he had taken over an army already in action and already attacking some points which he would rather have left unassailed. Lord Howick, Grey's son, had issued a temperate address, not very hostile to the Government, and without consulting Peel it was decided to put up a Conservative candidate to oppose Howick. The decision drove both him and his father more decidedly into

[1] Add. MSS. 40,405; 24.
[2] Graham to Stanley, Nov. 18, 1834 (Graham, I, 214).
[3] Duke to Aberdeen, Nov. 18, 1834 (Privately Printed Aberdeen Corresp.). Peel's *Memoirs*, II, 43.

the ranks of Peel's opponents. It was a decision that by no means earned Peel's approval.[1]

It is inconvenient to be summoned from Italy to govern your country; but what it loses in convenience it gains in romance. Hudson travelling with speed caught Peel in Rome. He saw Peel on the night of November 28th at his hotel, in full dress, having just come with his daughter from a ball at the Duchess of Torlonia's. It might well form a subject for one of those historical paintings in which that age so much delighted, with the added advantage that a mute picture would hide what legend reports, that Peel's only thanks were to show Hudson that by another route he might have come to him more quickly. That night Peel wrote cautious answers to the letters sent to him by the Duke and the King, merely telling them that he would come home immediately. He managed with a struggle to leave Rome next day by about three o'clock. Back he came with his wife and daughter by carriage over the difficult routes of those days; a handsome, portly, red-haired English statesman, pondering over the problems in front of him.

For twelve days they travelled, and eight nights. Part of a night had to be passed at Massa because of a rapid torrent that could not be ferried by dark; one night they slept at Susa before crossing the Mont Cenis; one night had to be spent at Lyons, owing to political troubles there, and one night at Paris waiting for letters which Peel wished to receive before he reached London. The other eight nights they passed in the carriage. It was no wonder that Peel had had a separate passport made out for himself in case his wife might be tired on the way, and that when he got home he often mentioned with pride that she had been with him from Rome to Dover. He left her there, and drove up through the winter night to London and his fate. For he had thought it all out while he travelled, and before he entered London

[1] Add. MSS. 40,410; 56 and 97.

very early on the morning of December 9th he had come to the conclusion that he must become Prime Minister.[1]

In truth Peel had not had very much choice. Even before the Duke had reached the King the matter was settled, since Peel and the Duke both apparently felt that they could not refuse to supply the King with a Ministry once he had appealed to them. It was a responsibility such as Peel had recognized in his memorandum of July. It is true that it was a responsibility he had refused in 1832. But then he had had a definite reason against it; he had been asked to take office to do what he was pledged not to do. It is true that this time also he had thought twice about it, but very little consideration had convinced him that he had no alternative but to become Prime Minister. He had determined that he could not reconcile it with his feelings to humiliate the Monarchy by compelling the King to receive back his old Ministers; that if he was going to refuse, it must be due to avowed disapprobation and with such reasons as should prevent him supporting any other Conservative Ministry that might come in his place.[2] It was a view of his duty likely to lead into many a strange and dangerous position, if he had always been ready to follow it. But rules for political conduct are made and obeyed by men, not by machines, and are likely to be in part explanations or excuses. There was probably another difference between 1832 and 1834—a difference of mood. Since 1832 Peel's politics had gained zest and vigour. He was better prepared to receive willingly such a summons from His Majesty. Perhaps he may even have allowed himself some sort of hope.

§ 3

Peel told the King when he saw him that the Government must be formed on a basis as wide as was compatible with the honour and consistent opinions of public men of high character, and that he must advise an invi-

---

[1] Peel's *Memoirs*, II, 26.   [2] *Ibid.*, II, 32.

tation to Stanley.[1]   Peel had always wished to base his
Government on comprehension, and as to the offer to
Stanley, that had universally been expected and desired.
Indeed, the Duke had included both Stanley and Graham
in the lists of probable Ministers which he had sent out
to meet Peel on his way home.   On this first day of his
return Peel wrote to them both.   He asked them to
join his Government, declaring that he had only appointed
as yet the Duke of Wellington to be Foreign Secretary
and Lord Lyndhurst the Lord Chancellor.[2]

It was the most important question of all.   With
those two exceptions he kept all his arrangements open
till he should have received some answer from Stanley
and Graham.   He wished to be entirely free to nego-
tiate for their support, and though he communicated
with those of the Conservatives who might form the
Cabinet, he does not seem to have appointed them.[3]
He was obviously ready to make considerable sacrifices
to gain Stanley and his friends.   They would spread the
basis of his Ministry, they would show that it was not
only the old narrow type of Tory Ministry escaped from
the rubbish heap.   They would give it a chance of
support from men who had been Whigs.   Stanley
answered by letter and Graham came up to see Peel, and
both, as was already agreed between them, refused his
offer.

Stanley founded his refusal on the fact that he had
so recently been a member of Lord Grey's Ministry, and
within the last four years opposed to Peel on important
matters, although recent events had narrowed their differences.   He admitted that since the Reform Bill Peel's
opposition had been moderate and fair, but some of his
followers had needed his restraining hand.   The Duke
had been the first man to be summoned by the King and
had become Foreign Secretary, and Stanley could not

[1] Add. MSS. 40,403; 15.
[2] Duke to Peel, Nov. 30, 1834.   *Memoirs*, II, p. 28, 33.   Add. MSS.
40,309; 316 and 380.
[3] Add. MSS. 40,405; 56 and 76 (Peel to Knatchbull, Dec. 11 and 12).

forget his attack on Grey and all his works, on the night of Grey's retirement. He spoke in general terms of the evils of coalitions, and of how he would be suspected if, having left office for conscience' sake, he should so soon return to it with his political opponents. He ended by saying that he believed, from the tone of Peel's letter, that he would be able cordially to support his measures. Graham also said in his interview that if Peel's measures were good they would best be able to support them if they were out of office.[1]

Their refusal was natural. They were still too much entangled with the Whigs, and it was said, probably with truth, that Stanley was very much afraid of having to take office under Peel and of enduring the reproach from his old colleagues of having abandoned his principles.[2] But, truth to tell, there were also dreams to disturb matters. Graham had thought in September that Melbourne might be willing to fall back on those who had retired.[3] In the present crisis Stanley had told Graham that they would support Peel from out of office on the condition of his passing certain measures which they deemed essential, whereby they would naturally gain not only private satisfaction but also public credit, and so they might strengthen their own party.[4]

Such calculations and hopes appealed probably more consistently to Graham than to Stanley. Stanley was a creature of moods, forgetfulness, and rash mistakes, as brilliant as spring sunshine and as inconstant. He was at one time hot and excited over politics, and at another time exclusively interested in a race meeting, while debate he regarded as a game to be won without too much attention to fact or tact. He was sincere but not determined, and he had not great resources of political courage. Graham's character was different. Creevey

---

[1] Stanley to Peel, Dec. 11, 1834 (*Memoirs of Sir R. Peel*, II, 36. Add. MSS. 40,405; 61). Parker's *Graham*.

[2] Add. MSS. 40,404; 265 (Greville to Col. Peel, Dec. 2, 1834).

[3] Parker's *Graham*, I, 208 ff.

[4] *Ibid.*, I, 214 (Stanley to Graham, Dec. 8, 1834).

spoke of "canting Graham." It is true that Graham's principles were at the time of speaking inconvenient to Creevey's party but the adjective may still be in part descriptive. Graham was an able administrator but at times a suspected and unpopular colleague. He was eloquent, and was one of those whose eloquence perilously intrudes into their private letters; for he was serious over what were really literary opinions. He was also busyminded, always active, often interfering, usually intent on some project or other. He was ambitious and yet timid, and tended to lean rather heavily on one favoured colleague. At that time it was Stanley. "Stanley," he is reported to have said, "was the right horse to back." He seems to have wanted Stanley's friends to come out into the open, to have hoped that Peel might be led to join them, rather than that they should join Peel, and he spoke of a third party of which they should form the centre. With Stanley he disliked Peel's "crew"; but he was already attracted by Peel's kindness in his interview with him, and he was already conscious of Stanley's defects.[1]

Their refusal was a heavy blow to Peel, though it was probably expected. They had not shown themselves to be unfriendly, and Peel could do something by announcing to everyone that the first thing he had done was to invite Stanley and Graham. Still he had started with failure. About this time, after Stanley's refusal, Croker called on Peel at Whitehall. Peel talked matters over with him, showed him Stanley's letter, and said twice over in a querulous tone that it would be only the Duke's old Cabinet.[2] It was very true. At that moment a junction with Stanley in office would have led almost to a coalition Ministry, especially since Peel had left almost all of his offices open for negotiation. As it was he went to the other extreme and this Ministry was markedly Tory.

[1] Parker's *Graham*, I, 214, 220, etc. For Graham's view of Stanley, see Grev., III, 250 (under April 9, 1835).
[2] Croker, II, 248.

The Cabinet was filled with Peel's old friends and old colleagues; and Peel and his advisers showed care to placate the most ultra-Tory Lords.   Lord Roden was offered high household office, although he was the leader of the dangerous Irish Protestants, and had just been writing menacingly to Ellenborough about their high expectations.[1]   Wetherell, the most violent of ultra-Tories, being angry at not being appointed Chief Baron, was offered the Attorney-Generalship.[2]   The sons of Tory Peers were put into subordinate offices, and their fathers were notified.   Thus age was conciliated and youth recruited.   There were also in the Ministry other young men worthy of note; Sidney Herbert, at that time distinguished for one notable speech and still more for being well connected; Gladstone, already started on his lengthy career, and Praed, already too near to the end of his short one.   One young man was recruited with characteristic difficulty.   A strange mixture of modest scruples and something like baffled pride made it singularly hard to include Ashley in the Board of the Admiralty, or even to understand his letters.   Granville Somerset, who was acting for Peel in this case, seems almost to apologize to Peel for having succeeded.[3]   But he had managed to add to the Ministry another name pregnant with importance for the future.

The Ministry was a strange welter of aristocracy, talent and Toryism, and unfortunately it was the aristocracy and the Toryism which contemporaries recognized.   There were many criticisms.   It was thought that Peel might at least have made his Cabinet smaller, and not have included so many objectionable names;[4] but this was the criticism of men not fully confronted with the insatiable demands of greedy desire and political exigencies.   It is possible that Peel was too much in the hands of his headquarters staff or too much imbued

---

[1] Add. MSS. 40,405; 251.   [2] *Ibid.* 40,316; 100 and 106.
[3] *Ibid.* 40,405; 7; 12; 95; 97.
[4] E.g. Grev., III, 189 (Conversation with Lyndhurst), Parker's *Graham*, II, 223.

with the old method of making a government by linking together a glorious array of satisfied Peers. Perhaps he was blind to the nobler possibilities of party, and too much unthinkingly committed to its commonplaces. The ultra-Tory Peers were likely to give him no trouble; before he had come home the Duke had circulated a letter to them, and had received favourable answers. Still, the refusal of Stanley had thrown Peel on his own party, and most Governments were at that time largely constructed by the light of that ignoble science of claims and influences; and Peel knew how to refuse.

He had shown this in another great failure, one redounding to his credit and increasing his anxieties. Before he came home Lord Chandos had been to Lyndhurst and told him that he and other county representatives would not support any Ministry that would not pledge itself to repeal the Malt Tax. They would agree to give their support to re-enact the Beer Tax, but the Malt Tax must cease.[1] Chandos was dangerous ; Lyndhurst told Greville that there had gathered under him a sort of confederation of counties, and when Croker called upon Peel he was told that the only thing that was settled was that Knatchbull and Chandos would be invited, that Baring would be in the Ministry, and that all the rest would be made up from the old odds and ends. Now Knatchbull, Chandos and Alexander Baring were, all three, leading agricultural Conservatives, and all had been supporters of the Repeal of the Malt Tax. It seems almost as if Peel's own diagnosis of his own Government was that it would be the agricultural interest, and the old odds and ends. The phrase might even be plausibly used as an analysis of Conservatism.

As early in the proceedings as December 12th Peel saw Chandos and apparently offered him office, or discussed it with him. Chandos would have liked office; he seems to have been most anxious for the success of Peel's Ministry. He stated his anxious desire and entire

[1] Grev., *Geo. IV and Wm. IV*, III, 152. Add. MSS. 40,316 ; 98 (Lyndhurst to Peel, Dec. 12).

readiness to accept office, provided that he could be assured in confidence that the partial or total Repeal of the Malt Tax would be recommended, and he alluded to his position with his constituents and indeed with the country on this question.[1] This pledge Peel refused. He expressed his views in a memorandum which he sent to Chandos. He declared that he had been engaged since he came to England in the harassing duties of Cabinet making, and that he had not yet turned to the immediate duties of the Chancellor of the Exchequer. But his present impressions were decidedly unfavourable to total Repeal of the Malt Tax, and to partial Repeal. Total Repeal must mean, in Peel's opinion, the reimposition of the Property Tax, and he was deeply impressed with the belief that the agricultural interest would suffer from the substitution. His present impressions, he said, were against partial Repeal. In the existing state of Revenue, and with his views of the paramount importance of maintaining public credit, he must be assured of a substitute to which Parliament would consent and which could be defended on sound financial grounds. He would be ready, he said, to consider with his colleagues such a substitution, but he could fetter himself with no assurances.[2]

There are perhaps the very smallest signs of a slight weakening on the question of partial Repeal, but the whole memorandum is clear, strong, resolute and to be admired. He wanted Chandos, for Chandos' importance and annoyance at the position taken up were not hidden from him. Lyndhurst warned him that Chandos might deliver himself of an address. Bonham, the Conservative Whip, told him that Chandos' powers of mischief at the moment were immense. Chandos himself, through a third party, got a letter to Peel, declaring that it was most important for the elections to have some declaration on the Malt Tax. A total Repeal would enlist all the country gentlemen who were prepared to

---

[1] Add. MSS. 40,406; 160.
[2] *Ibid.* 40,405; 116 (Peel's Memorandum) and 163.

support any government at all.   Chandos was obviously
moved at having to refuse office.   He spoke rather
strangely of this most unexpected obstacle, and said of
Peel's Government, "if he fail, what is left but ruin?"
But for all that he could not join a Minister who had
declared so directly against the Repeal.[1]

Peel would not conclude his arrangements without
making sure that Chandos would not come into office,
and on December 19th he wrote to him asking him to
make his final decision.   But Chandos was firm, though
friendly, and both he and his father were left out, since
the Duke of Buckingham had not been offered office
equivalent to Cabinet office such as he had held under
Wellington.   Later he offered to go as Lord Lieutenant
to Ireland, but his offer was not accepted.   Buckingham
was out and was angry, but Peel could not see that he
had any grievance, considering that he and Chandos had
had an offer such as had come the way of no two other
men standing in the same relationship.   But greedy
ambition could not be satisfied, nor honest obstinacy
over-persuaded.   Such were always the difficulties of
Prime Ministers.[2]

Knatchbull and Alexander Baring, the other two Agri-
culturalists, accepted office.   Baring was only agricultural because of his constituency.   Knatchbull was one
of those ultra-Tories who had led the revolt which had
pulled Peel down in 1830, and consequently his junction
was considered significant.   But neither had been of
late years so notably as Chandos the leader of the Agri-
culturalists; Peel had again failed in a most important
respect.

Still, he had few other failures in the construction of
his mosaic.   Peel's forlorn hope attracted many volun-
teers, too many, in fact.   Peel had to suffer the usual

[1] Add. MSS. 40,405; 235 (Chandos to——, Dec. 15). 40,407; 61 (Bonham
undated). 40,316; 117 (Lyndhurst to Peel, Dec. 21).
[2] *Ibid.* 40,406; 158 and 160 (Peel to Chandos, Dec. 19, 1834, and
Chandos to Peel), referring to the Duke of Buckingham's refusal. Add. MSS.
40,403; 192–4. 40,406; 67.

punishment of those who have been condemned to be
Prime Minister. He had to receive the absurd suggestions, the innumerable applications, the requests for
livings, peerages, baronetcies, bishoprics and offices
which were no doubt habitual under such circumstances.
He seems to have become the target for all human expectation, reasonable and unreasonable. The matter was
made worse by a widespread belief that he had a large
Civil Service patronage, when, as a matter of fact, he had
to complain at the end of the Ministry that he had not
a single opportunity to place in the Civil Service, in an
office not connected with Parliament, anyone with the
habits and training of a gentleman.[1] He began to groan
at his task. He began to talk to the angry and disappointed of the very false estimate put by the public
on the advantages of power.

On Christmas Day there was a slight pause. It was
a very slight one, for even on that day of-rest the post
he received prophesied incessant toil. But he took the
opportunity to write to a friend. "I never guessed,"
said he, "and doubt whether the most vivid fancy could
form a guess of what it is to form a Government." To
that hour, he declared, he had not entered the Treasury
or looked at a single point of real business, and yet at
the close of each day he had been obliged to leave undone
half of what ought to be done, even in the way of personal communication on matters relating to the personal
pretensions of candidates for office. "However, all this
seems essential to the success of that undertaking—in
which from no act, no wish of mine,—I am engaged and
upon the result of which very serious consequences
depend."[2]

§ 4

But all Peel's time up to Christmas Day had not been
spent in dealing with the insatiate claims of private
candidates. He had already done something to satisfy

---

[1] Add. MSS. 40,419; 3.
[2] *Ibid.*, 40,407; 229 (Peel to Hobhouse, Dec. 25, 1834).

the needs of the public and of high policy; he had already
done what was perhaps the most important thing he could
do in this Ministry; he had announced his intentions.
He had been prompted to do this by his party, and he
had been prompted what intentions to announce.   Even
before he had arrived from Italy many letters had come
in urging him not to appoint an ultra-Tory administration
or one too much redolent of the Duke, and to attempt a
union with Stanley.   On December 8th Goulburn wrote
to Peel that "all I see around me and learn from other
quarters confirms me in the opinion that the property of
the country desires a Conservative and not an *Ultra*-Tory
Government—meaning by that a Government deaf to all
improvement that comprises change."   Even Alexander
Baring's Essex true blue Tories talked of continuing to
be Reformers, and Baring had recommended candidates
to say that they had every disposition to reform real
acknowledged abuses.   He had sent letters to Goulburn
to show that, when their minds were not entirely occupied
by thoughts on Malt, such were the Tories' desires in his
part of the country.   Indeed all over the country it would
se n that the Party was turning to Peel and Moderate
Reform as to salvation.[1]
   Certainly the policy of cautious Reform agreed with
the whole bent of Peel's mind and of his conscious desires.
But in politics a heart of gold is not enough without lungs
of bronze.   The public must learn of Peel's good
intentions, and there was some fear among his party
that Peel might be condemned unheard.   Consequently
there were those who wished Peel to imitate Pitt's first
Ministry fifty years before, and to meet Parliament and
develop his measures before he dissolved.   But that
course was impossible; some other method had to
be devised for putting Peel's case before the country.
The question seems to have been considered by the
Cabinet on December 13th, almost immediately after it
was formed,[2] and by December 16th Peel had determined

---

[1] Add. MSS. 40, 333; 177; 179; 105.   40,404; 334; 312 (Parker, II, 261, 262).
[2] *Ibid.* 40,405; 202.

that every object would be answered by an address from himself to his constituents. The address was discussed and approved by the Cabinet at Lyndhurst's on December 17th. They sat, says Greville, till twelve o'clock upon it, and then it was copied out and sent to *The Times*, the *Herald*, and the *Post*; and thus was produced what ever afterwards came to be known and abused as the Tamworth Manifesto.[1]

It has been much abused. The destructive powers of genius have played round it, informed by events then in the future, and little influenced by the necessities of the time. It bears on it now the scars and wounds of later heroic strife, and the hands that have torn it were human hands, directed both by great human insight and also by human feelings. The fifth chapter of Book II of Disraeli's *Coningsby* is devoted to an attack upon it. Disraeli says that it was an "attempt to construct party without principles; its basis therefore was necessarily Latitudinarianism; and its inevitable consequence has been Political Infidelity." The party thus constructed was, he declared, a mere aggregation useful to encourage the timid and confused in perplexing times. It was no real party. When perturbation had quieted down, it was soon seen how empty was their confession. For all that Conservative principles stood to conserve were the prerogatives of the Crown, provided that they were not exercised; the independence of the House of Lords, provided it was not asserted; the Ecclesiastical Estate, provided it was regulated by a Commission of laymen. "Everything, in short, provided that it is a phrase but not a fact."

The manifesto was avowedly addressed by Peel through his constituents at Tamworth to that great and intelligent class of society "which is much less interested in the contentions of party than in the maintenance of order and the cause of good government." Peel told how the King in a crisis of great difficulty demanded his services, and said that he could not desert the Crown. Nor, said

[1] Greville, *Geo. IV and Wm. IV*, III, 178.

he, could he admit that he had been disqualified by the Reform Bill from obeying the choice of the King and from hoping that he might as Minister appeal successfully to the people.   Here was a dangerous and most practical assertion of the King's prerogative.

Peel said that he would not accept office at the expense of the principles on which he had hitherto acted.   Neither would he admit that he had been, either before or after the Reform Bill, the defender of abuses or the enemy of judicious Reforms; and he appealed to his currency and legal Reforms as a proof of his feelings.   As to the Reform Bill, he repeated his declaration that he regarded it as settled, and that he would not upset it.   But it was held that it was necessary nowadays for every Minister to act in the spirit of the Reform Bill.   If that spirit implied continual agitation, obedience to each popular whim and the abandoning of those greatest aids to government, the respect for ancient rights and the respect for prescriptive authority, then Peel would not undertake to adopt it.   But if it merely meant careful Reform and respect for established rights, he would pledge both himself and his colleagues to act in it.

He dealt with particular measures, Municipal Reform, Reform in Church Rates and in the Marriage Law.   He described his attitude on the various measures that concerned Dissenters, to prove that he had not shown an illiberal spirit towards them.   He spoke of other matters, of his desire to make a right use of pensions, of economy and of Church Reform, pledging himself against Lay Appropriation, but declaring for a useful distribution of Church property, for the reform of tithes by way of commutation, and for the abolition of all the abuses that hindered the work of the Establishment.   He declared for peace, for the maintenance of public credit and for an impartial consideration of what was due to all interests —agricultural, manufacturing, commercial.   Finally he expressed, among other things such as a resolution to persevere and a consciousness of upright motives, "the firm belief that the people of this country will so far maintain the prerogative of the King as to give to the Ministers of his choice not an implicit confidence but a fair trial." [1]

Such was the document, and one thing must immediately be admitted and perhaps as immediately excused. It was obviously and undoubtedly framed to satisfy Moderate Reformers, and with a view to winning elections. It had been held necessary to satisfy Moderate Reformers, both by Peel and by his party. His correspondence was full of it. The words of the chorus were unmistakable; the country wished the reforms to continue, the country would not stand an old Tory Government, it was essential that Peel should invite Stanley, himself a Moderate Reformer and a pledge to others. If anyone is to be accused for encouraging such comprehension, practically the whole of Peel's party must crowd with him into the dock. And Peel's defence could be expediency. Probably without such reinforcement the party would languish in impotence, even if it flourished in political novels. Without such reinforcement the Ministry would certainly come to speedy and disastrous collapse, and after all it was a Ministry that had been undertaken to protect the prerogative of the Crown.

But there is no need of excuse, for no charge can lie against what Peel said in this document in the way of conciliation. It is all honest. Peel was no liar when he declared that he could and would produce reforms of great benefit to his country, and who shall say he was not a Tory? Were acknowledged abuses and defects that crippled old institutions essential parts of the Tory creed? Or if they were, can an ordinary intelligent man be blamed for believing that perhaps they were not? To assuage the wrath of the Dissenters was probably necessary for the safety of the Church to whose defence he was pledged by all that was most Tory in him. It would be hard to assert that such things as the right use of pensions, the

---

[1] A Copy of the Tamworth Manifesto is given in Peel's *Memoirs*.

maintenance of credit, peace, or economy were not fit and proper objects for a Tory Minister.

The document is honest, the comprehension it aimed at was probably needful, and the objects propounded were honourable to the author, useful to his party and agreeable to his principles. Peel manfully produced what he had to produce as an honest Tory or Conservative. He spoke vaguely, but in tune with his party, against restless innovations and in support of reverence for prescriptive right. He declared quite clearly against lay appropriation of ecclesiastical property, a danger which is become dead mutton now, but by strange transmutation from being a lion in the way. Peel said nothing, announced no intention in this memorandum which was incompatible with his character as a Tory, or was to the disadvantage of the name of Conservative, and yet Disraeli's accusation really stands unaffected.

The accusation is, or should be in effect, that in this document and in the policy that followed it there was no appeal to any life-giving, party-inspiring and specifically Tory principles. It was not what Peel said or did, it was what he did not say or do that caused the fault, or perhaps what he could not say and could not do. At any rate, so might run the accusation, there resulted a tepid comprehension, useful for the moment, but in the light of time, history and truth, inevitably and deservedly ephemeral, a marriage of convenience without issue and without fidelity. It could not be a party, for its creed was unreal and deceptive. For what, asks the accuser with effect, did the Conservatives seek to conserve? Was it something real, or was it merely the empty bodies of things?

The question is too important to be settled by personal recrimination or condemnation, or else ingenious use might be made of the accuser's own later life and difficulties. History should probably be a laboratory, and not a law-court. Nor should the question be solely settled in relation to the Tamworth Manifesto. It spread its shadow over all Peel's policy and party-making, indeed over all Conservative policy and party-making.   What do you mean to conserve? must always be a proper question to ask of Conservatives.   At that date Conservatives would have been ready with their definite lists in answer. The Duke would have said without hesitation "the lives and properties of His Majesty's subjects."   The standing answer would be "the existing constitution in Church and State" or, with a side glance at Ireland and O'Connell, "the Protestant Constitution" in Church and State.   It was a proper answer even for Tories, but it was an equivocal one.   For it might be held that parts of the existing Constitution no longer really existed, indeed no longer could exist to affect decisively the history of the nation, whatever Peel or his accuser might have done. If that were so, the most stubborn defence could not tenant the empty castle, the most eloquent words could not put breath into a lifeless body.   It might be that the Conservatives were defending with blood and sweat much that was as empty and as valueless and as fragile as a broken eggshell.

The problem can only be resolved in the light of what follows, and with it many other questions.   It may be that Peel could not have suggested any principle that could give continued life and unity to his party, because principles except in their vaguest forms have little to do with the history of Parties.   Perhaps parties are only the chance creations of past accidents and present need, helped out by continuous organization and invested with an unreal unity, an imaginary consistency with the past, and an illusory belief that they inherit its ideals.   Passing fears and the anxieties of agriculturists might be the dominant unchangeable features of this situation, whatsoever were the ideals of the programme that Peel propounded.   Perhaps, though Peel might rebel or betray, he could neither fashion, nor control, nor inspire; and perhaps it did not matter a jot what he said in this manifesto.   These things may be true or partly true; but again the course of History must be invoked to try out the question.

Peel supplemented this appeal by a speech he made at the Mansion House, which was considered by some to be more Conservative in tone. Meanwhile the Manifesto had achieved immediate notoriety. "Of course," said Greville, "it has made a prodigious sensation, and nobody talks of anything else." [1] The Whigs talked of hypocrisy, while many Conservatives used the Manifesto with success and without hesitation at their elections. [2] Peel spread it widely abroad and sent it himself to most of the notabilities of his personal acquaintance. [3] He was curiously anxious to get his personal position clear in the inner circle of politics. He mentioned to many that he had tried to secure Stanley, even apparently challenging argument from those who might disapprove, and it may be suspected that an invitation to Canning's son, which was shown to several, together with Lady Canning's answer, was made with the intention of proving that those old differences were over, if—which he denied—they had ever been. [4]

Asides to the boxes were all very well, but what was really needed was something to penetrate to the gallery, or at least to the dress circle. It was essential to have a good press. The Duke admitted to Greville that in the past he had too much neglected the Press, and Croker instructed Peel in its importance. He wanted to know who was to manage Peel's Press, for managed it must be, and by a Minister. Peel, he believed, had no idea of what the Whigs, especially Brougham, did in that way, or how much literary good feeling they conciliated by their patronage. [5] Peel himself, thus instructed by his friend or possibly even by his own reflections, was fully conscious of the importance of the Press, and had already been so fortunate as to have the chance of valuable newspaper aid. *The Standard* had been offered to him, [6]

[1] Grev., III, 178.
[2] Add. MSS. 40,406; 122, 200. 40,410; 1. 40,412; 17.
[3] *Ibid.* 40,408; 162, 165, 171, 173. [4] Peel's *Memoirs*, II, 52.
[5] Grev., *Geo. IV and Wm. IV*, III, 150. Add. MSS. 40,321; 28.
[6] Add. MSS. 40,404; 304.

and his friends had secured the powerful assistance of *The Times*. Of late *The Times* had been at enmity with its old ally Brougham. It had opposed the new Poor Law with which Brougham had identified himself, and towards the end of the last Session it had covered him with personal abuse and had ended by casting doubts on his sanity. Perhaps by November 1834 it was empty and garnished and looking about for another source of inspiration. When the Whigs were dismissed it adopted a moderate tone towards their successors, and Greville brought this to the notice of the Duke, and helped to start negotiations between Lyndhurst and Barnes, the Editor of *The Times*. Even before Peel had come home, but with due regard to maintaining his freedom of decision, Lyndhurst and Barnes had struck an alliance and had sealed the matter at a dinner.[1]

The alliance was important. Next year Lyndhurst told Peel that *The Times* was worth all the other papers put together, and that it was the only paper read in the City. Indeed, Peel had already shown himself duly impressed in the matter, and had written personally to the Duke and to the King's Secretary for their influence to help Walter, the proprietor of *The Times*, in his Parliamentary election. Up till February Barnes communicated through various secretaries, and then at Lyndhurst's suggestion Peel selected a definite Minister to hold communication with *The Times*. It was an alliance of equals. *The Times* does not appear in any way to have been a tied paper. Once at least the tone of their articles led Peel to believe that they were only at single anchor. There was a slight ruffling of their relations when the King's Speech had not only leaked out before it was meant to appear, but had also leaked into the columns of the *Morning Post* before *The Times* got it. Yet on the whole the alliance was successful. At the end of his Ministry Peel thanked Barnes, and Barnes let Lyndhurst know that he would have no political connec-

[1] Grev., III, 149.

tion with the new Ministers, but wished to continue his relations with the Conservatives.[1]

§ 5

Peel had put his case to the country, and the country was soon to have the chance of deciding upon it, for Parliament was dissolved by proclamation on December 28th. Or rather the electorate was soon to decide on the fate of Peel's Government, and that not entirely by the means of dispassionate argument or with reference to the logical case of Peel or any other man. It would be as foolish to deny the many competing influences that still interfered in elections as it would be difficult to recount them. If the Borough of Eatanswill had perhaps been disfranchised by the Reform Bill, its spirit could find refuge in many other Boroughs and its methods still flourished. The employment of rival mobs and bands, the securing of public-houses, the retaining of drunken electors under lock and key to prevent their perversion or kidnapping—all the jolly corruptions of those days—still continued unaffected by the Reform Bill. Great noblemen and others still had their widespread influence over their tradesmen, tenants and dependents, though it was sometimes side-tracked by their agents. During the Reform Bill crisis Newark had revolted from the Duke of Newcastle, but it had returned to its allegiance and was ready to return young Gladstone. Perhaps it was the attraction of the patronage as well as of the prestige that made it desirable for candidates to be connected with the Government by some appointment or other before they fought a difficult election; at any rate many men made their election necessities an argument in pressing their claims upon Peel. There were many accusations of bribery by defeated candidates, there were many assump-

---

[1] Add. MSS. 40,316; 164 (Lyndhurst to Peel, Feb. 26, 1835), 165 (Peel to Lyndhurst). 40,310; 3 (Peel to Duke, Jan. 1, 1835) and 24, 42 and 40,302; 131 (Peel to Sir H. Taylor, Jan. 1, 1835). 40,316; 195 (Letter of Barnes to be shown to Lyndhurst at end of Peel's Ministry).

tions of the reality of influence on the part of the Conservative Whips. Consequently it is perhaps not too cynical to assume that the electors were affected not only by considerations of national importance when they gave their votes in this election.

Since there is so much and such picturesque evidence of these matters it would be probably very easy to exaggerate their effect, and to be unjust both to the electorate and to the candidates of that period. All votes could not be managed, and probably the results of general elections had some vague approximation to the national will. Still at that time, as always, organization was obviously as important as argument in the persuading of a nation. The Conservatives had an organization. Even before Peel came home a Committee had been active on the question of elections,[1] and it had reported favourably. It was probably under Lord Granville Somerset, who occupied the most responsible position on the Staff of the Conservative Party. He helped Peel in the construction of his Ministry, himself writing to some who were appointed, in order to relieve Peel in his labours. Another name to remember is that of F. A. Bonham. He was a Whip, possibly the only Whip at this moment, for a certain Holmes, who had been in some such position, was not generally trusted. Bonham's fault was his optimism. It was said that he devoured information "like a ravening wolf" and disgorged it with as little discrimination.[2] But he was straightforward and honourable and good-natured and very faithful to Peel, and it was to be of great moment for Peel to have such a follower in such a position.

Together with Granville Somerset other names appear as working on the elections, such as Lord Rosslyn, Peel's brother William, Ross, Sir George Clerk for Scotland and possibly Shaw for Ireland, and others. They suggested candidates, and they stimulated men to give their influence in various districts. Early in December 1834, as there had been in 1832, there was again a com-

[1] Add. MSS. 40,404; 245; 318, etc.   [2] *Ibid.* 40,341; 112.

plaint that there was no central fund.[1]   But some money
seems to have been entrusted to Granville Somerset, and
some money seems to have been forthcoming for candidates.   For instance, at Lyndhurst's suggestion it would
seem that £500 was given to Disraeli at his election.[2]
Only Lyndhurst can have guessed what they might have
got with that £500.

Most of the work must have been done locally.   In
some districts even before the election large sums had
been spent to bring back constituencies to the Conservatives.[3]   Sometimes money had been spent in very odd
ways.   Planta, a Conservative, reported to Peel that he
had an agent at Hastings who had bought up all the sea
front between Hastings and St. Leonards, nearly a mile
in extent, on which he was building houses each of which
would have a vote, and each, said Planta, with interesting
fore-knowledge, would be cast for him.   "This," as he
joyfully and truly confessed, "is doing things by whole-
sale."   At Hastings apparently this election, which was
to determine the affairs of the kingdom, turned on the
renewal of leases for some Crown lands in the neighbour-
hood, and the giving of foreign licences to the fishermen
of the district.   It was, therefore, of course, important
for Planta to be connected with the Government.[4]

How efficient was the work done by the men at the
centre and how widespread and effective were the efforts
of the more local Conservatives, it would be very hard to
tell.   It is always easier to discover causes than to
measure effects.   Various factors in the situation favoured
the Conservatives.   There had been a change of opinion
in the country.   There was fear in some quarters of the
development of Radical doctrines.   In Liverpool, for
instance, it was reported that Whig Churchmen had been
frightened at the rage of the Dissenters, and Whig men
of property at the name of Lord Durham, while with

[1] Add. MSS. 40,405; 30 (Melville to Rosslyn, Dec. 7).
[2] *Ibid.* 40,406; 205. 40,407; 114 and 146 (the last two *re* Disraeli).
[3] *Ibid.* 40,410; 269.
[4] *Ibid.* 40,309; 372.

many the Government had become discredited.[1] At
Denbigh a gentleman was so much alarmed at the Radical
sentiments of a candidate whom he had himself proposed,
that he voted against him.[2] Various Conservative
candidates seem to have found their constituencies very
ready to receive the Tamworth manifesto. Moreover,
there was help from the country districts, though the
complaint was fairly general that the small towns in their
midst still remained obstinately Radical, while game laws
and aloofness possibly divided the gentry from men who
might well have been their allies.[3] Still there was a
movement amongst the counties. In twenty-one counties,
or divisions of counties, apparently the Tories had gained
seats. It is to be wondered how much these new
members represented constituents like those whom
Alexander Baring described in Essex as speaking, thinking, and dreaming of nothing else but Malt.[4] The
dreams of constituents may be more embarrassing than
relevant.

The revival of influence after the excitement of the
Reform Bill might have its full effect on the very small
constituencies of those days. The farmers might dream
of malt, or hearken fearfully to the talk about the Repeal
of the Corn Laws among the Radicals in the towns; they
might naturally follow their squires, or necessarily follow
their landlords. Men might fear for their goods and
change their coats. Still there was a long way to go.
The garrison of Thermopylæ had to be turned into an
invading army, a miserable minority into a majority large
enough to support a Government. About 200 elections
had to be gained.

It was a very long way to go, and the Reform movement
had not yet spent itself. Nor were the Whig Ministers
altogether discredited. They still had a following, and
many felt that they had been hardly used. Though
Whigs were told by Conservatives that they must now

---

[1] Add. MSS. 40,404; 318.   [2] *Ibid.* 40,410; 118.
[3] *Ibid.* 40,410; 108 (respecting Perthshire), 209.
[4] *Ibid.* 40,333; 179, 181, 183.

choose between "Conservative and Destructive, Peel or
Durham, Church or Chapel, Monarchy or Mob," it was
found that old party ties were still very strong among
them. It was for this reason that men had been so
anxious for Stanley to be recruited, that he might form a
bridge over which many honest men might have crossed.[1]
Even so the rowdies would have been left. The power
of the mob was still to be reckoned with, if the Conservatives' very many complaints of intimidation are to be
believed. Moreover, influence was not by any means
confined to one side; and whatever might be done in
England, Scotland was obstinate and Ireland impossible.

Yet the Conservatives did well. Without Ireland and
Scotland they might perhaps have had a majority. Their
worst disasters were the loss of their official men, and
they were not successful in what were considered Government boroughs, although Government influence was still
real enough for Conservative candidates to squabble
about it. It would be true to say that the election results
were satisfactory, but they were not satisfactory enough
to allow Peel to hope solely to rely on those who confessed
the name and party of the Conservatives.

Very often the hopes that men cherish do not live
after them. They are swallowed up in disappointments
and denied in memoirs. Forgetfulness conspires with
the memory of failure to obliterate their record, so that
there is no need to give full value to the statement, in
Peel's memoir of his Ministry, that he had never had
much belief in its success. Others had had hopes.
Bonham had told Peel that he thought the chances
were very good. Aberdeen had told Princess Lieven
that they had reason to believe that they would gain
enough in the election to enable them to carry on the
Government.[2] But perhaps Peel was never deceived, or
at least never had expected adequate reinforcement in

[1] Add. MSS. 40,404; 318 (Sandon resp. Liverpool, see above). Add. MSS.
40,333; 179.
[2] Ibid. 40,406; 114 (Bonham to Peel, Dec. 19). Privately printed
Aberdeen papers, 1832-44 (Aberdeen to Princess Lieven, Dec. 19).

the elections. If so, it did not matter; he had other comforters. About Christmas-time, tired as he was with his task, his mind was suffused not with hope, but with a kind of satisfaction with what had been done, which avoided the necessity of the services of hope in guarding against the pains and consequences of despair. "How it will turn out I know not," but said he, "I have the consolation of knowing that whatever could be done by me has been done, with but one single object in view." [1]

The contemplation of your zeal and your integrity might seem to be but desperate comfort in a tight corner. It was not so with Peel. He was censorious at rest, but he was sanguine in action. His great capability for Government must have made him feel confident and effective, like a splendid machine running smoothly about its appointed task. Besides, he knew as well as do historians the purity of his own motives, and his mind was ready to furnish him with variations on the theme that honesty would be the best policy after all. Consequently in January, when the returns were coming in, Peel wrote to Lord Lincoln, "I think the returns are, on the whole, very favourable, all circumstances considered, but my confidence in our success, which is very great, does not rest so much upon returns as upon my conviction that we shall do whatever is reasonable and just, and that reason and justice will ultimately prevail." [2] But if reason and justice were to prevail they must come, not for the first time in their history, into collision with party, and by the end of January the returns had convinced him that his hope must be in the adhesion of moderate men not professing Conservative politics. [3] It was all of a part; since the beginning of this Ministry everything had combined to drive home the same lesson; he must gain the adherence of moderate Whigs if he was to hold his own. A policy of moderation and comprehension would have been forced on him, if he had not of his own nature desired it. The sequel was to

[1] Add. MSS. 40,407; 247.   [2] *Ibid.* 40,410; 24.
[3] Peel to Croker, Jan. 26 (Croker, II, 256).

show of what little avail was moderation and comprehension when opposed to the spirit of party.

§ 6

To have any chance of placating Parliament Peel must have Reforms to propose to it, and before the elections, before the turn of the year and even before his laborious Christmas Day he had been considering them. It is significant that the questions that first appealed to as much of his troubled attention as was left over from Government-making were those of Church and Dissent. On December 22nd he solemnly declared to the Bishop of Exeter that his main object in power was the welfare of the Church of England, and that he would gladly make the "very very small sacrifice of office rather than consent to anything prejudicial to the sacred objects of her foundation." This resolution was, of course, rightly tempered with wisdom and he urged the Church, through the Bishop of Exeter, to aid her friends to pursue the path of judicious Reform, that he might make, if possible, a satisfactory and final settlement.[1]   It is to be wondered with how much hope he pursued these final settlements.

Church rates and Dissenters' marriages, he told the Bishop, required immediate attention, and also—almost an afterthought in this letter—the problem of Reform inside the Church itself. Peel was harassed and overworked, but his mind was one in which measures grew rapidly into intelligible and practical shape. Apparently he soon intended to deal with Church Rates on the lines of Althorp's Bill, which implied that the State should find some money to repair Churches as a recognition to the Establishment. With regard to Dissenters' marriages, he was struck with the idea of not demanding a religious rite from Dissenters, although, as he constantly said with emphasis, he would encourage one. He would have them married by a civil process before a magistrate, taking due precautions both against clandestine marriages and

[1] Add. MSS. 40,407; 107. Parker, II, 165 (Peel to Bishop of Exeter, Dec. 22, 1834—not all in Parker).

against any undue attraction the facility might have for those who were not Dissenters.[1]

He communicated with various advisers on this question of marriages, and the measure took shape and was handed over to others. But the legislator is an artist in a most refractory raw material, especially when he is a Conservative legislator of 1834, practising his art on Dissenters. At the turn of the year, before they even knew what he would propose, the Birmingham Dissenters passed a resolution to the effect that nothing Peel could do would satisfy them. Peel answered that he was sure their language and sentiments were not those of the great majority of Dissenters in the country, and received back a stern and class-conscious letter from a Dissenter in Birmingham, declaring that the meeting's resolutions were the sentiments of the respectable and enlightened class of Dissenters, and warning him that he was ignorant of the wealth and power of a class of which the nobility and gentry knew nothing, because they did not mix with them. It was strange, said Peel's correspondent, that the son of Peel's worthy "*straight forward*" father should be so deceived. Peel had to learn, he added, the grand secret of good government, which was kindness, conciliation, and even-handed justice. The repartee was obvious, and Peel made it with self-restraint. There were not a few Dissenters, especially Irish Protestant Dissenters, who conveyed their sympathy to Peel and their disapproval of those who had been in such haste to condemn him. But a stubbornness had been displayed which was not to be affected by any obvious repartee.[2]

It was not long before he began to deal with Reform of the Church itself. In the middle of January he did a deed of great import and benefit to the Church; he constituted an Ecclesiastical Commission. The Commission was to use the money of large preferments to supplement small livings, to adjust the boundaries, duties

[1] Add. MSS. 40,407; 208. Parker, II, 275. See also 40,407; 289 ff., etc., etc.
[2] *Ibid.* 40,409; 15, 220-2.

and stipends of Bishoprics, and to prevent improper
pluralities and abolish ecclesiastical sinecures.[1]   It was
to abolish abuses, increase the Church's usefulness and
furnish safe reform at the hands of the Church's friends
while there was yet time.   Yet whatever it was ultimately
to do or to be, it was immediately a striking example
of the dual nature of Peel's inspiration.

Safety and sense were the progenitors of Peel's ecclesiastical policy. Apparently Peel was moved in this
matter by the danger to the Church.   Was it prudent
to have such abuses when the Church had powerful
enemies in the country?   That was a question of which
he would make frequent and forcible use.[2]   But there
were two spurs in his flanks.   As he considered the
abuses rampant in the Church, profounder and more
reputable motives shaped themselves in his mind.   He
looked to the Church's defence and saw her needs.   The
complications of Ecclesiastical History, the perversions
of the past, the slackness at times of her spirit, and the
disorderly growth of huge new industrial populations,
had created startling instances of a failure on the Church's
part to perform her duties.   Such instances were brought
to Peel's notice, and a new question framed itself in his
mouth, and intruded itself into his letters.   Was the
Church to be a provision for men of birth and learning,
or was its main object the worship of God?[3]   It would
be hard to exclude from the answer matters not related
to caution and safety.   It was often so with Peel.
Caution would institute or excuse a policy of Reform,
but good sense and good feeling would demonstrate its
necessity, and obstinacy and determination might ensure
its continuance, so that the end would be a confusion
of motives very hard for Historians to disentangle.
Hostages from the enemy might become the adopted
sons of the General.

[1] Peel to Harrowby, Jan. 12, 1835. Add. MSS. 40,410; 58. *Memoirs*,
II, 72.

[2] E.g. Add. MSS. 40,412; 323 (undated memoir in Peel's hand).

[3] Peel to Croker, Feb. 2, 1835 (Parker, II, 284).

It was Trinity College, Cambridge, that had the chief honour of whetting Peel's reforming zeal. It took £2,000 a year in tithes from the Parish of Monk's Kirby and gave £24 a year back to the vicar in stipend. It was a parish, said Peel, of 10,000 acres overrun with Dissent, and he felt so indignant about it that he mentioned it to Goulburn, to the Archbishop of Canterbury and to Croker, together, in the last case, with the fact that Kingston and Richmond were united in one benefice because King's College, Cambridge, could not afford to endow the two.[1]   Meanwhile he recognized the spiritual needs of the manufacturing districts,[2] and it was important that he should recognize those desperate spiritual needs, for the Established Churches of England and Scotland were at that time the natural media through which Conservatives might be brought to see and might try to serve the poor.

So Peel tried to save the Church with sincerity and determination.   He supported his Ecclesiastical Commission, he was exceedingly careful about his use of the small amount of preferment that fell to his gift while he was Prime Minister.[3]   He wrote to the great Dr. Chalmers about his sympathy for the Church of Scotland,[4] and he was ready to argue with the many Churchmen or Tories who objected to his policy.   Safety had suggested, good sense and good feeling had inspired, and who shall say that obstinacy or determination was not taking up its just and necessary part in the sequence?

Ecclesiastical questions certainly filled a large proportion of Peel's attention in the early days of his Ministry, but then in those days they filled a large part in many men's minds.   However, these were not the only matters over which Peel took trouble to prepare himself for the

---

[1] Add. MSS. 40,412; 103, 207 (Peel to Goulburn).   Parker, II, 283 (Goulburn's answer).   Add. MSS. 40,333; 271 (Peel to Croker, see above).   Goulburn's defence of his College should be read.

[2] Add. MSS. 40,412 339.

[3] E.g. *Ibid.*; 40,412; 321.   40,415; 134.   40,417; 266.   *Memoirs*, II, 77.

[4] Add. MSS. 40,411; 200.

battle before him. It is not to be wondered that his interests and activities were directed towards the old crucial questions of economy and pensions. On January 5th he circularized his government, declaring that they would gain much public goodwill if they could announce in the King's Speech that, notwithstanding all former reductions, the estimates of 1835 would be lower than in any preceding year since 1793, and he urged them on to all safe economies.[1] There were many currents in the other direction. A new Government in the middle of a period of economy is the natural target for the thousand appeals of men who feel that they have been hardly treated. But Peel was a good hand at refusing claims. He declared that he had been called upon to review half the decisions of the late Board of the Treasury, but that he had uniformly refused to do so. He even restrained, with respect, an inclination which the Duke seemed to show to go back on Palmerston's economies at the Foreign Office.[2]

He was peculiarly careful about honours and pensions. Baronetcies and Peerages were kept down to a minimum, to the distress and anger of many Conservatives who had lusted for them, or had thought they had claims. Pensions formed the proper stage for an interesting display of economy and virtue. Peel had mentioned in his Tamworth Manifesto that he had assented to a resolution of the House of Commons in 1834 as to the right use of pensions. He acted up to his declaration and, advised and stimulated by Croker, showed his principles by a series of scientific and literary rewards. He gratified science by giving, with suitable expressions, pensions to Professor Airey and to Mrs. Somerville.[3] He was as much, even possibly more, anxious to gratify literature. "Are there not," he enquired of Croker, "literary men of fair power and whose works have no stain of irreligion and immorality—who are struggling

[1] Parker, II, 274. Add. MSS. 40,310; 18 (Peel to Duke, Jan. 5, 1835).
[2] Add. MSS. 40,310; 26, 75, 77, 79, 80.
[3] Parker, II, 307 and 308 (Add. MSS. 40,414; 369. 40,418; 316).

with severe poverty?" He felt that the public would
not like literary pensions conferred upon persons of
tolerably affluent circumstances, but would welcome an
occasional pension as a relief from distress.[1]

Literary men of fair power and considerable respect-
ability were to be found, and at the beginning of February he communicated with Southey and with Wordsworth, asking them what he could do for them, and
later in the year Hogg also was helped. Nor, while the
sun and the smaller stars were tended, were the little
lamps forgotten which also burnt in public. Even Mrs.
Hemans was assisted.[2]

So Peel laboured and suffered in the fogs of London
to prepare his Ministry, his legislation and his case. He
was Chancellor of the Exchequer as well as First Lord
of the Treasury, and consequently in addition to his
labours as Prime Minister he had heavy official duties.
But the pressure was so great upon him that he could
not enter on these till the evening of December 30th,
and when he did he found immense arrears of business.
It is no wonder that he was too busy to go down to Tamworth for his election until the dinner after it.[3] He had
a short glimpse of Drayton in the middle of January,
during which he enjoyed a dance and some shooting.
He still comforted himself with the feeling that he had
left nothing undone, and that if he was driven out he
could retire with dignity and sometimes, after a day's
shooting, sit at ease with Croker in the new library at
Drayton.[4] He needed all his philosophy. He had to
come back to London and find that his labours imposed
upon him a sacrifice of "every enjoyment of every comfort excepting that which accompanies the reflection of
having acted on a sense of public duty."[5] Prime
Ministers ought not to overwork, they certainly ought

---

[1] Add. MSS. 40,321; 53, 61.
[2] Parker II, 304, 305, and 309–11. Add. MSS. 40,413; 16 and 40,419;
176 (Southey). 40,413; 124 and 212, etc. (Wordsworth). 40,413; 205 (Mrs.
Hemans). 40,412; 223.   [3] Add. MSS. 40,408; 195.
[4] Parker, II, 277 (Peel to Croker, Jan. 10, 1835).
[5] Add. MSS. 40,419; 53.

not to combine with their task the labours and responsibilities of another office.   There is a danger that they
should get a grievance against the society that they
govern.

But Peel was wonderfully strong and stout.   He was
strong enough to continue to hope, to believe in himself
and in the justice of his cause, and to confront with
courage insuperable obstacles.   Immediately on the
arrival from Ireland of Hardinge, their Chief Secretary,
the Cabinet took up the consideration of the Irish Tithe
questions to the exclusion, said Peel, of other pressing
claims on their attention, and he declared that of all
matters that ever were presented this was now the most
difficult, and yet that he and his colleagues felt the
necessity of proposing to Parliament an immediate
practical solution.[1]   A new Sisyphus was called to the
old stone.   Being confronted with an insoluble problem
was the immediate reward of Peel's sacrifices; this, and
the reflection of having acted entirely "on a sense of
public duty."

§ 7

Meanwhile, through a sense of public duty, private
pique or party principles, an opposition had been built
up against him.   It was true that some of the Whigs
had entertained such feelings as might possibly have led
them to support Peel.   In the first moments after the
Ministry's dismissal neither Melbourne nor Grey had
utterly condemned what had taken place, and they both
had fears enough for the future to make them wish to
step warily.   Both feared for the future of the Moderate
Reformers and in the minds of both Conservative feelings stirred uneasily.[2]   Grey blessed his stars that he
was rid of politics.   Matters of family and old feuds
may disturb the most retired of statesmen, and Grey's
complacence was shaken by the military way in which

[1] Add. MSS. 40,419; 9 (Peel to Archbishop of Armagh, February 14, 1835).
[2] *Melbourne Papers*, 224, 227 (Melb. to Grey, Nov. 14, 1834).   *Corresp.
Earl Grey and Princess Lieven*, III, 39, 47, 54.

R

his old adversary the Duke of Wellington dispossessed the late Government. Also two of his family were attacked in their elections by candidates apparently officially approved by the Conservatives; one of these seemed even to be an ex-Radical, in fact Disraeli. Nor did Grey believe that the Conservatives would be able to agree together on their schemes for Reform. Still he remained rather angry and doubtful, doubtful as to whether if the Whigs could turn out Peel's Ministry they could put anything in its place.[1]

Melbourne also hesitated. He had answered with mildness and exhortations to self-restraint two addresses that were sent to him commenting on his dismissal.[2] He put off deciding what should be done till it could be seen what would be the character of the new House of Commons.[3] When the elections seemed certainly to have produced a clear majority against the Ministers he was troubled. He told his friends that while the old Ministry had persisted he had thought it his duty to maintain it through its difficulties, although the men he had most trusted in it had left it. Now that was all over. It must be a new departure and—this he repeated —he must be free to decide with what principles and with what colleagues he would reassume power. He wanted to pause and to think things out, as can so seldom be done in politics. He asked whether he was justified in declaring a decided opposition to the new Government? Could he form a Government to succeed them? Would it be well to declare war on the King, the Lords, all the Clergy and two-thirds of the gentry of the country?[4] From the tone of his letters he was a little unhappy, but he was not free. He was merely the leader of a party.

[1] *Corresp. of Grey and Lieven*, III, 47, 54, 60. *Wellesley Papers*, II, 255 (Grey, Dec. 9).
[2] For text of Melbourne's answers to Melbourne and Derby addresses, see Torrens, *Melbourne*, II, 55 and 56.
[3] Torrens, *Melbourne*, II, 67 (Melb. to Lansdowne, Dec. 29, 1835). *Early Corresp. of Lord John Russell*, II, 69 (Melb. to L. J. R., Jan. 5, 1835).
[4] *Melbourne Papers*, 235 (Melb. to Grey, Jan. 23, 1835).

Most of the leading Whigs neither shrank from their task nor slackened their party feelings. If they harboured Conservative feelings they were rather led to comment on the danger of the King's action than to acquiesce in it, and if the Ministers showed reforming zeal they doubted whether it was genuine. A man may have to submit to have his clothes stolen, but it is going beyond human nature to expect him to praise their fit on the thief. This was the Party that had, as they said, for years resisted all improvement, and John Russell made a clever speech at Totnes ridiculing the Duke's possible claims as a Reformer.[1]

Their desires and their views were reflected in their intentions. Holland thought that necessity, honour and even reason, apart from passion, demanded that the Tories should be turned out and such a Ministry reinstated as Grey and Melbourne had presided over. He felt that Melbourne was bound to help, and comforted him with the thought that he could still choose with what colleagues he should re-enter the Government. Althorp thought that they ought to propose an amendment to the Address. John Russell and Palmerston and many others wished to oppose the reappointment of Manners Sutton to be Speaker. He was considered not to have adhered to his neutrality as Speaker, and it would be a great tactical advantage to show their majority at the very beginning of the session.[2]

They had not all turned into Radicals. But it was impossible for them merely to turn aside, to become inoperative, unworthy of the name of party men. Their pride and their principles would naturally lead them to resent and resist their summary dismissal by the King. With a party at their heels fresh from the polls it would have been probably not possible to desist, even if they had wished to, from trying their strength on their enemies.

---

[1] *Times*, Dec. 8.
[2] E.g. *Melbourne Papers*, 232 and 250 (Holland to Melb., Jan. 22, 1835, and Feb. 9, 1835). *Early Corresp. of Lord John Russell*, p. 63 (Dec. 4, 1834), p. 71 (Palm. to Russell, Jan. 22, 1835).

They were not Radicals. Lord John Russell himself, who was to lead their party in the House of Commons, told Spring-Rice that he did not wish to be towed further out to sea than he had been in Lord Grey's Ministry.[1] They feared that the King's action would place power in the Radicals' hands, since they were sure the present Ministry could not last. They felt, not unnaturally, that the best solution of all these difficulties was the speedy replacement of their Ministry, as it had existed before the King's mad act. If that was no solution it was the King's fault, not theirs, and Holland House chattered, speculated and hoped for the defeat of Peel, till Greville grew disgusted at their airy malice, and thought them intoxicated by faction, wilfully blind to the probable results of their desires.

They were to have allies to give effect to their desires. The formation of a Tory Ministry had given Whig, Liberal and Radical a common object, however lately and however greatly they had disagreed. The Radical Warburton and old Francis Place held conference together to consider how Warburton could induce Whigs, Reformers and the Irish to work together for such ends as were common to all.[2] Warburton wrote to O'Connell urging this union. There was to be a meeting of Lord John's followers at Lichfield House just before the Session, and Warburton procured a number of undirected invitations to it and sent them to O'Connell for his party.[3]

O'Connell and Lord John were not natural allies. When the late Ministry had been turned out O'Connell had rejoiced as much to get rid of the "Humbuggers" as, immediately before, John Russell had been anxious that no one in the Ministry should have communications

[1] Torrens, *Melbourne*, II, 78 (Lord John to Spring-Rice, Jan. 21, 1835). Grev., III, 188, 191. *Melbourne Papers*, 228.

[2] Graham Wallas' *Life of Place*, 335.

[3] O'Connell's *Corresp.*, I, 520. Spencer Walpole's *Life of Lord John Russell*, I, 219, ff.

with O'Connell. But prohibitions waver, and even humbug is embraced before the insistent demands of an important common enmity. O'Connell was afraid of the Orange faction remaining in power in Ireland, and he had recognized and noted their triumph at the formation of the new Ministry. Their ascendancy would mean, so he said, oppression and at the last civil war. Meanwhile Lord John was equally convinced of the necessity of removing these men for England's sake. O'Connell drew in towards the Whigs. During the elections he had said that he would support whatever Speaker the Whigs recommended and during the elections he had received some help from Duncannon.[1]

When he got the bundle of invitations from Warburton he wrote to Lord John to say that he would come with his friends to Lord John's meeting, and that they would work together to turn out the Tories. It was a sign, a portent, perhaps a challenge; and, like others of his party, Lord John had doubts. He was not sure whether he approved of having Radicals and Repealers in his meeting. He wrote two drafts for his answer, and showed enough hesitation to excite a remonstrance from Duncannon.[2] But the answer was favourable. O'Connell came to the meeting with his friends, and so did the Radicals. The alliance was formed. Later on in the Session there was a dinner, also at Lichfield House, at which O'Connell and the Radicals met Lord John Russell and owned him as their leader. Lord Grey was very much shocked, and the Tories and the newspapers had a most useful subject for humour, invective and noble indignation in what was called the Lichfield House compact.

It is declared that there was no secret treaty,[3] and it is most probably true. But O'Connell had his condi-

---

[1] O'Connell's *Corresp.*, I, 503, 507, 512, 518. *Early Corresp. of Lord John Russell*, II, 48, 81.

[2] *Melbourne Papers*, 233. Spencer Walpole's *Life of Lord John Russell*, I, 220–4.

[3] E.g. *Recollections and Suggestions*.

tions, on which he was prepared to give his support to a Whig Ministry.[1]   He would insist on various reforms but not on Repeal.   He was ready to put Repeal aside for the time being, and try what the Whigs would do for him.   He had various definite desires for Ireland. He wanted to clean its administration from Orange taint and bias, he wanted to reform its old Corporations, he wanted, perhaps less insistently in his innermost mind, to restrict the Irish Church.   These were realities and possibilities, while Repeal was something of a dream, the child of ungoverned hope, or of despair.

He was an honest man, one to be admired, if not wholly admired.   It is hard to judge Irish character for those days, to free it from the vulgar unrealities of the Erin of paddies and the poet Moore.   O'Connell was a patriot and a rhetorician.   He had a sincere love for his country and sane views for her welfare, if he was also sanguine, passionate, autocratic, boastful, verbose and vain.   He was wonderfully eloquent, though sometimes in blackguardly bad taste.   Rhetoric is the chiefest curse of all oppressed peoples, and it had done ill to him. But it had not destroyed him.   He did not live in an unreal world though he was constantly claiming successes over his enemies, would boast that each turn of events was favourable to his cause, and promised from time to time more than he could possibly perform.   He was ready to work in a sensible way for a practical and immediate goal and ready to lay aside Repeal for a time and ally with the Whigs.   But the fever was not cast out of the system; the passion was still there, and Repeal was still there.   The hardest problems of his country remained, while the intolerable difficulties and necessities of his position, and his old methods of mass agitation, were ready to reclaim him when the use of the Whigs had faded away.

It was so with them all.   There were many divergent tendencies among the Whigs, Radicals and Irishmen.

---

[1] O'Connell's *Corresp.*, I, 523 (February 27).   Hansard, XXVI, 408 (O'Connell's Speech on the Address).

They were three parties and not one.[1]   But they were none of them likely to be merciful towards Peel, whatever reforms he might produce.   The Whig leaders were ready to adopt hostile measures against him.   After investigating the matter with various leaders of his party, Melbourne decided that a new Speaker must be proposed against Manners Sutton, and that Abercromby, a Liberal, should be the man.[2]   John Russell wrote to Melbourne in February that he thought they must have an amendment to the Address, though the more cautiously worded it was the better.[3]   Melbourne so far agreed as to criticize its composition.   Some individual Whigs might be desirous of giving the Ministers a fair trial, but Lord John Russell was now to be their acknowledged leader in the House of Commons.   He wished to be cautious, but he was determined to condemn.   He thought it was necessary for England to remove Ministers from power "who do not profess, and as I believe never can obtain, the confidence of the country." [4]   He was determined to persevere with his mixed forces to his difficult victory.

§ 8

The Vote on the Speakership was to be taken on February the 19th.   It was not to be taken in the old House of Commons, for in October 1834 the old Houses of Parliament had been burnt.   They had retired from life into History, as had the rotten boroughs and much that was dirty and old and corrupt and had made England great.   The old House of Lords had been roofed over for the use of the House of Commons and the House of Lords was cooped up in a wretched dog-hole, bad enough for Radicals to declare that it suited their position in the Constitution.   The new

---

[1] N.B.—*Life of the Right Honourable William Molesworth,* 73, 74 (to his mother, Feb. 19, 1835).

[2] Torrens, *Melbourne,* II, 84.

[3] *Early Corresp. Lord John Russell,* II, 89, 90.

[4] Letter to O'Connell, see above.

House of Commons was not incommodious, although it was said that it looked rather too much like a Methodist Chapel.   It reproduced too many of the features of the old one for the liking of Roebuck the Radical, but then he was naturally without due affection for old inconveniences.   There were other complaints.   O'Connell complained that the new House of Commons was erratic in temperature, and Brougham that the new House of Lords smelt.   But bad temperatures and smells are irrelevant in the description of a desperate fight for a minority Ministry.[1]

There was much speculation and many bets on the result of the vote on the Speakership.   For some time everyone's mouth and mind had been full of calculation. There had been much fishing for individual votes, and Greville declares that each side prophesied its victory and yet guarded itself by saying that a defeat would not matter.   February 19th came in "sunshine and south wind," but the excitement in politics were hotter and less gracious than any February sunshine.   At twelve o'clock the doors of the House were opened and the members poured in.   Even Hansard is interested enough to report that in five minutes' time there were not less than three hundred members in the House, but it was some time after two o'clock when the debate began.   It was not very long.   Among others Lord John Russell spoke in favour of Abercromby, and Peel in favour of Manners Sutton, as also did Stanley, and with vigour.   The case against the old Speaker was feeble, but it was good enough to allow the Whigs to be conscientiously persuaded that he ought not to be elected.   Their calculations on victory had been correct, and Abercromby received 317 votes to Manners Sutton's 307.[2]   Stanley had supported the ministerial candidate, but that had not availed to save him, and the defeat was a severe blow to Peel's Ministry.   As Peel said next day, they had not

---

[1] Grev., *Geo. IV and Wm. IV*, III, 205.   Roebuck, p. 15.   Hansard, XXVI, 489 (Brougham), 853 (O'Connell).
[2] Hansard, XXVI, 2 ff.   Grev., III, 204 and 205, 212, etc.

quite expected it.[1] He had become very vehement in one passage of his speech, and now in defeat it was said by a rather hostile observer that he looked painfully downcast and very white. "There was a convulsive motion of his mouth that gave one pain to look at. He seemed to sink under the blow and walked out of the House as would a man stunned by a fall."[2] That night, when the members came in from the House, there was an uproarious dinner at Brooks's.[3]

Peel might stagger and the Whigs dine cheerfully, but the fight was not finished. Peel was not counted out, and he was to go through the next few rounds with great spirit and an ability that all could recognize. Nor was the task of the Whig leaders simple, for there was apparently a feeling in their party that Peel should have a fair trial.[4] Luckily the phrase was an elastic one, able like a magic spear to salve or to wound, to salve consciences or to wound enemies, but a direct vote of censure was going to be out of the question. The Radicals, however, would press on the attack, particularly Joseph Hume. His great strength had always been a consistent Radicalism, an unflagging obstinacy and assurance, with a great capacity for not doubting the imbecility and general bad faith of those who opposed him. They were useful qualities, but not suitable for the present occasion, so that Hume showed himself too eager to bring the Ministry's fate to a decision, and several times announced a vote of censure, or an equivalent, which he was not able to bring forward. Peel drew him out, for it was good tactics for Peel to show that he desired that his opponents would attempt a vote of want of confidence against him, especially when it was obvious that they would not, and Peel said in private that by his blundering and impudence Hume was a good friend to the Ministry.[5] Yet it is doubtful whether his friendship

[1] Add. MSS. 40,415; 218 (Feb. 27).
[2] Roebuck, *Life*, p. 65.   [3] Moore's *Diary*, under Feb. 19.
[4] E.g. *Life and Letters of the 4th Earl of Clarendon*, I, 85.
[5] Add. MSS. 40,416; 64 (Peel, March 3, 1835).

helped the Ministry much, or whether it was entirely in a friendly spirit that on one occasion Peel wrote a significant letter to Hume to ask him how he had come to say that Peel was not acting as a man of honour; at that time such questions hinted at an old-fashioned way of clearing up differences.   But the letter was probably not written in enmity.   Peel was a man, as Greville said, of prompt courage, during this Ministry he had already required another such explanation.[1]

After the Speakership came the Address, with the Whigs' amendment to it.   John Russell had written his amendment in a spirit of caution, and it had been emasculated.[2]   Consequently it was not a vote of censure, it merely insisted on the continuance of Reform while it deplored the dissolution of Parliament.   But the whole tone of the debate showed how strange and meagre was to be the Whigs' version of a fair trial.   It was not to mean much more than a grudging and suspicious permission to exist, on condition that certain measures were passed and certain predetermined principles adhered to, those principles being beforehand specifically avowed by the Ministers; and to this could be added a good deal of sneering at the flexibility of the Tory conscience if it could be passed through this gauge.   It was to be trial by leading questions and with, it was hoped, little chance of an acquittal.   For the doctrine was really obsolete, as it could not but be obsolete in any period when parties were self-conscious and labelled by principle.   Still attention must even be paid to obsolete doctrines.   The animus against Peel's Ministry was not enough to destroy it immediately, and even as it was, the amendment to the Address was only carried by 309 votes to 302, a very small majority in a full House.   Peel was still to be allowed some weeks in which he could partially produce his measures, in which he should undergo many defeats and score one victory at the expense of his friends.

Peel turned with courage to his task.   "Our hope,"

---

[1] Hansard, XXVII, 55.   Parker, II, 190–1.   Add. MSS. 40,417, 290–2.
[2] Spencer Walpole's *Lord John Russell*, I, 217.

said he to a friend, "must be by patience, perseverance and good humour to detach many of those who formed the last majorities."[1] Play might be made with the fact that he used not "is" but "must be;" but such subtleties are not certain enough to make them worthy of History. Others speculated on desperate remedies and, as was natural but futile, began to talk of his having recourse to another dissolution, but there was no chance of Peel's being unwise enough to try that expedient, and after an attempt, which he strongly resisted, to taint him with sympathy for the Orange Society in Ireland, he came to his one victory. On March 10th Chandos brought forward his motion on the Malt Tax.

Peel had not been idle over the question of Malt. While the clouds had gathered and frowned on his Ministry he had not been idle over his duties as Chancellor of the Exchequer. Sometimes these were trivial, as was the great question of the money for three chandeliers in the Waterloo Chamber of Windsor.[2] Sometimes they were unnecessary, as was the daily receipt, at this time, of ten or twelve schemes for taxation from various unknowns who wanted to assist the nation's finances and, perhaps, to be assisted in their own.[3] But for such a task, both for matters of triviality and for the great problems of national taxation, Peel had a clear head, great industry and frigidly sound financial views; and all of these incomparable qualities he displayed on the Malt Tax. In the small time at his disposal he showed his view of the importance of the matter by deep research into the Tax itself and into the arguments for its Repeal. Even his own agent at Drayton was instructed to look into the matter. Lord Chandos was again interviewed. Lists of taxes were drawn up which might possibly supply the place of the Malt Tax, on its repeal or partial repeal.[4] But it was no good, the wishes

---

[1] Add. MSS. 40,416; 64 (Peel, March 3, 1834, to Westmoreland, quoted above).   [2] Ibid. 40,413; 264; 268.
[3] Ibid. 40,416; 80.   [4] Ibid. 40,414; 114-18.

of squires would not coincide with the results of research. The arguments for the Repeal were found to be unsound, the tax was found to be necessary, and its repeal uneconomical and of very slight assistance to Agriculture. Peel was told from the Customs that there were no articles on which the duties could be increased, and several on which the duties should be lowered when the opportunity arose, in order to increase consumption or to diminish smuggling.[1] Peel himself was persuaded that the place of the Malt Tax must be filled by a property tax which would fall heavily on Agriculture. He seems to have made up his mind to be firm.

It would be hard to calculate what were his risks of failure. Croker supposed that the House would decide for the Malt Tax's repeal by 400 votes to 2, Peel and his teller. But Croker loved a striking statement for its own sake.[2] Apart from the question itself Peel could use the strong argument that it was improper to take such a division at that period in the session. But he would not allow the previous question to be moved on that ground, since it might raise expectations. He was resolute and austere. He would meet the matter with a direct negative in order to encourage no hope. He held a large meeting of the Party on the subject, and it was successful. The Conservatives who were concerned were determined to save the Government. Lord Grimstone, a member for Hertfordshire, told Peel that he had learnt that on this vote the future of Conservatism in that county depended, but Peel could not allow him to say that he had voted against the tax with his sanction. In the bitterness of having voted against his constituents' wishes another member applied, after the Division, for the Chiltern Hundreds, but Peel told him that he had been in such a position himself, and advised him to stay.[3] Peel had persevered and was successful. Duty and economics had again bidden him disappoint part of his

---

[1] Add. MSS. 40,416; 204.   [2] Croker. Add. MSS. 40,321; 98.
[3] Add. MSS. 40,416; 248, 267, 217, 219, 404. 40,417; 23. Croker, II. 267.

followers. Chandos' motion was rejected by the vast majority of 158, 192 votes for the motion and 350 against it. Greville, though he thought that the Government might have done wisely in allowing some of their friends to redeem the pledges they had given in the counties, remarked on the great ability of Peel's speech, and on his great and rising reputation. The ability and force of Peel's speech stand out from the pages of Hansard. Very strong, very able, very honest and at times peculiarly unyielding, Peel pursued his course towards his appointed end.[1]

Certainly his strength was needed for the rest of this Ministry. There were to be no more victories. Peel was to run strongly with the hounds at his heels. But they hesitated to pull him down. The obvious method of attack was to refuse or to restrict supplies. But this would be a very severe blow to public credit as well as to the Ministry, and was altogether too drastic. Hume introduced and John Russell apparently approved a proposal to limit supplies to three months. But many of the Whigs would not support it, and the project had to be dropped. Hume had to confess to Peel in the House that he did not mean to bring the motion forward, and to content himself by promising vaguely that someone would bring forward a motion of want of confidence at the first fit and proper moment.[2] It might be hard to discover what moments were fit and proper. That night Peel went on to produce a measure for the Reform of the Ecclesiastical Courts. It was not a party measure, nor was Peel's Government really responsible for its preparation. But Peel took the opportunity to draw attention to it as an earnest of his readiness to reform, and to taunt Hume with having withdrawn his motion through some subtle prognostication of the nature of the Government's measures. Hume replied with a reference to Peel hatch-

[1] Hansard, XXVI, 737. Grev., *Geo. IV and Wm. IV*, III, 224. See Add. MSS., Vols. 40,414 to 40,417.

[2] *Ibid.*, XXVI, 884 (March 12). *Early Corresp. Lord John Russell*, II, 103 (Grey to Russell, March 11, 1835). *Recollections and Suggestions*.

ing other people's eggs, which metaphor grew in his mouth in later debates to some rather mixed talk of a cuckoo and of stolen plumes.[1]

The next day Peel received a check, severe and damaging. At the beginning of his Ministry Lord Londonderry had desired to be appointed either Lord-Lieutenant of Ireland or foreign ambassador, particularly at Paris, or possibly the Master General of the Ordnance.[2] He had been named Ambassador of Russia. It was a most unpopular appointment; even *The Times* had reprobated it when it was first rumoured, for Londonderry's reputation was bad, perhaps undeservedly bad.[3] He was held to be a violent, factious man, noted for wild attacks on the foreign policy of Lord Grey's Government, and thought to have spoken unfeelingly about the Poles. Their cause was popular in England and it was essentially the concern of the country to which he was appointed. The appointment was attacked in the Commons. Peel put up a good defence, but the debate went against him, even Stanley deplored the choice of Lord Londonderry, and Londonderry had to resign with what grace he could.[4] The Ministry was damaged, and the matter was peculiarly serious because the appointment of an ambassador was part of the King's prerogative, and it was thought to be a dangerous precedent that the House of Commons should be allowed to intervene. On March 16th, the night that Lord Londonderry's resignation was reported, Lord John pointed out that what Peel called a fair trial seemed to endanger the respect in which the useful prerogatives of the Crown were held. In his heart, perhaps, Peel was uneasy. Again he complained that he was being continually threatened with votes of censure that were never brought forward. Lord John answered that he did not propose a vote of want of confidence, because if he did Peel might complain that he was not

---

[1] Hansard, XXVI, 908.   [2] Add. MSS. 40,309; 378.
[3] *Times*, Jan. 2, March 13, etc.   Grev., III, 228.
[4] Hansard, XXVI, 947.   Parker, II, 269 and 270.   Add. MSS. 40,417 140 and 142.

fairly treated in not being allowed to bring forward his reforms, and because it might not be passed.   If Peel's Reforms were wanted matters would soon come to their climax, for that night Peel announced that the Dissenters' Marriage Bill, the Irish Tithe Measure, and the English Tithe Commutation Bill were to be brought forward in the next two weeks.[1]

Peel was allowed to produce his best measures, but they had little to do with his fate.   They might be his pride, they were not his salvation.   The Dissenters' Marriage Bill and the English Tithe Commutation Bill were both received moderately well, the first perhaps more favourably than the second.   There were compliments from the opposition side of the House when Peel produced his well-prepared measure on Dissenters' marriage.   He was congratulated from various quarters on the friendly spirit towards the Dissenters in which he had conceived his measure and in which he had introduced it.   It was not universally approved.   The anxious eyes of Dissenters detected signs of inequality in it.   Some did not wish to be married by civil contract, some wished all marriages to be by civil contract, some felt that for a man to have to go before a magistrate and swear that he was a Dissenter was a "degradation not to be submitted to by any upright mind," [2] and some objected to the payment of five shillings to a clergyman of the Church of England for registration.   But it did not matter; the Bill was never going to become law.   The measure proved that Peel could introduce on some subjects sound Reforms in a liberal spirit, and the result proved that that was not enough.[3]

Meanwhile matters were not comfortable for Peel in the House of Commons.   Sometimes the House seemed to be in a haste to go the way the Government did not want, and it was inclined to take up its time in long debates arising out of questions put to Peel or his col-

[1] Hansard, XXVI, 1018–31.   [2] Add. MSS. 40,416; 323.
[3] Hansard, XXVI, 1073 (Dissenters' Marriages).

leagues.   It began to be difficult to get the supplies.
Hume questioned, abused, and introduced motions on
supply nights, and, as Peel confessed, the Government
had not weight or authority to prevent it, because they
were in a minority.   When they complained they were
told that the supplies were late because time had been
wasted by the change of Government and the dissolution
of Parliament.   The Board of Admiralty began to complain that they would get into difficulties through the
delay on their votes.   Peel declared in the House, after
another evanescent threat, that he "panted" for a direct
motion expressly to the effect that he could not be trusted
with the money.   But no such motion was granted to
him.   He was told that he would take the opportunity
to gain support on the ground that he was being refused
what was essential for the service of the Country.   Yet
the Ministry's position showed the unreality of the
policy on which the opposition leaders had to act.   Even
before the Ministry produced a definite cause for their
condemnation, the House did not give them enough
confidence to enable them to govern the Country.   Their
fate might nearly have resembled that of a man condemned to the death of a thousand cuts, merely because
it was feared that the axe would not go through in one.[1]

§ 9

But such was not to be their fate.   They were to fall
on a clear question of principle.   There was a principle
to which the Government had given their uncompromising adherence in opposition, against which all their
enemies were united.   The question in dispute may seem
to be far enough removed from the most important needs
and desires of humanity, nevertheless it was the question
which was to furnish for some time the strongest lines of
division between the parties.   It was the old-standing
question of the appropriation of the revenues of the
Established Church in Ireland.

[1] Hansard, XXVI, 1031 ; XXVII, 225, 315, 864. Supplies, see also XXVII,
204 and 279.

This fatal and dreary question was not dragged into undue prominence to confound Peel. Ireland and the Irish Church had dominated the politics of 1834. Ministers had retired over it; over matters relating to it a Ministry had been destroyed. Lord John Russell was in earnest over Tithe. He had told Melbourne, in September 1834, that the Whig Ministry must give a clearer and more determined lead on the subject. He told Melbourne, in early February 1835, that he would not join another Cabinet divided on the question. He had taken care to find out in January that Lansdowne and Rice did not, as the Tories asserted, disagree with their colleagues on the problem of Lay Appropriation, but were willing to use the Irish Church's surplus revenue for general education of all denominations.[1] His mind had been clear, consistent and very determined on the matter, long before the present state of affairs. Consequently there is nothing surprising in the fact that the matter presented itself to him now, as he described it long afterwards, as a good "experimentum crucis" for a Ministry to whom some of his followers insisted on giving a "fair trial."[2]

Yet if Lord John used the Irish Church and Lay Appropriation to try out Peel's Ministry, he would determine other fates beside that of the Conservatives. Many Whigs, probably Lord John himself, wished to avail themselves again of the splendid services of Stanley. Lay appropriation was the subject on which Stanley had left them, and while the Whigs legislated on such principles he could never come back. Lord Grey was conscious of this, and begged them not to press the matter prematurely. But John Russell knew that there could be no further compromise on the Irish Church.[3] There

---

[1] *Early Corresp. of Lord John Russell*, II, 46 (Lord John to Melb., Sept. 22, 1834), 90 (Russell to Melb., Feb. 11, 1835), 74, 79 (Russell to Spring-Rice, Jan. 23, Rice to Russell, Jan. 29).

[2] *Recollections and Suggestions.*

[3] *Melbourne Papers*, 239 (Grey to Melb., Feb. 1, 1835) and 252 (John Russell to Melb., Feb. 11). *Melbourne Papers*, 239 (Grey to Melb., Feb. 1, 1835) and 252 ; see above, John Russell to Melb., Feb. 11.

would be no going back. Stanley's career as a Whig was over. The Whigs had taken the turning. The road on which they had started would lead them away from Whiggery if not towards popularity; it would lead them away from Stanley and toward O'Connell; it would almost certainly lead them into hostile collision with the House of Lords.

Since the Whigs had resigned, the problem had remained urgent, with the harsh bloody insistence proper to an Irish question. Very little tithe had been paid, the clergy were in great difficulties, an attempt to levy tithe had resulted in an affray at Rathcomac, in which the military had found it necessary to fire on a crowd; O'Connell could have the people in tears by his descriptions of Rathcomac. Before the Session began Peel and his colleagues decided they must legislate on the subject as quickly as possible, and about the same time Ward, who had made the pace on Appropriation the year before, worried John Russell with suggestions for a motion upon it.[1] On the first night of the debate on the Address and on March 2nd Peel, under question, repeated the declaration he had made in the Tamworth Manifesto against lay appropriation of ecclesiastical revenues. For a time the report of the Commission which the Whigs had set up in 1834 on the subject of the Irish Church's revenues was delayed and Lord John postponed taking the matter up till it should appear in March. Peel struggled with difficulty through the preliminary stages of his tithe Bill. The report of the Commission was not yet in the hands of members, but Lord John was not prepared to postpone the matter any further, and he announced his intention of bringing forward a motion respecting the appropriation of the revenues of the Irish Church on Monday, March the 30th.[2] It would be a frontal attack on the Ministry. The butcher had taken his knife into his hand.

---

[1] Grev., III, 222. Spencer Walpole's *Life of Lord John Russell*, I, 226.
[2] Hansard, XXVII, 102, 313, etc., and 377.

Peel prepared for his end.   On March 25th he sent
round a memorandum to his colleagues, pleading the
difficulties and dangers of carrying on the Government
in a minority.[1]   There was the obstruction of public
business which they had not strength to stop.   There
was the danger, typically important to men at that time,
of the House of Commons getting into dangerous habits
of interfering through being controlled by no executive.
If the House of Commons should adopt Lord John's
motion there would be the great danger and difficulty
of administering Ireland on a principle rejected by the
House of Commons, and with the House of Commons
on the side of those who did not pay tithe.   These things
would seem to be sufficiently obvious.   But the grand
inconvenience of governing the country without a
majority in the Commons is that you have lost the best
excuse for ever going out of office.

The Tories were set against Peel's retiring.   Kenyon
told him that he must not leave office unless his honour
was stained.   Newcastle begged to be required to share
a scaffold with him.   According to Greville, there were
Tories who said that Peel would abandon his party if he
retired, and talked of struggling on with the Duke alone,
and numerous arguments were put forward by various
people to show that he need not resign over this motion,
any more than over his earlier defeats.   Croker also told
Peel not to resign, but to see whether the Whigs would
face pay-day and still dare to impede the supplies.
The Duke thought that he ought to fight on for a week
or two, although he wished to God he could relieve him.
And all this tumult was to prevent a wretched, hampered,
impotent Ministry from changing itself into a powerful
and effective Opposition.[2]

Of course it was important that Peel should show his
followers that he had stayed in till he could stay in no

[1] Parker, II, 292. Add. MSS. 40,418; 123.
[2] Parker, II, 294. Add. MSS. 40,418; 69, 133–279, etc.   40,310; 89.
Croker, II, 268 (Croker to Peel, undated. Peel to Croker, March 30, 1835.
Croker to Peel, March 31). Grev., III, 244.

longer.   But there could be no real hope, and Peel knew
it.   He heard that the Opposition expected to pass their
motion on Monday next by a considerable majority.
Moreover, not only were the Conservatives in a positive
minority but, as Peel said, their force was composed of
gentlemen with engagements in Society, while the evening
entertainments of the great body of his opponents "did
not connect them with the refinements of the fashionable
world."   As Greville said, the Opposition contained a
dense body of fellows who had no vocation outside the
House of Commons, who, if they dined at all, dined at
an adjoining chop-house, and thronged the benches from
the beginning to the end of the proceedings.   In the old
days the placemen had made it a habit to attend and
carry the business through, but now, said Greville, this
household phalanx was outnumbered by these blackguards.[1]   That placemen should usually be outnumbered
by independent blackguards might mean a very important
change in political history.

Either the increase of his difficulties, or the clarity of
his principles, or the bold decision of his character, made
Peel very anxious not to elude John Russell's motion.
He told De Grey, in a letter, that he should be very sorry
indeed to have a plausible pretext for acceding to John
Russell's motion.   He might have had such a pretext.
It was suggested that he might allow John Russell to
move the House into a Committee in order that he might
ask for his measure.   Stanley, who was in correspondence
with Peel on the matter, seems to have suggested it.[2]
But Peel was not pleased with Stanley and his friends.
He pitied them if they could not make up their minds
at such a moment.   The best punishment that they could
receive, he thought, was to leave them with the alternative of either giving a fair and honest support to a Government or themselves presenting a Government to the
country.   He saw no advantage in going out of his

[1] Add. MSS. 40,418; 188.   Grev., III, 225.
[2] *Ibid.* 40,415; 293 (Stanley to Peel undated, presumably Friday, March 27,
1835).

way to gain them.   Of course, he added, the Conservatives need not tell Stanley what they felt about him.[1]

Yet if futile hopes and useless manœuvres are a punishment, as perhaps they are, Stanley had already been
punished.   He was an obsolete Whig trying to lead a
party united on superficial grounds and without coherence, continuity or organization.   Before the Session
he and Graham and their allies had gone over lists, and
had analysed the House.[2]   Before the Address they
summoned a meeting of moderates which numbered in
the end about 40 or 50.[3]   In the debate on the Address
Stanley declared that he spoke for no insignificant body.
O'Connell jeered at him, and among many other things
quoted the anti-Jacobin about "the Derby Dilly, carrying
six insides," or some other slight variant from the
original, and Stanley's party came to be known as the
Derby Dilly.   They were more than six in number,
but they were never enough to decide any issue.   Stanley
and others who agreed with him voted for the Ministry
on the Address, and still the Ministry was beaten.[4]

The Dilly had achieved a nickname and no success.
The elusive dictates of moderation were not able to
recommend to them a consistent policy to be followed in
unity.   According to Greville, who had first hoped
great things of them, they showed at their meetings
considerable animus against the Government, to whom
they were supposed to be giving a fair trial, and at their
last meeting he reported that they were hopelessly divided
on the question of Appropriation which was Stanley's
own question.[5]   Meanwhile Stanley, for the sake of
consistency and independence, had to show himself a
Whig.   He attacked the Duke of Wellington's conduct
when the administration was formed, he exchanged
signs of marked friendliness with Grey when he came
up to London for the Session, very late, rather angry and

---

[1] Add. MSS. 40,417; 281 (Peel to De Grey, March 30, 1835).
[2] Parker's *Graham*, I, 231–2.
[3] Grev., III, 220 and 222.   [4] Hansard, XXVI, 398, 428–62.
[5] Grev., *Geo. IV and Wm. IV*, III, 228 and 237.

certainly impotent. Graham explained to Howick that
his and Stanley's attitude on the Irish Church was
based on real Whig principles, though as a matter of
fact it had been abandoned by the vast majority of the
Whig party.[1] Graham and Stanley had acted not unnaturally, but their Whiggery was out of date, their ambitions were futile, and they failed to do much more
than anger the Conservatives, whom when the test came
they had to join, and whom they could not save.

Yet they were to be important for the future. Stanley
and Graham might be splendid recruits for the Conservatives. Nor were they alone. They were the first
of a steady trickle of Whigs into the Conservative
cistern. For instance, the communications of Lord
George Bentinck with the Conservatives were from the
start of this Ministry so confidential and friendly, that
he was rewarded by attention to his recommendations
in the appointment to a living in Norfolk.[2] He had
tried to find an independent candidate for his borough
at Lymne. The Chancellor had offered him Disraeli,
but he would have none of him.[3] Certainly Peel was
being reinforced. Various streams of opinion were
finding their way into Conservative channels. But
Stanley, Lord George Bentinck, and Disraeli were not
names of good omen for Peel's future.

The approach of Lord John's Irish Church Motion
was the signal for the demarcation of parties. On the
28th March a dinner was held by the Opposition at
which John Russell was recognized as Leader by the
Radicals and the Irish, and at which the Whigs seem to
have pledged themselves to Appropriation. Whatever
thoughts Graham and Stanley may have had of urging
Peel to manœuvre, were abolished. On March 29th,
Stanley, answering a note from Peel, wrote to him that
he concurred with his views, that the alliance between

[1] Grev., II, 232 (March 21, 1835). Parker's *Graham*, I, 240 (Graham to
Howick, March 13, 1835).
[2] Add. MSS. 40,416; 272, 274. 40,316, 177.   [3] Grev., III, 170, 171.

the Whigs, Radicals and O'Connell placed matters on a new footing, that he and Graham were prepared to take the high line against their old friends. On the same day, March 29th, Peel sent another memorandum round the Cabinet discussing the necessity for resigning if they were defeated on the next day's motion.[1]

From the 30th March to the eighth day of April there were many debates. John Russell developed his theme on the appropriation of Church property in Ireland from division to division, and at each division Peel was defeated. He fought well and hard, with a cheering party behind him. But it was like a beaten pugilist showing pluck to the spectators. Lord John's first motion was carried in the early morning of April 3rd, and on that day Greville met Peel and walked with him. He seemed in good spirits, but he talked of the fight as over and declared he would have no tampering with his Tithe Bill.[2] He wrote to the Duke to provide him with matter to turn over in his mind before the Cabinet. He spoke of the danger that would arise from staying in Office with a minority in the Commons, of another Government forming itself there independent of the King's consent, not filling official places but virtually ruling the country, and—this was an argument well fitted for a specialized palate—of the danger of France taking advantage of an English official Ministry which they knew had no power in this country.[3]

Peel's brother told Greville that Peel was only staying in to show his supporters that he must resign. But the Conservatives were filled with enthusiasm and activity. Efforts were made by some unofficial Conservatives, through large meetings at Bridgewater House, to ensure a better attendance of Conservatives.[4] Peel was told by the tractarian, Palmer, that the same gentlemen

---

[1] Add. MSS. 40,418; 288 (Parker, II, 298. Stanley to Peel, March 29, 1835). 40,418; 286 (Parker, II, 301. Cabinet Memo., March 29, 1831).
[2] Parker, II, 302.   [3] Greville, II, 243.
[4] Add. MSS. 40,419; 240 (Lushington to Peel, March 28, 1833) and 196 (Egerton to Peel, April 8).

who affected the movement in favour of the Church were
going to do the same for him.[1]   He was told that out
of doors the people were on his side.   Yet in the House
of Commons Peel was beaten on April 3rd, 4th and 6th.
The majorities were usually about twenty-five, for—as the
fate of Stanley's party also showed—men who had been
prepared to vote for a fair trial were not prepared to vote
against lay appropriation.   At last, on the 7th, John
Russell proposed the strong resolution that without the
principle of the lay appropriation of the Irish Church's
surplus revenues no Irish Tithe Bill would be satisfactory.   Peel was beaten again by 285 to 258, and on
the 8th he resigned.

The Ministry had failed.   The country had returned
a majority against them.   Peel had not been able to be
Liberal enough to change his minority into a majority.
He had been Liberal.   He had adopted some of the
tone and style of Liberalism in his utterances.   At the
start of his adventure he had spoken of "mere super-
stitious reverence for ancient usages" in the Tamworth
Manifesto, and in his last speeches on the Irish Church
he had referred with apparent approval to the arguments
that had been used in favour of Catholic Emancipation.
There was nothing against the practice; it was agreeable to intelligent Conservatism.   It was good strategy
to occupy here and there the enemy's ground.   Still
there was the danger that his tongue might get used to
that vernacular, and though Liberal words are honestly
compatible with Conservative principles they do not
conduce to Conservative thought.   Indeed, the tongue
sometimes leads the mind.   But he had been in the
best sense Liberal.   He had produced good legislation,
he had made honest appointments, even refusing the
pleading of his friend Goulburn for his brother.[2]   He
had urged, for instance, his Executive in Ireland not to
be partisan but to be just and equal in their dealings.
But it would not do; he could not be Liberal enough to

[1] Add MSS. 40,419; 110.
[2] Parker, II, 272–3 (Add. MSS. 40,333; 245, 247. 40,316; 126).

satisfy Liberals. If the Irish Church had not been the cause of his undoing, it seems likely that the Municipal Reform Bill would have destroyed him. He failed by the touchstone of the Liberals' set principles, and he was not at the head of their party. Liberalism must, naturally, be a matter of set principles and parties, and if for the moment it is a fruitless principle or a sterile party, so much the worse for the country.

So Peel fell. He may have been tired. He had found it hard, significantly hard, to delegate his labours. There was again mysterious talk about his retiring from politics.[1] But he was cheerful, in good spirits, and not gloomy about the future. By his dissolution he had vastly increased his party in the Commons. He told Greville, on their walk together, that a party had been created strong enough to obstruct any violent measures on the part of their opponents, and to others also he expressed his confidence, if rather more equivocally.[2] He himself had added immensely to his reputation for ability, a reputation which would add to his power in the future, if that should interest or please him. Perhaps he had got rid of his dreams, hopes or expectations, or whatever they had been, of the chance of an administration formed by moderate Conservatives and fragments of the Whigs. He had learned that he could not yet form a lasting administration. He was enthusiastically cheered in his last speech, and when he resigned he was congratulated in many memorials. Though there were some unreasonable enough to think that he might have stayed in, yet on the whole he had done enough to please his party, and to the common observer he might seem to show, by the way in which he lost this battle, that he was capable of winning another. He had done very well.

So Peel resigned, and the reflections on his fall were as various as the breasts that entertained them. Peel said that as far as personal feelings were concerned he was heartily glad it was over.[3] Lady Holland soon

[1] Greville, III, 243.   [2] Add. MSS. 40,419; 169.   [3] *Ibid.* 40,419; 306.

found that now that they had gained their object she was not nearly as happy as she had thought she would be.[1] One man wrote to Peel to beg and implore him to make him a baronet while there was yet time.[2] Politics is a mixed broth—a mixture of vulgar ambition, faction, pertinacity, pride, sincerity, intelligence and blind endeavour.

[1] Greville, III, 254.   [2] Add. MSS. 40,419; 245.

CHAPTER VI

1835—THE MUNICIPAL REFORM BILL

In a boxing match, when an exciting round is just over and the air is full of the flapping of towels and other sounds which show that the seconds are at their work, there comes a moment when there is a general stirring in seats, a lighting of pipes, and above all a general buzz of conversation about the two men engaged, what form they are showing, how much each has left in him and which is likely to win. Then suddenly the seconds leave the ring, and the noise dies down as abruptly as it started. Such an occasion for comment was Peel's retirement from his Ministry.

On the whole men were pleased with Peel. He had received heavy punishment very well and had shown surprisingly good form, and if for the moment he had had the worst of it, it was felt that he had a good deal in hand for later on. Greville commented on the reputation he had earned,[1] addresses poured in on him, and even the *Annual Register* takes flight and grows rhapsodical in his praise. He had, indeed, been obviously the central figure of the episode, the cynosure of all, the heart of the battle. It was he who had sustained the struggle in the House of Commons, with great ability and almost alone. It was he who had been both Chancellor of the Exchequer and First Lord of the Treasury. It is true that he confessed that he thought that double task was too much for human strength, but it is a commonplace among moralists and tragedians that heroes may be the centre of much admiration and yet at the same time a little tired and strained.

His fame at least is of historical importance. It is probable that his Ministry might be chosen as a date from which men clearly saw Peel as the real leader of the Conservative party. As with a dead man whose character is buried under official eulogies, the Duke's name,

[1] Grev., *Geo. IV and Wm. IV*, III, 243 ff.

execrated or blessed, was to sink behind his military glory. He was to be universally respected. The real man was to remain with the Lords and his colleagues, but, for the rest, it might be said that a generation was to arise that knew not Joseph, but had heard of his services in the famine. His task was not yet over, but it was Peel's achievement and character, and not the Duke's, that were to dominate the next eleven years of Conservatism.

There were many addresses, a notable one from the London solicitors, and altogether there were a thousand signs that the party was eager. It was believed that the time was not far distant when they would see Peel in power again. Meanwhile the party was putting on flesh and muscle that would, in time, enable it to sustain a Government. There were new Conservative Associations in various parts of the country. There was, for instance, an Operatives' Association at Leeds with, for its style, "The altar, the throne, and the cottage," and with the twin and superficially contradictory principles of "subject ourselves to every ordinance of man for God's sake" and "Britons never never will be slaves." In Denbighshire Charles Wynn showed an interesting reluctance to be at the head of any political association, on the ground that it would produce irritation and check the exercise of individual judgment, although, as he said, he saw their friends promoting them all over the country. Perhaps the party was being everywhere imbued with those fine unthinking unanimities and jolly hostilities which are the backbone of concerted political action.[1]

There was other work being done for the party. On taking office John Russell had had to vacate his seat, and during his election he had declared that if their measures were rejected by either Lords or Commons they would appeal to the country. Bonham advised the immediate formation of a small committee to prepare for a dissolution lest they should be taken by surprise,

[1] Add. MSS. 40,419; 186. 40,418; 172. 40,420; 70.

which, said he, had produced much of the mischief of
1831. It would help to consolidate the work that Lord
Granville Somerset and others had done during the last
election. With or without the committee this work went
on, and they soon had a suitable and useful recruit in
Sir James Graham, who was able to transfer to them
influence that had been Whig. He seemed, said Bonham, to consider that in such matters they were all
embarked in the same boat, and in May 1835 Bonham
negotiated through him with Lord Stanley, George
Bentinck and the Duke of Portland, then at Newmarket,
for such distant things as the Duke of Portland's interest
in Ayrshire.[1]

The work was ceaseless, and undoubtedly useful.
Perhaps it might be said that the creator of the new
Conservative party was not Peel, but the body of gentlemen who thought so much and worked so hard to spread
their net over Great Britain. Nevertheless, Peel's fate
would be entirely settled by the nature of what was
created.

§ 2

The new Ministry took so long to form that there
were Conservative hopes that it would never come at all.
Peel was moved to write that considering the difficulty
of his opponents in replacing his administration they
might have abated a little the vehemence of their opposition.[2] Certainly behind the curtain there were difficulties and some despair. The leading Whigs and the
King combined in an attempt to get Grey to become
Prime Minister, but he wisely refused. He was present,
however, at the conferences with the King, and he
declared afterwards that there were times when they
nearly broke down. Melbourne at one time despaired,
and John Russell was not always hopeful. Success had
come to the Whigs, but its yield seemed laggard and
doubtful. "I can never remember," said Greville, "a

---

[1] Add. MSS. 40,420; 126 and 137.   [2] *Ibid.*, 40,419; 321.

great victory for which Te Deum was chanted in so faint and joyless a voice." [1]

The Whigs' difficulties centred round three men, Brougham, O'Connell, and the King. At the end of 1834 Melbourne had declared that never again either in Cabinet or in opposition would he work with Durham, Brougham and O'Connell, and now that the new Ministry was formed, poor Brougham was left out and O'Connell was not asked in. The blow was softened for Brougham by the Great Seal being put into Commission, and he contrived to seem moderately and temporarily reconciled. He was an intolerable colleague, but were the Whigs strong enough in talent to discard with impunity even the most intolerable man of genius? [2] And if the exclusion of Brougham might affect the fate of one party, the exclusion of O'Connell might change the future of two nations. Lord John Russell wanted him. Apparently at one time he was practically appointed Irish Attorney-General. But it was not to be. His appointment was revoked and another, a Liberal, was put in his place. He received compliments; Lord John Russell told him that he too would resign if O'Connell felt himself aggrieved, but O'Connell had accepted his rebuff with commendable calm. He put it down to the King. The King had certainly attempted to put a prohibition on O'Connell and others, and though Melbourne had firmly protested against all exclusions he may not have wished to press the matter. But Melbourne's own earlier exclusion must still be remembered as well.

At any rate O'Connell was not in, and he would have come in, on conditions. He dreamed that summer of becoming a Cabinet Minister in the next year, and of giving the people in Ireland justice, for he could at least dream of justice. Had he come in, he might possibly

[1] Torrens, *Melb.*, II, 103. *Early Corresp. Lord John Russell*, Vol. II, 107–8. *Letters of Earl Grey and Princess Lieven*, III, 98 (Grey, April 16, 1835). Grev., III, 254.

[2] *Melb. Papers*, 237 (to Grey, Jan. 23, 1833, quoted above); for formation of Ministry, 266 ff.

have made a union of the countries such as there never
had been and such as there never would be.   He might
have done something to prevent those unhappy politics
which should so often turn good into ineptitude, and
patriotism into rhetoric or gloomy hatred.   He might
have done this.   It is not likely, for ranged against him
would have been such bad habits and such forces of
religion and economics as could turn the sweetest milk
sour.

Even as things were, O'Connell had much to content
him.   He was given a sympathetic Irish Executive, for
Lord Mulgrave, the Lord-Lieutenant, and Lord Morpeth, the Chief Secretary, both pleased him.   He rejoiced to feel that the old Irish Protestant party were
down for ever, that the old gang were cleared out of the
Castle, and that the permanent Secretary was no longer
to be Sir William Gossett but one Thomas Drummond,
who was to make his name in Irish conciliation.   The
Government was to be friendly.   They would have a
Corporation Reform Bill and a new Registry Bill and
both objects were important for him.   The Liberal
part of the Bar would be encouraged, and—again and
again he repeated this—they were delivered from their
insulting Orange oppressors.   His spirits were buoyant.
He was going to be friendly, fatally friendly, to these
Ministers who could not let him in to their counsels and
would not let him in to their drawing-rooms; who could
not even perform all that they intended to do for him.
An alliance there was to be, if real union was never to
come at all.[1]

If O'Connell's spirits were buoyant at the change of
the Ministry, the King's were not.   As Peel's fall had
approached his state had become miserable.   He is
reported to have said, in remarkable phrase, that "he
felt his crown tottering on his head," and whatever
was happening on the top of the King's head, there was

[1] O'C.'s *Corresp.*, Vol. II, pp. 10–20 (for formation of Melb.'s Ministry),
also p. 33 (Sept. 4), 38 (Sept. 11).   Spencer Walpole's *Life of Lord John
Russell*, 233–4.

certainly perturbation and discomfort inside it.   He was
naturally very difficult during the formation of the new
Ministry.   He was anxious about the appropriation of
Church property, for the Coronation Oath perturbed
his conscience.   He was not allowed to appeal, as he
wished, to the judges on the matter, while Lyndhurst,
whom he was permitted to question, rightly refused
any answer.   Melbourne was firm; he told the King
that the new Ministry had come into office pledged to
the late resolutions of the House of Commons on the
appropriation of the surplus of the Irish Church's
Revenues.   He was firm that the King must not exclude
any subject legally qualified for office.   He insisted
that the accession of the new Ministry should be marked
by the creation of a certain number of Peers, not to over-
awe the House of Lords, but to balance the creations
of the last Ministry, and in order that it should be
generally understood that the King was willing to make
use of this branch of his prerogative.[1]

Melbourne was admirably firm, but perhaps he would
need to be most radically determined.   The Lords
would probably throw out the measure to which he
conceived his Government to be pledged, and other
measures as well.   Would he persuade the King to use
that branch of the prerogative?   Melbourne was entangled in an obsolete constitution with a moderately
Liberalized party and a moderately Liberalized electorate.   His obvious salvation was in the knife, but could
he, or would he, use it?   Perhaps he was not entirely
suited to his position.   He was like an old gentleman
who should have gone for a ride on a hack, and to whom
some fool in the stable had given a whirlwind.   Only
in this case it was a broken-down whirlwind; perhaps
better to ride it as a hack, after all.

At last Melbourne's second Ministry was formed,
and was but little different from his first.   Lord John
was Home Secretary, Spring-Rice was Chancellor of the

[1] Grev., III, 238, 250.   Melb. Papers, 269, 277.   Add. MSS. 40,316; 185,
187 and 189 ff. (H. M. Lyndhurst and Peel).

Exchequer and Palmerston Foreign Secretary. Hobhouse and Howick were in the Cabinet. They started
with a preliminary misfortune, for on vacating office
Lord John failed to be re-elected for Devonshire and had
to take refuge at Stroud. On April 19th Melbourne
spoke in the Lords about his Ministry and its difficulties,
and was immediately questioned about his relations with
O'Connell. He had declared that he had no compact
with O'Connell, had taken no means to secure him
and, most particularly, had made no terms with him.[1]
In the House of Commons O'Connell was led to call
Lord Alvanley, the questioner, a bloated buffoon.

§ 3

There had been much delay in the work of the year,
and on May 25th the Ministers announced that they
would not undertake to do more that Session than to
propose measures for Municipal Reform in England
and Wales, and the regulation of Tithe in Ireland.[2]
Municipal Reform was important enough without the
addition of Tithe. It was to be founded on the labours
of a Commission, who had just been delivered, and it
had already thrown its shadow over the debates of the
year. John Russell said it would affect two millions of
people, while in the Freemen of the old boroughs it
disenfranchised very many who had been Parliamentary
voters. The Municipal Corporations were spread over
the length and breadth of the country, and many were
corrupt and some not a little absurd. Municipal Reform
might well be considered as one of the four great
measures of the Reform Era. It was the last of those
four measures.

Liberals, Moderates, Conservatives and ultra-Tories
were all profoundly interested. Sir James Graham
approached Hardinge, using Conservative language,
wishing to know what concessions on Corporation
Reform Peel would be inclined to make. He wanted
previous concert with Peel, for he asserted that if Stanley

---

[1] Hansard, XXVIII, 998 ff.   [2] *Ibid.*, XXVIII, 60.

T

and Peel differed, Lord John would probably try to make his plan conform to Stanley's views. The suggestion seemed to hint at that management and finesse which Peel had so warmly and so often condemned; moreover Peel may not have yet forgiven Graham and Stanley, for it is an axiom that neutrals are usually peculiarly hard to forgive. On receipt of Hardinge's news Peel wrote to the Duke telling him what he felt at the moment about Corporation Reform, and how little he was inclined to adapt himself to Graham. He told the Duke that he would much rather consider what was prudent and safe than accommodate his line, for mere temporary purposes, to that of Lord Stanley and Sir James Graham. "My first wish," said he to the Duke, "in office or out of office will be to confer with you." For his own conviction was that they both felt more interested in protecting the monarchy and the public interests involved in its security than in fighting a mere party battle. To Hardinge Peel said that he had not read the Corporation Report with proper attention, that as far as previous pledges went he would vote as he liked upon it, that he was as free as air in the Corporation question. Air can be strong and very undisciplined. No one can foretell which way the wind will blow.[1]

The Duke seemed remarkably pleased with Peel's letter. "I am very much flattered," said he, "by your desire to consult with me the course to be taken on the Corporation question. I don't doubt that without much concert we should have come to the same conclusion upon it." It was a slight superstition with him that Peel and himself usually reached the same conclusions without much communication. He liked to comment upon this, and no doubt it was a comfort to him when they had had no communication at all. He put forward his views on Corporation Reform, and towards the end of his letter came the old bitter complaint that what was necessary in this country was a Government. The slightest accident would destroy the country's power and

[1] Parker, II, 312 ff. Add. MSS. 40,314; 89 (Peel to Hardinge, April 25).

influence through the world. There was danger in China, and could anyone believe we should maintain the dominion over Canada? He was therefore ready, he said, to make sacrifices of opinion upon some of the questions with a view of keeping a party together which should be strong enough to govern the country. It was a readiness that he would find it hard but important to remember towards the end of the session.[1]

But in these letters Peel and the Duke show much the same views on Municipal Reform. Both agreed that there had been abuse over Corporate Funds and that there must be Reform in that. Both dreaded the increase in the principle of popular election with a constituency of ten-pound householders, while Peel added a specific fear of his own, that annually recurrent elections should poison social life and let loose a new flood of bribery. The opinions of other Conservatives were various but violent. Curious and uncharitable readings were put on the Government's motives. Radical uniformity was feared, together with the entrusting of the control of finance or of the police to the poorer classes. There was very great indignation about the abolition of vested rights, and it was also felt that the Government's Bill was aimed at the political strength of the Conservatives. Lord Falmouth told Peel, among many other things, that the reaction had been worked in his part of the country by "the quiet influence of the Corporations." In that district, said he, without their assistance hardly a single Conservative member would have been returned, which last statement seems to have been too strong for Peel, for he made Falmouth modify it. Yet, modified or unmodified, such opinions were not confined to Lord Falmouth. There was kindling ready, and touchwood, if any wished to light a fire.[2]

On June 5th John Russell moved for leave to bring in the Bill to reform Municipal Corporations in England and Wales, and Peel proved himself cautious but condi-

---

[1] Add. MSS. 40,310; 101.
[2] *Ibid.* 40,420; 186, 201, 206, 217, etc.

tionally agreeable. He agreed that the time had come
for municipal reform, and he accepted the principle that
Corporate Revenues should be applied to public and
municipal purposes, and that those exercising corporate
authority should be under popular control. He would
afford cheerful consideration to the principles of the
measure and co-operation in its details, provided that it
was not a mere pretext for transferring power from
one party in the State to another.[1] It was not that he was
reconciled to his adversaries or liked their Bill. In fact
he entertained privy suspicions that it was especially
framed to annihilate large numbers of Conservative
Parliamentary voters.[2] With some wit and a great
use of the Commissioners' Report he attempted to con-
vict John Russell of a party presentation of the case.
He fruitlessly attempted to amend the Bill with amendments that seem to have been decided on by a joint
Committee of the Conservative leaders in Lords and
Commons.[3] He spoke often, felt scornful and Conservative, and yet he never imperilled the existence of the
Bill itself. He acknowledged with apprehension the
justice and necessity of the elective principle with regard
to Corporations, and above all he never argued, as did
Sir Robert Inglis and others, that Parliament was going
beyond its powers in depriving men of their chartered
rights. On July 21st the Bill went up to the House of
Lords.

Peel's position had apparently been accepted by the
Conservative leaders in the Lords, and it was blessed
by the open alliance of Stanley and Graham. Their
neutrality had shrunken, and with it their party; they
worked openly with Peel, and, abruptly and rather
foolishly, they had even crossed the floor of the House.[4]
Peel's distrust of Graham seems only to have been the
creation of a moment's ready suspicion, and at last
Stanley and Graham stood beside Peel, a pledge of

[1] Hansard, XXVII, 558.   [2] Croker, II, 278.
[3] Add. MSS. 40,420; 222 (Ell. to Peel, June 14).
[4] Grev., III, 272 ff.   Hansard, XXIX, 199 ff.

strength, an argument for moderation and, as Peel would find, a new fetter for the independent House of Lords. Stanley and Graham had important parts to play in Peel's destiny.

But before the Lords could consider the Municipal Bill another element in the situation had been developed. On June 26th the Ministry had begun to introduce their Tithe Bill, which included the arrangements for that appropriation of the Irish Church's revenues on which Peel's Ministry had fallen, and to which he could never consent. He let the Bill reach the Committee stage, and then moved an instruction to divide the Appropriation Clauses from the others, so that they might be dealt with separately. Of course he was supported by Stanley and Graham, and of course his motion failed. The Ministry were pledged to appropriation, and could not leave it out of their Bill. Without that Bill no tithes would be levied for the Irish Clergy's support, and the Government must probably proceed against them for the money which had already been advanced to them. Yet the House of Lords had already in 1834 rejected the Government's Irish Tithe Bill which had not then been one that embodied appropriation.

§ 4

The Irish Church and Tithe Bill was not read a third time till the 12th of August, and before that date the Ministry was facing the implications of its position. They were indeed already threatened by what was dangerous and obsolete in the Constitution. The King was in a state of minor eruption. From the first he had shown himself absurd, and personally discourteous to this Ministry. As Greville said, he would not swallow his bitter pill, but rolled it in his mouth and made grimaces. He notably avoided asking Ministers to dinner. He grew anxious and very excited about the Militia. He burst out into a speech in the Council on the appointment of Sir George Grey to be Governor of Jamaica. He gave the most extraordinary instructions, not without blasphemy, to Lord Gosford who was to be the Governor of Canada. "Mind me, my lord," he said on this occasion, "the Cabinet is not my Cabinet; they had better take care, or, by God, I will have them impeached."[1]

It was only a foolish old man, over-excited and under-controlled, who could not keep his temper nor withhold his speeches. There were no subtle plots or very clearly defined designs in his mind, while there was, in fact, much honest if rather misty intention, and a great deal of very good nature. But the fine indignations that are natural and not unpleasant before the smoking-room fire of a Service club are out of place in the closet and dangerous in the council. It is true that the King had given his assent to the introduction of the Municipal Corporations Bill and the Irish Tithe Bill,[2] and that Melbourne could deal out his reprimands with courtesy and firmness, to which the King would submit. Yet the matter was dangerous. Even the virtuous and foolish can go too far. The King undoubtedly dreamed of having another Conservative Ministry, and he had those about him who wished to commit him. He might drive out this Ministry, although sane men knew that no other could succeed it. Some had their fears, and in this case as in others leading Conservatives found it their duty to try to teach one of the branches of the Constitution its duty and its impotence.

It was about the middle of July that Croker and Peel both wrote to Sir Herbert Taylor, the King's secretary, about the King's behaviour and the rumours that pre-vailed of an intended change ´of administration. Tay-lor's answers reveal that useful and sensible man in a position of grave discomfort. He had conveyed Croker's remarks and reasonings to the King, but he had not felt at liberty to read him Peel's letter. He concurred in all that Peel said, and he declared that he had lost no oppor-tunity in trying to impress those views upon the King. At times he had succeeded in making the desired impres-sion and at times he had failed, or the King had been

_____
[1] Grev., III, 272. Broughton, IV, 40.   [2] *Melbourne Papers*, 282–8.

led away by the excitement of the moment to the use of language that was much to be regretted. "Indeed, I may add that I was not present when he so committed himself." It is a hard task to hold the leash of a King.

Taylor told Peel that he was alone in his task, and was counteracted by others. It need hardly be said to whom he chiefly referred. Early on in the session Taylor had told Peel that the Duke of Cumberland's attempts, direct or indirect, had failed. Now, on July 15th, he admitted that although Cumberland's influence had not increased, yet he had continued to make mischief, and it had been intensified by casual circumstances. He traced to Cumberland the mischievous reports of an intended change of administration and the constant desire to produce excitement and to commit the King. Cumberland had nearly succeeded in obtaining the refusal to the Western Railroads Bill. On July 14th he wrote, through the Queen, very violently on the subject of His Majesty's consent to the introduction to the Irish Church Bill by placing his Irish Patronage at the disposal of Parliament. A refusal on this point would, as Taylor pointed out, have led to the dismissal of the Ministers. Cumberland's influence, said Taylor, was nil, and his manner of intruding his opinion irritated. But he had a great inclination to mischief, and possessed in the highest degree the merit of perseverance. He took credit for what he had failed to effect, and reports went out on his bare assertion, rendered plausible by his free access. He had done this, said Taylor, since the reign of George III.

What seem to be Taylor's recommendations to the King were sensible, if rather elementary. Communications should be made in a conciliatory tone, the conduct observed on all occasions should be courteous and gentlemanly; that the intercourse should always be free and familiar could not be expected. Perhaps such instruction would seem more fit for the schoolroom than the closet. But few men ever really leave behind them the need for a governess, and Taylor's commonplaces were healthy and needful. He believed that the King should act on the advice of his confidential and responsible servants, and that if he differed from them great care should be taken to guard against interference with the matter from outside.   Taylor did not mean formal interference on great public questions such as could be claimed by Peers and Privy Councillors, but such proceedings as those of the Duke of Cumberland, which both Peel and himself condemned.

Above all Taylor agreed with Peel on what must have been the most important point of Peel's letter. He agreed that the King and the Lords could not maintain a Government unable to command a majority in the House of Commons.   It had been proved that a Conservative Ministry could not survive, and that fact controlled the situation.   But would it control the malice of the Duke of Cumberland or the folly of the King ? [1]

§ 5

The King was one, but only one and that the lightest, of the bonds which the constitution laid on the Ministry. He was absurd, but he was weak, well intentioned and manageable, at least to a point, and he himself would have to face the consequences of his actions.   He had allowed the introduction of the Corporation Bill, and at the end of July the House of Lords was preparing to consider it.   The question of importance was whether the Government was prepared to consider the House of Lords.   Lord John had declared, during his election for Devonshire, that the Government would dissolve Parliament if their measures were rejected by either Lords or Commons.   But such a resolution may have been dashed and such a dissolution made more improbable by Lord John's defeat, and apart from Lord John's declaration it would be hard to say what the Whigs had determined to do, should the Lords throw out their Bills.   Perhaps they had never been clear on that question themselves; some of them seem even to have trusted in one case to

[1] Add. MSS. 40,303; 238, 239. 40,321; 154.

a limit to what they would call the madness of the House of Lords.[1]

On July 27th there was a meeting of about 70 or 80 Peers at the Duke of Wellington's, and they agreed to allow the second reading of the Corporation Bill to pass unopposed. Ellenborough, describing the meeting in a letter to Peel, said that they must hear counsel on this Bill according to precedent. But it was agreed that the hearing of counsel should not be allowed to constitute any very grave delay in the course of the Bill. Nothing had been decided, said Ellenborough, with respect to the amendments upon which they should insist. There was a general inclination to make no alterations not supported by reason and justice, and since it seemed not improbable that Peel might be called upon, as First Minister, to propose a Corporation Reform Bill, it was a primary object with the Lords to pledge themselves to no course to which Peel could not adhere. Yet Ellenborough admitted that there were those among them who wanted to amend the Bill very drastically indeed, and he urged Peel to communicate to the Lords how far he would go. Obviously the Conservative party would need careful leadership. Unfortunately leadership is a game at which two can play. The winning cards are position, prestige and prejudice, and tricks are not infrequently won by prejudice. Peel had too few Tory prejudices in his hand.[2]

On July 28th the House of Lords decided to pass the Bill through its second reading, on condition that the principle of the Bill should be discussed by counsel at the bar of the Lords on the ground that the Bill preferred accusations against the existing Corporations and deprived them of their rights. It was agreed that the cases of the various Corporations which had petitioned were to be compressed to the pleadings of two counsel, so that the Bill should not be delayed by taking an indefinite number of cases. The counsel chosen were a lawyer named Knight and that odd ultra-Tory Sir Charles

[1] Grev., III, 247.   [2] Add. MSS. 40,421; 7.

Wetherell, and July 30th and 31st and Saturday August 1st were largely occupied in hearing their speeches, mainly those of Sir Charles Wetherell, and they were well worth hearing.

Wetherell was one of the strangest characters of the time. He had that brutal irresponsibility and sterile honesty which is sometimes developed by old lawyers who are party men but have not often been Ministers. He was a man of great parts, something of a wit and something of a grotesque. It is well known how he would free his trousers for ease while speaking, so that an interval of shirt would appear above them. His speeches were remarkable and violent, and Sergeant Buzfuz seems to suggest himself, but that would be robbing Wetherell of the high strain of individuality which passes even the filter of Parliamentary reporters. He attacked the Bill and he attacked the Report on which it was founded, and he attacked the Commissioners who had drawn it up. He spoke of the "garrulous trash and the ribaldry and the gypsy jargon of the report," he spoke of its "partisan prattlings," he said that it was so vulgar as to be only fit for the circulating library of a watering-place. He spoke for three hours in this strain on the first day, until he was exhausted, and on the next he started again, and his speeches went to the heads of the Peers like new wine.[1] It was possible that the Peers might get out of hand.

Indeed, they had already got out of hand. The reins were already broken. On Monday, August 3rd, Peel told his wife that the old ultra-Tories were playing their old game. On the previous Friday and Saturday he had had two unsatisfactory meetings with the Peers at his house, and he had told the Peers who had been in his Cabinet that he would not be responsible for other peoples' actions, especially when he disapproved of them. On Saturday night he was out at dinner when in came Wetherell and the Duke of Cumberland, fresh from the House of Lords and very violent. Cumber-

---

[1] *Times*, July 31 to August 3.

land seemed intent on taking a line different to that of
Peel in the Commons; he talked of honour and conscience. Peel quarrelled with him in so notorious a
way that it got into the pages of Greville.[1]   The omens
were indeed bad when the Duke of Cumberland talked
of honour and conscience.

Peel spoke to his wife of the Newcastles and Winchel-
seas who were the regular figures in ultra-Tory politics,
but the man to be watched is Lyndhurst, a figure more
splendid than those respectable scarecrows.   There is
possibly a profounder plan in action than is likely to have
been involved or supported by their unenlightened and
honourable honesty.   But it is a matter of controversy,
and the best authority for it is a high-spirited genius,
young, and enthusiastically in touch with a really exciting
political intrigue.   It is Benjamin Disraeli, who seems
by this time to have been in Lyndhurst's close confidence,
and matters of this sort must have received an unreal
importance to Disraeli in the atmosphere of wit and
titles, of brilliant dinners in Lyndhurst's house to "eighty
people of the supremest ton and beauty," of charming
women and political hostesses, of glittering chandeliers
and gilded saloons, the atmosphere which he loves to
describe in his novels, and in which he loved to move.
Yet though brilliant chatter and interesting whisper perhaps may not produce very good witnesses, they may
have offspring, even inconvenient offspring, in the politics
of the time.
   In Mr. Monypenny's first volume of the life of
Disraeli there is a curious staccato account of Lord Lyndhurst's policy in 1835 and 1836, written by Disraeli at
the time, and it is supplemented by an appraisement of
Lyndhurst's character which Disraeli wrote at the time
of Lyndhurst's death in 1863.   These are supported
from outside by a memoir on Lyndhurst which appeared
in *The Times* of 1863, and it must be remembered that

[1] *Private Letters of Sir Robert Peel*, 153 (Peel to Lady Peel, Aug. 3, 1835).
Grev., III, 283.

The Times would have opportunities of knowledge, since it was in very close touch with Lyndhurst at this time.[1] There are obvious traces in Disraeli's letters to his sister that something was afoot in 1835. Lyndhurst, unfortunately, burnt his own papers.

In his narrative Disraeli declares that in 1835 Lord Lyndhurst first formed his great plan of stopping "the Movement," which was the name used at that time for the progress of democracy. Lyndhurst tried his plan on the Municipal Bill. The Duke surrendered the leadership and Lyndhurst determined to accept the Premiership if offered, having received hints from Windsor. Brougham was to be his Chancellor, Graham and Sir William Follett were to lead the Commons. Ten seats in the Commons were to be provided for younger men of Lyndhurst's choosing, one of whom was to be Benjamin Disraeli.

All this Sir Theodore Martin, Lyndhurst's biographer, passionately denies, having read of it in *The Times* but not, probably, in Disraeli's narrative.[2] His best argument is that Lyndhurst declared in a speech on the Municipal Bill that his ambition was satisfied with his position as an eminent lawyer. It is probably true that Lyndhurst was so satisfied. Disraeli declares, in his appraisement of Lyndhurst, that he was offered the Premiership by the King in 1836, and seemed disconcerted and distressed by the offer, but that a friend talked him over; and here a capital D has been inserted in the manuscript. Lyndhurst was not ambitious, and he was liable to be bored. He could be bored by Londonderry and Cumberland;[3] yet his actions often conformed to their dearest wishes. He did not yearn for greater place. He was a charming, weak, sweet-tempered man with no need or desire for gilded dreams. He acted under the impetus of strong effective opinions which were held with sincerity, if there was no depth. Perhaps he enjoyed the exhilaration of a dashing campaign and of grand oratorical

[1] Buckle and Monypenny's *Disraeli*, Vol. I, 301 and 329.
[2] *Life of Lord Lyndhurst*, 342.   [3] E.g. Add. MSS. 40,316; 153.

displays in the House of Lords.   Others stronger than
he could hope, speculate and pass rumours for him and,
it might be, urge him towards a goal which he by no
means desired.   This year or the next he may have been
encouraged to undertake a destiny which dismayed him.
Under the compulsion of the words "duty" or the
"King's wishes" he may even have assented or almost
assented; and it certainly seems clear from Sir Herbert
Taylor who it was that was always prepared to supply
the hints from Windsor.

Whatever Lyndhurst desired or Cumberland whispered, there was a feeling among many more ordinary
Conservatives that the Whigs' hold on power was slight.
There seemed to be signs that the electorate was turning
against them.   The Ministry were held to have no
longer a strong hold on the country, and one old Conservative hope budded and blossomed which should have
lain sterile till Doomsday.   There was possibly a chance
of an anti-popery cry in the country.   The weakest
point in the Ministry's position was held to be their
connection with O'Connell and the Irish Roman Catholics, and there were signs that this was being turned to
account.   The Irish Church Bill naturally excited Protestant susceptibilities, and when it was being debated
there were meetings in Exeter Hall, and *The Times* dealt
savagely with the Church of Rome along the usual lines.[1]
The Ministers were known to be uncomfortable at
Court, they were known to be weak in the House of
Lords, and it was held even by so cautious a man as
Aberdeen that they were in the power of Sir Robert
Peel to reprieve or to destroy when he liked.[2]   Aberdeen
and the wiser heads doubted Peel's power to replace the
Whigs with a lasting substitute, but from the tone of
the casual remarks of Londonderry and Cumberland and
Disraeli it does not seem that they were much troubled

---

[1] E.g. *Times*, July 7, 2nd leader; July 9, 2nd leader.   Meeting at Exeter
Hall, July 11. *Standard, passim.*
[2] Privately printed Aberdeen Corresp., p. 40 (Aberdeen to Lieven, May 8,
1833).

by such forebodings. It was less than four months since the Conservatives had failed to maintain a Ministry, but hopes will often grow up with the rank vigour of weeds in poor soil.[1]

On August 3rd there was another of the many meetings of Tory Peers in Apsley House. They now decided to take evidence against the principle of the Bill. The Duke objected, but Lyndhurst, so Greville was told, insisted upon it, and the Duke gave way.[2] A few days later Londonderry talked of the Duke's not liking to be over-ruled,[3] and it was probably at this meeting or at one held on the next day that the Duke, according to Disraeli, surrendered the lead of the party to Lyndhurst. There was hot debate that night in the House of Lords. Lord Lyndhurst made a great speech in favour of taking evidence. He attacked the Bill as a Whig Bill produced for Whig party purposes, by Commissioners who were Whigs and often something more. He attacked it as revoking Chartered Rights merely because they were inexpedient, and reminded their Lordships how many of them possessed their titles and seats in the Lords by letters patent which might be held to be inexpedient too. He spoke with great energy and eloquence, and wrestled with Brougham. Melbourne, said Disraeli, seemed quite wild and scared, and the Whigs were surprised and confounded. The Lords determined by a huge majority to take evidence on what counsel had said.[4]

Counsel's speeches and Lyndhurst's speech seemed to imply not the amendment of the Bill but its rejection, but the Lords had not voted for this; they had merely voted to hear evidence. Consequently they had not had the advantage of the votes of the older and simpler ultra-Tories, and they still retained the support of the moderate

---

[1] Maxwell's *Wellington*, II, 30, for some project in May 1835 of Buckingham, Cumberland and Londonderry of throwing out the Governmentt.

[2] Grev., III, 283.   [3] *Courts and Cabinets*, II, 196.

[4] Hansard, XXIX, 1346. *Lord Beaconsfield's Corresp. with his Sister*, p. 39 (Aug. 5, 1835).

Peers, such as Wharncliffe and Fitzgerald. But things looked ill for the measure and for the peace of the future. The division between Peel and the Lords was notorious. It was commented on by the *Morning Chronicle*, perhaps the main Whig paper,[1] which was itself preparing for a struggle with the Lords. Place was told that the Lords were going to throw out the Municipal Reform Bill, and joined others in making those preparations which they had used for a like crisis in 1832.[2] A crisis between Lords and Commons had seemed very possible since the reformation of Lord Melbourne's Ministry. Now perhaps it had come. Lord Melbourne started proceedings on the Municipal Corporation Bill by an earnest warning to their Lordships not to trifle with public opinion. Was it not possible that they were about to disregard or disbelieve in his advice ?[3]

Peel was preparing to leave London. He was disgusted and angry. It is probable that the hard work of his late Ministry had told on him, for towards the end of August he was under Doctor's orders to rest in the country. He managed to avoid the fish dinner which heads of parties or Ministries seem to have held at the end of each Session. He said he would stay up in town for the next debate on the Irish Corporation Bill, and that then he would go to his beloved Drayton. He was told that his going would be the signal for a general flight, and he said that he could not help it. He was told by Wharncliffe and Lord Fitzgerald what had happened at Apsley House on Monday, August the 3rd, and he believed that the ultra-Tory party had completely succeeded. He heard an immediate adjournment foretold, or a resignation of the Ministers, and he declared again, with firmness and italics, that he would not be made responsible for the acts of the Lords.[4] His mood was sulky and dangerous, justifiable and most unmanageable.

---

[1] E.g. *Morning Chronicle*, Aug. 3.
[2] Graham Wallas, *Life of Place*, 344.   [3] Hansard, XXIX, 1133.
[4] *Private Letters of Sir Robert Peel*, 153 ff.

From the 4th to the 9th the Lords were occupied in the preparing of evidence. The King was in high spirits, very discourteous to his Ministers, moved to many speeches on delicate topics at the dinners he attended, and moved on one occasion to take wine with Peel ten times. Disraeli was so excited or so full of secrets that he could hardly trust himself to write to his sister on politics. Londonderry had heard that though Peel disapproved of the Lords' course, the Duke now agreed that Lyndhurst's line was the right one.[1] Lyndhurst became indisposed owing to his great efforts, and Peel left town suddenly, without even telling the Duke of Wellington.[2]

§ 6

Yet Peel was strong even in absence, for there was one fatal weakness that spoiled the plans of all these adventurers. If they were to be strong, if they were to attempt anything, if they were ever to hope for a Conservative Ministry, they must maintain a united party. They must keep the alliance of the moderates, and above all they must keep the support of those who were in the House of Commons and would have to face the electorate. Peel had his allies among the peers, Aberdeen, Wharncliffe, Ellenborough and, in his own way, the Duke. For the moment the closest ally of all was Lord Fitzgerald, his old friend Vesey Fitzgerald who had lost the Clare election in 1828. In a memorandum among his papers Peel refers to his correspondence with Lord Fitzgerald for this crisis. Unfortunately there is but one-half of this correspondence among the Peel papers. For the letters he wrote to Lord Fitzgerald Peel presumed were in the hands of Fitzgerald's executors, and he had kept no copies. There is another misfortune, too, connected with this correspondence. Fitzgerald was an admirable man in many ways, he was a good friend to Peel, indeed for this year almost his

---

[1] *Courts and Cabinets*, II, 196 (Londonderry to Buckingham, Aug. 6, 1835).
[2] Maxwell, *Life of the Duke of Wellington*, Vol. II, 309.

agent in the House of Lords.   But he had two very bad
vices.   He often failed to date his letters, and at times
his hand is illegible.[1]

Apparently on Wednesday, August 6th, Fitzgerald
saw the Duke and Wharncliffe.   He did not conceal
from them Peel's feelings with respect to all that had
passed, particularly with respect to Lyndhurst, and the
Duke admitted that Lyndhurst had in his speech gone
too far against the principle of the Bill with reference to
what had passed with Peel and with the rest of the Conservative leaders.   The next Saturday the Lords brought
the evidence to an end, and on Monday there was a
meeting of above a hundred peers at Apsley House, at
which the Duke said that he was anxious for the Bill to
go into Committee, and Lyndhurst gave the outline of
his amendments.   The simple ultra-Tories, Mansfield,
Winchelsea and the like, wished to meet the Bill with a
direct negative, but Londonderry and Cumberland
pressed the need for union, and the meeting agreed to go
into Committee on the Bill on the next Wednesday.

It was not what Lyndhurst's earlier speech had implied,
and Fitzgerald thought he would be embarrassed in
proposing amendments after what he had said.   Indeed
Fitzgerald told Lyndhurst that Peel felt he had reason
to complain of that speech.   Lyndhurst was annoyed
and talked mysteriously.   He said he could not help
following that course and that he would explain it hereafter.   There was nothing left now, he felt, but compromise.   He had presumably then intended a course
which did not imply compromise, and he had failed.[2]

Lyndhurst's present policy, as explained by his allies,
implied no love for the Bill.   It was union that Londonderry and Cumberland had urged in their speeches,
union that was vastly important for purposes which they
and their dreams alone knew.   "If we had divided our
party, we were lost," was what Londonderry wrote to
Buckingham concerning this meeting.   But now, with

[1] Peel's Memo., Add. MSS. 40,323; 239.
[2] Add. MSS. 40,323; 292 (Fitzgerald, undated, "Monday").

their great majority, they had hopes of turning the Bill into a Conservative arrangement. They could not have taken the leap of total rejection, said Londonderry. Now if it were to be an entirely new Bill "the House of Commons will be those that reject it, not us." [1] The preparation of the amendments had been entrusted to Lyndhurst, and their outline had already been shown to be effective enough to content the majority of the Conservative Peers. Fitzgerald began to believe that when they learnt the extent of the changes, the Whigs would throw up the Bill, and that very probably they would throw up the Government too.

On August 11th Goulburn obtained the outline of Lyndhurst's amendments, and sent them to Peel. They were sufficiently extensive. Perhaps the most striking was the provision for Aldermen appointed for life and constituting a fourth of the Town Council, who were in the first place to be, if possible, appointed from the Councils already existing. Peel did not approve. He told Goulburn that the amendments went far beyond those discussed at his house earlier in the Session. He disapproved of the Aldermen's Clause and the retention of part of the existing Councils; he felt that Lyndhurst's speech had been directed against the principle of the Bill and excluded in logic all attempts at amendment. Some of the Government, so he thought, might be willing to take the opportunity to retire, in order to settle their differences with the King by causing him to be driven back a third time to their counsels. He saw no good in repeated attempts to dispossess the Government of office. The Conservative party could not govern the Country with the existing Parliament, and he held that it had no hopes from a dissolution. A dissolution might break down the private fortunes of the staid friends of good order, for elections, said Peel, were ten times more expensive to them than to the Radicals; another failure would be a mighty stride towards the destruction of what little balance there was left in the Government. So

---

[1] *Courts and Cabinets*, II, 198 (Londond. to Buckingham, Aug. 10, 1835).

Fitzgerald told Peel's late colleagues in the Lords that
Peel would assume no responsibility in forming a Government if the existing one were broken up by a course to
which he had not been a party, and which he did not
approve. Peel's refusal was not meant as a weapon but,
like the man who dropped a coal-scuttle on his wife, he
might find it none the less effective. It remained to be
seen whether sulky refusal or dash and rhetoric controlled
the event.

Like men who have strayed, rather than betrayed,
Peel's old colleagues were now anxious to shape their
course as nearly as they could to that of Peel. The Duke
of Newcastle intended to move the rejection of the Bill
on its going into Committee on Wednesday, the 12th,
and it was decided by a small Committee, formed of the
Lords who had been in Peel's Cabinet with the addition
of Fitzgerald, that the Duke should make a conciliatory
speech declaring that he was prepared to admit not only
the necessity of a general corporate Reform, but also the
principle of popular suffrage with the rate-payers as the
elective body, with due consideration for the rights of
property and vested interests. They decided to vote
directly against the Duke of Newcastle. All was not
comfortable. Lyndhurst did not see how he could vote
against Newcastle after his earlier speech, the Duke was
depressed and anxious, and Fitzgerald thought that they
would make a great hash of it in Committee, and that
when the Government knew to what extent it was proposed to amend the Bill they would throw it up if they
did no worse.[1] So the Bill went into Committee.

It went into Committee on August 12th and continued there till August 27th, when it was reported.
Lyndhurst produced his amendments in fine dashing
style and carried them through with crushing majorities.
Brougham squabbled and blustered, fighting Lyndhurst
with great ability and, often enough, producing scenes
in the House. When the Aldermen's Clause had been

---

[1] Add. MSS. 40,333; 334 (Goulb. to Peel, Aug. 11). Parker, II, 314
(Peel to Goulb.). Add. MSS. 40,323; 269 (Fitzgerald to Peel, Aug. 12).

produced, Greville met Howick and Duncannon open-
mouthed at the Lords' amendments, declaring that this
last, at least, could not be stomached. Howick spoke of
the "Lords being swept away like chaff" and of "the
serious times that were approaching."[1] Yet Cumberland, Buckingham and Londonderry were still unsatisfied. Lyndhurst would work the matter, said Londonderry, into a much higher key if he dared, but Wharncliffe
and Ellenborough played Peel's game, and they would
end in so modified a form that the Commons would take
the Bill as a first step. It might have been supposed
that such would be the natural desire of the men who had
troubled to amend it. But Londonderry continued:
and really he did not see any party willing to take the
Government. If Melbourne resigned, he doubted if
Peel would accept office and risk a dissolution. Nothing seemed likely to happen that year. Then he
mentioned to Buckingham a possibility not unlike something which had seemed probable to Disraeli a few days
before. If Melbourne retired and Peel refused, why
should not Lyndhurst accept the call of the King and
party? A dissolution would be the first step, and after
that the young Conservatives, Follett and Praed, might
lead the House of Commons, "Peel supporting, of
course, the arrangement." "Of course" must represent
here rather necessity than likelihood.[2]

But what would the Government do? That was the
question to be speculated upon, whispered over, rumoured
about, with great and growing force, while the Bill
suffered in Committee. Fitzgerald's own colleagues
would not share his fears of the Government's throwing
up both Bill and office, and grew half impatient when he
stated them.[3] As the Committee went on his appre-

[1] Grev., III, 290 (under Aug. 19, 1835).

[2] *Courts and Cabinets*, II, 199. (N.B.—In this letter, as in others in this
volume, the names are eviscerated till they are only an initial and a series of
stars. They must therefore be to a certain extent a matter for speculation.)
Beaconsfield's Corresp. with his Sister, p. 40 (Aug. 12, 1835).

[3] Add. MSS. 40,323; 278 (Fitzgerald to Peel, with postmark Aug. 13), 286
(Fitzgerald to Peel, undated, "Friday").

hensions wore off a little. On the 15th and 19th he
believed there was no chance of their resigning, and
Wharncliffe and Ellenborough, who were in some sort
of communication with Melbourne and Lansdowne,
believed that they would accept the Bill.[1] Bonham and
others in the Commons who were in a position to collect
information, continued to believe that the Government
would throw up the Bill. It was said that the Radicals
would be firm, there continued to be rumours of the
Government going out. On August 20th Disraeli
told his sister that he thought the Government would
retire over the Appropriation Clause to the Tithe Bill.[2]

For the Irish Tithe Bill had passed the House of
Commons, and on the 20th of August started its career
in the Lords. They allowed it to go into Committee
for the sake, as Londonderry said, of the famishing
clergy, and there they amended it and expunged the
Clause about Appropriation, so that Melbourne threw
it up on the 24th. The clergy would get no tithes, and
as things stood would probably have to pay the money
that had already been lent to them. In fact they were
still famishing.[3]

In the House of Commons attendance was thin, and
Conservatives might say it was reduced to its dregs, for
O'Connell and Hume persisted, while others went about
their business. On August 21st there was a demon-
stration by Hume and O'Connell against passing any
more supplies, in order that they might not relinquish
their Constitutional control. Fitzgerald thought that
this had shaken the Government.[4] The town was full
of rumours, many of them about Peel and his difference
of opinion with the Lords. The Government were
known to be collecting their men. The time drew near
for the consideration of the Bill in the Commons, and still

[1] 40,323; 288 (Fitzgerald, with postmark Aug. 15).
[2] Add. MSS. 40,323; 265. 40,421; 18 ff. *Beaconsfield's Corresp. with his
Sister*, p. 42 (Aug. 20, 1835).
[2] *Courts and Cabinets*, II, 204 (Lond. to Buck., dated Aug. 28, which must
be wrong). Hansard, XXX, 715, 872.
[4] Hansard, XXX, 822. Add. MSS. 40,312; 248. 40,323; 300.

no one knew what the Government intended to do, or what they could do in the Commons.

The leaders of the Lords began to consider the desirability of getting their friends to attend in the Commons for the divisions which were imminent, and the Duke applied not to Peel but to the leaders who were in or about London, to Goulburn and Hardinge.   On August 25th he wrote to Hardinge in terms which showed the dangerous division of Conservative councils.   His practice, he said, had for many years been never to interfere, even with an opinion unless it were asked, on matters in the Commons.   Yet matters were becoming critical. The Duke understood that the Ministers intended to propose a Bill to suspend for a year the repayment of the million pounds which had been lent to the Irish clergy. He could not tell what they would do with the English Corporation Bill.   He did not wish, it seems, to prevent his friends from taking any course that they might think proper.   He understood that Sir Robert Peel disapproved of the course which the Lords had taken upon the Corporation Bill.   He should be very sorry if anyone should say a word in approbation of that course contrary to Peel's opinion.   But he thought that his friends in the Commons should support the Government if they tried to suspend the repayment of the million or to pass the Corporation Bill, and should give the Ministers an interest in preserving a good understanding between Lords and Commons.[1]

The letter was sent on to Peel, and Goulburn also wrote to him.   He was still at Drayton, and still angry. He had been ill used, and the strength and pertinacity of his fits of sulkiness were one of the most decisive features in the politics of his time.   On August 23rd Croker wrote to him to regret that he had seemed to have abandoned the field while his feeble followers fought on their miserable stumps about questions of more importance than had occurred since the reign of James II.

[1] Add. MSS. 40,410; 114 (Duke to Hardinge, Aug. 26, 1835).   Add. MSS. 40,323; 305.

Peel answered on August 26th that he was out of town partly under doctor's orders and partly out of sheer mental fatigue after his Ministry, and partly because he disagreed with the course taken on the Municipal Bill. He would not be responsible for that course. Had he stayed on in London he would have been perpetually asked to consider a policy in the Lords to which he was not an assenting party. He thought it better to stay away. Indeed, so strong was his reiterated opinion against Lyndhurst's amendments that he found himself unwilling to discuss them. He told Goulburn in one of his letters not to quote him, and he refused to give him an opinion as to what should be done when the matter came to the Commons.

He may have assumed this attitude to avoid the exhibition of schism, or perhaps, and more probably, to avoid all chance of responsibility for what might be done. To a tired man under provocation all may perhaps be excused. But excuses modify condemnations, they do not alter results, and the attitude was unfortunate. He let the Lords know too little of his feelings on the matter, and he should not have kept away from London during the crisis. Fitzgerald was admirable at communicating Peel's views, yet his admonitions usually arrived after the Lords had committed themselves. Peel should have kept the link closer. On the whole it does seem likely that Peel could in some way have exerted a more modifying effect on their counsels, even though they had already diverged from his desires; while his communications with the Duke of Wellington seem to have been incomplete and inconsiderate. Peel may have been right, he may be certainly pardoned. Still if ever the reins are dropped they may have to be picked up and pulled with a jerk.

The matter in dispute was not only, not mainly, the various clauses of the English Municipal Corporations Bill. They were very important, no doubt, and fit subject for earnest consideration and passionate dispute. But the House of Lords was stopping the career of other Bills as well, as for instance the Irish Tithe Bill, so mangled as to be fit only for refuse.   There was a problem in hand well worthy of even greater passion, even longer dispute, and that was the power of the House of Lords itself, its right, as Goulburn said, to act as an independent branch of the legislature.   Peel did not deny that right; he only feared, as he said, that it would be admitted, and an antagonist right contended for, and probably enforced, on the part of the House of Commons.

Collision between the two Houses, said Peel to Croker, was already inevitable.   It was inevitable on a great principle on the Irish Church Bill, it was inevitable on the Irish Municipal Bill.   Collision on the Irish Church Bill, from the importance of the principle and of the practical consequences involved, presented the best of battle-grounds.   It saved the honour of the Lords, asserted their independence, and was ever a point upon which the Conservative party in the Commons was the strongest, most united and most in harmony with Lord Stanley and his few adherents.   But the present mode of dealing with the English Municipal Bill took no count of the strength of the party in the Commons, or of their relations with Stanley and his friends.   So a course other than what Peel thought wise had been taken. Did he personally complain of it?   No.   Men very often do not complain personally of courses whereof they are prepared at some length to point out the folly.   But he was not, and this he was ready to repeat a good many times, he was not going to be made responsible for it. And he remained in personal felicity and political nullity at Drayton, while the half of his party that was in the Lords seemed to swim off into splendid heights like a gay but captive balloon whose rope has been broken, and which haply may sail quite away.[1]

On August 22nd Goulburn had told Peel that it was very desirable to know what course Peel advised taking

---

[1] Add. MSS. 40,333; 336 (Goulburn to Peel, Aug. 22).   Parker, II, 315 (Peel to Goulburn, Aug. 23).   Add. MSS. 40,321, 158 (Croker, Aug. 23). Croker, II, 280 (Peel to Croker, Aug. 26).

in the Commons with respect to the English Corporation Bill, and it was on August 23rd apparently that Peel had discovered his difficulty in giving any opinion at all. On August 26th Goulburn wrote to Peel in some doubt. Unless they gave notice it would be extremely difficult to assemble a decent number of their friends, and if they were merely to betray differences between their party in the two Houses they had better take no part whatever. Yet it was disagreeable to take no part whatever on a matter which might be of extreme importance. Peel would judge what was best to be done. Those who were in the Commons had a perfect right to object to some of the Lords' amendments; the Lords had an equal right to adhere to them or to listen to argument against them. It would be best to try to understand each other. Acting independently would certainly lead to more misunderstandings and wider separations which were above all to be deprecated, and, said Goulburn, there was a general desire among Conservatives that Peel should come up.[1]

The last letter to be found from Peel before the debate in the Commons is that to Croker on August 26th. His motives and motions have been doubtful before, but now they become almost unknown. It is as when the gauze curtain, sometimes used in theatres to make actions at the back of the stage seem dim and mysterious, has been changed to an opaque one, to prepare for a transformation scene. It can however be known what facts reached Peel from the letters he received. It was still doubtful what the Government would do. Other Bills besides the Municipal Bill and the Irish Tithe Bill had been destroyed by the Lords, and it was thought that the Government were angry. It was known that the Government intended to pass a Bill, actually proposed on August 29th, to suspend for the year the payment of the money which had been lent to the Irish Clergy. On August 28th, when the Corporation Bill was brought down to the Commons and ordered to be reprinted with the Lords' amendments, Hume and O'Connell used strong

[1] Add. MSS. 40,333; 340 (Goulb. to Peel, Aug. 26, 1835).

words against the other House, and the fact was duly
reported to Peel.¹   The Government were known to be
gathering men, but for what purpose?   To throw out
the Bill or to face the Radicals?   The Bill was to be
considered on Monday, August 31st, and on that day the
Government were to have a great meeting of their followers.   There was little talk now of their resigning, but
as for their passing the Municipal Bill, perhaps they
would and perhaps they would not, or perhaps they could
and perhaps they could not—the best opinion seems to
have been that they were still undecided.   And all these
facts and speculations were sent by various hands to the
absent leader of the Conservative party.²

With them came one letter which does show some
light on Peel's intentions.   It is from Goulburn, and its
probable date is the 28th August.³   It is in answer to a
note from Peel which brought Goulburn to town immediately.   In it Goulburn speaks of various things, the
day on which the Lords' amendments would be discussed in the Commons, the doubt as to the intentions of
the Government, the number of men the Conservatives
would probably have in the Commons, the general
expectation and desire that Peel should be there, the
possible course of events.   At the end he says that he
will call on Monday at Peel's house in London in the
hopes of seeing him.   There is a rustle and shiver from
behind the curtain; there was at the least a likely chance
of Peel's coming up.

In London the Lords were in no mood for compromise.   On Sunday, the 29th, there was a meeting of
about sixty Peers at Apsley House to decide what to do
in case of collision, and to impress them with the need of
not going out of town.   The Duke of Wellington was
cautious, but there was a spirit of courage and obstinacy
in the meeting, proper to ancient chivalry if not to
modern times.   The Duke of Cumberland spoke strongly

¹ Hansard, XXX, 1093.
² Add. MSS. 40,314; 91 ff.   40,323; 310, 315, 240.   40,421.
³ *Ibid.*, 40,332; 342 (Goulburn to Peel, "Friday evening").

against concession and was loudly cheered.   There was
cheering again when it was said in another speech that
the Lords' Amendment on the Town Clerks was important.   The Duke of Wellington deprecated discussion,
but "rather let out that he should surrender no principle," and there was loud cheering.   The Duke, it
seems, wished to wait till the Government had disclosed
itself, he would not go into conference until he knew
their ultimatum.[1]   He had wandered far into dangerous
regions, and he did not know their danger.   His rewards
had already been too great, the sinews of his heart were
too hard and his eye was too clear, to let him be deceived
by any passing dream of a Conservative Ministry.   It is
unlikely that he was journalist enough to have a comprehensive plan of stopping "the movement."   He had
desired, with success, that the Bill should go into Committee, and why should he go back from a position
he had assumed, from amendments to which he had
assented?   Not, certainly, because the amendments
should not have been imposed by the House of Lords.
The Duke seemed set, and how if the Government were
set also?

§ 7

Monday came, and with it the climax of the crisis.
At one o'clock there was a meeting, at the Foreign Office,
of the various supporters of the Government.[2]   There
were, says Greville, between two and three hundred
present.   Lord John Russell told them what amendments he would accept, or modify, and what he must
refuse.   He was too conciliatory for Hume, who according to Greville made a violent speech deprecating all
concessions, while O'Connell was moderate, recommending compromise.   The difference is important, effective
and very significant.   It is the old division.   At this
time Hume was a man of principle and O'Connell a man
of government.   To Hume, Grote and Roebuck it was
important above all things that the Peers should not

[1] Add. MSS. 40,323; 250 (Fitzgerald, undated).   [2] Grev., III, 303.

"tread on the rights of millions," that a body of irresponsible persons should not oppose the just rights of the people and the course of Reform.   O'Connell was not naturally moderate; he had no peculiar affection for the House of Lords.   Their politics he detested, his Reforms they blocked, and he would willingly have urged their drastic amendment with what eloquence he might.   But there was something more important involved.   There was the life of the Ministry, which meant to him the good administration of Ireland.   O'Connell felt that he stood well with the Government.   He felt that he might possibly join it, if it continued in power.   Numerous and various were the benefits which he expected it to effect for Ireland.[1]   He thought that opinion was ripening against the Lords, but it was not likely that he would risk such good things as the Government might bring, by opposing what might be necessary to its existence, its own counsels of moderation; and so John Russell had the advantage of O'Connell's support at his meeting.

Later in that day the House of Commons met to consider the Lords' amendments and the debate was opened by Lord John Russell.   He was temperate and conciliatory, although he mentioned the unfortunately irritating proceedings with which the Lords had prefaced their arrangements.   More than once he showed himself ready not to stand rigidly to what he had said when the Bill was discussed before, while he conceded an amendment which he thought inconvenient.   He ended with a peroration about reforming in a spirit of peace, without disturbing the industry of the people or curtailing the constitutional powers of either branch of the legislature. He was as conciliatory as he might be, yet there was still a broad gap to be bridged.   He radically altered the Lords' clause about Aldermen, he altered some and he rejected others of the Lords' amendments.   He had brought the torch of compromise as far as he could, but it might be dropped there and left to smoulder out in the muck of ennobled obstinacy and party contention.

[1] *Corresp. of D. O'Connell*, II, 33 (Sept. 4, 1835).

It was picked up and carried on by the next speaker. The curtain has lifted; it was Sir Robert Peel.

He had arrived suddenly and unexpectedly in London and he intervened in the course of events with the abruptness of an act of God rather than with the consideration and caution of a party leader. Goulburn may have expected him but not so Hardinge, who was also an intimate, nor apparently the Duke of Wellington. From his letters beforehand it would have seemed that he had not meant to interfere. If he had so intended, it seems strange that he should have been even averse from recommending to Goulburn what they should do in the Commons. The actions of a brooding man are often as surprising and incomprehensible as the sudden gusts of wind on a day of long menacing calms; perhaps, revolving matters in his mind, he had decided that he could not in duty be absent from the debate. Or perhaps there had been something to press the trigger. From a reply to a letter from him at the time, and from part of his speech, it would seem that he wished to settle the matter, to obviate agitation during the coming months of recess.[1] He said in his speech that he had come to aid a settlement and to resist, if need be, any amendment or resolution interfering with the honour and independent character of the House of Lords. He defended the Lords for a time from some of the attacks upon them and then, "as everybody said (some with rage and others with joy)," writes Greville, "threw the Lords over." For he abandoned the Aldermen's clause and cricitized it fully, and though there were some amendments which he supported, there were others in which he disagreed with the Lords or supported Lord John. He ended with another mention of the perfect independence of the House of Lords, adding his hope that he might be instrumental in procuring an amicable settlement. If this were so he would not regret his presence there that night. Yet the word amicable had not been made the more obedient by his method of coming.

[1] Add. MSS. 40,421; 42, 44.

There was cheering during his speech, but from the wrong side of the House. Greville, who was a visitor in the House at the time, met a sulky Tory member under the Gallery. He asked him why they did not cheer Peel, and was told that the Whigs were cheering him enough already. That night, in the House and in the Travellers' Club, Greville listened to the grumbling of angry Tories. Even Lord Harrowby, who was a moderate, complained that he had heard that Peel had abandoned the Aldermen. "I have a great affection," said he, "for the Aldermen." The danger was that the friendship formed by Lyndhurst for his Aldermen would be inextinguishable.[1]

The battle was not yet over. Next day Londonderry told Buckingham that he had heard from Cumberland that Lyndhurst was firm and that so would be His Royal Highness, while the Duke was in a dilemma between inclinations and friends.[2] On Thursday the 3rd they would meet to decide. Meanwhile Lord John Russell put through the House of Commons his amendment to the Bill as it now stood, and they passed the Bill for the remission for the million paid to the Irish clergy. The Tithe Bill would have to wait till next year, as would the Irish Municipal Reform Bill, which the Government had started but never sent up to the Lords.

On September 3rd the Lords met at Apsley House to decide on the amendments made by the Commons to their amendments in the Corporation Bill, and perhaps to decide more. "I never was more nervous," wrote Wharncliffe to Peel, "than upon going into the room at the Duke of Wellington's this morning where our Peers were assembled." "I could not help feeling," he said, "that the very existence of the party who have hitherto voted together in resistance to Revolution was at stake." There was reason for fear.

At first, says Fitzgerald, the discussion wore a very angry appearance. The Duke spoke first, not decisively,

[1] Hansard, XXX, 1131. Grev., III, 303 ff. (Sept. 1, 1835).
[2] *Courts and Cabinets*, II, 206 (Sept. 1).

expressing his wish to withhold his advice and even his opinion, until after he had heard the sentiments of the Peers. The Duke was in a dilemma. He hesitated between amendments in which he believed, a policy for the House of Lords in which he saw no impropriety, and a party and party leader in the Commons in whom he had invested his trust. He was followed by De Grey, who recommended moderate courses and spoke of the Conservative party's prospects in both Houses if a schism took place.

Then came the charge of the reactionaries, a wedge of impossible opinion. De Grey was followed by Cumberland, Mansfield and Falmouth. Then, after Wharncliffe and other moderates had spoken, there seems to have come the speech which of all others that evening was psychologically the most interesting. Lord Lyndhurst, being loudly called for, went into a review of his whole conduct, stating with truth that he was only the agent of the Peers generally, and seeming to Fitzgerald rather to lay on others the responsibility for the measures he had pursued. He could not, said he, under any circumstances stultify or degrade himself by taking any part in offering the amendments of the House of Commons or in retracting his own. At first he said he should be content to withdraw on such a question, but, on receiving encouragement from others, he rather indicated that he looked for support to the view he had taken. His arguments turned on the Aldermen's clause.

Encouragement from others had been the key to Lyndhurst's position. The man was only an eminent lawyer, twice rewarded already by being Lord Chancellor, and there was a third time to come. He asked no more. The day after this, with perfect truth and perfect sincerity, he told the House of Lords that he asked no more. "My ambition has been gratified. I have no wishes unfulfilled." He had been asked by Lords, with whom he had acted for years, to lead the opposition to the Municipal Bill, and he had led it. The Duke and his old colleagues had asked him to prepare the amendments

to the Bill, and he had prepared them.   Perhaps someone else had asked him earlier on to throw out the Bill,
for he had overruled the Duke and had gone as far as
he could to throw it out.   Perhaps someone at some
time had or would ask much more of him, and he would
say or try to say that he was merely a lawyer and not
suited to such adventures, and he would be right.   He
had acted no doubt as a lawyer who disliked this revolutionary Bill, and for the rest he had done what he was
asked to do, and in a moment he was to do what he was
asked to do again.

For about this time in the meeting at Apsley House
came the speech which seems to have decided the matter,
not with Lyndhurst, but with stronger machinery.   It
was by Lord Harrowby, the moderate.   He spoke at
length, beautifully, as it seemed to Fitzgerald, and with
great effect, urging an accommodation with the House
of Commons.   He would fight, he seems to have said,
the battle of the Houses to a finish, but on more tenable
grounds, with more public support, for the sake of some
higher principle and with the hope of more auxiliaries
in the House of Commons.   After Harrowby, probably,
Lord Abinger spoke, hesitatingly; and then, like a
thunder-cloud drifting away, muttering but undelivered,
the great Duke relented.   He spoke, greatly affected—
or so thought Fitzgerald—admitting all their difficulties.
He had taken, he seems to have said, so active a part
respecting the Aldermen's clause, which was the critical
clause, that he would not retract his opinion; yet the
wisest and most politic course for the House to take would
be to accede to the amendment by the House of
Commons.   There was no other course, said he, which
would not involve the Lords in greater difficulties.   The
battle was won; many Lords wished to act on his advice.
The Duke had moved at last, and the rest of the flock
crowded after him, bleating, into the pen and to safety.[1]

They decided to adopt the Commons' suggestions on

[1] Add. MSS. 40,421; 16 and 21 (Wharncliffe, presumably Sept. 3 and 5);
40,312; 250, 254, 256. 40,323; 318 (Fitzgerald to Peel, Sept. 3) and 282.

the Aldermen's clause, but to insist on some of their amendments, and to amend some of the others that came from the Commons. Lord Lyndhurst was good enough to consent to abandon his earliest intention of absenting himself from the House, and to propose the concessions of the Lords. This, thought Aberdeen, would incalculably increase the dignity and popularity of their course. All seemed fair for compromise. The evil spirit had gone out of the Lords. For the Duke of Cumberland had left town, and Falmouth and Mansfield promised to do no mischief. On September 4th Lyndhurst proposed the Lords' amendments and concessions, save that he had a scruple about proposing their concession on the Aldermen's clause which, he declared in his speech, he must leave to others.[1] Then, after the Lords had given formal reasons for dissenting in some points from the Commons, Lord John Russell proposed to the Commons that the Bill be accepted as it now stood, not as approving it all, but in order that the Reform might be secured, and in the hopes of altering some points in it in the future, when they might seem less important to their Lordships. Hume spoke amicably of the Government, but in favour of a Reform of the Lords, and others spoke in favour of that, more wildly. The Bill was passed, on September 10th the Parliament was prorogued, and a long crisis was over.

§ 8

It may form an apt parallel with the Reform Bill, for they are like enough to expose their differences. In each case there was an important measure in danger, each case raised the question of the powers of the House of Lords. Only in 1835 the people did not care. "There is something inconceivable, a sort of political absurdity," said Greville, "in the notion of a country like this being on the eve of a convulsion, when it is tranquil, prosperous and without any grievance." He was right. It was inconceivable, but unfortunately in politics absurdities

[1] Hansard, XXX, 1340.

x

sometimes move the fears and passions of men, and inconceivable things are not seldom conceived. Even Greville went on to attribute results more dangerous than was likely to be possible from the rage of parties. Even Peel, so said Croker in the September of 1835, was at last thoroughly "I will not say frightened—but convinced that the Revolution is inevitable, and talks of resistance."[1] Men might talk and men might tremble, but still it seems true that the people did not care. When, in this crisis, Francis Place began to elaborate such machinery as he had used in the Reform Bill crisis, he started a paper called "The Municipal Reformer," but it failed from lack of support and lack of interest.[2] The failure to arouse any excitement against the Lords encouraged Disraeli. Goulburn grew surprised how little sensation had been created by the Corporation Bill.[3] Mrs. Partington was active and efficient and, behold a wonder, the Atlantic was retreating.

For the position was no longer suitable for a contest between the two Houses. Increased prosperity, or distrust of the Whigs, or dislike of O'Connell, or reaction from the unusual preponderance of one party, had altered the state of opinion in England. Excitement had died. There was now no great difference in numbers between the two parties in the House of Commons. The Government did not wish to push matters to extremities. Even the Radicals, even Joseph Hume, had become a little unwilling to embarrass Ministers, and Place growled and snarled at the puling people who talked of revolution and feared to oppose the Government.[4] The times were propitious for Mrs. Partington. She might splash and flourish with her mop in security; for, as is not unusual on the sea shore, the tide was going down.

Yet the English Municipal Bill had not proved the independence of the House of Lords. Both Whigs and Tories had asserted that doctrine. In the last debates

---

[1] Croker, II, 282.   [2] Graham Wallas' *Life of Place*, p. 343.
[3] Add. MSS. 40,333; 336 (Aug. 22).
[4] Graham Wallas' *Life of Place*, p. 345.

on the Municipal Bill Lord John had spoken of not curtailing the constitutional powers bestowed on either branch of the legislature. This independence had already become one of the chief articles of the Tory Creed, and Peel himself was very ready to fight for it. But common consent and eloquent asseveration are not good evidence of reality. Men have fought, and not seldom have died, for a meaningless motto. The Lords had not done what they wished. They had been forced to pass a Bill which, had they been left to themselves, they probably would not have passed. They had not even kept the amendments that they had made in it. The moral of the crisis was this. The Lords were forced to be dependent on the views of the Conservative party in the House of Commons, and the Conservative party in that House were ultimately dependent on the views of the people.

So the Lords were already dependent on the views of the people. The change that the Radicals desired had already, in part, taken place. A constitution may be changed by abrupt and violent methods; you can, for instance, take off a King's head and blot out the offending clauses with the blood of the deed. Such methods are usually a sad waste both of time and of temper, and they are, besides, uncertain in action. It is better, if possible, that the constitution be naturally and logically changed by the realities far behind its portico. Only such a method may be long and dreary and cloaked in the folds of a thousand unknowing deceits; and such changes also may be incomplete.

CHAPTER VII

1836—THE LORDS' INDEPENDENCE

In 1835 there had been no open change in the constitution. Indeed it can hardly be said that there had been a secret one. His Majesty had not lost his sting nor had the House of Lords been swallowed up in a victory for the Commons over the Municipal Bill. Yet though the Lords had forfeited, in 1835, no power that they really possessed, and had paid no calculable penalty for their exuberance, they had certainly managed to excite the most active feelings of hostility among their enemies. Hume spoke of raising the question of House of Lords' Reform next year, and after the session O'Connell toured England and Scotland in a pilgrimage of crusade against them, for his desire to retain the Ministry did not necessarily stop him from attempting to rouse the people. Nor did it make him gentle with his adversaries, and he called the Duke of Wellington a stunted corporal and took the opportunity of saying that Sir Robert Peel was as full of political and religious cant as any canter that ever canted in this canting world.

For Peel had been canting lately to some effect. On September 5th, just after his successful raid on London and the Lords' Amendments, he had made a speech at a dinner at Tamworth, ransacking all History and Politics to prove the danger and tyranny of single-Chamber democratic government. The speech was unjust to the Radicals, who did not desire a single Chamber but pursued, as have so many others, that phantom chameleon, a reformed House of Lords. But the speech helped to dissipate the legend of an illicit friendship between Peel and the Ministry, and was a fair statement of his own ideas. He was really no Liberal, but was as ready, in spirit, to defend as to restrain.[1]

But, Liberal or not, Peel had his difficulties when he confronted the situation at the end of 1835. Without

[1] For Peel's speech see *The Times*, Sept. 5, 1835.

doubt his course on the Municipal Bill had strained his
relations with some of the Conservatives. Rumour
exaggerated the position, but certainly Peel's correspondence with the Duke had dropped to nothing since
he had determined that concert between them would be
his chief satisfaction in opposition. However, the
estrangement did not last long. Characteristically it was
the Duke who made the first advance. He took the
opportunity to write to Peel in November on the subject
of the election of an Irish Representative Peer for the
House of Lords, and got a kind answer which pleased
him. Communications were resumed, and when they
next met the Duke found "as usual" that their views were
the same. Later on in 1836 Arbuthnot laboured, with
the assistance of Hardinge, at his accustomed task of
reconciling his two principals, but by then the reconciliation, if such should be the word, had been already effected.
Certainly it was not Peel's most difficult duty to keep in
with the Duke of Wellington.[1]

Unfortunately for Peel he had not only a companion
in the leadership, he had a greater and more fatal difficulty,
a party to lead. It was a party with which its chief
organizer, Lord Granville Somerset, was not altogether
contented. Corn and currency, fools and farmers, were
again causing trouble. At the end of December 1835,
Granville Somerset told Goulburn of the great disapprobation and dismay with which he had been
regarding the proceedings of a body called the Central
Agricultural Association, especially as regarding the
currency question. He detected among its leaders an
intention to make it a stepping-stone for their future
popularity among the farmers, and a latent hope of
causing a split among the Conservatives. Chandos was
trying to allay the mischief, but the admission of Thomas
Attwood to their councils, and the speeches of Lord

[1] Add. MSS. 40,410; 117 (Duke to Peel, Nov. 11, 1835); 40,314; 108.
Privately printed Aberdeen Corresp., 1832–44, p. 55 (Duke of Aberdeen,
Jan. 18, 1836. Narrative by Duke of reconciliation). Parker's Peel, 319 ff.
Add. MSS. 40,314; 123 ff. 40,341; 1.

Stanhope, showed Somerset how far gone they were in Agricultural Radicalism.[1]

His anxiety was natural, and there was something ominous in the way men could be led astray by their own private view of the needs of agriculture. The agricultural interest was the strength and bastion of the Conservative party, but it was not inspired by pure Conservative feeling. It remained an interest, after all. No doubt agriculture was largely represented by Conservative men; perhaps its pursuit led to Conservative feelings, but it was also agricultural. Successful appeals could be made to it by men who were not Conservatives, such as Cayley of the Agricultural Association, and issues could be raised which would throw Peel into contact with what Whips called "fanatick Agriculturists." The Conservative party represented both a political principle and also the life and livelihood of its supporters; and while principle may inconvenience life, or even at times usefully direct it, life may annihilate principle. So it was significant that enthusiasm for an interest seemed to suggest to these men courses, companions and beliefs repugnant to party principles, and Granville Somerset found reason to accuse them of Agricultural Radicalism.

Equally significant with the cause of these troubles in the party was the cure that Granville Somerset suggested. He asked that pains should be taken for concert with their own Agriculturists before the Session began. On this, and on the Church question, "members would not be curbed unless it is by previous concert." Men might be made tolerably obedient to Peel's wishes if he would give an idea of them beforehand, and demonstrate that he meant to continue leader. It was, said Lord Granville, "necessary for our leader to give us good council and show an interest in us," or else they might run wild. The machinery of party was to restrain the particularities of partisans. Peel was to control or direct by taking the trouble to lead.

One of the possible duties of party leadership is the

[1] Add. MSS. 40,332; 346 (Granville Somerset to Goulburn, Dec. 26, 1835).

substitution of exciting topics for embarrassing ones, and the question immediately ahead was whether or no to move an amendment to the Address.   The party was in a high state of excitement, partly, said Goulburn, owing to the success of the Northamptonshire election, partly because they had been stirred by the recent defeats of the Conservatives in the elections to the new Municipal Corporations.   They wanted to fight, and the question was whether they should be provided with a battle-field. It was a question that earned considerable thought.   Peel produced a memorandum upon it, which, said Goulburn without intended sarcasm, included all arguments for and against an amendment except the effect which its moving would have upon the attendance and co-operation of their friends in the House of Commons.   An interesting selection of subjects had been suggested.   One suggestion was an amendment on Protestantism.   Before 1828 Protestantism had been the mainstay of the Tory party, and with strange pertinacity its fires still smouldered and spluttered in the people's hearts.   Their Irish legislation and their dependence on O'Connell were likely to be the weak points in the Ministry's defence, and with commendable ability and regrettable violence *The Times* and many others had seized on this point and were prepared to use it for what it was worth.   Another possibility was an amendment about the Church, but in so far as Peel approved of having an amendment at all he leaned towards one on the privileges and authority of the House of Lords. Even from this he shrank, but his choice is important. It combines with other statements by Peel and his colleagues to prove that at the beginning of 1836 one subject seemed to dominate the political situation and the destiny and the duty of the Conservatives, and that was the problem of the integrity of the House of Lords. It remained to be seen what effect that issue would have in helping to found a living, permanent and unanimous Conservatism.[1]

[1] Add. MSS. 40,333; 352 (Goulburn to Peel, Dec. 31, 1835).   Parker, II, 318 (Peel to Goulburn, Jan. 3, 1836).   Croker, II, 301 (Peel to Croker,

§ 2

Before the new Session started there was much business
and bustle among the Conservatives, meetings at Drayton,
regrets at the success of the Radicals in the municipalities,
speculations as to whether Stanley was not negotiating
with the Whigs, and much other rumour, conference
and conversation. The Duke stayed at Drayton and
found Peel wonderfully approachable; disposed, as he
said, to act more rationally than he had ever known him
to be before. "I," said the Duke, "conducted myself
towards him as I always have done; with unaffected good
temper and cordiality."[1]   That the Duke had always been
unaffected does not need his own confident assertion, and
in spite of this it may be wondered whether his cordiality
may not at times have been as strange as was always his
use of semicolons. But whatever was decided at Drayton, the language of the Speech from the Throne, by
appearing to pledge the House to reform Irish municipalities on specific principles, seemed to demand an amendment to the Address, and Peel in the Commons and the
Duke in the Lords concurrently moved one. To the
surprise of many, Stanley made a Conservative speech,
while to the surprise of the Conservatives Peel was beaten
in the House of Commons by the majority of 41.

This caused bitter disappointment, for, according to
Disraeli, Conservatives had thought that since their
resignation in 1834, they had gained enough in isolated
elections to put them into a majority, and that O'Connell
had been fatally damaged by an election scandal.[2]   But
the Ministry seemed as strong as ever. Men's hopes had
proved false, mere symptoms of the facile expectations to
which the party was liable, and Parliament settled down
to the real work and the real problems of the Session.

These problems were to centre round the troubles in

Jan. 12, 1836).   Privately printed Aberdeen Corresp., pp. 49, 51 (to Princess
Lieven, Sept. 8, Oct. 22).
    [1] Maxwell, *Life of Wellington*, II, 310.
    [2] Monypenny, *Life of Disraeli*, I, p. 327 (written Sept. 1836, quoted above,
resp. 1835).

Ireland.   First of all there was an important debate on
the question of the Orange Society, which had surprisingly large ramifications both in Ireland and England
and other parts of the Empire.   Various Tory Peers were
implicated, notably the Duke of Cumberland, who was
Grand Master.   The Society was attacked, John Russell
made a much-admired speech, and the Society was dissolved.   Then the time approached for the two great
contested Irish measures, the Irish Municipal Bill and
the old miserable problem of the Irish Tithes.   The Irish
Municipal Bill was taken first, while the Ministry, as
Disraeli said, propitiously postponed the Irish Tithe Bill.

   The Irish Municipal Bill was then to be in the forefront
of Parliamentary controversy, and it remained to be seen
whether it too, like the English Municipal Bill, would
alienate Peel from his party, and anger the House of
Lords.   Luckily Peel was prepared to take a severe view
of what was likely to be the behaviour of freely elected
Irish Corporations, and early in February he and his
colleagues in the Commons decided on a policy in the
matter which was agreeable to all but extreme ultra-
Tories.   They would permit the present Irish Corporations to be destroyed, admitting their corruption, and
then they would propose that Irish towns should be
governed without any Corporations at all.   Thus they
would prevent Irish Corporations from being merely
transferred as tools from the old Protestant faction to the
Roman Catholic Repealers.   O'Connell had said that
new Corporations would be normal schools of agitation,
and the phrase put the Conservatives' point, and very
often garnished their speeches.

   This policy seemed to form a good basis for party
action, and it was a hopeful sign that both Stanley and
Graham, largely through Graham's mediation, assented
to it.   They were getting into step.   Peel noticed strong
signs of willingness on their part to act with the Conservatives, and after an interview with Graham he wrote to
the Duke that he believed that the only impediment to
a good understanding with them was the Duke of

Cumberland and the Orange system. The Duke re-joined eagerly, agreeing with everything. He agreed about the danger of the King attempting another Con-servative Ministry, which Graham had deplored to Peel, and he launched out into a condemnation of the Duke of Cumberland which gives an impression of accumulated violence reminiscent of a double-shotted broadside. There was no one, he said, who felt more than he did the inconvenience of the Duke of Cumberland. He felt it "every day, and all day." Cumberland's whole busi-ness, he said, was to pass the time. His amusement was mischief, preparing for it, hearing parties about each other, and talking of it afterwards. But the Duke could never discover that he felt any real interest in any ques-tion, or entertained any serious opinion. Yet the Duke felt that with all these disadvantages it would be better to keep in communication with him and have his support for the time being, for, he said, "as long as we are engaged in measures which have for their object only to prevent the Government from doing mischief, I don't see what harm the Duke of Cumberland and those whom he affects to lead can do, excepting annoy me and the few persons who must keep him in order." [1]

It must have been about this time that Lyndhurst, according to Disraeli, had a conference with Cumberland, and formed another and still more comprehensive plan of stopping the Movement, to which Peel assented, and to which the Duke must have agreed if it had been adopted at all. Perhaps Disraeli knew something of what Lyndhurst and Cumberland desired, but he did not know much of what was in Peel's mind, or of what sort of thing happened behind the sudden and sawing nasal laugh and the husky voice of the Duke of Wellington.

The Duke had concurred in Peel's plan for the abolition of Irish Corporations, and it was tried on the Bill in the House of Commons with profoundly little

---

[1] Parker's *Graham*, II, 244. Parker's *Peel*, II, 322 and 323. Add. MSS. 40,310; 123.

success.   The Conservatives moved an instruction to the
Committee of the Bill embodying it, and were defeated
by the increased majority of 64.[1]   It was a severe defeat,
and there was great joy among the Ministers at the levée
next day, with much talk about the Conservatives not
being able to make their men attend, and of their having
trusted too much and too long to mere abuse of O'Connell.   O'Connell himself became exuberant, and fancied
that the Lords would pass the Bill.   But the game was
not over.   A day or two after the division Greville met
Lyndhurst in the street.   "Well," said Lyndhurst in his
laughing, off-hand way, "we are done, entirely done."
Greville asked him what they meant to do.   Oh, said he,
the Lords would pass Peel's Bill, and the Government
would be glad of it.   It would give them the power which
under their own Bill O'Connell would obtain, and they
would prefer to have their own influence rather than
O'Connell's augmented.   Here was a light heart indeed,
and light reasoning to go with it, but perhaps that was
only produced for unnecessary conversation.   Nevertheless Lyndhurst could prophesy what would be the actions
of the House of Lords.[2]

§ 3

The Irish Municipal Bill passed the House of
Commons on March 28th, and underwent its second
reading at the hands of the Lords on April 18th.   Lyndhurst opened the proceedings with admirable oratory.
He showed no off-hand tone in debate.   Greville was
present at one of Lyndhurst's later efforts that Session,
and it seemed to him in the finest style of speaking.   "So
measured, so grave and earnest, nothing glittering and
gaudy, but a manly and severe style of eloquence."[3]
Lyndhurst's eloquence did not flag while the Bill suffered
in Committee, and it emerged from thence in the form
that Peel and his party had attempted to recommend to

[1] Hansard, XXXII, 119.
[2] Grev., III, 347 (March 10 and 12).   O'Connell's *Corresp.*, VI, 48.
[3] Grev., III, 353.

the House of Commons. It now abolished the Corporations that existed in Ireland and put in their place direct
local Government by the Crown, while Lyndhurst was
held to have ravaged the feelings of Irishmen by saying,
in words which he denied and which are not to be found
in Hansard, that the Irish Roman Catholics were aliens
in blood, in language and in religion. Whether Lyndhurst said them or not, they were words very generally
reported against him—indeed John Russell asserted that
he had heard them with his own ears [1]—and Lyndhurst
was going to find it difficult to leave them behind. This
Bill was more transitory, and it was passed by the Lords
on May 18th, and went down again, an unacceptable
changeling, to its first parent. The Commons would
have to amend it back to its original form.

So there was frank collision between the Houses. The
Ministry was at last confronted with the realities of their
position. Their defeat by the Lords in 1834 had been
cloaked by the Session ending. Their defeat in 1835
had been masked by the success with the greater part of
the English Corporation Bill. Now their position was
naked. They were in the middle of the Session. There
was no likelihood of compromise from the ranks of the
Conservatives, and their defeat on the Irish Municipal
Bill had the cumulative effect of the Lords' actions in the
previous Session behind it. The matter had been clear
before, it was unavoidable now, and they could do nothing.

On June 5th John Russell called the attention of the
Cabinet to their position. It was evident, he said, that
a majority of the House of Lords were combined, not
to stop or alter a particular measure but to stop or alter
all measures not agreeable to the most powerful, or in
other words the most violent, among their body. In this
state of things both Tories and Radicals had the advantage
of a definite course. The Tories praised the Lords'
wisdom, and wished to maintain their power un-
diminished; the Radicals complained, and proposed an
elective House of Lords. But the Ministers confessed

---

[1] Hansard, XXXIV, 231.

to the evil, and would not consent to the remedy. Of course public opinion was some check on the Lords, but on Irish questions it was a very imperfect one. It was certainly possible to wait till the next Session before some definite course was taken, but John Russell owned that he thought it better to take every opportunity to increase the strength of the Liberal party in the Lords. He thought that it was possible, even probable, that the Tories would be cowed by the signs of a steady and gradual creation of peers, since at the time of the Reform Bill they had been coerced by the mere threat of a large creation. He suggested, therefore, that this opportunity might be taken to create eighteen or twelve peers, and that the Ministry should be prepared to advise a similar action whenever provoked.

John Russell might suggest, but the Ministry would do nothing. He might think to grapple with circumstance, but he was not Prime Minister, he was certainly not King, and circumstance was outside the range of his actions. He sent this paper to Melbourne, begging him not to send it round the Cabinet if he was not of the same opinion. Presumably it never went round, for Melbourne wrote back that what was suggested was a very serious step. He had no doubt it would lead to the resignation of the Government and to attempts to form another. "What may be the consequences of this it is impossible to foretell, and I own that at present I am loth to be the immediate and proximate cause of bringing it on." [1]

So nothing was done, and nothing could be done. No doubt Melbourne knew that such a suggestion meant dismissal by the King. If in the ordinary course of events there was danger of the King getting rid of his Ministry, what would he do if he was asked to intimidate the House of Lords. The Whigs were held inert by the Constitution. They were faced by sodden, sullen deadlock, a mire in which their path would be checked and their persons soiled. Like so many other paths to

[1] Spencer Walpole's *Life of Lord John Russell*, Vol. I, 266.

glory theirs had seemed to end, not over a precipice as it should do from the fables, but in a broad and shallow slough. It may seem that there was an alternative open to them. They might have advised and retired. They might have precipitated that struggle whose end Melbourne could not foresee. Such a policy would have been quite practicable, it would probably have been quite harmless, if it is by no means certain that it would have ended in the success of the Whigs. But it must be remembered that in men's minds there were still memories and fears of revolution. The smell of old gunpowder was still hanging about, and it is little wonder that Melbourne shrank back and wished to consider the matter. Possibly even Lord John Russell would have had some reluctance in leaving office. These men were not Radicals and they were Ministerialists, so they shrank from the knife and preferred the lingering and dangerous disease.

Of course some had thought that the Government would act differently. Disraeli had started the year by finding every indication of a crash in the political world. "It is understood," he told his sister in January, "that the Whigs have at length resolved to dissolve Parliament." In March, according to Disraeli's letters and narratives, Lyndhurst developed his plan and the Peers pledged themselves not to falter, while a dissolution was generally apprehended among the well-informed. Earlier in the year there had been boredom and lassitude with regard to politics, but in June men were excited. "The crisis goes on," said Disraeli, "the general impression is that the ministers are going to play 1832 over again, and resign with the idea that we cannot form a Government." Disraeli did not believe that there would be a dissolution, but he looked forward to a struggle. "Lyndhurst," he said, "who has been dining with the Duke, confirms what I have heard, the battle cannot be fought better than at present." [1]

[1] *Disraeli's Corresp. with his Sister*, 1832-33 (Jan.-March 25, June 13, 1836, pp. 48, 50, 53). Add. MSS. 40,321; 171 (Croker to Peel, Jan. 14, 1835).

Presumably this battle was to be fought to establish the independence of the House of Lords, to curb the Government's power of doing mischief, to stop the Movement. The word is heroic. Lyndhurst's eloquence was splendid on June 27th, when the Irish Corporation Bill returned from the Commons with some concessions, but in the main amended to what it had been before. He denied and explained the saying attributed to him with regard to aliens. He thundered and lightened over his opponents, and lit up O'Connell, who was in the House a few minutes later, with an annihilating bolt and an apt quotation from Cicero on Cataline. Very splendid was his eloquence, very decisive his victory, for he threw out the Commons' amendments by the large majority of 97. At the next Cabinet meeting Melbourne is reported to have opened proceedings by saying that under ordinary circumstances they would resign their offices; but that since they came in with the declared opposition of the Peers, since the Peers had at the very beginning of the Session been against their Corporation Reform, they knew nothing now that they did not know before, and their resignation would not be justifiable. His opinion, therefore, was that they ought to go on quietly now, and try a new measure next Session.[1] In effect Melbourne's advice implied that the Lords should be left immune for the moment; and if for this moment, why not for any other? The battle was not joined, it was won. Heroism was rewarded, eloquence crowned. The Lords were truly independent, they could do as they pleased. They had already shelved the Irish Tithe Bill two years in succession, they could and would put it off a third and a fourth, and even more. They had now succeeded in having the Irish Municipal Bill postponed to another year, and there seemed little reason why that should not happen again. A noble vista of perpetual obstruction might open before them. The Duke's dreams of 1834 might come true, and he might be able to congratulate himself on being able to stop effectually and for ever the

---

[1] Broughton, *Recollections*, Vol. II, 87.

Government's mischief. Perhaps Lyndhurst might congratulate himself on the success of his plans for stopping the Movement; and as for Disraeli's narrative, it takes wings with success, until enthusiasm even dispenses with verbs.

Disraeli may rejoice, but the historian must hesitate. The Movement was not stopped. The victory was not really very decisive, nor really very resounding. For one thing no victory can seem more than ordinarily laudable when it is won because the enemy is largely on the side of the victor. The Lords depended for their immunity partly on the restraint of the Whigs and partly on the indifference of the people, especially upon a matter connected with Ireland, and both were necessary conditions to their success. If the people were roused or even if the Government resigned, the Lords would be in difficulties; and the next year was to prove that such difficulties still had their power over them. The Lords were not independent, and their work was not lasting.

After all, the hardest task for Conservatives is not to obstruct, but to provide men with alternatives. Their alternatives must have some small chance of coming into action, and apparently they must be alternatives in harmony with the conditions, the cant and the commonplaces of the day. In this case the Conservatives in the Commons and Lords had provided an alternative to the Irish Municipal Bill; yet, in spite of what Lyndhurst may have said in his off-hand way, there was never the remotest chance of its being adopted. No doubt the Conservative leaders, as in the Commons so in the Lords, were honest and sensible; the Duke and Lyndhurst were not peculiarly foolish or self-seeking. It can easily be understood that they did not wish to hand over Irish Protestants and Irish towns to men who they believed would use them for every sort of treason, by means of every sort of tyranny and intimidation. But unfortunately their ideas were dead, and nothing that they could do would bring them to life.

The Irish Municipal Bill was, however, only one of
the two contested Irish measures. With regard to the
other, the Irish Tithe Bill, the inspiring metaphors of war
seem even further from place. The battle had been
going on so long that it is hard to conceive it as anything
so stirring as a battle. There were rumours that the
Government intended to yield upon the strategic point
of the Appropriation Clause. Perhaps a Government
which could not use force on the Municipal Bill, might
reduce its difficulties by concession on the Tithe Bill.[1]
Indeed so strong were these expectations that when the
Appropriation Clause appeared in the Irish Tithe Bill it
was held to betray disgraceful subservience to O'Connell.[2]

The fated Tithe Bill crawled on towards its destruction
with much less speed and with much less support than
the Irish Corporation Bill. "It would never do," said
Graham to Stanley, "to oppose the plan of the Government without tendering another and a better measure in
its stead,"[3] and so the Conservatives agreed on a measure
which removed, as said Graham to Stanley, "every well-
founded objection to the present Establishment." This,
or one like it, Stanley put forward in the Commons, there
was a division upon it on June 3rd and the Ministers'
majority was 39, much smaller than their majority on
the Municipalities Bill. The Appropriation Clause,
which, as all knew, damned the Bill to destruction, was
kept as an essential part of it, appropriating to the uses
of general education a surplus whose existence was
warmly and drearily debated. On July 4th the Commons
divided on the Clause in Committee, and the ministerial
majority was found to have shrunk to 26.

At the same time came news of a Conservative election
success and, as Greville says, Conservative stock rose
considerably. The Bill took its way to the Lords on
July 25th; it was altered in various respects and the
Appropriation Clause struck out. It was clear, as in
truth it must have long been clear, that it could only be

<hr>

[1] E.g. Add. MSS. 40,422; 71.   [2] Disraeli's *Correspondence*, p. 32.
[3] Parker's *Graham*, II, 243.

Y

either by concession or force that they could ever get this Bill into law.   It might still be by concession.   Men still spoke of John Russell's consenting to drop the Appropriation Clause.   All agreed that a Tithe Bill of some sort was undoubtedly necessary for the pacification of Ireland.   It was prevented, it would be perpetually prevented, by the stubborn retention of one clause in it, and that a clause which was supported by a small and possibly a diminishing majority in the House of Commons.   After the late division in the Commons, many of the Government's supporters wanted to take the Bill without the Appropriation Clause, and Greville, with the ready determination of those not in politics, declared that the Government were in a scrape, that they had got the country into a scrape, and that it was their duty to get the country out of it, whatever it might cost them and to whatever reproaches they might render themselves personally liable.[1]

But there were two effective obstacles to this course. Unfortunately the Ministers had a past and a party, a past that had exalted them and a party that sustained them. It was John Russell's past that most troubled them.   He had pledged himself so openly and so plainly to Appropriation, and on that principle he had lifted the Ministry into power.   The Ministers might, perhaps, if they were prepared to provide their adversaries with abuse, jettison their own consistency for their country's good.   They might use, with some show of reason, the ancient excuse of Ministries that none but they could provide His Majesty with a Government, but they would hardly be able to retain John Russell as Leader of the Commons, nor yet to keep the allegiance of a number of those whose support kept them where it was their duty to be.

§ 4

For the Government's position depended in part on their relations with the followers of O'Connell, and also in part on their relations with the English Radicals.   In

[1] Grev., III, 353 ff. (July 9 to 18).

1835 the Radicals had helped the Whigs to come into office, but some of the Radicals had still hoped that theirs would be a separate party, and some of them thought indeed that their party was doomed to swallow up the Whigs and the Tories.   When the Whig Government had been formed it gave the Radicals good reason for discontent.   In 1835 the taxes on knowledge, that is on newspapers, were untouched, and at the end of that Session the Government had adopted a conciliatory tone to the Lords, and had submitted to the partial amendment of their Municipal Bill.

Nevertheless the Municipal Bill had been something to satisfy them, and there were still enough of them desirous of sparing the Government to throw old Francis Place into the most picturesque rage.   "People, silly puling people," said he, "aye, and those who ought to know better, are talking of 'Revolutionary measures.' To oppose ministers is to promote violent bloody revolution, plunder, rape and the Devil knows what besides." All of them agreed that the House of Lords must be reorganized.   They were grand reorganizers, said Place, "who take a kick like dogs, wag their tails, and take another kick."   As to revolution, he reassured himself with the pregnant reflection that there was no likelihood of revolution while the people had faith in the House of Commons.[1]   Yet in spite of this storm some of the Radicals on whom it had been poured were, at the beginning of 1836, satisfied with their prospects, if not in love with the Ministry.   Joseph Parkes, the Radical who had been largely responsible for the Municipal Reform Bill in its original state, wrote to Place highly pleased with its results.   Things were going well.   There would be, said he, no resurrection for the Tories.   The Whigs would, of course, raise their bidding as the peoples' power and demands grew.   To Parkes the Whigs seemed an unnatural party, standing between the Peers and the People.   Their hearse, said he, is ordered.   Yet if it was ordered the undertaker was to be intolerably slow in

[1] Graham Wallas, *Life of Place*, 345, etc.

bringing it, and if the Tories were not to be resurrected at least they were going to make effective raids upon life from the tomb.[1]

Hope and complacency are not necessarily bed-fellows, and even Parkes at this moment expected, which is often the Radical for hoped, that the Whigs would be abolished. Nevertheless for the first half of 1836 Whigs and Radicals remained in alliance. The connection was cared for by Ellice, the Liberal Government Whip, but it was uneasy and Ellice was anxious, as seems to be shown by the way in which he was bluffed by the Radicals into joining in the foundation of the Reform Club.[2] The roads lay apart. There was still some desire among Radicals not to jeopardize the Government's existence, but during 1836 there seems to have been the growth of a doubt.

It is true that 1836 saw one cause of discontent partially abolished, for the taxes on newspapers were considerably reduced. It was not enough to satisfy all the Radicals, but it was something; the Government still did one or two things which could gain Radical approval. But at the end of June, and during July, there came signs of a rift. On June 30th there were signs of Radical discontent, when Lord John moved firmly but mildly the rejection of the Lords' amendments to the Irish Municipal Bill. Hume reprobated the policy of delay in dealing with the Lords, and Roebuck spoke more vigorously, and so did O'Connell. He, too, denounced the Lords, and he denounced the insult to Ireland. But he added a rider. He would continue in his experiment of trying to obtain justice for Ireland without repeal; he knew that there was no alternative between a system of uncompromising despotism in Ireland and the maintenance of the Ministry. He would support the Ministry.[3]

In the course of July the Ministry were engaged in carrying forward in Parliament various measures for

---

[1] Parkes, 127 (Parkes to Place).
[2] *Ibid.*, 140. *Life of Molesworth*, p. 73.   [3] Hansard, XXXIV, 1967.

Reform in the English Church which were the result of
the labours of the Ecclesiastical Commission; for the
Whigs had continued Peel's Ecclesiastical Commission,
only changing those who were members of it by virtue of
their official positions under Peel's government. The
measures suggested did much to reorganize the Bishoprics and redistribute the endowments of Chapters and
other Sees; they gained Peel's support, but they did not
satisfy the Radicals. These complained that some of the
Bishops' salaries were still too large, while the poor working clergy were still neglected. They complained with
something like violence, and on July 19th Charles Buller,
a Radical, speaking about some of the Government's
proposals, protested that the Government seemed to be
inspired with the unfortunate notion that with Liberal
professions they could conduct the Government of the
country upon Tory principles. "It is placing them,"
said he, "in the position in which they were in 1834, and
which enabled their adversaries for a while to eject them
from office." [1]

The words were serious, and the Radicals were excited.
According to Greville a deputation, headed by Hume,
waited on Melbourne to remonstrate, and reported that
the interview was very civil, very good-natured and
very unsatisfactory. On July 23rd John Russell called
the Ministerialists together at the Foreign Office and
harangued them, but the English Radicals were not to
be appeased, and announced that they would oppose the
Bill at every stage. Again there was help from elsewhere. O'Connell declared that the Government was
of vital consequence to Ireland, and that there should be
no appearance of disunion in the party. The Government should have his support.[2]

The Radicals were angry. Greville managed to fasten
on that high-spirited Radical, Tom Duncombe, as he was
coming away from the meeting, and he told Greville

[1] Hansard, XXXV, 350.
[2] Grev., III, 357. Lord John Russell's account of his own speech, *Early
Corresp. Lord John Russell*, II, 186.

how angry the Radicals were.   But the Radicals were not yet prepared to sacrifice the Government.   This much Duncombe told Greville, and on July 25th Charles Buller himself declared in the Commons that he did not wish to disturb the Government's stability.   It is true that some of the Church reforms had to be dropped for the Session, but things had not reached their danger-point.   The Radicals were angry, but as yet they would not destroy.

Yet their anger might at least be a sign.   It might be a sign that the alliance which had driven out the last Ministry from office would give way, and that Peel, whatever he wished, would be precipitated back into power.   The very ineffectiveness of their anger might come to show that if there were still any power in Liberal disgust or in popular discontent, it had fled from Parliament and taken refuge elsewhere, and men might find some truth in what Place had said about there being no fear of Revolution while the people had faith in the House of Commons.   But as far as the present was concerned, what was most significant was that the Ministry must go on with their task, mainly trusting the active support and good wishes, not of the English but of the Irish Radicals, and most especially of Daniel O'Connell.

§ 5

Most men took that to mean that there was no chance of the Government's retreating on the Appropriation Clause,[1] and certainly whether the deterrent fear was of O'Connell or of enraging the Radicals, in 1836 there were no more signs of a compromise.   On August 2nd Lord John Russell moved the rejection of the Lords' amendments to the Irish Church Bill, in language both vigorous and unyielding.   The division was made the object of great party exertion and, as was usual in such cases, the accidents of nature were either resented or ignored.   The blind and the infirm were dragged into the House, and a death was regretted because it deprived

[1] Grev., III, 357 ff.   Parker's *Graham*, I, 245.

a party of a vote.   The result was a slight increase in the Government's majority on the question, which was now 29.   "The whole affair," said Greville, "went off tamely enough, everybody in Parliament knew what was to happen and out of doors people don't care."   Out of doors, so he said, there was great material prosperity and industrial activity, and it was idle to think of political excitement.[1]

So the great constitutional struggle was partly unreal. If it is true that no one cared, the issue can hardly be held to have been between the House of Lords and an indignant people.   It was merely a quarrel between the majorities in the two Houses of Parliament.   The Whigs desired neither to force it to a decision nor ease it by a compromise.   Consequently the controversy must go on, without end as it was without reality for the people. But if politics continued to centre round unreal quarrels there might be approaching one of those periods when life would be sadly needed by politics; periods which may become tragic if they coincide with a moment when politics are sadly needed by life.

Yet though debates in the Commons might be tame, in the other House Lyndhurst soared undaunted, wild and free.   Towards the end of the Session the Government's Bills were struck down in a holocaust as they came up to the Lords.   According to Disraeli Lyndhurst became the virtual leader, and there can be no doubt as to his prominence.   He became the object of great abuse, but he did not seem to care.   He should have been pleased, for it must have seemed that his plan was succeeding.   The Movement was being stopped in the massacre of its projects.   The House of Lords was preventing the Government's mischief.   They had some excuse for their butchery, for they were apt to be kept idle for the first part of the Session and then towards its end an attempt was made to rush a great number of ill-digested bills through their House.   But their actions

[1] Grev., III, 358.

certainly did not seem to be wholly inspired by the quiet spirit of peaceful revision.

To crown his work Lyndhurst finished the Session in very fine style, with a long prepared speech of great force and telling invective in defence of the House of Lords. He struck hard, justifying the House of Lords as having acted with moderation and forbearance, merely rejecting after careful consideration what was vicious in the Government's measures. He taunted the Government with having had to drop part of their Ecclesiastical legislation, owing to the opposition of the Radicals, and with having had another of their Bills altered by the House of Commons. In the House of Lords, he said, the opposition was forced to perform the duties of Government, while in the other House measures which Ministers admitted to be concerned with the most important interests of government they abandoned tamely and without scruple at the dictation of any section of their supporters. "Yet thus disgraced and trampled upon," said he, "they still condescend to hold the reins of Government."

It was the forerunner of many like accusations. The Ministers were to be accused of disreputable persistence in office, of being, not base or tyrannical, but shabby and lingering like a poor relation at a dinner party. They would be told that they stayed in to enjoy not power, but their pay. It was an accusation easy to make and often made, but on this occasion a fair answer was given. If Lyndhurst thought so ill of the Ministers why did he not move for their dismissal? The answer was, of course, that he could not command the assent of the country. The state of affairs was such that the Lords might mangle but they dare not slay, and it was not a desirable state of affairs. Lyndhurst could thunder, but Melbourne need not retire. "As to holding office," said Melbourne, "I have only to say that I conscientiously believe that the well-being of the country requires that I should hold it— and hold it I will—till I am removed."[1]

Yet for all this, the political situation, the Lords' activi-

---

[1] Hansard, XXXV, 1282.

ties, the weaknesses of the Government and the ordinary nature of political humanity were bound to raise in men's minds the question of a change of Ministers. To many Conservative politicians it must have been naturally an end always to be dreamed of if never fully considered. If we can trust Disraeli's novels, such a change must have meant to Taper and Tadpole the fulfilment and the completion of the "great Conservative cause," and for those for whom he says politics were entirely a struggle for £1,200 a year, its meaning was concrete. If we can trust his narratives, it must have been just as much a delightful probability, full, it may be, of glittering promise to one whose desires rose higher if his ideals were also more lofty. It is in this year that Disraeli records that the King offered the office of Prime Minister to Lord Lyndhurst, his patron. The end of his narrative, written in September 1836, is full of the rumours of exciting events. A son-in-law of the King had told him at the Carlton that the King wanted Lyndhurst to be Premier, but feared that he was inextricably bound to Sir Robert Peel. Another Peer, with whom he dined alone, told him that the Duke anticipated a daily break-up of the Government, but himself wished it postponed. The Duke, it was said, wished himself to be in Cabinet without any office, thought that Peel must be Premier, but thought that Lyndhurst, with an Earldom and the Home Department, would be almost the same as Premier. It is notable that in the story in *The Times*, which does not assign the events to any year, Lyndhurst was to have had an Earldom and, with the title of Earl Copley, was to have led the ranks of reaction and to have dictated the policy which the country was now evidently preparing to receive from a Conservative Ministry.[1]

Perhaps this is but the froth of politics, light rumours of foolish thoughts. Even so, they may be significant and they might have been harmful, for whether true or false the story contains one dangerous probability. The Lords' obsolescence was not apparently dangerous, but

[1] *The Times*, Oct. 13, 1863.

there was nothing to prove absence of danger from the
King. They might succeed in crippling the Ministry,
but he could drive it out. He might appeal to someone
to try an impossible Government; there was probably
much obsolete constitutional doctrine abroad with regard
to the way such an appeal should be received. Obsolete
constitutional doctrine has a way of reviving in strength
when it suits the convenience of fools. According to
Greville it was obvious that the King was waiting with
the greatest impatience till his Ministers should resign.
After the final reduction of their majority on the Appropriation Clause, he was assailed from all sides to dismiss
them. There were at Court specific rumours of their
approaching resignation. At the end of the Session the
King refused to two of his Ministers leave of absence
abroad, and Melbourne told Hobhouse, who was one of
them, that he should not be surprised if they were soon
to be turned out, imprudent as such a step must be,
since the people, as in 1834, might sympathize with them,
and the House of Commons might refuse the supplies.
But His Majesty, said Melbourne, was all but crazy,
and that, added to his dislike of his Ministers, might
bring about the catastrophe.

It might be dangerous for the Ministers to be turned
out, it was certainly miserable for them to have to stay
in; indeed the moment was a miserable one for all Liberals. The Liberal party, or rather alliance, was in
dissolution. The Radicals were at variance with the
Government and quarrelling among themselves, exhibit-
ing or so it would seem, all the signs of the confusion of
failure. The Court was against the Ministers, as were
the English Constituencies so far as they knew, and the
House of Lords. They had nothing, said Hobhouse, in
their favour but an insignificant majority in the Commons, and that only on doubtful and unpopular questions.
It is hardly to be wondered that Hobhouse reports that
even quiet and courageous Lord Melbourne began to
give way and to tell his colleagues that he had doubts
whether it was right and becoming for them to go on

with the Government in their present condition.   "Lord
Melbourne," he reports, "said that a man must have the
patience of an ass to stand against such odds."[1]

The prospect may have been gloomy, nevertheless it
seems very probable that in the depression of the moment
they were under-estimating their strength.   Above all,
they still had, and, for all that they said, they were going
to retain, the support of a majority of the House of Commons.   They were not beaten yet, and Melbourne had
said that he considered that the well-being of the Country
demanded that he should continue to hold it.   And Melbourne's will was not always quite as light and airy as his
conversation.   Men have called him a saunterer, but
Hobhouse has called him quiet and courageous, and both
Hobhouse and Parkes, the Radical, were independently
moved by their experience of him to testify to his qualities.   It was for Melbourne now to reflect that an ass is
a useful animal.

Parliament was prorogued on August 20th.   The
Session had not been entirely sterile, for the Ministry
among other things had passed a marriage law for the
Dissenters and an act for the Commutation of English
Tithes, but it had not been satisfactory, and the prospect
of the holidays was not satisfactory either.   The King
was still in a high state of excitement and the speeches
would keep coming out, against his ministers in Council
or, at his table, against the Duchess of Kent, the mother
of the Princess Victoria.   Melbourne felt that having
got rid of his Parliament, and with five clear months in
front of him, the King would not be unwilling to drive
him to resign.   In time the King quieted down and grew
good-natured again and very convivial, but then the
money market began to give trouble.   There was little
respite for Melbourne during that recess.[2]

§ 6

But Peel could go on a holiday, and he went to Norris
Castle in the Isle of Wight and there, overlooking the sea

[1] Broughton, V, 59, 61. Grev., II, 358.
[2] Spencer Walpole, *Lord John Russell*, I, 268. Torrens, *Melbourne*, II, 208.

and the white sails of the peaceful yachts off Cowes and the trees completely covered with their tired August foliage, he told his friend Goulburn that he could find nothing to read for mere amusement and interest half so attractive as the Memoirs connected with the French Revolution.   Portly, handsome, intelligent and absorbed, he read of the recall of Necker, the abolition of tithes, the discharge of political prisoners, the cry for democratic municipalities, the condemnation of the vote of the Nobles, the denunciation of yesterday's demagogues, and the disillusionment of ministers who made concessions to the people, until "all these things," said he, "following in rapid succession made me doubt for a moment whether I was not reading the Annual Register of 1836 instead of the Mémoires de Bailly."[1]

Singular and significant doubt for so able a man in so quiet a room with so safe a future.   Farther east along the South Coast, within sight, there was living the man who was partly responsible.   Croker was violently interested in the French Revolution.   It furnished him for his articles in the *Quarterly*, but it meant more than a magazine of thunderbolts.   His was a sincere, consuming and devouring passion, and three separate times in his life he seems to have made a collection of papers and books on the subject, each of about 10,000 pieces.   He bought for Peel also, and no doubt Croker's activity kept Peel's attention alive upon the French Revolution,[2] while his interest was whetted by the strange facility with which he was able to apply the details he found to those of his day.   But his thoughts were more natural than accidental; they bear a deeper significance.   The French Revolution was still the fecund mother of potent dreams and also of potent nightmares.   The cries of the mob and the gleam of guillotine still performed their part in many men's minds, and there was much vague talk of precipitating anarchy which must end in military tyranny. It must be remembered that these men had seen some-

---

[1] Parker, II, 328 (Peel to Goulburn, Aug. 22, 1836).
[2] E.g. see Croker, II, 283 (Croker to Peel, Oct. 1833), etc.

thing of rioting, and had at least lived in the times of
Napoleon. It is well to be just to their fears, and it is
certainly well to remember that they were haunted by
ghosts. While one party was failing, the thoughts of
those who would have to take up their burden were distorted by the continual consciousness of the terrible and
irrelevant past.

This past troubled Goulburn also. He answered
Peel's letter, saying that he was not surprised that Peel
should read about the French Revolution. He himself
could not read it without fear, for "all the same wild
opinions as to Government and religion are now abroad."
But Goulburn addressed himself to modern movements
of opinion also. There was, he believed, everywhere a
strong party opposed to the Poor Law. They made but
little noise at the moment, but they were acquiring
strength. His belief was true, and things were being
said and suffered in England at that moment which happened to be more relevant to the destiny of parties than
the precedent of the French Revolution.[1]

The bitter hatred which the cruel severities of the new
Poor Laws excited was going to bring grave unpopularity towards the Whigs. It was going to combine
with other things to pull them down at last. If so, it
would set the Tories up. But would it make them
popular? It might. Many of them were opposed to
the new law and had been since the beginning. Country
gentlemen who were magistrates, in spite of the benefits
the law brought to Agriculture, because of their humanity,
because of the obvious necessities at times of their districts and because of their pride, disliked the interference
with their powers of relief. *The Times* urgently opposed
the new Poor Law. Religious Conservatives were
moved in the matter, and some perhaps were inspired by
the possibility of a "good cry." The new Poor Law
might be a source of popularity to many Conservatives,
but not to their leader. Peel had not committed himself
in the debates when the Bill was passed, but signs soon

[1] Add. MSS. 40,333; 360 (Goulburn to Peel, Sept. 2, 1836).

came to show what manner of opinion his was.   In the January of 1835 he was applied to by a magistrate who was in great difficulties as to providing, as he was attempt-to do, for the distress in his district.   He wanted Peel to restore to the magistrates the power of compelling overseers to relieve the poor.   Peel answered him kindly, but objected, declaring that he would be most unwilling, without an overruling necessity, to interfere with the late experiment in the improvement of the Poor Law.   He would decidedly object to the restoration of the power which magistrates, as magistrates, formerly possessed in respect to the administration of relief from the Poor Rates.[1]   Again it was a conflict between science and sense at the head of the Conservative party, opposed to feeling at its extremities.   The sense was good and the feeling not always ignoble; and the feeling was fiercely shared by a large part of the country.

There is further evidence of Peel's position with regard to some of his followers.   In February 1836 he declared in debate that he believed that great benefit would result to the agricultural interest from the alter-ation in the Poor Laws.   He said he had done what he could to enforce the improvement in his own neighbour-hood, though he gave his reasons for not setting too high the permanent reduction of expense on the poor which the new law had effected.   The debate in which he thus spoke was on another subject of potential division be-tween Peel and some of his followers.   It was on the proposal to form a Committee to enquire into agricultural distress.   Peel did not think much good would come of the Committee; there might be some help to be given, indeed he made one or two suggestions, but he could not help thinking that he saw in the great prosperity of our trade and manufactures a more encouraging prospect of an improved condition of agriculture than in any other definite cause.   One thing, however, appeared to him self-evident.   He held it to be clearly as much for the interest of agriculture as for that of commerce that we

[1] Add. MSS. 40,408; 310, 313.

should adhere to the present standard of value.   It had long appeared self-evident to Peel, but not so to all agriculturists, nor did his convictions on Currency matters, nor yet his view of the probable uselessness of trying to assist agriculture, appear self-evident to all of them now. In effect the same clear intelligent mind was at work on agriculture as on the Poor Laws: and in each case it divided the leader from the forces that would carry him forward to power.[1]   It is not good, though it may be inevitable, that a leader should be so divided.

Peel was divided from some of his followers, but in spite of that he was certainly a Conservative.   His fears were enough to claim that title for him.   He believed that he was struggling for the Constitution as it existed. In 1836 he had tried to defend the Protestants of Ireland from being handed over to what he thought would mean Roman Catholic tyranny, and ever since 1833 he had been attempting to defend the integrity of the Irish Church.   He was a friend, according to his lights, of the English Church, and he sincerely wished to use and defend the House of Lords.   His position was both hard and intelligible.   But in order to explain his difficulties men said then, and have said since, that he was by nature a Liberal who had got by a hereditary mistake and early parental pressure into the wrong camp, and had remained there long after he was a grown man and a responsible statesman.   The theory is hard to digest.   If there had been a mistake, Peel himself must also have made it, he must have made it continually and blindly over nearly if not quite the whole of his life.   It is hard to conceive an honest and an intelligent man, from mere habit, force of position and reasonless error, acting continually for thirty years with those with whom he was in essential disagreement, against those who were his natural allies. It was not as if some of his enemies and some of his own friends had not from time to time pointed out, even with violence, that he had possibly got out of place.

There was, in fact, no mistake.   But a man's creed

[1] Hansard, XXXI, 158.

may be true while his policy is not effective. It may be said that Peel's policy was, alternatively, one of ultimate surrender or of unnecessary defence. But it would be as well that Peel's policy should at least be compared with those that were proposed in competition to it, whose only strength seems to be that they were never effectively tried. There was Lyndhurst's great plan of stopping the Movement, which would have left the Conservatives with the incubus of a rejected reform of the English Municipalities; there was Chandos' Agricultural policy which would have gained Conservatives an embarrassed exchequer, and there was Inglis' Ecclesiastical pedantry which would have retained for them an ineffective and indefensible Church, for Inglis' school objected to the work of the Ecclesiastical Commission. There was always to hand King William's madness, to ensure constant futile and probably dangerous attempts to install the Conservatives in power. And it is for the sake of such possibilities that Disraeli sneers at Conservatism, during these years, for only attempting to conserve the prerogatives of the Crown provided that they were not exercised, the independence of the House of Lords provided that it was not asserted, the Ecclesiastical Estate provided that it was regulated by a Commission of laymen, everything provided that it was a phrase and not a fact. Well, it is better, even from a Tory point of view, to be a phrase than a folly.

Nevertheless this can be no complete justification for Peel's policy. It must not escape by mere criticism of its critics; there are many questions still to be asked. Could Peel's work have been made lasting where it was only temporary, could he have dealt in realities where he was occupied with illusions, and could he have made the institutions he was defending really and obviously useful to the people? for that must be the foundation of both Toryism and Conservatism. Could he have criticized to bed-rock what he was opposing, and from bed-rock itself built up something acceptable and different? for that is probably the difficult task of Conservatism and men in opposition.   Lastly, could he have foreseen the fate of himself and his party, and could he have prevented it? The harsh and unjust task of criticizing a man with the aid of the knowledge of what was to happen must be undertaken for these years of increasing Conservatism. But it is most nearly fair to let the facts develop the matter, and where possible to let Sir Robert Peel speak, if he will, for himself.

§7

Peel was soon to have an opportunity of speaking for himself.   In the middle of November he learnt that he had been elected Lord Rector by the students of Glasgow University.   The significance of the event was urged upon him from all sides.   Brougham had been followed as Rector by Stanley, and now Stanley by Peel.   The trend of opinion was obvious, and the young men who had elected Peel were said to be the descendants of Whigs not only of 1688 but also of 1832.   Moreover, the effect of Stanley's speech two years ago had been to unite the Tories and the Church Whigs, a union which was apparently easier in Glasgow than with the obstinately obsolete Tories in Edinburgh.   Peel, it was hoped, would consolidate this.   He was urged to accept the Rectorship in order to show his interest in the Church of Scotland.[1]

For the Church of Scotland was the key.   The Whigs had attacked the Established Churches or, rather, had stumbled against them.   In Scotland, as in England, Churchmen felt that the Government was faithless and untrustworthy, secretly inclined to the voluntary system, unduly anxious to conciliate Dissenting supporters and patently under the influence of Irishmen and Papists. The Church of Scotland saw, so Clerk told Peel, evidence of the Ministers' unfriendly feelings in their constitution of the Church Commission for Scotland, she feared what their policy might be with regard to education, and augured ill from the character of their acts in England

[1] Add. MSS. 40,422; 155 ff.   Parker, II, 327 ff.   Parker's *Graham*, I, 246.

z

and Ireland.[1] Moreover, the best Scottish Churchmen, such as Dr. Chalmers, were thwarted in their noblest desire, which was to extend the facilities for preaching the gospel to the poor, which they wanted to do at least partly at the public expense.[2] The Whigs doubted and dallied and listened to Dissenters on this question of Church Extension in Scotland, while Peel in his short Ministry had put it into the King's Speech. The subsidizing of the philanthropic efforts of an Established Church came as a natural duty to Conservatives, even if it was one that could never be fulfilled.

Thus as a defender of Churches and of Protestantism Peel could even appeal to some part of the obstinate Scotch race. His speech at Glasgow would show that he was ready to make full use of those assets. For Peel proved not to be insensible to the claim of the reaction in Scotland, and acting, as he told the University in his address "upon the impulse of feelings that were better counsellors than doubts and deliberations," he accepted the office, and in this ardent and generous mood not only consented to give a Rectorial address but also to accept the invitation to speak at a vast Conservative banquet to be given at Glasgow in his honour. His courage did not evaporate, and up through winter and the North he came, to be inaugurated into his duties on January 11th, 1837.

His address on that occasion was not political, but an eloquent expression of those suitable commonplaces which are ordinarily addressed by eminent men to Academic youth. It went down very well, and evoked the admiration of Miss Edgeworth and the labours of translators into other tongues. But his political speeches at Glasgow are possibly of more interest to historians.

There was a short reply to an address given to him from the Conservative Operatives, and a very long speech at the dinner. The reply to the Operatives was also exceedingly suitable. Peel showed them that no

[1] Add. MSS. 40,422; 192, 221, 226 (Clerk to Peel, Nov. 1836).
[2] E.g. *Memoirs of Dr. Chalmers* (Hanna), Vol. IV, Chap. II.

portion of Society was more deeply interested in the maintenance of peace and order, in the protection of property, in the respect for Constitutional privileges, than the working and industrious classes, and that the monarchy and mixed form of Government gave better security for this than purely democratical institutions. He praised Glasgow, with its infinite gradation of classes and the constant changes of condition among them, prompted not only by fortuitous but also by moral influences. To ensure the continuance of this he wished to maintain the ancient institutions of the country and that form of national worship which, had its means been coextensive with the increase of population, would have made the Scots, so he said, the most moral, intelligent and religious nation of any on the face of the earth. On January 13th he made his speech at the great public dinner.

This was held, not in a Hall but in an erection put up for the purpose, "an immense temporary saloon" with tables laid for no less than 3,432 guests. They were 3,432 ardent guests; for they punctuated his speech with applause, having received him with tumultuous enthusiasm and what the reporters called "literally deafening cheers." The cheers continued at very short intervals while Peel endeavoured in what he called the most simple and familiar phrases to express his gratification at being there, and while he described a riding and walking tour he had taken after his degree at Oxford, to satisfy the burning anxiety which he confessed to have had to see Scotland. He had seen Glasgow and various other parts which he particularized, amid applause, and he had met a Highland shepherd, the narration of whose virtues and religious exercises led Peel on to eulogize the education the man had received, founded on the Bible and guided by the Church, and further eloquently and vehemently to deprecate the day when men in authority should be unwilling to support the National Church of Scotland "to extend its ministrations, to advance its banner into the desolate and unclaimed wastes of religious indifference and profligacy"; at which, of course, there was loud and continued cheering.

Encouraged by this, Peel desired that they should try whether they had common sentiments as to the danger which imperilled their institutions and a common resolution to avert it. The task that he now approached was not entirely easy. For there were converts present who must be appeased or at least not offended. Stanley, before the event, had speculated whether Peel might not be under some embarrassment at this dinner from the zeal of his Scotch Tory friends; however he had had no doubt that Peel would dance the tight rope with great skill.[1] To whatever he owed his balance, Peel certainly made out a good case for the alliance with him of those who had supported the Reform Bill. He quoted the pledges of adherence to the acknowledged principles of the constitution, the prerogatives of the Crown and the authority of both Houses of Parliament, which had accompanied the Bill and which those who had supported it ought to maintain by assisting him. If they still demanded improvement he was ready to improve without meddling with the vital functions of the machine. If they were still hostile to corruption, what had he or those who listened to gain from corruption?

Apparently he carried his meeting with him. Loud cheers, great cheering, loud cheering and laughter, follow each other in the report at very regular intervals, and when he made a humorous allusion to men wanting more *movement* in the engine of State, the universal applause was enough to prevent the sentence from being finished. A more sublime effect, however, was immediately to follow. After declaring he would come to the point (cheers) and not gain their support by hoisting false colours (great cheering) he said, "I mean to support the National Establishment which connects Protestantism with the State in the three countries." "And here," to use the words of the report, "the whole company rose and responded to his avowal with loud cheers and wav-

[1] Parker's *Graham*, I, 247.

ing of handkerchiefs which had a most imposing effect
and lasted for several minutes." It must have been a
supreme moment for National Churches and for Protestantism. Peel continued on the theme for a time,
making a very reasonable and obviously much appreciated
case for National Establishments, and then proceeded
to another great and perhaps not unexpected avowal.
"I avow to you, moreover, that I mean to support in its
full integrity the authority of the House of Lords,"
said Peel, and the report adds that the enthusiasm with
which this sentiment was received "baffled all description."

He meant to consider that integrity, he said, as an
indispensable condition for the continuance of the mixed
form of government under which they lived, and he
meant to consider all propositions affecting the settled
institutions of the State with regard to their ultimate
tendency to undermine the independence of the House
of Lords, and when he asked the company whether they
concurred in that opinion there were loud and universal
acclamations and cries of "We do." Whereupon Peel
begged his company to exert themselves, if those were
their sentiments, and endeavour by their efforts and their
use of the franchise to avert the peril that threatened
them. "For the time is come," said he, "believe me,
the time is come for bestirring ourselves and not trusting
to others what we can do for ourselves." He had read
speeches of late delivered by those whose special duty
he would have thought it was to defend the British
Constitution in all its integrity, which made him unwilling to trust its defence to their official exertions; and
Peel poured fine scorn on the Government supposed to be
rummaging in their pigeon-holes for paper schemes of
a reformed House of Lords. Against all such attempts
he produced a strange metaphor about an oak whose
roots had been severed, but which had been propped up
by artifical machinery and would succumb to the first
gust of popular passion.

He went on defending the House of Lords by argument and, as he said, dispassionately. It was hereditary principle which gave it stability, as a breakwater should not float on the surface which it was to control; and besides that the monarchy was also hereditary. True the House of Lords was not responsible; neither was the Electorate, some 500,000 or 600,000 persons, responsible; and here Peel was able to attack the ballot. He challenged the opponents of the House of Lords to prove that it was at variance with the spirit of the people and the march of social improvement; he reviewed the number of Reforms that the House of Lords had passed, albeit sometimes unwillingly, as proving that they had not obstructed the current of public opinion. Were they now to be blamed, he asked, if they refused to place implicit confidence in that combination of public men which had only one bond of connection—spoliation of the Irish Church? And with much severity on the Government, as allied to O'Connell, and with much accustomed argument against appropriation of the Irish Church's revenues Peel implied, still amidst cheers, that the House of Lords was not to be blamed.

Then he defended, as he had done before, the institutions of his own country by means of a comparison with the fate of others, for which his wide reading no doubt fitted him, and when he said that he felt assured that the time would come when the ancient heart of England and of Scotland would rally round their institutions, the people, disregarding the difficulty of the sentence, again "simultaneously rose and continued cheering for many minutes." On that sentiment he ended, speaking eloquently of the proud keep of the British Constitution standing "girt with its double belt of kindred and coeval towers" to protect the rich from spoliation and the poor from oppression. The faith and the establishments in the three parts of the National Kingdom intended for its promulgation and protection should survive as a part of a solemn national compact. The pure faith they professed should find in the diffusion of sound knowledge a new source of strength, and if exposed as it might be, to the storms of adversity, should come forth purified by the trial to take a yet deeper root in the convictions, the affections, the hearts of a Protestant people; and here "the Right Honourable Baronet resumed his seat amidst continued rounds of the most vehement applause." [1]

Such was Peel's creed at the opening of 1837. Perhaps there were elements in it not without a feeling for truth and the promise of life. But how much of it had dealt with what were in reality illusory dangers, irrelevant religious emotions, imaginary needs?

[1] A correct report of the speech delivered by the Rt. Honble. Sir Robt. Peel, M.P., on inauguration into the office of Lord Rector of the Univ. of Glasgow (Jan. 11, 1837), and at the public dinner at Glasgow (Jan. 13, 1837). 7th Edition, Murray, 1837.

CHAPTER VIII

1837—A NECESSARY COMPROMISE

Peel's Glasgow speech did one thing. It certainly pleased a great many people. Peel himself told Graham that the cheers were overpowering, and that "in the assemblage there was but one mind, to defend to the last extremity the Monarchy, the Peerage and the Church." Graham was persuaded that the Liberalized tone and the avowed abandonment of the ultra-Tories were the immediate cause of a portion of the enthusiasm.[1] Hardinge believed that the two principles which Peel had upheld—the maintenance of the Protestant Church in the three countries, and the preservation of the House of Lords in all its independent privileges—would serve as a clear rallying-point for future Conservatives; and "our friends," said Hardinge, "are delighted at the uncompromising tone of the speech"; which possibly reflects on what they had expected to hear.[2] Peel had found a creed on which there could be comprehension without concession, firmness without folly, and unity together with clarity. He was on his legs this time, even if he was going nowhere.

Moreover, there were other places besides Glasgow where gentlemen had dined that Ministers might hang. The last months of 1836 had resounded with the noise of Conservative dinners, with the clink of glasses, the clatter of knives and forks, the hubbub of dinner-table conversation now and again to be hushed for fiery denunciations of O'Connell and the Ministry, and praise of the Peerage. Such sounds drummed the great party on to political victory, since a victory might well seem near if, as Bonham told Peel, they would gain fifty seats on an election with the Conservatives in.[3] There was Conservative activity both in England and Ireland, while

---

[1] Parker's *Graham*, I, 252 (Graham to Stanley, Jan. 15, 1837).
[2] Add. MSS. 40,314; 173 (Hardinge to Peel, Jan. 17, 1837).
[3] *Ibid.* 40,422; 289.

on the other side Lord Morpeth put up a defence for the
Ministry at Leeds, and January showed that even the
Radicals could dine.   But the Radical dinners mainly
serve to show that the Radicals were sharply divided
between those who wished to press on with the matter,
and not be compromised by any silly respect for the
Ministry, and those who had talked of the necessity of
union among Reformers and wanted to keep the Ministry
in office, and who excited in the grim bosom of Francis
Place the deepest and most general disgust.[1]

The Radical quarrels at the beginning of 1837 seem
to spell Radical failure, for when the wolves tear each other
it should be a sign that the shepherd is safe.   But the
whole situation at this moment points to deadlock and the
diseases of stagnation.   Lyndhurst held the House of
Lords in an iron hand, and the Government could pass
nothing but what was agreed to by all parties.   The
King would not allow them the means to get round that
obstacle, and the Government would not resign, and if
they did it might be hard to find a set of men who could
take their places; for in spite of Bonham, it is probable
that the Reformers had still a slight predominance in the
country.   The metaphor seems inevitable of the stream
and the dam that must some time break, a metaphor that
seems so useful in deadlocks and is so inaccurate in its
implications.   This time it has the appearance of reason,
for the Whig measures were of such a sort that it was
unlikely that opinion would finally go back from them;
but even then it would be wrong to imply that the pressure of public opinion in their favour would be without
intermittence.[2]   Moreover, it would be found that the
Lords who formed the obstruction could be influenced
by other things than direct pressure.   The King was not
immortal, nor, for that matter, was Lyndhurst's hand of

[1] E.g. Leader's *Roebuck*, 81–91. Parkes, p. 154 ff. *Molesworth*, 119 ff.
[2] N.B.—For description of affairs at the end of 1836, see Stanley's *Arnold*,
398 (Arnold to Platt, Nov. 28, 1836).

iron.   It was a very human hand inside an iron glove.
The surface seemed hard, but the fingers were soon
inclined to get tired with the strain of it, and to get bruised
with the pressure of so much holding on; nor was the
owner a man who would like to disregard these pains and
inconveniences.

At the end of the Session of 1836 Lyndhurst had gone
off to Paris to live, so Greville said, the *vie de garçon*,
and make himself in some respects rather ridiculous.
He was certainly happy, for he met Greville there in
January and told him that he had never passed such an
agreeable time as the last four months; not a moment of
ennui.   "He had become acquainted with a host of
remarkable people of all sorts, political characters of all
parties, and the litterateurs such as Victor Hugo, Balzac,
etc., the latter of whom he says, is a very agreeable man."
It can well be believed that after such a life the Duke of
Cumberland may have palled, and even the House of
Lords seemed at times a little slow.   London did not
attract him.   He could not bear the winter smoke, it
meant for him more abuse and political and judicial
drudgery, and he felt that at Paris he was near enough
to be within call.   He said to Greville, so Greville
reports, "I suppose the Government will get on; I am
sure I shall not go on in the House of Lords this year
as I did the last.   I was induced by circumstances and
some little excitement to take a more prominent part than
usual last Session; but I don't see what I got by it except
abuse."   And he complained how he found concentrated
in Galignani the English newspaper abuse which he had
thought to avoid in Paris.   This was not the man to
toil uncomfortably for an uncomfortable ambition, to
face, without caring, inevitable abuse, or to stop the
Movement, however much circumstances might suggest or a little excitement encourage.   Charming, sensitive, pleasure-loving men do not change the course of
History, no matter how manly their style of speaking, or
how unchanging their front in debate.[1]

[1] Grev., III, 378.   Martin's *Lyndhurst*, 370 (Lynd. to Barlow, 1836).

But even if Lyndhurst should keep away from the Lords in 1837, it might not make much difference. The Duke by himself would continue the policy of obstruction. "I believe," he had told Lyndhurst in October, "that we in the House of Lords must follow the same course as last year." [1] The same sequence of events seemed likely to recur. The House of Lords would be kept inactive for the first half of the Session, and then difficulties between Lords and Commons would blossom out into their usual summer profusion.

§ 2

There would also be in 1837 the same concentration of interest or at least of controversy upon Ireland. The Ministry's failures had provided matter to sharpen controversy in Ireland, and so also had its success. For the Irish Executive which Melbourne had appointed in 1835 had been successful. The protagonists in this had been Lord Mulgrave, the Lord-Lieutenant and Thomas Drummond, the Permanent Under-Secretary. Mulgrave and Drummond had greatly changed the methods and bias with which Ireland was governed. They endeavoured to weed Orangemen out of the police, and to make the police do their duty in repressing the excesses of Orangemen and in stopping the faction fights which, it was said, Government had winked at before as a safe outlet for the hot blood of Irishmen. Lord Mulgrave went on progresses about Ireland, releasing men out of prison in order to further the cause of pacification, while Drummond wrote many letters refusing the aid of police or soldiers to levy tithes or to serve writs for the landlords, or in fact to do anything but keep the peace. The Attorney-General, O'Loughlin, refused to pack Protestant juries. They made great use of stipendiary magistrates, they gave posts to Roman Catholics; in effect their policy was successful, consistent and Liberal, pleasing to their friends and disgusting to their enemies. O'Connell was delighted, the Whigs declared

[1] Martin's *Lyndhurst*, 368.

with statistics that outrage and crime were decreasing
and the country unusually tranquil, while the Tories
attacked their conclusions and declared that tithes were
abandoned, Orangemen inequitably treated, and the
labours of justice vitiated by indiscriminate mercy.[1]

But though the Ministry was successful in administering Ireland, they had not been able to legislate for her,
and in 1836 O'Connell had looked round for new
weapons to assist him.   At the beginning of July he had
written to Ireland to announce his intention of forming a
new general Association in Ireland to procure adequate
Municipal Reform and such a settlement of the Tithe
question as should be satisfactory to the people of Ireland.[2]   The Association was formed and a rent collected
for it, thus giving further cause for anger on the part of the
Tories, and for fierce comparisons of the toleration of
O'Connell's association with the condemnation and suppression of the Orange Lodges.   However, in spite of
his Association, O'Connell was still anxious not to
jeopardize the Ministry's existence and the work that was
going forward in Ireland.   Most especially he wished
they were decently freed from the dangers and embarrassment of the Appropriation Clause, which he seems
to have valued at very little.   Indeed, in December 1836
he took the trouble to convey such views to a quarter
from which he may have known they would pass to the
ears of John Russell.[3]   Perhaps on the Appropriation
Clause even O'Connell would assist at the task of compromise.

On February 7th, 1837, the Irish Municipal Reform
Bill was reintroduced.   It was much the same as the
Bill of 1836, and perhaps the most striking thing in the
debate was a passage in John Russell's speech introducing
the Bill.   He declared that he considered it a vital

---

[1] For Administration in Ireland, see *Thomas Drummond, Life and Letters*
(R. Barry O'Brien).
[2] O'Connell's *Correspondence*, II, 72 (O'C., July 2, 1836).
[3] Spencer Walpole, *Life of Lord John*, I, 273 (O'C. to Warburton, Dec. 29,
1836); cf. with O'C.'s *Corresp.*, II, 78 (O'C. to Fitzpatrick, February 18, 1837).

question for the Administration, and that he was fully
sensible of the evil of bringing forward Bills year after
year and suffering them to be lost without taking any
further steps on the subject; and he plainly hinted at
resignation.   The debate then became in the main
violent bludgeon work on the details of the Irish Administration.   But at the end Hobhouse rubbed in Lord
John's hint, and asked Peel whether, if he came into
office, he would be able to govern Ireland by Orangemen
and against the will, on this point of the Municipalities,
of a large majority of the House of Commons.   Peel
answered with spirit, and asked in return what Hobhouse, who was now in office, would do with regard
to the Irish Church; for he was convinced that the
formation of the new Municipalities would put power
in the hands of the organized enemies of the Irish
Church.

Peel's retort brought significant words from John
Russell, who closed the debate with a speech in which he
plainly pointed at concession with regard to the Irish
Church and its tithes.   It looked as if the Government
were strong on Irish Municipalities and yielding on
Appropriation.   Perhaps by an exchange of pieces the
parties might end this wearisome game.[1]

But there was no immediate sign of concession.   On
the Irish Municipal Bill going into Committee the
Conservatives moved, as last year, an instruction to
abolish Corporations in Ireland.   A prolonged debate
followed, in which the usual accusations were made by
the Conservatives against the Government, and in which
Sheil, the Irish orator, was the cause of a scene which
made a considerable effect on contemporaries.   He had
come to an eloquent passage denouncing Lyndhurst's
expression about aliens, which was rarely left to rest
while these debates proceeded.   He asked, with telling
phrase and much eloquent declamation, whether these
aliens had not done their duty in the Peninsula and at
Waterloo; and his attack on Lyndhurst was direct, for

[1] Hansard, XXXVI, 209, 380–403.

that handsome man was sitting under the Gallery.   Then
for ten minutes there was a scene of what was usually
called in those days indescribable confusion.   There
was tumultuous vociferous cheering.   The Irish members all stood up and turned to Lyndhurst and shouted
and hooted and gesticulated, until it almost seemed that
they were going to attack him.   Lyndhurst played his
part admirably well.   He did not attempt to move, nor
did he change a muscle of his face.   He was well fitted
to play such a part in such a drama.   More important
perhaps for the purposes of history was the fact that the
Government defeated the Conservative motion by as
many as 80 votes.[1]

The Conservatives were, said Greville, prodigiously
depressed at their defeat.   There was strong complaining
against sickness and death as having robbed them of votes
on this occasion, and there were renewed complaints of
slackness in attendance on the part of Conservative
members.   There may have been casualties, but for all
that it was obvious that Conservatives would find increasingly that this question of Irish Municipalities was for
them an exceptionally bad one, and at the same time
disquieting rumours came to the ears of the leaders.
There was talk of the Government retiring.

Hobhouse had met Stanley in the House of Commons,
and apparently told him that they were going out.   He
even gave him the date, April 8th.   However, they were
determined, so Hobhouse was supposed to have said, to
do all they could to prevent the success of any other
Government.   They would not have resented defeat
by the House of Commons, but they were resolved to
bring it to the test whether the House of Lords should
or should not appoint a Government against the will of a
majority in the House of Commons.   "All this seems
very extraordinary," wrote Peel to the Duke, "but you
may depend upon it that the conversation, as I reported
it, passed.[2]

[1] Hansard, XXXVI, 925 (for Sheil's speech, Grev., III, 389).
[2] Parker, II, 335 (not in Add. MSS.).

Extraordinary was a word which expressed in the early nineteenth century a powerful mixture of surprise and reprobation.   In this case it is a little hard to share either; but the Duke enjoyed both, though his surprise was stylistic rather than real, since he confessed that he had long had reasons for expecting as much of these honest servants of the King.   "But," said the Duke, "the House of Lords will be as much surprised when informed that they are appointing a minister, as the gentleman in the play was when told that he was talking prose.   The only crime that I know of which the House of Lords has been guilty, is that it is an independent body." [1]   The surprise, as in the play, would be both naïve and significant.   Whether crime or not, to be an independent body meant the obstruction of that legislation which must be the main justification of a modern Government.   Consequently in rendering such a Government inoperative they risked its resignation, and consequently it could be said with truth that they were appointing its successor.   But the Duke did not understand the needs of a modern Government; he put government first and legislation a very long way afterwards.   He did not recognize the unavoidable. nature of the demands of past promises and a present party.   For him a Government had to govern and not to work out a programme, and in the contrast of those two conceptions a vast amount of constitutional development is signified.   It was lucky for him that the Government was not quite modern.

But an independent House of Lords was incompatible not only with the modern idea of government, but also with the modern idea of an opposition.   The Conservative leaders were never quite sure that they ought to be in opposition.   Opposition was a difficult and degraded word, soiled by long application to Whigs. It seemed to imply in the eyes of Conservatives factious manœuvring, unholy combinations for the unnatural seizure of office and an unprincipled hampering of His

[1] Parker, II, 335.   Add. MSS. 40,310; 162 (not all in Parker).

Majesty's Government, and both Croker and his friend Peel talked of a Conservative Opposition being almost a contradiction in terms.[1] The Conservative leaders' inclination in opposition was not to try to regain office, but rather to be content with impeding what was mischievous. For the practice of such strategy, if it were practicable, an independent House of Lords would be a very suitable weapon. But luckily such strategy is impracticable. At one time or another duty or, it may be, necessity teaches every Opposition that they must be ready to take office with a reasonable chance of retaining it, and then they may learn how much they will be hampered by mischief which they have impeded but not abolished. At this moment Conservative leaders could not avoid the consciousness that they might have to take office, but as yet it did not affect their policy, although it must have been obvious how much they would be hampered by the unpassed but popular Irish Municipal Bill. But Peel made no suggestion about it and the Duke said in his reply, "I don't think that this information ought to make any difference in the course I intended to pursue." Peel and the Duke had yet a lesson to learn in politics.

The strength of the Conservative position, both in Parliament and in the country, was in Church matters. Indeed some of Peel's followers wished him to bring forward the Irish Church in order to withdraw public attention from the Irish Municipal Bill, but Peel refused on the ground that that course would unjustifiably endanger the Irish Church;[2] and it was the Government itself that provided the diversion. On March 3rd they brought forward a proposal for the abolition of Church rates. The burden was to be put on the money raised by the better management of Ecclesiastical Estates, on pew rents with modifications and on the money saved by the abolition of certain fees. The measure would deeply violate Conservative principles. It robbed religion, and

[1] Parker, II, 338. (Add. MSS. 40,425; 301), last para. Croker, II, 282 (Croker to Hertford, Sept. 30, 1838).   [2] Parker, II, 338.

it robbed the poor.   It was a concession to the voluntary
system, which the Ministers had forsworn, and to the
ungovernable incommensurable conscientious scruples of
Dissenters.   It could be proved from their own words
that the measure was a step in the Dissenters' assault
on the Church; and the Bishops stood to arms.

From February onwards the Archbishop of Canterbury and the Bishop of London had been busy writing to
Peel on the Church Rate Bill as a measure raising the
question whether they should have a Church Establishment or no, and one that would be followed by more
decisive measures.[1]   In March the Bishops came openly
into the field.   On March 9th eighteen of them met
at Lambeth and protested, and that night, on presenting
petitions in the House of Lords, the Archbishop launched
himself in assault on the Government and the Bill.
That mild man came on very stoutly and resolutely,
while the Bishop of London was sharp and effective in
support, his abrupt and animated exordium, so Greville
reports, being very much admired.   Meanwhile for the
time that the Bill was before Parliament the Bishops struck
work on the Ecclesiastical Commission, for they had
consented to continue to serve there when Melbourne
came into power, under an agreement of which this Bill
was an undoubted breach.[2]   There still were fears in the
Church's breast and there was fire in her defence.   The
incident showed how strong was her position.   The
House of Lords would be stubborn as oak on Church
Rates, and in the House of Commons Whig members
seem to have shown a tendency to stay away, or even to
vote against the Government on a matter that nearly
touched the sacred principle of Establishment.[3]   So this
Bill had an unpromising future and an uncomfortable
present.   At the outset of its career in the Commons
it was only passed by a majority of 23 votes, and on

[1] Add. MSS. 40,423; 21, 50, 83, etc.
[2] Spencer Walpole, *Lord John Russell*, I, 278.
[3] Add. MSS. 40,423; 206.   *Melbourne Papers*, 331.   *Memoirs of Sir Thomas
Fowell Buxton, Bart.*, p. 399.

A A

May 23rd on the second reading it obtained 287 votes
against 282, a majority of 5. After that, not unnaturally, the Bill was abandoned. Perhaps it might be confessed that the Church was safe.

But there was still the Irish Municipal Bill to embarrass
Conservatives. The first small majority for the Government on the Church Rates had made a great impression,
and men began to approach Peel with anxiety that there
should be no division on the third reading of the Irish
Municipal Bill to spoil its effect. Peel was so heavily
pressed on the subject that he wrote to the Duke about it,
putting the case for and against a division, and then
wrote another letter before he could receive the Duke's
answer, definitely declaring that he thought that they
ought to divide. The Duke answering the first letter
told Peel that he saw the force of the argument against
division, and would be satisfied with whatever Péel
decided, although an efficient debate and a division would
be a great assistance to the House of Lords; especially
since he had some waverers there on the subject.

But the Duke knew that there was more in the matter
than the mere effect of a division upon either House of
Parliament. The Government were surrounded by
difficulties abroad and at home, in the colonies and everywhere, and the Duke felt sure that, encouraged by his
waverers, they would use this measure as the first opportunity of running away. They would be further encouraged to persevere in this if the minority in the Commons
manifested anything like indifference by avoiding division and discussion on the third reading. To show all
that was involved it was very desirable that Peel should
bring out forcibly the points on which the two parties
differed, and declare himself ready to uphold the
Protestant religion, the Church of England in Ireland as
well as England, and the independence of the House of
Lords.[1]

---

[1] Parker, II, 340.   N.B.—Not all of Duke to Peel, March 23.   Add. MSS.
40,310; 168, is in Parker.   For description of whole crisis up to April 11, see
Add. MSS. 40,316; 206 (Peel to Lyndhurst, April 18).

§ 3

Peel sent this letter on to Graham, begging him to communicate it to Stanley, thus showing how intimate had grown his relations with Graham and Stanley.[1] Peel had wanted those two and now he had got them, the allegiance and assistance of both of them and the ripening friendship of one; for, pertinacious, sententious and prone to reverence, Graham was a natural friend for Peel. Stanley and Graham were still in a semi-detached condition with regard to the party and it was through Graham that Peel communicated with Stanley, and with Graham also that Peel was most usually in intimate conference. Graham agreed with the Duke about the division, and said he was going to see Granville Somerset and Bonham, and that they would endeavour to ensure a strong muster for it. On March 27th he reported a conversation with Stanley, his friend.

Stanley also agreed with the Duke, readily acquiesced in dividing and, with the Duke, believed that Ministers would resign on the first adverse vote on the Irish Municipal Bill in the House of Lords. But he developed this idea in a way that the Duke had not. The principal difficulty which a Conservative Government must overcome was this problem of Irish Municipal Reform. They would have to be in agreement upon it, and they would have to legislate upon it, for they had already admitted that there were abuses in the old exclusive Protestant Corporations. Consequently by moderation and caution they must render the violent measure of resignation on the part of Ministers unintelligible, and they must keep the present Bill alive in the Lords so that they could legislate as soon as they got into power. He therefore suggested that before the third reading in the Commons they should come to a distinct understanding with the Lords, to the effect that they should not reject the Bill on its second reading, but rather postpone it for two months. But this could only be done in

---

[1] See Croker, II, 311 (Croker to Hertford, Feb. 8, 1837).

good faith if there was some intention of making a conditional concession, and Stanley also suggested that they should be prepared to say that in the event of their obtaining a good Irish Tithe Bill without Appropriation, and a good Irish Poor Law, they would concede the extension of Corporate Privileges to the larger cities in Ireland.

There would be an excuse for this course. A better Poor Law would make a great change in the civil condition of Ireland; it might, for instance, provide a safe basis for Electoral Qualifications. A good Irish Tithe Bill would remove the objection urged against Irish Corporations, that they would merely form centres of agitation against the Irish Church. Arguments on this line could be used, so Stanley thought, in the Commons on the third reading, but he also thought that the suggested concessions should come from the Lords. He wished, therefore, to come to an understanding with the Duke and the Peers on the question. Also he put his finger on what was indeed the key to the problem. Concessions could not be made in government by men who in opposition had strenuously opposed them, and they must now when still out of office make a reasonable tender.[1]

Such were Stanley's views, and great was Peel's embarrassment. The Duke was obviously not much attracted to the plan when he heard of it. It is true that he did not consider himself pledged to any one course on the Municipal Bill, and was therefore ready to amend it. But he saw difficulties in the plan, did not think that they would get a reasonable Irish Poor Law or Tithe Bill and through them a reasonable Municipal Bill, and was not sure how he would stand with the Lords. At the end of his letter, in sentences instinct with years of suspicion and more than usually bespattered with semicolons, he explained that he did not see how, even if the plan were followed, they would

[1] Add. MSS. 40,318; 60, 64 (Graham to Peel, March 24 and 27, with enclosure in last on G.'s conversation with Stanley).

avoid the main difficulty, the resignation of the Government, which had been determined upon from reasons quite distinct from the course the Lords would take upon the Irish Corporation Bill. All that he could say was, "I think you had better speak to Lyndhurst about it."[1]

Now speaking to Lyndhurst was just what Peel could not do. Lyndhurst's daughter was ill and he was with her, and in fact again in Paris. His absence did not weaken Graham's urgency in recommending Stanley's proposal to the consideration of Peel and the Duke, and he talked to Peel of the dangers to the Peers and to the Protestants were the opportunity lost. Peel was determined not even to form an opinion on the scheme till he had communicated with those Peers with whom he had always immediately acted on the Irish Municipal Bill. Yet Lyndhurst was still in Paris, the third reading in the Commons was getting uncomfortably close, and might decisively affect the course of action in the Lords, while Stanley and Graham seemed to Peel fixed in their determination. Peel called a meeting of his old Cabinet, delayed it in the hope of Lyndhurst returning and then held it without him at Aberdeen's on April 9th, the day before the last date to which he could contrive to postpone the Bill's third reading. And on that day or just before it he got, through the Duke, a letter from Lyndhurst urging that the Bill should be "disposed of" on the second reading in the House of Lords.[2]

Of course the Lords' independence was not responsible for Stanley's scheme or Graham's pertinacity, or Lyndhurst's absence and airy resolution. Those were misfortunes which might happen to any man who had to have colleagues. Nevertheless this present embarrassment had its origin in the independence of the House of Lords. The House of Lords is often attacked as the

---

[1] Add. MSS. 40,310; 174 (Duke to Peel, March 31).
[2] *Ibid.* 40,318; 75, 77 (Graham to Peel, April 2 and 4). 40,310; 178, 179, 183 (Duke to Peel, April 7, and Lyndhurst to Duke, April 6). Parker, II, 344 (Peel to Duke, April 9). Add. MSS. 40,423; 160.

dead hand in the Constitution; it had been something much worse; it had been the hand that had kept alive. It had kept alive the controversy over the Irish Municipal Bill, and in consequence the Conservatives were still chained to a question in which they were increasingly unsuccessful, and which prevented their having any hope at this moment of retaining office if they had it. The Lords might keep alive all Conservative failures, and encumber and stifle what was lively and likely in the Conservative creed with the lumber of past defeats. They might never let the Conservatives succeed, if they would never let them utterly fail. Such was the effect of the sacred independence of the House of Lords.

There must be no exaggeration; the Lords were useful in some things. They enabled the Conservatives to bargain with a very weak Government. They were able to prevent some of the Government's Ecclesiastical Legislation, which was not very popular. In effect, they were successful in killing the dying, and the dying might still have done harm. This was not independence, for it depended ultimately on the Electorate; it was not glorious, it was not lasting, but from a strict and very narrow Conservative point of view it was certainly useful.

And of course there is a defence. Clear eyes and unambiguous phrases are not generally vouchsafed to men amid the dust and declarations of politics. It was natural for the Conservatives to maintain what they called the independence of the House of Lords; and in politics there is always vagueness to succour inadequate thought, and inconsistency to resolve dangerous formulæ. Peel probably never entirely meant what the words "Lords' independence" seem to mean, and in his Glasgow oration, using the curious extempore debating thought of a political speech, he had spoken of the Lords being in some way amenable to public opinion, and had strangely enough given their forced submission to the Reform Bill as an example. In the past he had not considered it right that the Lords' Independence should ultimately block Roman Catholic Emancipation, and now, in a lesser matter, stimulated from outside, he was going to help modify the Lords' position on Irish Municipalities.

At the present, however, he was in difficulties. He warned Stanley and Graham that he could not form an opinion without a full communication with his friends in the Lords. He told them also that more entered into the question than the mere abstract practicability of the scheme; among other things, the position of the House of Lords in respect to that measure and the bearing of any particular upon its honour and independent character; for he showed all through this crisis a very nervous and sensitive loyalty to the Lords. As a man lost at sea clings to a board, he clung to the moral principles involved, and he, too, insisted on the retention in office of principles upheld in opposition, and on the duty of giving the present Government a chance, before they retired, of considering the terms of any compromise to which the Conservatives were going to assent. Indeed both of these wise and uncontroverted reflections so filled Peel's mind that he impressed them upon the Duke of Wellington's as well.

April 8th came, and the old Cabinet had to meet at Aberdeen's without Lord Lyndhurst. Probably they could decide upon nothing. But they did not adopt Lyndhurst's suggestion that they should destroy the Bill immediately, and Peel was authorized to tell Stanley and Graham that they were all of opinion that the Bill should be read a second time in the Lords, and also that they would be ready, when Lyndhurst returned, to discuss the whole matter. The way for concession was still open, while Stanley and Graham's views had received unconscious and spontaneous support in the letter of one of Peel's colleagues who could not attend.[1]

[1] Add. MSS. 40,423; 160 (Peel's Memoirs on his communications with Stanley and Graham after March 27). Parker, II, 344, *v.s.* Add. MSS. 40,423; 115 (undated notes probably on this meeting), 149 (Memoir read by Peel at meeting at Lord Aberdeen's, undated), 131 (Ashburton to Peel).

The third reading in the Commons passed off without incident. Peel took a line founded on what seemed to be the sense of his committee at Aberdeen's, emphasizing the dependence of the Government's Irish Municipal Bill on their Irish Poor Law and Church Bill. Then he taunted the Government with the difficulties all round them, and with anxiety to retire. There would be vigour enough in the country, said he, to find successors to them. There may have been surprising vigour in the country, there was certainly something like surprising complacency in the orator at the success of this taunt. "You never"—he told Croker afterwards —"saw men confounded as the Government were at being taunted not with pertinacious adherence to office but the contemplation of its cowardly abandonment." To be able to change quickly from the one taunt to the other and back again would be indeed a position of great tactical strength. However, Peel told Croker that the Government had changed their plans, and he probably meant had been frightened from resigning. But there were still exciting rumours current, and on April 16th the story of a plot by the Government seems to have been distilled from the ordinary fog of politics, that is, from newspaper articles and diplomatic reports. It made Stanley excited enough to wish to prepare the King for it through Sir Herbert Taylor; but Peel restrained him, declaring, with wisdom if inaccuracy, that he had always refused, when out of office, to hold any communication with those in the immediate confidence of the King. Meanwhile, to give body to the rumours of the Government's intention of forcing the Conservatives to a contest on the Irish Municipal Bill, the Irish Tithe Bill was not yet introduced nor was the Irish Poor Law very far forward, while the Irish Municipal Bill proceeded up to the House of Lords, as if chosen and segregated for the purpose of resignation, suspiciously alone.[1]

[1] Hansard, XXXVII, 1095. Croker, II, 305 (April 14, 1837). Add. MSS. 40,321; 214 (Croker to Peel, April 16, 1837). 40,423, 147 ff. (Stanley to Peel, April 16, 1837), etc.

Perhaps these fears are not important except in so
far as they kept the Conservatives face to face with the
salutary dread of having to take office.   For concession
was not dead.   There were signs of it in the House of
Lords and out of Parliament, and the work was pressed
forward in the Conservative party, although the difficulties were great enough to cause Peel to write a memorandum about them a month or two later.   He spoke of
Lyndhurst's position, of the disposition of a great party
in the Lords to refuse any compromise, of the determination of Graham and Stanley, and he declares that it was
only after much discussion, and many threatening appearances of open dispute, that they came to an agreement.

But Peel was led to speak more generally in the
memorandum.   "Few people," said he, "can judge of
the difficulty there has frequently been of maintaining
the harmony between the various branches of the Conservative party."   There were those two branches of the
party, the great majority of the Lords and the minority
in the Commons.   As well as this there were some of the
foremost supporters of the Reform Bill and some of its
most determined and unforgiving opponents, and the
course of debate had to be regulated so as not to revive
the half-extinguished animosities of the Reform Bill and
of Roman Catholic Emancipation; while there was the
perpetual difficulty of conducting a Conservative opposition and of avoiding any factious alliance with men of
extreme opinions.   The past divided and the present
complicated, but perhaps Peel was a match both for the
past and the present.   Even in the future the party was
not to be split simply along the old lines of Lords and
Commons, Reformers and Anti-Reformers, Peel and
Lyndhurst.   Lyndhurst's great plan of stopping the
Movement was to be laid quietly aside, though in time
one of its most junior adherents was to come forward
disastrously with strange ideas and a surprising invective.   For Peel could succeed in tasks which he could
understand.   He was to succeed in dealing with these
difficulties in 1837.   What could be done by judicious

speech and sense and cautious action he was honestly well capable of doing; and he had also always at his elbow a powerful spirit, obedient, natural, a little aloof and a little absurd, like a rustic god, who was often of use in disciplining the Lords.[1]

The Duke had been at the committee at Aberdeen's on the Irish Municipal Bill. He had not been fully conscious of everything, for when he received a letter from Peel upon it he had to confess that the fact was "that I don't hear half of what passes." But he had heard enough, for he remembered that he was to persuade Lyndhurst not to reject the Bill on the second reading, and apparently to confer with Stanley and Sir James Graham.[2] The Duke was in good hands. Divagations of policy sometimes commended themselves to him in the intervals, but he could always be put right, and though he walked in the incomplete indefinite lonely world of the deaf, he could always be trusted to do his duty. So all went well.

When Lyndhurst returned Peel told him all that had happened, and he seems to have seen Peel and the Duke and Graham and Stanley and he probably assented to Stanley's policy. Certainly on April 23rd, when his party Cabinet met again—this time at Lyndhurst's—Peel read a paper in which he adopted the thesis of Stanley and Graham; and since they discussed the terms of settlement on the Corporations problem, and since the course recommended was followed, it seems probable that his "Cabinet" adopted it too. Perhaps it might be said that the cause of concession had won. It was the cause of reality; but it was a denial of the Independence of the House of Lords.[2]

There was yet the whole body of the Lords to manage,

[1] Add. MSS. 40,423; 301. Parker, II, 336 and 346 (Peel's Memorandum, July 4, 1837). (Peel wrote an addition to it after 1846.)

[2] *Ibid.* 40,310; 195 (Duke to Peel, April 15).

[3] *Ibid.* 40,316; 204 ff. (Peel to Lyndhurst, April 18, *v.s.* Lyndhurst to Peel, April 15, 16, 20 ,21). 40,423; 176 (paper read by Peel at Lyndhurst's, April 2, 1834), 116 (points reserved for future discussion by all who met at Lynd hurst's), 113 (undated).

and the very next day a large meeting of them was held at Apsley House. The Duke apparently pressed that the Irish Municipal Bill should be allowed to pass its second reading, and stated on that question the reasons that had been dwelt on the day before. "When asked," said the *Annual Register*, "what he would do with it in Committee, the noble Duke is reported to have answered that it would be time enough to think of that when it was there." Really he did say a little more on the point, for he spoke of the necessity of considering this Bill with the other two Irish measures. No objection was made by anyone, says Fitzgerald, until the Duke of Cumberland invited Lyndhurst to give an opinion. He did so, briefly, in unison with the Duke but rather more sharply against the Bill. Cumberland then expressed his assent, and in the end the meeting was unanimous with the Duke, who managed it with great skill so Fitzgerald reports, though he adds that if Lyndhurst had not promptly declared his concord with the Duke of Wellington it was plain that the Duke of Cumberland would have dared to resist. Perhaps there was confused and mischievous anger behind those bushy whiskers and moustaches, as he asked again across the room if Lyndhurst was satisfied. The next day the Bill passed its second reading, and on May 5th its committal was postponed by the Lords to June 9th, with the express intention of seeing the result of the Commons' deliberations on the Irish Tithe and Irish Poor Law. But the Government had already introduced an Irish Tithe Bill which by no means satisfied the Conservatives.[1]

§ 4

For the Government were not yet ready to become a party to the compromise. Their views were too little settled and their position too much confused. There continued to be signs of the existence of restlessness and discontent among the Radicals. There had been

[1] Add. MSS. 40,323; 364 (Fitzgerald to Peel, undated). Grev., III, 397. *Ann. Reg.*, 1837, (History) p. 52.

long and strong speeches, by Roebuck, and Radical
motions which sometimes made some of the Liberal
members of the Government tug at their mooring chains.[1]
But violence and virtue and the voice of the future
resounding without much effect in the Commons are not
nearly as disagreeable or dangerous as discussions may
be in the Cabinet room; and there had been such disagreements in Cabinet that Melbourne told John Russell that they had better, if possible, not bring the question of the Appropriation Clause again before them,
for he feared that their course might be hampered by the
wrong-headedness of some of his colleagues. But John
Russell himself was restless—and dangerous.

Lord John Russell was set on being both Liberal and
Whig, and was therefore very obstinately dissatisfied with
their position. He continued to entertain the idea of
making two or three Peers to frighten the Lords; and
he had his uncomfortable moods. It was in one of
these that he had called the Irish Municipal Bill a vital
measure, in the first debate on it that Session. Indeed
his mood had betrayed itself beforehand in conversation,
for next day the Prime Minister wrote to him in natural
anxiety: "I hope you have said nothing damned foolish.
I thought you were rather teeming with some imprudence yesterday." It must be remembered that, in 1834,
when John Russell had teemed he had suddenly boiled
over with irrecoverable consequences. Certainly at
various times during the Session he had thoughts of
resigning when the Lords threw out the Municipal Bill.
He obviously talked to Melbourne about it, for on
April 1st, Melbourne told him his only two scruples
against resignation were a fear, which he admitted might
be chimerical, lest they should produce a state of affairs
in which it would be hard to form a Government, and a
fear lest his friends should think themselves abandoned,
which he put forward as a very material consideration.[2]

[1] *Melbourne Papers*, 315 (Melbourne to Poulett Thomson).
[2] Torrens, *Melbourne*, I, 213 (Melb. to Lansdowne, Dec. 29, 1836). Spencer
Walpole's *Lord John Russell*, I, 275–6, 280 (note 3). Melb. to John Russell,
April 1. Grev., III, 393. O'C.'s *Corresp.*, II, 89.

Melbourne's were old-fashioned arguments, for may-be modern principle would risk the unlikely dangers of resignation, and would certainly have the claim of friendship kept firmly under the control of the claims of consistency and of the party organization. But Melbourne was old-fashioned, and so he kept resolutely on his way, and gave the Lords no idea that they were going to resign. Meanwhile John Russell still suffered from the itch of principle, of principle thwarted but potentially popular, and on April 11th, he said again in the Commons that he considered the Irish Municipal Bill a question most vital to the present administration. But he did not match his words with action. Something —his own interests as a ministerialist, his colleagues' influence, or perhaps the Lords' change of plan—managed to defeat the demand of principle. On May 8th, after that vital measure the Irish Municipal Bill had been postponed by the Lords, John Russell declared that the Ministry would continue in office while they retained the confidence of the House of Commons.

They were words Melbourne himself had used, and they contained disastrous implications. Greville spoke to Tavistock, John Russell's brother, of inconsistency, but was told that Lord John must choose his own time for resignation. That time was not to come that year; indeed it would never come in time for consistency, for credit, or for command of the future.[1]

If the Irish Municipal Bill might have been the occasion of resignation, the Irish Tithe Bill was the key to concession as far as the Cabinet were concerned. A Tithe Bill which should satisfy Conservatives must at least make no attempt at Appropriation. Before the Session there had been serious talk in the Cabinet of dropping the Appropriation Clause,[2] and from the beginning of the Session John Russell had shown in the Commons some readiness to compromise on Irish Tithes generally. But the Cabinet were divided, and

[1] Broughton, *Recollections*, V, 69. Grev., III, 397.
[2] Torrens, *Melbourne*, II, 213.

when Morpeth, the Irish Secretary, produced his Tithe Bill, though it was without the old Appropriation Clause, it had a provision for money for undenominational schools which, to Conservatives at least, still implied the old principle of the Appropriation of Church property. There were other provisions to which the Conservatives objected, so that the Bill, as it stood, could plainly form no part of a compromise. Nor was John Russell content that the Lords should so use it, and he rendered it impossible for them to consider the three Irish Bills together, by agreeing to fix the second reading of the Irish Tithe Bill for June 10th, the very day to which the Lords had postponed their Committee on the Irish Municipal Bill. On June 10th, Lyndhurst again postponed the Committee, and that in a speech of some violence.

John Russell was suspended between heaven and hell, position and principle. He had not resigned, but he would not facilitate a compromise; and principle is too near to peevishness to look well when it is only an obstacle. His principle was of no use to any one, it only hindered the settlement of a sterile controversy. Things were different with Melbourne. On May 12th a debate sprang up in the Lords on the presentation of some petitions in which Lord Wharncliffe attacked the Government about John Russell's choice of date for the second reading of the Tithe Bill in the Commons.[1] The tenor of the various speeches made Melbourne ask Stanley's friend, the Duke of Richmond, whether the Lords had changed their tone or were still ready for compromise. Richmond asked Stanley, got the proper assurance and tried to induce Stanley to enter into negotiations as a Conservative plenipotentiary. That, of course, was not permitted. But Richmond's conversation convinced Stanley that Melbourne would accept any terms of agreement, if satisfied that they were compatible with reason and honour, and that he had will and power to force his Cabinet to do the same. Meanwhile Mel-

[1] Hansard, XXXVIII, 817.

bourne had said some strange and interesting things in
a conversation he sought with Wharncliffe in the House
of Lords.

For one thing, to Wharncliffe, an opponent, he called
Lord John Russell's choice of a date for the Irish Tithe
Bill "petulant folly."   He asked why, if the Lords were
anxious for a settlement, they did not declare what they
proposed to do.   He said he thought they would give
up the Appropriation Clause without much difficulty,
and when Wharncliffe asked the obvious question about
his approval of Lord John's Appropriation motion in
1835, he said that he had tried to stop his friends from
turning out Peel's Government upon it, but they had
answered that they could not carry an ordinary vote.
And as they drove away together in his carriage from
the House Melbourne told Wharncliffe that he thought
things were soothing down.   Wharncliffe said he could
not see much sign of soothing down.[1]

§ 5

Soothing down: Lord Melbourne's words seem to
summon up the man, the great Whig nobleman in his
carriage, the sturdy figure, the broad attractive face
whose kindness and graciousness still show from his
portraits, and the easy natural manners of the most agreeable society there has been in England, the old fashionable and intellectual Whig high society.   He was
something of an unprejudiced Liberal and something of
an intellectual reactionary.   His Government had been
struggling since its formation for a principle to which he
had not wished to be pledged, his own wish had merely
been the old one to keep things going, to keep His
Majesty supplied with a Government.   His words are
eloquent of his desires; and Wharncliffe's is the kind of
inappropriate answer a Conservative would naturally
make.

Perhaps things were soothing down.   It is true that
men could still talk of deadlock and point to the fact

[1] Add. MSS. 40,423; 209-38.

that of the Ministry's great measures this Session, the
English Church Rate Bill, the Irish Tithe, Poor Law
and Municipal Bills, none were likely to pass into law.
It is true that Roebuck the Radical could talk very
angrily in the House of Commons of hopes miserably
disappointed, of promises shamefully broken, of a
doomed Ministry and an indifferent people. But
probably these things are compatible with soothing
down.

Also, Roebuck was not well supported in his attacks on
the Government, and unsupported eloquence is a poor
stimulant. Also, for these Radicals there was in preparation the best soporific of all for violent, over-prin-
cipled men, the soporific of extinction and failure. They
had already suffered a blow. The old aristocratic
Radical, Sir Francis Burdett, had of late become Tory,
and in April he had stood, on a vacancy, for the old
tumultuous Radical seat of Westminster, this time in
the Conservative interest and warmly supported by the
Carlton. He was opposed by Leader, a Radical of the
period. Him he defeated, and was received by the
Conservatives in the Commons with cheers and exul-
tation. All Liberalism was held to have suffered a
reverse, but Melbourne said he was glad that Leader
had failed, or otherwise the Radicals would have become
unmanageable.[1] It probably helped the process of
soothing down.

The Reform Bill had not helped to soothe things, but
the force of the Reform Bill was by this time patently
losing its impetus. They had passed most of its respectable sequelæ, and the disreputable ones, the ballot and
the like, were being successfully opposed by Conservatives and Whig Cabinet Ministers. Things had been
disturbed by the danger to the Church, especially the
Church in Ireland. But the Church in England should
by now have seemed safe, after what had happened on
the Church Rate Bill. The Church in Ireland was still
embarrassed, but even those affairs were tending towards

[1] Grev., III, 398 (supported by Add. MSS. 40,423; 227).

a settlement, while in Parliament Church matters were reaching equilibrium.

It is true that there was still room for debate upon them and sometimes for passionate controversy. Peel had during this Session been putting forward the claims of Scotch Church extension, the Government was to dabble in education, but neither were to be disturbingly effective. There were still angry parsons who detested the doings of the Ecclesiastical Commission. The Whigs were still wicked. In 1836 they had given a new sign of it by appointing to the Regius Professorship of Divinity at Oxford, Hampden, who was known to be heretical, if anyone had had the pertinacity to read his unattractive works. They were always sullied by alliance with Papists, influenced by alliance with other Dissenters and infected by Liberalism. But on the whole they were deservedly impotent, and some of the High Church Party do not seem to have felt that the Conservatives were very much better. The Church was safe if not satisfied; though there were still to be religious matters to excite ardours and quicken tempers. The Scottish Kirk question and the High Church problem were about to begin. Angry clergymen were to rage horribly against each other, or against patrons, or even against State interference or in favour of State aid. Ecclesiastical members of Parliament were to have their ineffective indignation, their unjustifiable expectations. But they would not disturb the equilibrium; and, indeed, unrepresented passion and ineffective hope are two of the primary conditions for soothing down.

And while religious problems came to an equilibrium the problem of the House of Lords would be modified to a compromise. They would ultimately pass an Irish Municipal Bill and yet continue to refuse those measures which could not be promoted effectually. That battle was won and lost, though the Conservatives might still put the independence of the House of Lords in the forefront of their programme. For a concentration on

bygone political issues is of great importance when
politics are soothing down.

But there is no need to be angry.   It is usually unjust
when the present taxes the past with its sins of omission.
Men are not to be blamed for labouring on controversies
which seem dreary and sterile, uninteresting to the
people, unfruitful for posterity, but which were not yet
finished.   After all, the compromise which was to resolve
the difficulties of the House of Lords was left incompleted
by the Session of 1837, and the men who contributed
to deadlock were not mere seekers for places, but were
able and conscientious statesmen whose policies were
largely inevitable, and in part intelligent also.   There
is no need to be angry, but there may be a temptation.
It is not pleasant to contemplate years in which politics
seem to become ineffective and discredited, when they
seem to provide little principle for the present and therefore little preparation for a difficult and momentous
future, when party politics seem to be by no means an
organization of hope.   If it were to such uselessness
that politics were soothing down, a man might very well
be tempted to say in his haste that they were being soothed
into the sleep of the dead and into the impotence of the
damned.

§ 6

But such haste is unjust.   A historian must wait on
events, and must merely report that some of the old political difficulties had started to pass away, and that there
were new difficulties at the doors, and unsolved difficulties even inside the House.   At any rate there was one
event in the June of 1837 which would alter profoundly
the appearance of the situation and even some of its
realities, which would close this useless Session and dissolve this Parliament, which would even give strength
to the Ministry.

It will be remembered how in Disraeli's novels during
that June the great political ladies were speculating, with
their sons' elections in view, whether the King was only

suffering from hay-fever. Perhaps this ignorance is a poetic exaggeration, but certainly in clubs, lobbies, dinner-parties and drawing-rooms men and women were speculating, murmuring and fishing for information about the King's health. His death would appear to mean so much, it would remove the Tories' great friend and replace in his high and difficult place a young girl who had just reached the age of eighteen and attained her legal majority. She had always lived completely concealed under the shadow of her mother, and though it was thought she might be under the Radical influence of Lord Durham, practically no one really knew anything about her at all. No wonder men talked while the King lay ill, no wonder that O'Connell seems to have found it next to impossible not to be pleased at the prospect of the King's death. Meanwhile it is well to remember that there had been much innocence, good nature and good intention in the King during his reign, even if his actions had sometimes been dangerous and his words almost always embarrassing. At any rate he had not done the things that his brother Cumberland wanted him to do. This is the moment to enumerate his good points since, as all grew to know in time, he was certainly dying, and at six o'clock on the morning of the 20th June, the Princess Victoria was awoke by her Mamma, got out of bed and went into her sitting-room, alone, and dressed only in her dressing-gown, to learn that she was Queen.[1]

[1] Letters of Queen Victoria (*Queen's Journal*, June 20, 1837), I, 75.

CHAPTER IX

THE NEW REIGN—1837–38

The last days of June and the July of 1837 were occupied with the bustle and business of the start of a new reign. There was the dead man to be eulogized and put away, with much empty pageantry, where he could never embarrass anyone again, and stock had to be taken of the small and determined young lady who had taken up his duties in his stead. On the first day of her reign she came, dressed simply and in mourning, into her first Council, with the eyes of all upon her. She seemed cool and self-controlled, and read her speech simply and effectively, giving full meaning to her words. Her Council listened and were charmed. There was something very appealing about the combination of her obvious youth and her position, and when they went to their homes they were full of sentiment and her praise. She had started very well.

Naturally everyone was anxious to learn what they could about her, and soon stories began to come through to throw some light on her personality. She was industrious, it was said, and careful of detail. She had completely established her independence of her mother, the Duchess of Kent, and Greville began to deduce that when she gained confidence and her character began to develop, she would evince a strong will of her own. He called her cautious beyond her years. Still she was young, so young in fact that it was obvious to those about her that she enjoyed her new position, could play her part with a zest not always usual in monarchs and, for that matter, laugh in a very natural way indeed. But frank enjoyment and rather downright laughter may perhaps be permitted to one who could behave in public with the most exemplary propriety, and who had a crown and not more than eighteen years.[1]

[1] Broughton, IV, 76. Greville, *Journal of the Reign of Queen Victoria*, Vol. I, e.g. 20 (under Aug.; 30).

But however childish or precocious or cautious or determined she might prove to be, one thing was certain. The Whigs had found a friend.   For Melbourne indeed it was particularly delightful, for it might almost be said that he had found a daughter, but for them all she was a very good exchange for William IV.   It was even possible that they could not have remained in office much longer if he had lived, it was exceedingly improbable that he would have let them try to mend their fortunes by a dissolution of Parliament.   But now they had a Sovereign whose prejudices and predilections were if anything in their favour.   Since they had to dissolve Parliament within six months of the King's death they could dissolve at once under what were held to be the best possible circumstances for them and, as was to be expected, Melbourne made full use of his opportunity.   He quickly cleared up the remains of the futile Session which was in progress, and dissolved Parliament as soon as he could.

Consequently in July and August the country resounded with the confused noise and struggling of a general election.   There were the usual accounts of brutal rioting, of intimidation by mobs or men of property, the usual stories of bribery, of treating and of Government influence; and each party was prepared, no doubt with perfect truth, to bring suitable accusations against the other.[1]   The Queen's name was extensively used, and the *Annual Register*, which was Conservatively inclined, saw something discreditable and amusing in elderly Whigs citing as their chief claim to the suffrages of the people their unavoidable toleration by a young and inexperienced girl.[2]   However, the Whigs not only played their Queen for themselves, they were also able to throw a King in the teeth of the Tories.   In Hanover King William could not be succeeded by a woman, and there the Tories' old friend, the Duke of Cumberland, came to the throne.   While the election in England was going on, the news came that he had overthrown the

[1] Add. MSS. 40,424; 82.   [2] *Ann. Reg.*, 1837 (History), p. 239.

constitution he had found there. Of course his action was used to discredit his old Tory associates, as for instance one who was called on the hustings "a bloody Hanoverian and the enemy of our Reforming Queen." "He is a delightful coadjutor," said the Duke of Wellington of his old friend, the new King.[1]

It would be hard to say how much these cries affected any issue; perhaps they were really rather the poetry of battle than its substance. Certainly they did not bring victory to the Whigs. The reasons for Whig ill-success were manifold. There was probably a continual drift of the old Whig landed interests into the Conservative party. Melbourne said that the Church had been too much for them, and Hobhouse added that the Dissenters had only been lukewarm.[2] They suffered from the unpopularity of their Irish Roman Catholic allies and of their work on the Poor Law. Above all they were damaged by time and disappointment and the inevitable wastage of office, while the Conservatives showed all the signs of natural growth. Instead of having about 180 candidates in possession, as in 1835, they had now over 300. Instead of starting only 390 candidates, by July 19th, 1837, they had started approximately 445, and after the election there were several complaints that they could have risked more candidates in the country constituencies.[3] The old giant was putting on new strength, but to do what? Did he himself know?

At any rate the party was drawing level with the Government. In the English Boroughs, according to Conservative calculations, their gains and losses exactly balanced. But the English counties fell to the Conservatives, as if, so the Radicals said, they had an epidemic disease, and they gained 23 seats among them and lost 1, for Sir James Graham in Cumberland paid with his seat for having changed his party. In Scotland gains and losses balanced. In Ireland O'Connell was successful,

---

[1] Add. MSS. 40,424; 65. Privately printed Aberdeen Corresp., 1832–42, p. 92.
[2] Broughton, V, 93.   [3] Add. MSS. 40,423; 346, and e.g. 40,424; 69.

and the Conservatives had a loss of nine on what they had had before. Altogether the party had gained a balance of 13 on the whole election, and the Whig majority had become very thin and insufficient; indeed on Church matters the Conservatives believed that they held an absolute majority of the whole House. With the aid of Scotland and Ireland the Whigs might still maintain themselves in the Commons, but it would be with difficulty, and perhaps not without degradation.[1]

And if the Whigs had just managed to hold a little less than their own, others on their side of the House had fared worse. All over the country there was evidence of the growth of Conservative feeling, even where the Conservatives had not themselves been successful. There were cases of very greatly increased Conservative minorities, while Greville reported that the applications to the Reform Club for candidates were always for Whigs and not for Radicals. Many of the Radicals in the field suffered heavily. Grote just got in by the breadth of a hair, Hume was defeated and given a seat by O'Connell in Ireland. Roebuck was out, and many of his fellows. There were, it is true, Radical successes; there were even Radical gains, but Radicals of the old type who centred round London and Benthamism were going into eclipse. They represented opinions and ideals which were losing strength and coherence, and their places were to be taken by men of different habits and traditions; indeed the only comfort that they could get out of this election was that it had fully demonstrated the need for the Ballot.[2] Yet there was a great part to be played by some of the Radicals who were left behind.

Election figures are simple, their significance is often impenetrable. The incidents, characters and special circumstances are often so various that the noise of an election, which should be the voice of the people, seems more like the confused roaring of the inarticulate sea.

---

[1] Add. MSS. 40,424; 97, 44, 65. 40,333; 372, etc.
[2] Grev., *Vict.* I, p. 15 (under July 29). *Life of George Grote*, p. 121.

In this case it is hard to see what lay under the network of intimidation, bribery and interest. It is true that principles were expounded from the hustings, as were personalities exposed, in very great profusion, but the former are usually trite and the latter are naturally irrelevant. The Conservative gentlemen still spoke much of the existing Constitution, of the House of Lords, of the Protestant Established Church, and also of Reform which should be safe. They deplored the use by the other side of the Queen's name, and they continually abjured and abused O'Connell and the Irish Roman Catholicism. Perhaps these things may not seem, as they stand, to be a very enlivening creed; but from them was formed a very large part of the speech of one who was called the first statesman of his age.

For Sir Robert Peel said, very skilfully, at his election at Tamworth, much that he had said, very skilfully, before. He spoke of the preservation of Church and State, of preserving the Monarchy and the ancient Constitution of the country. He said that he was preventing the Reform Act of 1832 from being destroyed by those who had been its friends and now wished to destroy it in their disappointment, and he described to his constituents, with humour and vigour, how often he had protected the Government from being outvoted by their own supporters on Radical measures. It was the old story, but Peel did not tell it without interruption. While he was talking of the number of times he had had to support the Government there came a cry from the crowd, "You supported the Poor Law Bill!" Peel did not flinch. He admitted it and declared that his opinions on the measure were unchanged. He was convinced that the law would have beneficial results for the Poor; but at the same time if there was any hardship in its operation he would be glad to see it corrected.

Peel had not flinched, but he had been forced. Probably he would never have mentioned the Poor Law if the crowd had been quiet; he never mentioned it at all in his speech at his election dinner. There was nothing disgraceful in that. Many a Conservative speech was made at that election without touching the Poor Laws; they did not necessarily come into a review of Conservative principle. Nevertheless other Conservatives were abusing the new Poor Laws and being powerfully assisted in this election by the hatred inspired by a measure of which Peel himself approved. Obviously Peel had not spoken loudly enough to prevent his friends speaking the other way, to control, that is, the forces that would elevate him to power. It was a condition of affairs on which his enemies did not scruple to comment. Yet he himself was completely satisfied with the sufficiency of his declarations on the Poor Law, as he was satisfied also no doubt with the programme and principles with which he had endowed the Conservative party. But for all Peel's satisfaction there seems to have been in this case a division between the sentiment which was the source of power and the intelligence that determined its use.[1]

Parliament was to meet in November, late enough to give men ample time to consider the election results, or to endeavour to forget them. Peel occupied the interval with sport and sciatica in the country, but one repercussion of the election first claimed his immediate attention. His opponent at the Tamworth election had made so wild a personal attack upon him that Peel found it necessary to dispatch a friend and to gain an apology, which did not come before Bonham had smuggled a pistol case in a handkerchief out of Peel's house at Whitehall.[2] The incident was finished soon enough, and it was rather for Peel's opponents that serious trouble came out of the election, for a wounded honour is more easy to cure than a damaged majority. Melbourne was

---

[1] Peel's speech on the hustings, *The Times*, July 25. Add. MSS. 40, 424; 158 (corrected report of Peel's speeches at the hustings, July 24, and dinner at Tamworth, Aug. 7, 1837).

[2] Parker, II, 350. Add. MSS. 40,314; 133, 184. 40,424; 131.

reported by a Conservative lady to have said (with his usual oaths) that things looked bad, and John Russell wrote gloomily to Melbourne. It was no use, said he, concealing the difficulty of their position. He did not think, as some comforted themselves, that this House of Commons would be any more steady than the last had been, and he had always been sure that the Whigs as a party would be destroyed by the Reform Bill. His only hope lay not in his own strength, but in his belief in the difficulties of Peel's position, especially with regard to Ireland. It is a desperate, unhealthy kind of hope which is merely centred in another man's weakness.

However the most depressed and uncomfortable of ministers must decide on a policy. John Russell proposed a policy of compromise and comprehension, compromise with his adversaries, comprehension towards his possible friends. He could not escape compromise. He told Melbourne that no one could expect that they should now carry the Appropriation Clause, and that he was ready to abandon it and to accept the reasonable compromise which had been offered with respect to Irish Tithes. But upon the Appropriation Clause John Russell had climbed up into office in 1835, and it was not the only one of the Ministry's most controversial measures that he was now ready to shelve.[1]

Now controversial measures are obviously the very badges of consistency and the children of principle. But part of the brood of principle may be abandoned while the mother is retained. Like any other domesticated wild animal she may keep her home, if she does not keep all her offspring. Lord John had not abandoned his principles. In his speech at Stroud, after laying many sins of omission and commission at the doors of the Tories of the past, he endeavoured to keep them down for ever by putting the entire cost of the Napoleonic Wars on their shoulders. He then proceeded to explain the difference between the modern Conservatives and the Reformers by showing that Luther, Galileo and the early

[1] Spencer Walpole, *Life of Lord John Russell*, Vol. I, pp. 285 ff.

Christians were Reformers, while Leo X, the Inquisition and Nero were the Conservatives who opposed them. Such words could only have come from a sane man if he was still completely inspired by his party principle.

Lord John was still a Whig and he was still a Liberal. He was Whig enough to stand with courage by the Whig pledge that the settlement of 1832 should be final except in its details; a pledge which it was the more honourable to remember since it was impossible to maintain. Meanwhile his Liberalism was active and futile. He desired Liberal allies, he wished to adopt where he could a Liberal policy, or at least a policy which would conciliate Liberals. He suggested to Melbourne that they should allow members of the Government to vote as they pleased on the ballot, which the Government had hitherto officially opposed. But Melbourne would not allow the ballot to become an open question, and he also refused to admit any Radical into the Ministry, for he wanted to avoid the harassing discomfort of Lord Durham's company. So the Ministry remained unquestionably and unhopefully Whig.[1]

On the other hand the leaders of the Conservative opposition on their side were prepared to remain not only unhopefully Conservative but also contentedly in opposition. "We are," said Aberdeen early in 1838, "unfortunately in a false position, viz., that of an opposition without the desire of obtaining office, and doubtful of the power of retaining it if obtained." "Many of us," said he, "are perfectly satisfied to remain as we are, fully possessed of the means of preventing all legislative mischief, and able to expose the misconduct of the government."[2] Unfortunately, but not unnaturally, many of their friends were not so satisfied. "They do not understand," said Aberdeen, "these cool speculations." They were too cool, for instance, for the

[1] Spencer Walpole, *Lord John Russell*, I, 282 ff.

[2] Privately printed Aberdeen Corresp., 1832–44, p. 113 (Aberdeen to Princess Lieven, Feb. 7, 1838).

Marquess of Londonderry. In September 1837 he confessed to a friend that he was sick of this policy. "The statesmen of the present day seem not to know that a body acting together must have the rewards of ambition, patronage and place always before their eyes and within their expectation and belief of grasping, as well as the fine expressions of love of their country, and the patriotism which is a virtue." Nevertheless he was forced to admit that there was but one man and one party for them, and "bad," said he, "as the Conservative chance may be, rely upon it, if that party is split into any sections the Whigs are in power for ever," which was not a consummation to be desired by Lord Londonderry.[1]

Lord Londonderry was frank enough in what he said to require no comment, but possibly near enough to the truth to require some consideration. Supposing that what Aberdeen said was true, ought anyone to have been satisfied, as were the Conservative leaders, with the mere prevention of legislative mischief, and with the ability to expose other men's weakness and misconduct; satisfied to stand with irresistible power to prevent, but none to create, to restore or to govern? After all, there are more profitable dreams than of drawn battles, more reputable tasks than perpetual criticism, more useful consummations than stale-mate. Moreover if the leaders really lacked ambition, and did not wish for or think about office, their habit of mind would not only cripple and chill their own visions and their friends' loyalty, it would also limit the extent of their coolest calculations. If a man never contemplates victory, then victory may become, as so often, the most embarrassing accident of warfare. If a statesman never tries to think what his party will do in power, he is less likely to understand, what must always be difficult to understand, how much he must know and control his party in opposition.

Of course it was very hard for the Conservative leaders to see these things. They were obstructed by their incomplete knowledge of the rôle of a modern opposition,

[1] *Courts and Cabinets*, II, 288 (Londond. to Bucks., Sept: 1, 1837).

and their principles mainly instructed them in the duties
of prevention and preservation.   They conceived of a
Government rather as dealing with matters as they
occurred than as carrying out a programme for which it
had already, while in opposition, prepared its party and
the country.   They followed faithfully their limited view
of their duty; they forbore to hitch their wagons to a
star, while some of their followers hitched theirs to a
Star and Garter.   In consequence there was always
friction among the Conservatives in opposition, and when
the time for a Conservative Government came it may be
that the leaders paid in full for that dullness of desire,
that limitation in the conception of their duties, which
their followers diagnosed as lack of ambition.

§ 2

In November the members of Parliament began to
gather in London, for the new Session was to start on
the 18th.   Peel arrived full of spirit, Lyndhurst looked
plump and rosy and most gaily attired, and among the
lesser known Conservatives came a new member of
Parliament who had already achieved some notoriety by
his novels and political writings, a gorgeously dressed
young Jew whose name was Benjamin Disraeli.   But he
was only one among the many of whom it was said that
there had never been so strong a party in opposition.
They were very good-humoured but naturally very eager
and determined, and even Peel grew desirous that the
opportunity for a good party division should arise.[1]

However the first political development in that Parliament divided others rather than Peel from the
Government.   The Radicals brought forward an amendment to the Address, in which they pressed for the usual
Radical demands, an extension of the suffrage, a shorten-
ing of the length of Parliament, and the vote by ballot.
They abused the Conservatives, accusing them of bribery
and of the bullying of tenants and tradesmen at the

[1] Parker's *Graham*, I, 254 (Peel to Graham, Nov. 21, 1837).

elections, but they spoke harshly of the Government, demanding with appeals and threats that it should produce more numerous and more effective Reforms. John Russell followed them in debate, declaring against the ballot or any alteration in the duration of Parliaments or the constitution of the electorate. The Reform Act had only been passed five years, and had been permitted to be extensive in order that it might have the prospect of being final, and he said that he could not feel it wise, or in his own case justifiable, to propose alterations which went beyond it. Lord John had proved himself a Whig, and a courageous one. He was complimented by Whigs on his adherence to principle, but his declaration earned him the nickname of Finality Jack and was noted, regretted or abused by all manner of Radicals. They could not know how large a fund of Liberalism he had, as yet unexpended, or that he was anxious that his colleagues should be allowed to vote for the ballot which he himself was so courageously and consistently to resist. So for the moment the Radicals were inclined to indulge in despair, or in hopes for the future which did not include the prosperity of the Whigs.[1] As was their nature and duty, they criticized the size of the Civil list granted to Queen Victoria, but there was a more interesting field at hand for their activities.

At the end of 1837 the problem of Canada had become acutely critical. In all the British North American colonies difficulties had arisen from the problem of combining representative Assemblies with the irresponsible administration of a Governor appointed from home. These were especially important in Upper and Lower Canada, and most of all in the province of Lower Canada, where the majority of the population was French, with an increasing British minority pressing upon them.[2] The Assembly in Lower Canada persisted in refusing

---

[1] *Life of Rt. Hon. Sir Wm. Molesworth*, by Mrs. Fawcett, p. 134 (Molesworth to Mrs. Grote, Autumn, 1837).

[2] A good epitome in Lucas' *Durham Report*, Vol. I.

to appropriate money for the Civil servants, and the home Government, trying to be reasonable, succeeded in being muddled and indecisive.   In such a quarrel the Radicals' duty was plain, and a plain duty may be one which does not give a man time to think.   A popular assembly was desiring its rights from an unelected Government; possibly a Colony was demanding its right to secede, and the precedent of the United States, whom they very much admired, engaged their minds.   They objected eloquently when, as in the spring of 1837, the Whig Government took drastic measures against Lower Canada, and when at the end of 1837 the news came of open rebellion in both Upper and Lower Canada they were in haste to sympathize enthusiastically and unwisely, even desiring the failure of British Arms.[1]

The Conservative leaders, on their part, were not un-interested in the matter.   Stanley, who had dealt with the Canadas as Whig Colonial Secretary, was greatly excited and was ardent against the Lower Canada Assembly;   the retention of the Colonies had, since the Reform Bill, been one of the Duke of Wellington's most grievous anxieties, and Aberdeen and Gladstone, who had been at the Colonial Office in 1835, were involved in the problem.   Peel gave the matter his attention.   He too commented on the decay of order and authority.   In 1837 he had told Gladstone, "You have got another Ireland growing up in every Colony you possess," by which he probably meant to reflect on the tendencies encouraged by the feebleness and truckling of the Government.[2]   For though an opposition may not be able to diagnose, suggest or foresee, at the least it will always be able to criticize.   Indeed there was much in the Government's actions deserving of criticism, especially when the Whigs tried to pursue a meandering path on the frontiers of concession and firmness, and the Colonial Office was dominated by the verbose and conscientious confusion of Lord Glenelg, the Secretary of State.

[1] Hansard, Vol. XXXIX, 1467 (Molesworth's speech).
[2] Morley's *Gladstone*, Chap. III (Diary, March 4, 1837).

In the first weeks of 1838 the Canadian problem engaged the attention of the Conservative leaders. It was a matter in which the initiative had to be left to the Government, and they intended to support any measures that the Government proposed for putting down the revolt. But Stanley wrote to Peel full of criticism against the Government, and his letters induced Peel to write at length on Canada both to himself and to the Duke. Every effort, Peel said, should be made to suppress the revolt, even at the expense of war with the United States, with whom complications had arisen. The honour of the country, her immense Empire, her position with regard to Ireland demanded this. Her honour also demanded that if the great body of British settlers desired to persist in the British connection, there was no option but to maintain it. But if that was the case, it was intolerable that there should be an obstructive and hostile popular Assembly dominating the mouth of the St. Lawrence. They had a right to require that the friends of the British connection should have a predominance in the local councils. If it were for him to advise, he would therefore suspend the Act which gave Canada its constitution, provide an intermediate administration, and consider all the North American Colonies together, in order to discover the best method of providing against the risk and charge of defending them in a war with France or the United States.

Such in brief was Peel's general view. It was a cold one, and he does not show much belief in the intrinsic value of that part of the Empire to England. If it was to be retained, it must be because we owed it to those who had settled under our protection. Stanley, commenting, thought that Peel underrated the importance for this country of the possession of the Canadas, or rather the importance of their not being possessed by the United States, in itself a strange way of expressing the value of Canada to the Empire. But Peel was kept steady in the service of the Empire by his regard for the honour of his country, an expression by which he seems to have meant sometimes its prestige and sometimes its good faith. He was the steady servant of a future which he could hardly understand.[1]

But the Ministers were the slaves of the present. It was for them, it could not be for anyone out of office, to put forward proposals for the subduing and settlement of the Canadas. The subduing was easy, indeed the revolts were quickly put down in Lower Canada by the troops, and in Upper Canada by the people themselves. For the task of settlement the Ministry proposed to send out Lord Durham with dictatorial powers to discover a solution. Lord Durham was the leader of the Radicals. He went out to Canada sustained and surrounded by Radicals, but the Ministry did not thereby avoid all Radical criticism. Their previous conduct, their present suspension of the Canadian constitution, all came in for attack from one Radical or another during the debates on their proposals in the early part of the Session of 1838. Nor were the Conservatives sparing in their accusations, and the Bill which gave Durham his powers was criticized by Peel in the most useful and humiliating manner. Peel showed great ability and the Bill great deficiencies, so that the Government had to submit to its alteration, while Peel did not conceal his contempt. Again men repeated the sneer that it was Peel that really governed the country, while the Ministry took the pay. Yet Peel's position was not without its difficulties and complications.

One of these complications was the Duke of Wellington, who proved again that he was a good patriot but a bad comrade in party warfare. At a time of national difficulty he could not keep up the kind of disapproving support of the Government which an Opposition usually finds suitable to such periods, and at the beginning of the Session he broke out and exonerated the Government from his friends' accusations of their having sent out too few troops. However, Peel had a graver problem to face in the House of Commons than explaining away the words

[1] Parker, II, 355. Add. MSS. 40,424; 287, etc.

of an old incalculable Duke.   By the middle of February
it was known that the Radical, Sir William Molesworth,
would move for the removal of Lord Glenelg from the
Colonial Office.   It was a motion in which the Conservatives might easily join with the Radicals.

The passage of time had robbed the Radicals of neither
their taint nor their terror.   To forget the fears of the
Conservatives would still be to misunderstand them.
They had commented very gloomily on the strength of
the support given during that February to a motion in
favour of the ballot, one even saying that it was the
beginning of the end, that end, presumably, which was
so often beginning.   To join with the Radicals upon this
motion against Lord Glenelg would be both shameful
and unwise, as Peel, the Duke, Stanley and Graham were
all in haste to point out.   As Graham said, "they force
on this motion because they think the juncture favourable
to their wicked designs."   A victory gained by a coalition
between Radicals and Conservatives would discredit the
Conservatives and set them up in a minority Government,
with matters at a crisis in Canada and probably in Ireland
as well.   Yet the Radical motion condemned a Government which the Conservatives also condemned, and the
Conservatives were strong enough to encourage the more
foolish among them to desire a more active opposition.
Men felt that nothing was gained while a Whig ministry
remained in office.   Too great restraint would lead to
anger and discontent in the party, and possibly to some
Conservatives voting with the Radicals against Peel.
The party would have to be led delicately.

Peel was aware of the difficulty.   He reminded the
Duke, who needed to be reminded of it, that it was of
great public importance to keep the Conservative party
together.   A powerful minority, said Peel, acting in
concert, was an immense check upon Radicalism, it was
a great encouragement to that half of the Government
who were not Radicals, and a great support to the House
of Lords in its resistance to what was dangerous and
unjust.   Since the Reform Bill Peel had been most

intelligently anxious about his party's unity. Yet the
ends for which he always proposed to keep his party
united were purely defensive, to be achieved by a cautious
opposition, uninspiring and unenterprising, which
naturally tended to secure the recurrence of such dangers
as the present one to the unity which he so much desired.[1]

Nevertheless the Canadian corner was turned. On
March 7th Sir William Molesworth proposed his motion
against Lord Glenelg. In his speech he produced much
indeed that showed an enlightened and far-sighted view
of the possibilities of the Empire, but much also that
proved his desire to replace the present Government by
one which should be Conservative in name as well as
deed and to which they would have a truly Liberal
Opposition. But the Conservative leaders had produced
in secret an amendment for which Peel had carefully
prepared his party. It not only abused the Government,
it also abused the revolted Canadians in such a way that
the Radicals could not support it. The manœuvre was
successful. Molesworth's purely Radical motion was not
even pressed to a vote, and Peel was able to lose his battle
with vigour and dexterity.

§ 3

Canada was not the only disturbed country with which
they had to deal in 1838. Ireland was always with them,
and they were, during that Session, to get rid of part of
the paralysing controversy respecting Irish measures.
As Lord John now desired, the Ministry tried to avail
themselves of the suggested compromise on the Irish
Poor Law, Tithe and Municipal Bills. The three Bills
were introduced in a conciliatory order, the Irish Municipal Bill being kept till last, as the Lords had declared
that it could only be considered in the light of what was
decided on the Irish Poor Law and Irish Tithes. The
Irish Poor Law was passed with comparative ease, for it
was nearly an agreed measure and only violently opposed
by O'Connell and a number of the Irish members of all

[1] Parker, II, 358 ff. Add. MSS. 40,424; 343 ff. 40,318; 116, etc.

parties and creeds.   An acceptable Irish Tithe Bill was ultimately produced without Lay Appropriation, which put the payment of tithes on a temporarily satisfactory basis, and passed the House of Lords and became law. The Irish Municipal Bill alone was unfortunate.   It formed the subject of much consideration and research among the leaders of the Conservative party, and it did not seem to Peel that its details permitted it to come under the compromise.   He objected to the qualifications laid down for Municipal electors, which he held should be as high in monetary value as what was exacted in England. Consequently after the Bill had been passed through the Commons it was so amended by the Lords as to be dropped for the Session.

Something had been effected in the clearing of the stage, but not without controversy.   The Conservatives did not trust Whig faith in their proposals, and the whole Session was filled with a constant elaboration of explanation and counter-explanation in the House of Commons, of questions formally asked by one party leader and cautiously answered by the other.   The Conservatives suspected that the principle of Appropriation was concealed in the Government's Irish Tithe resolutions, and in order to establish their principle and prevent a precedent, they insisted on attempting to rescind the resolution in favour of Lay Appropriation which had driven Peel from office in 1835.   On May 14th, two days after a dinner to Peel in the Merchant Taylors' Hall, they were led in assault upon the Appropriation resolution in the House of Commons.   They cast 298 votes against 317, and thus showed their strength as an Opposition. And they were not only strong, they were being emancipated from their commitments.   The Irish Tithe Bill was passed, and the principle of granting to Ireland elective corporations was now accepted by the Conservatives both in the Lords and the Commons.   A settlement was at hand of the long dreary deadlock between the two parties and the two Houses of Parliament about the treatment of Ireland.

Of course it was not a settlement of the troubles of Ireland. In the course of the debates on the Municipal Bill, Disraeli asked that the principle of the compromise might be explained. He hoped that this settlement was not a mere attempt to elude difficulties against which they must finally contend.[1] The question was typical of the question , but it does not seem to have taken the attention of ae House of Commons. Nor · was the compromise only an evasion of difficulties. The Irish Poor Law was a serious measure. The Irish Tithe Act would lay the payment of tithes upon the Irish landlords who were mainly Protestant, rather than directly upon their Roman Catholic tenants, and would dispose of various irritating questions which the controversy had left open. Ireland would now ultimately gain the benefit of open and elective Municipal Corporations. There was some gain here, but nothing decisive. Irish poverty and bad Irish economic conditions remained ready for a tragic and a terrible culmination. What Irish peace there was depended on O'Connell's alliance with the present Government, and O'Connell's fangs had not been drawn, nor his desires obliterated. He had refused, at some cost to himself, the Irish Mastership of the Rolls, in order that he might continue to serve Ireland. He was not satisfied with the Tithe settlement, he still desired Repeal in his heart and was ready to start on its violent agitation, and he still hated the Conservatives who persevered in their abuse of him and his religion.

Meanwhile Irish Conservatives were eloquent in their complaints of the peril to life and property in their country. They enumerated outrages, they believed in a general conspiracy and they clamoured for an enquiry into the condition of Ireland under the present Executive. Peel would still have to face terrible adversaries in Ireland and to consort with impossible allies. No peace had been prepared for Ireland, nor any end to her troubles. Settlements by compromise are necessary, but you cannot compromise facts, and it needs more than the arrangement

[1] Hansard, XLIII, 514.

of a deadlock to cure the cruellest social difficulties, the harshest of political antagonisms. Disraeli's question was relevant, yet to what advantage was it to ask relevant questions?

§4

Besides Canada and Ireland other problems must confront the Conservative party in 1838 and the years which followed. There were to be troubles in Europe and in England itself, a bad harvest in 1838, another in 1839, and food prices rising, especially in 1839 and 1840. There had been and were to be financial troubles and commercial dislocation. There was to be unemployment, misery and starvation, and the nation's misery would fester into politics. The strain that there was already on the new Poor Law would become intoler, able. There would be armed rebellion in the country-and the next few years would be remarkable for that strange coalition between the old-fashioned political Revolution and that of the economically disinherited, which is called Chartism. Meanwhile, less melodramatic but more fatal, the agitation of the Corn Law League was about to be started, and on all sides men of all parties would be moved on various questions by the emotions of hatred and pity. Both are dangerous emotions.

And while difficulties increased, Conservatives would find increasing evidence of the ineptitude of the Government. Their word for the Government was "Shabby," a word which Graham produced and Stanley was fond of repeating. They meant by it a kind of mean cowardice which by despicable evasions betrayed its trust, and laid on others the responsibilities of office. For instance the division lists in the various debates on the ballot and also the troubles of Canada would supply to Conservative minds many instances of Whig truckling, while the real Whig incompetence over finance would rightly alarm them with year after badly budgetted year of repeated deficiency. These years were to confront Conservative leaders with difficulties, with dangers, with apprehensions, with a troubled Empire and a weak and shabby Government, and also with the menace of the burden of power.

Peel approached his task and his future with Conservative principles. On May 12th he had been entertained to dinner in the Merchant Taylors' Hall by over 300 Conservative members of Parliament,[1] He spoke in response to his toast, and described his political objects. He had chiefly laboured, he said, to lay the foundations of a great party which, existing in the popular will, should diminish the risk and deaden the shock of collisions between the branches of the legislature, which should be enabled to check the too impatient eagerness of the well-intentioned for hasty and precipitate changes and say with a voice of authority to the restless spirit of Revolutionary encroachment, "Here are the bounds by which thy vibrations shall be stayed."

He was still thinking, in 1838, of the defence of the institutions of the country against the Whigs and the Radicals, of what his task had been since 1832. It was natural that he should continue to think of it. It was not obviously finished. If the Conservatives were for the moment successful in that struggle, it seemed to be only by their own efforts. As Peel pointed out to his followers, it was they, with but little help from the Whigs, who had defeated in the House of Commons motions for the ballot, for removing the Bishops from the House of Lords, or for repealing the Corn Laws. As Stanley said the same evening, the Church was only not in danger because the Conservatives were powerful and united. Given broadly Peel's premises it was natural that he should continue to concentrate his mind on his old objects. But in the broad light of History would it be enough?

Would it be enough? Would the appeal to such objects hold together his party when new controversies were active, when the Church and the Lords were not obviously faced by any immediate peril, or when Peel was in power? Did such objects foreshadow the work of any

---

[1] *The Times*, May 14, 1838.

Ministry, or prepare men for the policy to be followed
by any Government of which Peel would be the Prime
Minister?   It is true that men knew that Peel would be
a safe reformer, but safety is the object of all men's
reforms.   Would such objects definitely imply the cure
of any of those evils that would distress the country?
Perhaps a Conservative should promise not only to
defend institutions but to use them for the good of all,
and so to overwhelm foolish desires, especially in the
ignorant and suffering, with right-minded hope.   What
hopes had Peel for the poor?

The question is not one of those challenges of History
which are like the trial of a man in a language he does
not understand, when men are accused of having had the
opportunities of the past without the knowledge of the
present.   This challenge was made both by Peel's
circumstances and by his contemporaries.   The circumstances of the time had already made other Conservatives
take up the immediate cause of the poor and the
oppressed.   No doubt that is always the cause of parties
in opposition, as it is always possible for oppositions to
scavenge up the scraps and tit-bits of popularity which
any Government must discard.   Nevertheless, on two
subjects that cause seems almost naturally to have
enlisted the support of Conservatives.   One was the
new Poor Law, the other was the question of the restriction of hours of labour in factories.

The Whig Poor Law was certainly harsh, whatever
were its virtues, and whatever might be its effectiveness
in curing more or less permanent pauperization its
methods were intolerable, indeed impracticable, when it
was confronted with industrial unemployment.   In the
manufacturing North, especially, the feeling against it
had grown strong, bitter and very articulate; and in close
connection with this was the agitation about factory
hours.   Outside Parliamentary circles this agitation
really aimed at a Bill for the restriction to ten of the
hours of labour of adults, but in Parliament it was as yet

only possible to touch child labour. The controversy centred round the Act of 1833 for the protection of children in the textile trades. This, though originally proposed by Lord Ashley, was, when heavily amended, taken over and passed by the Whig government. It was obviously insufficient and certainly ineffective. From the moment it came into operation it was evaded, while offences under it too often came before magistrates in sympathy with the offender, and were neither impartially tried nor adequately punished. Yet the Whig Government would not willingly assent to the remedy of these evils, and in 1836 they even tried to take back part of what they had granted. Here were two causes which might well appeal to the humanity of men in opposition, or to their desire for popularity.

Both the cry against the Poor Law and the cry for Factory Reform were already associated with Conservatives, both in Parliament and the country. Richard Oastler, a remarkable land agent from near Huddersfield, was one of the central figures of the agitation in the North, and he called himself a Conservative. In 1835 he told Lord Ashley that he had long laboured to unite the aristocrats and the people,[1] and when the elections of 1837 came he stood himself as a Conservative candidate, and supported others on the hustings. But he was a strange kind of Conservative. His feelings and his oratory brought him to speak to ignorant and excited people in language of violence certainly unsuitable in a Conservative or a Conservative ally, while the language of his movement was often half-way and more than half-way to the language of violence and revolution.

But that need not prevent Conservatives from sympathizing with the objects for which Oastler worked. Conservatives had joined in the condemnation of much of the new Poor Law. Agricultural Conservatives were not disinclined to vote for factory reform, and religious-minded Conservatives were moved to support it. Inglis

[1] *Shaftesbury* (Hodder), Vol. I, 214.

was on its side and Goulburn voted for it, while its chief champion in the Commons was Lord Ashley, who had taken it over from another Tory, Michael Sadler.   With such movements and desires in his party perhaps it might be said that the circumstances of the time had issued their challenge to the leader of the Conservative party to become, obviously, the servant of the suffering poor.

To make the challenge clearer, some among Peel's contemporaries gave words to it.   It was not only that the Conservative party considered itself to be the party of religion and the Established Church, although Ashley was there to put the claims of humanity to it on that head.[1]   But there was also to be in some quarters a feeling for benevolent aristocracy in the air.   It was a time when Democracy faltered or was very foolish, and some theory of Aristocracy was likely to appeal to the generous or the disappointed.   In 1839 Carlyle was to publish a volcano of a tract upon Chartism, in which he passionately called men's attentions to the question of the condition of England and in which also he made some sort of appeal to aristocracy.   But Carlyle condemned everyone, and would appeal to no party; for at best Carlyle was only a prophet.   It is possible to come nearer home.   Disraeli was already in Parliament.   Men could have learnt already something from his political views, and the years were soon to come when he should produce at its full in *Coningsby* and *Sybil* his view of the true functions of aristocracy and Toryism, and its relations to the people.   Meanwhile there were already at Cambridge the young Tories who were to start the generous and philanthropic Young England movement. So there would be ideas in the air that could have inspired Peel, and might have served him.   There were to be most pressing needs for a right use of Conservatism, and apparently golden opportunities.   There was to be popularity available, and one man of great talent, even genius.   Yet Peel made no use of all these favours.   It is not to be wondered at that men have dreamed, with

[1] *Shaftesbury* (Hodder), Vol. I, 300.

easy injustice, that with Disraeli's insight and popular
sympathy Peel might have outbidden Cobden and
changed the whole history of England.[1]

§ 5

It is a dream to be enjoyed and considered, but with
it must be considered, if not enjoyed, other points in the
question.   Politics are not only a matter of insight and
popular sympathy; they are also unluckily concerned
with the difficult and dangerous and delusive science of
economics.   Some very honest men may live by intuition
alone and gain the rest by the way, but others, perhaps
equally honest, may have convinced themselves, possibly
wrongly, of the truth of various economic propositions.
Peel, for instance, was convinced that it was economically
unwise to imperil the New Poor Law or to interfere too
much with the hours of labour, yet the popular movement
to which he should have addressed himself was concerned
with the restriction of hours and dominated by the
Anti-Poor Law cry.

Nor is it fair to take Peel from his context.   He was
struggling to save the Constitution in Church and State.
Unlike Disraeli, he had been for some time in the thick
of that struggle, and he and all his friends, including
Lord Ashley, still continued to see signs that it was active
and urgent.   It is not to be wondered if that need filled
up too much of his imagination, or if it prevented him
from considering or approving a coalition with intemperate popular forces.   Nor indeed is it in the least
probable that any such coalition would have been as
effective or lasting as the dreamers would have it.   The
popular movement, on which Peel should have built,
largely evaporated in Chartism.   It would be hard to say
that there was any chance of preventing this, and it should
be still harder to say with any assurance that, if he had
wished, Peel could with any other popular appeal have
withstood Cobden and the powerful cry for cheap corn.

Unfortunately there is something more to be said.

---

[1] E.g. Monypenny, *Life of Disraeli*, Vol. II, 87.

It is not likely that Peel or anyone else could have effected much that was permanent by a popular alliance, and it would have been wrong for him to attempt to do so by compromising his opinions in Economics. Yet popular sympathy might have enlivened his party principles or enlightened his economic opinions. Fearless honesty has too often guarded insufficient thought or insufficient humanity. But it is fairer to consider Peel's actual opinions on the two decisive subjects Factory Reform and the Poor Law.

Peel's father, the great cotton spinner, was an early pioneer in the cause of the protection of factory children, but Peel himself seems to have early imbibed the current fears of any interference with the operations of the factories. Restriction in the freedom of trade might cripple it, and so produce unemployment ensuring the misery of the very children it was desired to protect, and in 1825 Peel had preached to the House of Commons the need of caution and hesitation in legislating for the factory children.[1] However, minds may enlarge with the years. In 1836 Peel had spoken on the question. In 1836, the Government made their attempt to recall some protection promised to children by their Act of 1833 on the ground of that Act's deficiencies. Ashley opposed them, and was able to win enough support to stop them. But Peel spoke on the other side to Lord Ashley. Part of what he said was very reasonable. The Act was admittedly defective, he would support the Government's proposition in order to consider its amendment. But the background of his mind had not changed. "He was quite opposed to the adoption of any severe restrictions of labour, from the belief that they were calculated to undermine the Commercial Energies of the country and thereby to strike a blow against the happiness and comfort of the people." It is true that he said other things in his speech. He said he was convinced that legislative interference was necessary, because he

[1] Hansard, XIII (New Series), 422, 645, and 1010; see also Clapham, *Economic History of Modern Britain* (The Railway Age), p. 377.

was afraid that the natural affection of parents was not to be trusted. He attacked the arguments about the danger of foreign competition, saying that that was a good argument for lowering the duties on cotton wool, but not a good argument for endangering the health of the factory children. He thought that the laws should prohibit the undue working of children.[1]

For his background of the freedom of trade was only a background. His mind was not so packed with that conviction that there was no room for anything else, and there were other things in his mind. He had a natural humanity and undoubted piety. He professed respect for Lord Ashley, and it was not only parliamentary respect. He desired his co-operation in the party, and that possibly not only because he wished for the prestige of his high moral character. Probably, and this was a large part of the trouble, he only thought of these and other economic problems intermittently. His great talents and what imagination he had were mainly engaged on the safety of the Constitution, the safety of the Church and the perils of the French Revolution. But he never could lose and he never did lose the background of his world, the need for that unencumbered trade which must support all interests, labouring, manufacturing and agricultural. His instinct would be rather to reform tariffs than hours in factories.

In 1838 the Factories Question came before the House of Commons. This time Lord Ashley urged against difficulties the necessity of amending the Act of 1833. Peel too urged the Government to settle the matter, for the sake of humanity and of trade. But he was perhaps less conciliatory than before towards Factory reform. This time he could not fail to perceive the competition with which the country was threatened. He mentioned again, as an unquestionable fact, that they would deprive the children of prospective employment. He never took, said he, the popular side of this subject, but from the division lists and the debates upon it, that seems to

[1] Hansard, XXXIV, 782.

have been the side taken by his friend Goulburn and
many other Conservatives.¹   So Peel was held back by
his economic scruples, and the main question for justice
seems to be whether he realized to the full the unen-
durable conditions in which he felt he must leave the
factory children, and whether he had thought enough
on the point.   They are rather questions for the Heavens
than the Historians.

Then there was the New Poor Law.   Early in 1837
a Commission had been granted to inquire into that
matter.   Its terms did not satisfy and its enquiry did
not silence the critics in Parliament.   In 1838 Conservatives among others, both in the Lords and the Commons, alleged scandals against its operation.   Most of
them shrank back, indeed, when Fielden the Radical
moved the repeal of the New Poor Law in the Commons,
although in the tiny minority of 17 who voted with
Fielden most were Conservatives and one was Disraeli.
But Peel did not wish to hamper the New Poor Law
by criticism.   He was afraid that propositions for inquiry
might in some way cast doubts on Parliament's resolution to maintain the principle of the law, although he
wished to find out how he might mitigate the severity
of its operation.   He believed that the measure would
elevate the moral condition and promote the independence of the poor.   He was for continuing the experiment.   It would be easy to be satiric.   It is always easy
to be satiric when any man talks about the moral condition of the poor.   Sometimes it is even just, but it is
also just to remember that there was at that time fair
reason to believe that the Poor Laws, by diminishing
rates, would enable men to be employed who might
otherwise be paupers, and that a strong case had been
made out that the old Poor Law had been demoralizing.
It is bad, even for the poor, to be demoralized.   In
1838, only four years after the passing of the New Poor
Law, an honest man might think it was worth a longer

¹ Hansard, XLIII, 974.

trial, and Peel always said that he was ready to do what he could to inquire into its worst severities.[1]

So on both the Poor Law and Factory questions Peel spoke as a man who took a comprehensive view of the condition of the poor, and who realized that those who differed from him were moved by a commiseration for individual and personal suffering. He was certainly affected by not insincere philanthropy and not entirely unsound economics. He was an Opposition leader who consciously and steadfastly refused to be factious and popular. But his comprehensive view perhaps over-looked more than details. His economics were not impregnable, and they vitiated his philanthropy, while his party waxed powerful in opposition with the enthusiasms which he did not share. He had the strong hands and the stout heart which there should be in an Aristocrat, but had he the restless mind and keen eyes as well?

§ 6

There is little more to record of the rest of the Session of 1838, except perhaps to mention the moderation with which the Duke of Wellington spared the Government in the Lords, and the annoyance to which that gave rise with some of his followers and with Lord Brougham, who wished heartily to injure the Ministry that had abandoned him. However, the year 1838 was still to provide much matter for politics. Canada was still unsettled. Lord Durham's career there was short and highly controversial. His task was hard, his dictatorial powers doubtful in extent and obviously repugnant to lawyers, his temper too ardent and his instincts impru-dent. He was built for the exercise of strong popular principles and unquestioned authority, and not for dif-ficult co-operation with a weak, suspicious and consti-tutional Cabinet. He produced an ordinance to deal as humanely and safely as he could with some of the political prisoners, and his action seemed to be tyrannical, and certainly went beyond his powers. When the news of

[1] Hansard, XL, 1415; XXXVI, 1088.

it came home, Brougham took the matter up in the House of Lords with an edge to his passion, for not only did it bear on the Ministry, but he had also an old feud with Lord Durham; and the Conservatives joined Brougham in condemning the ordinance and its legality.

The matter came up in late July and in August while the Session of 1838 was drawing wearily to its end. Decisions were difficult and hurried, the ordinance was hard to defend, while Melbourne seems to have always distrusted and disliked Durham. Ministers in the Lords first made a show of defending Durham, but when Brougham brought in an indemnity Bill for the illegalities of the Ordinance, they first abandoned one point and the next day announced that they had advised the Queen to disallow the whole, while they submitted to Brougham's Bill, to which they ineffectively tried to add a proviso. It passed through both Houses with Government support, though John Russell gave Durham a better defence than had been offered by Melbourne. During the autumn matters marched swiftly. Durham felt that he was betrayed, and threw up his office in Canada, having issued a proclamation which seemed to appeal to the Canadians against the Queen's Government. He came home full of rage against his employers, amid violent and not unjustifiable abuse from the Lords on account of his proclamation and the desertion of his post at the hour of danger. Hot foot on his heels came the news of another revolt in Canada. And yet from Durham's mission date those principles on which the Government of the British Dominions was to be founded.[1]

But there was political activity elsewhere than in Canada that autumn and winter. On all sides new issues were being added to politics. For one thing the Cabinet decided to take up Education. For some time there had been a growing talk of popular education on a national basis. It had had various advocates. In the Lords there was Brougham, the old friend of popular

---

[1] *Melbourne Papers*, 423. Spencer Walpole, *Life of Lord John Russell*, I, 307–10. Torrens, *Melbourne*, II, 268. Broughton, V, 161.

instruction; in the Commons, up to the last election, Roebuck had been the most notable champion of national education. But from a national point of view too little had been done. Neither Roebuck nor Brougham were likely to be very helpful to their cause, the religious were already full of the argument that education without religion was a great deal worse than no education at all, and the Church had claims to be the natural controller of the popular education in England. In 1833 it is true a grant of £20,000 had been voted to be divided between the National Society, which was the Church Education Society, and the British and Foreign School Society which was undenominational. It was given in proportion as each provided sums to meet it. It was not enough. It was not adequately controlled, nor was it very satisfactorily divided, for the Church, being the richer body, won most of it, and it was said that the proportional system did not help to found schools in the poorer districts where funds could not be collected. Something more was desirable, state education was in the air. At the elections of 1837, John Russell had mentioned education, while later that year something had excited the susceptible nerves of Robert Peel.

On November 12th, he had written to Croker a letter in which he seems to assume that education was about to be taken up as a mere ground for agitation and because previous agitation had failed. He believed that the Church could confidently defy this agitation by instituting an independent and purely voluntary system of her own.[1] Characteristically, then, he was driven to wish a service performed for the nation because he desired to outbid an objectionable proposal. Characteristically he believed that the best effect would be served by voluntary effort and not intervention by himself or by the State, even for the benefit of the State Church, and it is characteristic of his position that the service was one which no voluntary effort would ever be able finally, fully, and satisfactorily to perform at all.

[1] Croker, II, 321.

Characteristically also his view of the subject was vitiated by that worst danger to the judgment of a statesman, his routine contempt for the motives of his antagonists.

However he would have to speak further on the matter, for in 1838 it appeared to the Cabinet that the question could neither be escaped nor deferred. The next step would have to be an advance towards a national system under the control of the State. In the Prime Minister, as in Peel, education proposals produced typical reactions. Perhaps he never really said that he did not believe in education "because the Pagets got on so damned well without it," but certainly he was against a change because he thought education stood upon better grounds than any upon which they would be able to place it. He thought that the attempt at a combined system would fail, though he was ready to yield his opinion and try; he was not going to stand in the way. As Howick said to him in Cabinet, "Thank God there are some things which even you cannot stop, and that is one of them." [1]

Meanwhile other politicians were adding their characteristic contributions to the last months of 1838. The Duke of Wellington was anxious about the defence of the country and its strength on the sea, and he hastened to communicate to the Cabinet strange rumours that he had heard of the intentions of Russia. O'Connell was active for Ireland. The Ministry, he said, was weak, many of them anxious to retire; they were not strong enough to serve Ireland effectually. Moreover he realized that there was great discontent abroad on the Continent and in England; the moment might be a propitious one for pressing Irish claims by agitation. So, as always, he resorted to his old methods. He wrote manifestoes for the papers and he founded an association to whose members he gave the strange name of "Precursors." They were to agitate for full Corporation Reform, extension of the suffrage, adequate representation in Parliament and a universal appropriation of

---

[1] *Melbourne Papers*, 384. Broughton's *Recollections*, V, 168.

tithes, while their absurd name reflected the fact that
the demand for Repeal might revive. The Ministry
showed their disapproval of the Society. An episode in
Irish History was drawing to its end. The alliance
between O'Connell and the Whigs would continue for
a little, for O'Connell continued to fear the Tories' return
and Orange persecution. But neither his satisfaction
with past favours nor his belief in the Whigs' strength
and good-will were enough to make the alliance real or
lasting. When they began to fail there came naturally
to his mouth the old phrase that Ireland's only hope
was her own vigour and there came inevitably to his
mind thoughts of Repeal. Some time a new campaign
for Repeal would certainly begin, and it would be necessary to turn to a new page in Irish History, on which
were not written the words of peace.[1]

§ 7

Nor were the words of peace being written at large
over England. There were others who stirred in sympathy with the seething and spluttering of popular discontent, who despaired of the Whigs as O'Connell did
at times, and who were even now prepared to act for
themselves. There was a cause, long supported among
Radicals, which was now to be roused by the chill winds
of these years of high food prices and manufacturing
depression, and to become lively and dangerous. There
had been an Anti-Corn Law Association before, and Anti-
Corn Law pamphlets and lectures and Corn Law debates
in the Houses of Parliament. But those were light
gusts, making nothing but ripples. In the years before
1837 the complaints of the landlords were louder in
Parliament. Now the cause was to be undertaken in
the country by strong men and powerful orators, with
argument and with passion; there was to be, as never
before, a widespread organization to forward it, and altogether such a storm would be raised as would shake a

[1] *Correspondence of O'Connell*, II, 147 ff.

whole kingdom and, in the end, engulf a Conservative statesman. There would be a stronger Radicalism, rooted not in philosophy but in the provinces, a middle-class movement which would drag the Whigs lagging in its train. On September 24th, 1838, at the York Hotel, Manchester, the famous and final Anti-Corn Law Association was founded.

Its founders were soon at their work. At the end of 1838 they managed to carry, through the Manchester Chamber of Commerce, a petition to Parliament for the Repeal of the Corn Laws. In 1839 they founded the Anti-Corn Law League, to send out its emissaries all over the country. But it was in 1838, and very soon after the foundation of the original association, that they were vouchsafed their most remarkable weapon. For they were joined in their early days by a young Manchester manufacturer of thirty-four years of age. He had travelled widely and written very well about his travels. But he was not only an author, he was also a politician and had stood as a Liberal for Stockport in 1837 and had been barely defeated. He now came to ensure the life of a cause which was to ensure his fame. He had the vigour of his own steam engines and the rest-lessness of the fire which drove them. He could reason for his Cause and could elaborate its arguments, yet it was also a religion with him, affecting and colouring everything, filling him with moral conviction and moral hatred. But, with him, it was without unction. It left him a natural man, lively, untainted with man-nerisms, attractive, angry, unjust but nothing worse. He was Richard Cobden, the scourge, and at the end, the admirer of Peel.

That winter, also, there were other men stirring and striving through England with shriller cries and more Revolutionary desires than the Anti-Corn Law Associa-tion. The pinch of unemployment, the hatred of the New Poor Law, the fermentation of democratic ideas, were producing effects not controlled by Manchester manufacturers. Attwood, the Currency fanatic, had revived his Birmingham Political Union to use what popular strength he could, and what threats of force he dared, in the interests of his Currency proposals.   The orators who spoke against the new Poor Law surpassed themselves in wildness and vigour, and there was already in action another man who was going to take over the lead of the popular indignation.   Fergus O'Connor had been an Irish Member of Parliament but had quarrelled with O'Connell.   He was wild, ungoverned and vain, ready to use threats of force that he would never fulfil but that his audiences delighted to hear.   He was a bully and a coward and a true demagogue, whose thought was negligible and his oratory intoxicating.   He was now to become the leader of the Chartist Movement.

For in the autumn of 1838 the Chartist Movement had come into existence.   It was hostile to the Anti-Corn Law League.   That was led and inspired by the middle classes, and it had an economic objective which could be shared by employers and their workmen. The Chartist agitation was a working-class movement. It was inspired by the delusive hopes of a political programme, and the points of the Charter were such things as Universal Suffrage, Vote by Ballot, Payment of Members, and frequent general Elections.   The Charter had been provided by the politically conscious London artisans, but Chartism drew its strength not so much from London as from the various local distresses in the manufacturing parts of the country.   As with the cry against taxation and pensions which had so much assisted the Reform Bill, economic misery and dissatisfaction was trying again to find in politics the old and easy way out.   So the most dangerous recruits were probably such men as the distressed hand-loom weavers of the North and Midlands or the wild and mysterious miners of South Wales.[1]

In the late summer of 1838 all the various working-

---

[1] For Chartist Movement, see especially *The Chartist Movement*, by Mark Hovell, and "Chartism," by M. Halévy, *Quarterly Review*, Vol. 236, p. 62 (July, 1921).

class Radical movements converged into one. This was at first under the hegemony and impulse of Attwood, and on August 6th, 1838, under his auspices, a meeting was held at Newhall Hill, which is always held to be the official beginning of the Chartist Movement. But Attwood and his friends were out of place. They were merely courting dangerous allies to forward Currency ideas which could not possibly retain anyone else's enthusiasm. They shrank from men who thought with greater delight than themselves of the possibility of force. The movement quickly passed out of their control, and before Christmas O'Connor had captured it. Meanwhile the agitation had spread, and during the winter of 1838 the Chartists took to the exciting and melodramatic habit of meeting at night by the wavering light of torches smoking like their own fiery desires.

Partly against this background, perhaps partly combating these desires, Peel and his friends were to work out the fate of Conservatism. They were not unconscious of what was happening. O'Connell's society, Durham's mission, the Chartists, all had their comments in the letters of Conservatives. They are unquestionably the comments of party politicians in opposition. Peel, as usual, was in correspondence with his friend Croker and, as usual, was discussing with him points in the study of the French Revolution. In December, however, he wrote on graver matters, with reference to an article Croker was to write in the *Quarterly*. He suggested the question of how the Government accounted for the internal condition of the country. In 1830, said he, there had been some disposition to tumult and insurrectionary violence in the country, which was convulsed by the example of the French Revolution of that year. Then, the Whigs had had their explanation of it. Maladministration and the denial of reform were then the unquestionable causes of all disorder, and the specific was Reform. The present tumult could not be the swell of that old storm, for the reformers had never ceased from boasting of the improved state of the country or from attributing it to Reform, to the influence of the popular will and to the contentment and satisfaction of the people. Yet there were no torch-light meetings in 1830, no threatenings of physical force half so undisguised as at present. "What"—asked Peel almost in triumph—"makes the people so discontented?" [1]

Peel did not try to answer that question. It was to be put to the Whigs in controversy. He suggested a false answer that they would give, and went off into a long defence of himself and his party as having supported and not attacked the new Poor Law. He had asked the question in controversy, not in a spirit of inquiry. He was merely making a debating point, and after all it is a party leader's duty to make them. But it is hard not to ask how much of Peel's life and thought was spent in debating? How far did his sensibility occupy his mind only with feeling and repelling the charges that opponents made against him, or with altering his case or his conduct of affairs that he could the better repel them? Much of his best work seems to spring from this habit, but there is too much debating, even in his most intimate letters. In this case he was faced with serious trouble, and his mind was occupied with the problem, what would be his adversaries' arguments about it. His eyes were fixed more on them than on the world he might have to govern. Of course Peel's business was party warfare. Yet here there arises a burning if an unjust desire that Peel had asked of himself as well as of the Whigs, what made the people so discontented.

The events of that recess were having their vivid effect also on Peel's colleague, Sir James Graham. He wrote long and eloquent letters to his friend Bonham, the Conservative Whip, filled with arrangements for the elections, speculations for the future, fears for the party, contempt of the Government and metaphors for everything. He was particularly interested in the return of Durham from Canada. He felt that it might destroy

[1] Croker, II, 335.

the Government, through the division and disclosures
that it would cause. He wished all the parties concerned
to be exposed to shame in their "nakedness and real
deformity." He had great confidence in *The Times*
exposing both Durham and the Government with thunder
and truth. "With such a mirror as *The Times*," he
thought, "the full glare of the truth should be flashed
on the eyes of the British nation, till it dazzles them with
its intensity."

To such fire and rage and party hopes each of the
events of the moment moved Sir James Graham. Indeed,
he was much nearer than was Peel to what was really
party feeling, for one danger was continually present
to this ardent man. He was conscious of a dangerous
and unruly spirit in the party. Men complained of the
slackness of the leaders in the last Session. Graham
was afraid lest an amendment to the Address might be
got up at the Carlton, embraced by a large number of
the party, and made a matter of negotiation with the
worst Radicals. The cards, he thought, might be
forced from the hands of the Duke and Peel, who were
so well able to play the game. But he himself wanted
the Government's blood and his own party's victory.
"What Peel, Stanley and the Duke may decide on doing
I shall be disposed to adopt, but they never will ask me
or any gentleman of our party to take a course which
shall imply that these men are to be trusted with power."
And yet, for all Graham's confidence in this trinity,
Peel was cautious, Stanley not sanguine and the Duke
desperately anxious that these men should never again
be driven from the power they so much disgraced.[1]

Graham's views must be typical. Eloquence is not
granted to everyone, nor yet complete faith in political
leaders, but no doubt many other members of his party
had something of the eagerness to which the events
of politics had excited him. He himself gives evidence
that they shared with him some part of his wrath against
the Government and his distaste for their continued

[1] Add. MSS. 40,616; 57 ff (Graham to Bonham, Autumn, 1838).

existence.   Perhaps some were more crudely ambitious
and factious, but very many of them tended, as did Graham and even Peel, to see all that happened honestly
but exclusively in the medium of party political warfare.

Before 1838 is put away the touchstone of one of
its earlier situations must be tried on one other Conservative, one of the rank and file.   In March, when
the Whig Ministry had been in danger of defeat, Peel
received a proffer of help from Disraeli.   "In case the
present affairs lead to any result," said he, "there is no
doubt the Whigs will attempt instantly to raise an out-
cry in the country.   It might be advisable to anticipate
them and take the wind out of their sails.   This
might be done by a species of manifesto of the views
and principles of the Conservative party, which though
published anonymously, might be couched in such a
tone as would, I conceive, arrest public attention."
The address, he said, might be published widely, and
backed by the daily press, about which there would be
no difficulty; it would, he thought, exercise a considerable effect on opinion.   He had his ideas who the
author might be.   "If you think there is anything in
this suggestion, and do not deem me incapable of exe-
cuting it, my services are at your command, nor, in
order to be prepared, would I grudge the labour even
if thrown away.   In that case, however, I should like
at your convenience to have the honour of a few minutes
conversation to strike the keynote.   I assure you it is
with unaffected and even painful reluctance that I even
venture to trouble you and only with a full conviction
that you are much too generous to misinterpret my
forwardness.   Ever, my dear Sir Robert, your sincerely obliged servant, B. Disraeli." [1]
Disraeli was not yet very important, but the letter has
prophetic interest, since Disraeli was not always Peel's

[1] Add. MSS. 40,425; 413 (Disraeli to Peel, undated, but dated by watermark
and reference on bottom of paper to the Marylebone election).

sincerely obliged servant nor always fully convinced of Peel's generosity. Perhaps also it has some interest through the contrast of Disraeli's habits of mind with those of Graham and Peel. His tendency was to have resort to a confession of faith, a new expression and elaboration of the party's principles, which he intended should be popular. For instance, in the Irish debate of 1838 he had called for some principle in the settlement of Ireland. He was inclined to seek for something more generalized and more profound than the ordinary accidents of politics would afford, for he was not yet a party leader and the sport of all the accidents of politics.

But is even the discovery of a new party principle always evidence of the profoundest, most honest, most usefull and most difficult thought? And do even party principles make sure of party unity? These problems are better abandoned than answered, or at least left over to be developed a little by the Parliamentary Session of 1839.

CHAPTER X

PEEL AND THE QUEEN—1839

Dangers and perplexities, reports of murder in Ireland and of sullen and armed discontent in Yorkshire, prophesies of the loss of the Colonies, and of the Government's drowning all in the Corn Law controversy hung like clouds about the opening of 1839. In such an atmosphere what must be the Conservative policy? They must decide, as usual, whether they were to try to amend the Address, they must decide ultimately whether they were to try to govern the country, and in discussing the minor point Peel was led to give an opinion on the more important matter. Arbuthnot had forwarded to him a letter from the Duke in which that great and gloomy man apparently said that he was against ever attempting a Conservative Government again. The old wound from the Reform Bill had opened and the Duke felt, flat against all the evidence, that the popular cry was against them. With much in this letter Peel expressed his entire agreement. But he added one qualification. They must keep the party together, and not annihilate their influence by shrinking from opposition to the Government when it was justifiable or necessary. They must take the consequences of this steady maintenance of their principles, and that meant that they must not shrink when the time and the necessity came for the assumption of office. This showed that Peel realized, in a way, the responsibilities inherent in opposition. He knew that his party might have to stumble against that for which others have passionately and vehemently struggled. A Conservative Ministry might not be a matter for desire or design, but it might be the unavoidable result of their doing their duty. And Peel had declared that they must not shirk their duty. He was right, he was resolute, he was very courageous; but these are cold words with which to ascend to a throne.[1]

[1] Parker, II, 373 ff. Add. MSS. 40,341; 44 ff. 40,310; 252.

Peel did not want to move an amendment on the Address. There must be a debate, and he held it would turn on two points, Canada, as was obvious, and the Corn Laws. This shows how the Anti-Corn Law Association had already managed to put their question in the forefront of political controversy. It filled the letters of leading politicians, and it occupied some of the space of the most important newspapers. Most startling of all, *The Times*, the party's great ally, took up the Anti-Corn Law cry. But the defence of the Corn Laws had not yet swamped Conservatism. For instance, when Graham saw *The Times* attacking the Corn Laws he wrote to Bonham that it was a great misfortune but he trusted "that this is not the prelude to a more serious and general breach with us." [1] There were Conservatives who did not take up the defence of the Corn Laws automatically. Hardinge told Peel that the question would divide them from some of their friends,[2] and at least two eminent Conservatives compromised in these years with Anti-Corn Law feeling, for election purposes. There was Sir George Murray at Manchester in 1839, and in 1840 Peel's brother-in-law, Dawson, at Devonport. Dawson afterwards told Peel in private that his mind was entirely open on the subject and that the present system of Corn Laws always appeared to him far from satisfactory. But since he also added that without his declaration he never would have the slightest chance of being returned, his state of mind cannot be taken as typical of ordinary Conservatives without votes to gain.[3]

They are small exceptions. Conservatism without a vigorous defence of the Corn Laws was even then a possible creed, but it was not a usual nor a probable one. There was not much effective Conservative opinion that would be seduced by the Anti-Corn cry, for as Graham said, "at present in the purely manufacturing towns we have not much to lose." [4] Without much

[1] Add. MSS. 40,616; 120.   [2] *Ibid.* 40,314; 266.
[3] *Ibid.* 40, 428; 44 (Dawson).   40, 427; 140, 143 (Murray).
[4] *Ibid.* 40,616; 123.

thought and without any question the Corn Laws were
numbered with the other institutions the Conservatives
had to preserve.   It all seemed to hang together, and a
clerical orator at a Conservative dinner in Buckingham
could describe perfectly naturally how destructive opinion
lay· like a tiger ready to spring out alike on the Corn
Laws and the Church.   As he remarked nobly, but
perhaps irrelevantly, it was "unlike the lion which is
said to flee or calmly crouch to virgin purity." [1]

The leaders slipped naturally into the controversy.
Without comment Peel resumed the task of the Corn
Laws' defence.   Graham was more explicit.   He discussed the matter in a letter he wrote to Peel in January
1839.   They could not refuse, he said, to join issue
in defence of the present Corn Law.   He believed it to
be the best protection for Agriculture which could be
devised; "and without Protection the greatest interests in
the country will be involved in ruin and fatal confusion."
When the principle was attacked it was dangerous to
talk of concessions in details.   He approved the present
principle of a sliding scale which made the duties on
corn fall as the price of corn increased, for he thought
that no fixed duty would be of avail when prices were
high through scarcity.   However, he felt it to be fortunate, with these discussions pending, that Lord Chandos, the great agriculturist, had been promoted from the
Commons into the Lords by the death of his father, the
Duke of Buckingham; and, said Graham, "while every
protection that agriculture really requires must be
defended, every concession that can be made to trade in
its close rivalry with foreign skill and industry is justly
due."   Then he went on to say that the Tax on raw
cotton was bad, and that a substitute was necessary
in which land should bear its share.[2]

Graham had the right premise, but he had alien
anxieties.   He took it for granted that without the
protection of corn the greatest interests of the country
would be involved in fatal confusion, and this was in

[1] *The Times*, Feb. 5, 1839.   [2] Add. MSS. 40,318; 131.

tune with the social and political values that pervaded his present party. He was anxious about industry, in its rivalry with foreign competition, and about the activities of some of their agricultural colleagues. Even Peel, who assumed his part without comment, had shown himself concerned for the prosperity of industry, and there had been moments when the desires of fanatic agriculturists had been frustrated by a responsible Conservative leader. But perhaps these things would have no counterpart in the battle for the Corn Laws which would open in 1839.

At any rate, the real problem for Peel at that moment was what the Government would do, for in the middle of a fight you must study the movements rather of your enemy's weapon than of your own heart. This problem perplexed him and filled his letters. There were signs that, as several of his correspondents assumed, the Government meant to take up the Anti-Corn Law cry. The Government papers had begun abusing landowners, and just before Parliament John Russell announced in a public letter to the Chairman of an Anti-Corn Law meeting in Stroud that his individual opinion was in favour of a moderate fixed duty, which he would be ready to support with his vote in the House of Commons.[1] On the other hand Melbourne, who after all was Prime Minister, had announced with emphasis during the last Session that he was against a change in the Corn Laws. Moreover there were still enough Whig Lords and gentlemen attached to the interests of Agriculture to form a brake on the Government's proceedings.

The language of the Government press seemed to foretell that the Corn Laws would be taken up officially, but John Russell's letter implied and Melbourne's language demanded that the most they should do would be to make the Corn Laws an open question on which Whigs and Liberals could vote as they pleased and go their own road. As a matter of fact Melbourne had

[1] *The Times*, Jan. 26 (page 4, column 6).

been subjected, at the end of 1838, and the beginning
of 1839, to considerable argument on the matter of the
Corn Laws.[1]   The time might come when this pressure
might be successful and the Government and their party
might leave the cross-ways and take the road which
John Russell would suggest.   But that time had not
come at the beginning of the Session of 1839.

§ 2

It was on February 5th that the Queen drove down
to Westminster, greeted by very little cheering except
from the ladies in the balconies, while men held up
placards bearing the significant words "Cheap Bread." [2]
On that day there had also gathered in London two
other Parliaments, not opened by the Queen; the Chartist Convention at the British Hotel, Charing Cross, and
at Brown's Hotel, Palace Yard, the Anti-Corn Law
Conference.   Three Parliaments had met, rubbing
elbows together; only one of them could constitutionally
control the present; which would control the future?

In the Westminster Parliament Corn was not introduced into the Queen's speech; the Government showed
little sign of taking up the cry against the existing duties,
while Melbourne avowed himself still unprepared for
any alteration.   However, the Corn Laws afforded Peel
a notable debating victory when they discussed the
Address in the Commons.   G. W. Wood, the President
of the Manchester Chamber of Commerce, spoke in
favour of the Repeal of the Corn Laws, but prefaced
what he said by exuberant comments on the recovery of
trade after the danger which had been caused two years
before by the exigencies of banking, and on the marvel-
lous increase in the value of the country's exports.   It
was the complacency habitually induced by successful
manufacturing, but the Anti-Corn Law thesis was that
the Corn Laws crippled the exporting power of the
country, and laid its industry open to the risk of losing

[1] *Melbourne Papers*, 387 ff.   [2] Broughton's *Recollections*, VI, 75.

foreign markets to countries where the cost of living
was lower. The opening was not lost on Peel. When
his turn came he pressed home the point. He
thanked Wood for his opinion, he begged a rather
crestfallen Wood to regain his old cheerfulness about the
country's position, he often retailed Wood's statement
of the increase in the exports and asked the House
whether, merely because of the inevitable effects of a
bad harvest, they were to undermine a system which
had produced such unheard-of results.

He then went on in his speech to make another point
in debate. He talked of the violence of language which
had been used in the last year up and down the country.
He quoted specimens of it, he complained that the
Government had not taken earlier steps in the matter
and that Lord John Russell, as all Conservatives thought,
had encouraged disorder by a speech he had made at
Liverpool.

Then Peel made the point he had suggested to Croker,
and he made it with a vigour that seems to show that he
felt it. The people had not been satisfied with the Reform
Bill. The Radical amendments declared that they were
disappointed. He had prophesied that disappointment. He had told the Reformers that they exaggerated
the popular satisfaction and the new ability that Reformed
Parliaments would bring to their task; he would not
have been believed if he had said that they would have
as bad disorders in 1838, as they had laid to his charge
in 1830. Again he issued a warning. Men would
not achieve satisfaction or finality in any extension of
the franchise until it was universal and unlimited, until
the Constitution had ceased to be a monarchy, until
under bitter experience of that change they might
perhaps tell Peel that he was not a false prophet.

There were to be no bitter experiences of the sort
that Peel foresaw, yet he was not wholly a false prophet.
He was right in implying that no demand in franchise
would be final until the sources of franchise reform had
been exhausted; he was right in implying that demo-

crats had no right to prophesy that democracy would make men satisfied with their own Governments. Perhaps he had been a better realist than his opponents. He had seen and foreseen one of the continual disappointments of democracy. It might be said that while some of the people are poor they will never be satisfied, and while they are many no Government can for long be their own; and they will always be encouraged by democrats to believe that satisfaction will come when they have removed the next impediment to the popular will. If Peel was not likely to go as far as this, he could at least see how exaggerated had been the promises of some of his opponents, he could see how they had laid all ills and all popular discontent to the charge of Tory corruption. To prick delusive hopes, to disclose how futile is the habitual diagnosis of public evil by means of personal accusation, these are the constant tasks of Conservatives; but should there not be something else for them to say? Peel went no further. He could only end his speech with a helpless wish, that they had not left their old standards, and a desperate prayer that it might yet be possible to "preserve the inestimable benefits of a mixed and mild constitution." Could he only regret what he could never revive? [1]

The Corn Laws continued to occupy their share of the time of Parliament. The controversy on the question of exports was brought up again. The Anti-Corn Law men tried to prove that there was a decline in those exports which were most largely the production of labour, and were therefore affected by the high cost of living, and Peel had resort to statistics.[2] On February 18th, Villiers, a Radical who had long devoted himself to this question, brought in a proposal that the petitioners against the Corn Law should be heard at the Bar. It was a proposal to which even those who were favourable to a change in the Corn Law had grounds to object, and it was easily defeated. But there was a heavier trial to come. On March 12th, Villiers produced his annual

[1] Hansard, XLV, 94.   [2] Ibid., XLV, 228.

E E

motion upon the Corn Laws which allowed the subject
to be argued more generously. This second debate
showed the importance to which the subject had attained
in 1839. It went on for five days, immensely long,
intolerably redundant, seared with statistics, and spotted
here and there at intervals by a Latin phrase to give
point and elegance to an argument. In both debates
Peel spoke, and from the references of the enemies of
the Corn Laws it seems that they had begun to regard him
as the protagonist against them. He was joining battle,
he was joining his last battle as a Conservative leader.

He relied largely on statistics. As before, he tried to
prove that Trade was expanding even in articles that
demanded a high proportion of labour in their production. He dealt with the question of profits being
diminished by the Corn Laws, spoke of new factories
being erected and tried to demonstrate, by the use of
figures showing the increase in the amount deposited
on small accounts in the various Savings Banks, that the
Corn Laws had not entirely reduced the working classes.
Peel relied on statistics, and his enemies relied on statistics, and it would be hard to show that the use which
either made of them should have been impossible to an
honest and intelligent man. Perhaps Peel may have been
misled at times by the comparison of 1838 to 1837,
for 1837 was a year of depression. But he was certainly right in concluding that the trade and manufactures of the country had increased with a wonderful
resilience in spite of the duties on corn, and was probably right in declaring that, whether or no there had
been Corn Laws in Britain, foreign factories, as in
Saxony and the United States, must inevitably have
sprung up in twenty years' peace. But perhaps Peel
should not have been satisfied with his treatment of the
question of the working classes. Probably the test of
the Savings Banks deposits was not satisfactory, although
it was a test that Peel, and not only Peel, would use
again in debate. But there was further controversy
to come about the welfare of the working classes.

Peel could destroy to his own satisfaction what were presented to him as his opponents' chief arguments. He could do this the more easily because their arguments were often inflated, and they probably often exaggerated the effect that the Corn Laws had, and that their Repeal would have, upon foreign competition. There had been prosperity in spite of them, and when there was depression other causes could be found for it beside these Laws, such as the fluctuation of the American trade during these years. Such causes Peel could be trusted to diagnose and portray. But there was also a positive side to his case.

Perhaps it was weaker. He talked of the special burdens of Agriculture : he spoke swiftly and currently about such things as the Malt Tax, Poor Laws, and County Rate, and used as he had done before the protection on other commodities which afflicted the farmer. After he had tried to prove that the variable duty was not responsible for the variations in price, he talked of the danger of sacrificing the home production of Corn and risking the effects on the country of famine on the Continent. He referred to the danger of War, since he at least had the sense to declare that commercial intercourse was not in itself a guarantee of peace. Then he called emotion into use in defending Agriculture and the Agriculturist. The Agriculturists would find it difficult to transfer themselves to other callings. Under the influence of protection they had drained the land and extended tillage to the hill-top, they had improved the health of the people and prolonged life; and he implied that he would find something to regret should his opponents manage to provision the country from the cheap labour and fertile deserts of Poland, and so succeed in making England the workshop of the world and a dull succession of enormous manufacturing towns, strung together by railways intersecting the wastes which it was no longer profitable to cultivate.

Such, in the rough, was Peel's case. His statistics had reduced to nothing his sense of the pressure upon

him of his opponents' arguments.   His positive case for
the protection of corn was respectable, and he buttressed
it with a sentiment in favour of Agriculture which may
have been purblind, but may also have been not utterly
contemptible.   Some of his case was true, much was
ingenious, all was tenable; the question was how much
of its positive side was real enough to him to dominate
his future and direct his desires.

He also produced strictures on his opponents and
provisos on his own resolution to maintain the Corn Laws.
For he condemned the Whigs for their temporizing and
the Anti-Corn Law League for its agitation.   And he
talked as he had done before of the close connection
between the interests of agriculture and trade, and
declared as well that if the Corn Laws could not be
proved to be consistent with the general interests of the
country, and especially with the improvement of the
condition of the labouring classes, then the Corn Laws
would be practically at an end.   The time would come
when he would be pressed harder by those who advocated the end of the Corn Laws.[1]

Villiers' motion in March was to go into a Committee
of the whole House upon the Corn Laws.   It was supported by various members of the Cabinet and Government such as Hobhouse, Howick (Lord Grey's son),
Palmerston, the Chancellor of the Exchequer and Lord
John Russell.   But it was beaten by 342 votes to 195.
Peel called this an excellent division and calculated that
about 70 of their usual opponents had voted with the
Conservatives.   He was immediately annoyed by the
folly of his agricultural followers, led of course by the
new Duke of Buckingham, who wished to improve on
the occasion very dangerously.[2]   On the other side the
Anti-Corn Law Association broke up their camp in
London, not to end their activities, but to start them
elsewhere.

[1] Hansard, XLV, 678, and XLVI, 749.
[2] Parker, II, 383 (Peel to Duke, March 19, 1839).

§ 3

But after this the interest in the Repeal of the Corn Laws had already begun to slacken so much that Greville thought it had failed and fancied that he had noticed that *The Times* had dropped it.[1]   Certainly there were other things ready to fill the stage.   Other men besides those interested in the Repeal of the Corn Laws had come up angry and excited at the beginning of this Session.   Bitterness and fear could have been found among the Irish Conservative members of Parliament.

1839 had begun with an Irish murder.   On January 1st the Earl of Norbury was shot, nearly within sight of his house in Ireland, and on January 3rd he died. He was a man well known and well spoken of, and his death had stirred the depths of the already embittered Irish quarrel as to whether proper protection was afforded to life and property under the present Irish Executive, with its liberal use of the prerogative of mercy.   Ireland was already the seared battlefield of political passions.   It had little needed this murder to exasperate them.   Irish Conservatives had for long been eloquent to their leaders on the terrible danger of Irish affairs, while Irish outrages and O'Connell's activities had naturally attracted the noisy attention of Conservative journalists.   Moreover it had seemed both profitable and right to give the religion of the majority of Irishmen the full blast of Conservative invective.   As Graham wrote to Bonham at the beginning of 1839, "Protestantism is the only weapon with which we can encounter Republicanism."[2]

There were eager hands and hot heads always ready to embark on the crusade.   At the end of 1838 the *Quarterly Review* published an article on Papal Usurpations and the spirit of Popery.   Large parts of this were served up again by *The Times* with added abuse, alternated with wild attacks on O'Connell and unkind com-

---

[1] Greville, *Vict.*, I, 164, 174.
[2] Add. MSS. 40,427; 67, 70, 73.   40,626; 103.   Parker, II, 382.

ments on the state of Ireland, and on the Ministry. The Anti-Popery cry was popular, and was apparently sincere. Lord Ashley records in his diary that it was he that had set agoing the article in the *Quarterly* and stirred up *The Times* in the matter. He called Peel's attention to the article, and even Peel answered that he had long thought "there were fearful indications of a great religious struggle which will probably be co-extensive with Popery and Protestantism in Europe." [1]   However, to do him justice Peel did not let this struggle intrude into his own politics; he never indulged in violent attacks on Rome. He wished to be and to seem moderate and just, and he was resolved not to go back on Emancipation.

Indeed it was the complaint of Protestant fanatics that he made it impossible to take up Irish questions in Parliament in a "religious" sense. Again, a passion which he did not share was helping to drive him on to a position of power in which he would not satisfy it. It is the old problem. Passion is often the source of power and it is often a passion which no statesman should share. The problem must have a solution, party politics themselves must furnish it, but it seems a bad solution to have a moderate leader and passionate followers. Lord Norbury's murder gave fuel to Irish controversy. There was already friction between the Irish Executive and the Conservative Irish magistrates. When the Tipperary magistrates had memorialized the Government on the crime in their county, Drummond, the Lord-Lieutenant's Secretary, had replied with the galling truism that property had its duties as well as its rights, and the magistrates who met to consider the murder of Lord Norbury resolved that this declaration had excited and emboldened the feelings which had led to the murder; nor were matters made the sweeter by the report that O'Connell had insinuated that Lord Norbury had been killed by his own son. Small wonder that

[1] *Shaftesbury* (Hodder), I, 241 and 242.

Parliament was to hear something of the anger of the Irish Conservatives.

But their anger was perennial if increasing, and the controversy was not new. It would have done little harm and not much good if the question had been confined to the House of Commons, but there was trouble in the Lords. Unfortunately, although the Duke of Cumberland had disappeared, the House of Lords was still not entirely submissive to the Duke of Wellington's wishes, or patient of his moderation towards the Government. Indeed it must be confessed that that moderation had grown and was growing to an exasperating degree. The Duke seemed to become increasingly afraid of hampering the Government or of succeeding them. He now believed that the country would never allow the Conservatives, if they were in office, enough strength to do what it would be their plain duty to do, especially in the way of giving the country a sufficient army and navy which, as he complained, it did not by any means have at present. Consequently he did not wish the Conservatives to risk taking office, and he was inclined to defend those who occupied it already. His attitude came in part from the despair, natural and habitual in a professional soldier, of ever providing adequate armaments in peace-time, especially armaments adequate for times of troubled peace; and it came in part from the hopeless mistrust of an ageing Conservative for a new and incomprehensible world which he had never accepted. Rather naturally the course of action thus prompted did not appeal to all his followers, and there was always in the Lords the embarrassment of the anger of Brougham. Brougham raged and stormed like an able, eloquent and ennobled washerwoman against the Ministers who had abandoned him. He was always trying to throw out feelers towards the party in opposition, and he succeeded after a sort, so that the Duke's restraint was a perpetual annoyance. "Westminster Abbey is yawning for him," said Brougham.

No yawning sanctuary had yet managed to engulf

the Duke, but his followers might sometimes trip him
up, and in March 1839 they contrived to gain his sanction for the appointment, in the House of Lords, of a
committee to enquire into the state of Ireland since 1838.
The Duke gave his consent in the mistaken belief that
Peel approved.   It is probable that no one had consciously deceived him, but the incident caused him considerable annoyance.   He told Peel that "the truth is that
this affair is like every other.   We have—we must have
—followers.   They think that they know what ought to
be done better than you and I.   They don't care a pin
about our opinions."   They would risk, he said, the
public interests or any outrage against the independence
of the House of Lords in order to enjoy a momentary
triumph, while some perhaps acted in the futile expectation that a triumph in the House of Lords would dissolve the Government.   Those were the people on
whom they must depend if they undertook office in all
the dangers of the present moment.   They disgusted
the Duke.   Unfortunately they had also, probably innocently, outmanœuvred him.   On March 21st, Roden,
an Irish Protestant peer, had been allowed to move for
the committee.   Of course he carried his motion, and
the Government thought the matter to be serious enough
to require, if they were to continue in office, a counteracting vote of confidence on the policy of the Irish
Executive on the part of the House of Commons.

Peel thought Ministers were taking the opportunity
either to escape from office and their troubles, or to
rally their party on their Irish policy which was the one
policy on which they were all likely to agree.   He
noticed how few of John Russell's own supporters
joined him in resisting a motion which Hume brought at
this time on Household Suffrage.   Certainly the doctrine of finality was proving hard to sustain.   The professed Radicals would have been glad to destroy the
Government if they could, while Lord John, the Whigs'
strongest man, was tired and broken by the death of his
wife.   Lord John's own relations with the Radicals were

not comfortable, and after a minor scene in the House the best that could be said to him was the chilling comfort that he was not so unpopular with them as he had been last year. Even the Government's own paper, the *Morning Chronicle*, had taken to urging them to conciliate Liberal opinion by adopting a more Radical course. It is true that a large section of Liberal opinion still apparently remained faithful, and that O'Connell, in spite of the Precursors, could still be relied on. But a very few Radicals voting with the Tories would serve to defeat the Government.

Yet the Government had remained resolute and high-principled in the maintenance of their doctrine of finality. Lord John was not allowed by Melbourne to make what concessions he would to Liberalism, and himself stood forward manfully to oppose any attempt to carry Franchise Reform beyond the Reform Bill. Indeed he published an address to the electors of Stroud, reiterating his unpopular opinions, and his friends wrote to him admiring letters promising him immediate failure but lasting credit.[1] As was natural this situation had bred talk of some form of coalition between the Conservatives and the moderate Whig leaders; and there can be small wonder that the Government were accused of beginning to use the Irish motion to rally their followers or to retreat. A coalition would have left the Whigs sterile and the Conservatives crippled. A Whig defeat would have left the Conservatives dangerously embarrassed. Luckily there could only be war between Whigs and Conservatives, and fortunately for themselves the Conservatives were still able to lose, at least in this Irish battle.

For Whigs, Liberals and Radicals were certainly united over the proceedings of the Irish Executive. On April 12th Lord John brought forward the Government's Irish vote of confidence. All went well. Peel in a dexterous speech moved a dexterous amendment in which he criticized the Government, but declared that the Lords' motion could not be construed as a

[1] Spencer Walpole, *John Russell*, I, 367.

vote of censure. He was comfortably beaten by 318 votes to 296. All the Radicals voted with the Government; yet there were omens. One of the Radicals thought it necessary to add an amendment about further reform in the representation of the people in Parliament, for which he obtained 86 votes, and Grote declared in his speech that he supported the Government on this Irish question, but upon no other. It would only have taken the transfer of 12 Radical votes to have turned the decision against the Government.

It was not the last time that they treated with Ireland in that Session. Peel's free-trading instincts led him to oppose a proposal for the improvement of the condition of Ireland by the subsidizing of the Railways. The Irish Municipal problem again came up for solution and again was left unsolved. The Conservatives again proposed their amendment about raising the electoral qualification to ten pounds and carried it in the Lords. When the Bill reached the Commons again, it was decided that one of the Lords' amendments trenched on the Commons' privileges. The Bill could not be proceeded with, and by that time it was too late in the Session to bring in a new one. The Whig Ministers seemed to be desirous of settlement. Perhaps the next year would put an end to that wearisome struggle and these futile debates.

Yet these debates possibly display symptoms of differences among the Conservatives which might last when the next year was over. In the debate on the Government's vote of confidence in their Irish Executive Peel formally declared his desire that Roman Catholics and Protestants should be equal before the law in Ireland. No doubt the principle was trite and the assertion necessary for the purposes of debate, but too much can be discounted even from a statesman's trite and formal declarations. On the other hand, though some Conservatives openly deplored the delay in passing the Irish Municipal Bill, others in the Commons wished to go back on the agreement by which, having gained an Irish

Poor Law and a satisfactory Irish Tithe Bill, they were pledged to grant open and elective municipalities in Ireland. They declared that they knew of no such agreement, and led by Inglis they opposed the Bill's second reading. But Peel and Stanley said that as men of honour they were pledged, and they piloted the Bill through the second reading, to be amended in committee. When the Bill reached the Lords the Duke himself showed disquieting symptoms. He thought men were tired of the measure, and he wished to return to the position of refusing municipalities to Ireland. But he was kept in his rank, and the Conservatives were able to preserve the Bill until they wrecked it by amendment.[1]

The Conservatives had maintained unity of action on Ireland, but was there any sign of a uniform depth of passion? Was there much sign that all the party had learnt to sympathize with the obligations and tolerations of its leaders? Early in May a mysterious incident had occurred which might have enabled Conservatives to try whether the use of power would be altogether determined by the passions which had facilitated its possession.

§ 4

The cry against slavery had not died down with its abolition in 1833. Though the negroes had been liberated, they had been kept till 1840 in a state of apprenticeship which was not entirely different to slavery. The Anti-Slavery cry had increased greatly in force in 1838, and a proposal for the immediate liberation had been passed in Parliament against the opposition of the Government. The Assembly of Jamaica had protested against the right of the Imperial Parliament to interfere with them, but had consented to abolish apprenticeship. Meanwhile, the Government at home had received a very serious report on the state of the prisons in Jamaica, and at the end of the Session of 1838 they

[1] Add. MSS. 40,427; 76, 89, 91, 95, etc.

passed an Act through the Imperial Parliament to remedy it. This time the Jamaican Assembly would only protest against the assumption of power, and that in very violent terms. The Assembly was tiresome; it was obviously difficult, perhaps impossible, to secure the emancipation of the negro with their assistance, and in 1839 the Government brought forward a Bill to suspend the Constitution of Jamaica. Peel objected to this as hasty and harsh. He wished to give the Colonists greater opportunity to repent, and he opposed the Government's measure.

The division upon it was taken at about two o'clock on the morning of May 7th. Such Radicals as Grote, Hume and Molesworth and others voted against the Government, with the result that the Government majority sank to 5, and on May 7th the Cabinet decided that in view of the hopelessness of the division and the desertion of the Radicals they could no longer attempt to continue in office.

But it was one thing for the Ministry to go out of office, and another for their successors to come in. The relations between the Queen and Melbourne had been charming but inconvenient. Melbourne had been continually with the Queen, riding with her out of doors, or dining at the Palace in a chair reserved for him at the Queen's side. Greville wondered that he who was used to the brilliant and free atmosphere of Holland House could restrict himself to the constraint and dullness of a Court. But Melbourne was a man whose happiness and affections in the past had been entrusted to things less healthy and stable than Queen Victoria. It was natural that his affectionate nature should crave what had been denied to it, and he delighted in the company of his youthful and royal charge. To the Queen, after her escape from the strains and strictness of her youth, Melbourne was naturally irresistible. He was so frank and open, he explained so much so simply, he was so delightfully funny about the Bishops' Copes after the Coronation. The Queen, whose nature was warm, grew deeply attached to him and to his Cabinet, while the wives and sisters of her Ministers entirely surrounded her person. For, partly by accident, the whole of her household was Whig, and Lady Lansdowne, the wife of the Lord President of the Council, was First Lady of the Bedchamber. One sister of Morpeth, the Irish Secretary, was Mistress of the Robes, and another was a Lady of the Bedchamber, as was also Lady Normanby, the wife of the late Lord Lieutenant of Ireland, whose policy was still continually the centre of party strife.

On the 7th May Melbourne had to tell the Queen that the Ministry had determined to resign. He advised her to send for the Duke of Wellington and the Conservatives, since the Radicals had neither ability, honesty, numbers or leaders of any character; but he showed some natural anxiety, in the course of his advice, to ensure so young a Queen's independence against a strange Minister. Most especially did he warn her to insist on having the Duke of Wellington in office, if it should be Peel that should construct the Ministry. No doubt he felt that the Duke would be a protector.

That day was a black one for the Queen. She appears to have cried when she took leave of Lord John Russell, and as for Melbourne, she was as eager to keep in touch with him as a child with its parents on the first day of school. Like a child, simple and self-centred, she gave him a careful chronicle of all her grief. She told him how she had been in a wretched state till nine o'clock on the 7th, when she had managed to calm herself, but on waking next morning "all that had happened in one short eventful day, came most forcibly to her mind." During the course of the morning she felt better, but neither at night nor in the morning was she able to touch a morsel of food. She was anxious to see Melbourne who called on her that morning at eleven. But Melbourne had to tell her that he could no longer dine with her as before, and at ten minutes to one she went into the yellow closet to find there the Duke of Wellington.

The interview was short and not entirely disagreeable. The two children got on very well together. Both were simple and direct, and both Queen and Duke had one very strong feeling in common. They both thoroughly regretted that the Duke's party should come into power. When the Queen spoke of Melbourne as having been quite a parent to her and when, as she said, to show her great fairness towards her new Ministry, she warned him that she would often see her friend, the Duke replied very sympathetically. But it was not with the Duke she would have mainly to deal. He told her that he had no power whatever in the Commons. If, so he informed her, he said black was black, they would say it was not. He would rather not have been in office at all, though he would consent to serve if it was thought necessary, but for Prime Minister he advised her to send for Sir Robert Peel, and Sir Robert Peel was accordingly sent for at two o'clock.

Of course Peel was prepared for this; indeed he was overprepared and not cheerful. He was already familiar with the danger that he might have to form a Ministry, though this actual crisis seems to have come as an unpleasant surprise. The prospects that presented themselves to him were bad. Since the Speaker, Abercrombie, intended to resign, he was faced as in 1835, with an immediate contest for the Speakership. There were great difficulties pending in Canada, in Jamaica and in the condition of Great Britain itself. Ireland was said to be his chief difficulty and on that subject the House of Commons had a week or two before recorded a vote against his party. There was certainly not the same fire in him as there had been in 1834, and just before he went to the Queen he wrote to a friend how sensible he was of the great difficulties confronting him. Moreover he had also just been warned almost too urgently of his own personal drawbacks, having been told by a friendly Conservative lady that he did not possess Melbourne's open manner which the Queen admired.[1]

---

[1] Add. MSS. 40,426; 226. Parker, II, 389.

It was enough to make a highly sensitive man still more reserved, and to encourage him to retire behind that elaborate and statesmanlike language from which caution and circumlocution seemed to have expelled any meaning at all.

He arrived after two, with his burden upon him, and stood before his Royal Mistress, looking as she noticed "embarrassed and put out," and no doubt also very stiff and inhuman. The Queen told Melbourne afterwards that she was very much collected and betrayed no agitation during these audiences, but for all that there was probably something about her eyes or her mien or her voice to show how hot and resentful she was; it was always the case that the more uncomfortable Peel was, the more frigid and incomprehensible he became. He made the very worst impression. Grammar fled before the Queen's feelings when she described him to Melbourne, and the first person singular intruded irreverently on the Royal third person. "He is such a cold, odd man she can't make out what he means." "The Queen don't like his manner after—oh, how different, how dreadfully different to that frank, open natural and most kind, warm manner of Lord Melbourne. The Duke I like by far better to Peel." In this bad atmosphere she heard what Peel had to say about his Government. He was not sanguine, and he declared that he felt unequal to his task. He told her whom he should propose for the various chief offices of State, agreed that the Duke should take office, and talked of the contest for the Speakership after which, he said, if he was beaten he might have to dissolve.

The Queen made some difficulty about dissolution. Peel told her that he would require her to demonstrate her confidence in the Government, one of the marks of which would be the composition of her Household. The Queen answered this apparently by repeating something which she had said to the Duke about those of her Household who were not in Parliament, to which Peel would give no answer at present beyond saying

that everything should have her knowledge and approbation. When she talked to him about Melbourne
Peel became odd and unintelligible, though not entirely
unsympathetic. It was agreed that Peel should report
progress on the day following, and he left the Queen feeling
herself among the enemies of those she most esteemed,
among people who seemed to have no heart, and worst
of all deprived of the sight of Lord Melbourne. As
she told him in her letter "afterwards again all gave
way."

Meanwhile Peel was endeavouring to construct his
Government. He saw or had seen the Duke of Wellington about his taking an office. He held a sort of Cabinet
at which he alluded to the question of the Household,
although, since he does not refer to it in his minute on
his first interview, that cannot yet have appeared to him
as a matter in controversy. However, he had in mind
his own method of dealing with the Queen's Household,
and next morning he summoned Ashley. Ashley was
the man to put in charge. He was acceptable to the
Queen, and his moral character was so high as to be a
complete guarantee of the moral excellence of the Household appointments. Apart from any question of the
public effect Peel was himself profoundly anxious for
the good moral tone of the companions of this young
woman on whose moral and religious character depended
the welfare of millions, for he himself said as much to
Lord Ashley when he came. Ashley did not like the
suggestion in the least. He had an aspiring mind and
a sensitive vanity. He shrank from the trivialities of
Court life and from what men would say of him when
he was engaged in them. Peel's mental relegation of
Ashley to Court duties was one of the things which
would go ultimately to the alienation of Peel and Ashley.
But this time Peel succeeded in sounding the right note,
and Ashley records that he never saw a man in a state
of heart more solemn, more delicate and more virtuous. Unfortunately it is one thing to show delicacy,
solemnity and virtue to a friend while yet safe in your

own home and another to keep control of matters in
the Royal Closet with an angry and unhappy young
woman.

The next day Peel waited again on the Queen. He
told her what ministerial appointments he suggested
and they were accepted, if not very graciously. They
then came to the Household and started with a disagreement as to what the Queen had said on the
day before, which the Queen seems to have inter-
preted to Peel's disadvantage. However, Peel was able
readily to accede to her request that she should have
Lord Liverpool in her Household, while she on her
part said she would like Lord Ashley. It was probably their last moment of agreement. Soon after this
Sir Robert said, "Now what about the ladies?" He had
determined with Ashley that he must replace those in
the higher Household posts, who were directly connected with his chief political adversaries, and to make
no change in all the rest. But it did not matter what
he had determined, he had pulled off the trigger.

The Queen said she could *not* give up *any* of her
ladies, and to all Peel's questions she replied that she
meant to keep *all*. She told Melbourne afterwards she
had never seen a man so frightened. She was convinced that the request was outrageous, and she had
been ready to be angry. There was no precedent for
changing the ladies as well as the Lords. She was
sure she never talked politics with her women; she
would like to know, she wrote with deep satire to Melbourne, whether they intended to give the *Ladies* seats
in Parliament. She was sure that Melbourne would
never have dreamt of such a thing. Peel "was quite
perturbed." He fetched Wellington to see her. He
saw her again himself. But to all their arguments
the Queen was immovable. Peel went to consult his
Cabinet and they determined that without such a sign
of confidence the Ministry could not go on. The Queen
said she would reflect, but that she felt certain she would
not change her mind. She would write that evening or

next morning, and Peel said that meanwhile he would suspend further proceedings.

The Queen was not only firm, she was transported. When Peel had gone to fetch the Duke of Wellington she wrote, in order to prepare Melbourne, such a letter as would have stirred the feeblest heart and the slowest sword in an era of Romance. "But this is *infamous,*" said she, and again, "I was calm but very decided, and I think you would have been pleased to see my composure and great firmness; the Queen of England will not submit to such trickery." [1]   Melbourne had already urged her not to put the negotiations off upon the question of the Household, and not to be offended by Peel's bad manner. Again he urged her to listen to what Peel and the Duke had to say. But he did not think that Peel was right. He thought they were pressing her more hardly than any Sovereign was pressed before; he quoted to the Queen what seemed to him to be precedents against Peel's demand, he thought the case, taking all things together, could not be resisted by Peel when it was put to him.

It would not have been natural if he had judged the case dispassionately and on its merits. The Queen had written to him as to a father, and he only knew what had happened through her impassioned letters. The Queen had said nothing of Peel's ineffective desires to be moderate in his demands; probably she never even allowed herself to be conscious of them. The Queen was young, alone, and a woman, her Ladies were very important to her comfort and independence, and these demands were surely being urged on her in a manner which was both harsh and peremptory. He went with John Russell to see her that evening and both thought her case was good, and were moved by her appeals. Melbourne talked the matter over with Grey, who felt that by every obligation of duty and gratitude he ought to support the Queen if he could. Late that night he

---

[1] *Letters of Queen Victoria,* I, 161 (Queen to Melb., May 9). Neither phrase appears in *Girlhood of Queen Victoria,* II, 168.

summoned his Cabinet, one from dinner and another from the opera, and they agreed to stand by the Queen. They were apparently under the impression that Peel demanded the dismissal of all the Queen's Ladies.

Late that night, or rather very early on the morning of May 10th, the Whig Cabinet sent their message to the Queen with the advice to resist Sir Robert Peel's proposition. Later on the 10th Peel's letter came, resigning his Commission and declaring respectfully that he could not have attempted to conduct the business of the country in the first instance with the aid of the present Parliament, without public proof of the Queen's confidence in making some change in that part of her Household which she had resolved to maintain entirely without change. She put this letter into Melbourne's hands. "He started at one part," says the Queen, "where he (Sir Robert) says 'some changes' "—but some or all, I said, was the same; and Lord Melbourne said, "I must submit this to the Cabinet." When the letter was shown to Grey he felt the same about it as Melbourne. "It certainly varies the case," he told Melbourne, "and is artfully constructed enough to put himself in the right." But no artful construction that Peel could do could now put himself in office or even alter Grey's advice. So the Whigs returned to office and there was an end to the crisis of the Ladies' of the Bedchamber.[1]

It was a miscarriage in the Constitution. No change of Ministry ought to have been prevented by such an accident. But it is hard to distribute the blame. The Queen was passionate and unreasonable. Apparently she never allowed Peel to declare how many Ladies he desired to dismiss, or even tried to give him her complete confidence. She would not subordinate her own personal likes and dislikes or her sense of her own comfort to the

---

[1] *Letters of Queen Victoria*, I, 37–61. *Girlhood of Queen Victoria*, II, 159–96. Parker, II, 388. Add. MSS. 40,426; 204 ff. *Melbourne Papers*, 396 ff. (Grey to Melb., May 10 and 11). *Corresp. of Princess Lieven and Earl Grey*, III, 297 (Grey to Lieven, May 10). Grev., I, 199 ff. Shaftesbury, I, 245–48. Broughton, V, 189–98.

needs of the country. On the other hand it would be agreed even nowadays that the personal independence and freedom of a monarch ought to be a matter of national consideration, and in the case of a young girl this independence was especially connected with her having freedom of choice in her companions. The precedents were difficult and confusing, partly because the last Queen Regnant was Queen Anne. The Queen had lived in an atmosphere which had not prepared her to trust the Tories, nor did she believe their Government could last. She had excuses and some reason on her side, and in palliation of all it must be remembered that she was only nineteen.

Perhaps Peel ought not to have pressed so hard on such a Sovereign for so worthless an object as the dismissal of the Bedchamber Ladies. Yet he only wished to replace the wives of his chief opponents; he did not desire to strip the Queen of her friends, a fact of which he seems to have found it impossible to apprise the Queen. He had a hard task in front of him. The last reign had proved that the danger of Household influence was by no means a thing of the past, and the last election proved that the claim to the Queen's confidence had still its importance in politics. It cannot be denied that it would have looked strange and significant if the Ladies surrounding the Queen were, practically without exception, wives and sisters of those who were leading the opposition against her Ministers. If the Queen wished to be independent she ought also to be free from any party.

Probably the Whigs ought not to have supported the Queen's mistake. Having largely educated the Queen, and having just resigned, they were under special obligations to see that their adversaries had a fair chance to succeed them. There is also the technical charge against them that they advised the Queen officially, as a Cabinet, on the evening of the 9th before Sir Robert Peel had surrendered his Commission on the 10th. But the Whigs have against all charges the excuse that the Queen was young and unprotected and their benefactor, who, so they thought when they committed themselves, was being treated much more harshly than was the case. The action of the Whigs may not have been wise, but it was natural, and since it involved them in a position neither advantageous nor comfortable it was not dishonourable.

As for the Constitution it is true that a development of public policy was indefensibly frustrated by what were on the whole purely private desires. But this was only because it was a change of doubtful necessity for the public service. Peel was unwillingly undertaking a minority government, otherwise he might have demanded the Ladies' resignation with more authority, or need not have asked for it at all. The situation was made possible by the fact that the Whigs could return to office and stay there. The scales had to be very evenly balanced for the Queen's hands to weigh down either side.

But if it is hard for a historian to apportion the blame, when the story came out few contemporaries found equal difficulty. The news of the hitch soon galloped through London, and hot on its heels came accusation and counter-accusation. The hubbub of political conversation and the noise of the press grew like a storm at sea. Nothing, said Greville, could surpass the excitement and amazement that prevailed. Disraeli describes in *Sybil* how the strange rumour changed in Tory circles into unappetizing truth. Men had already begun, as Peel's papers show, to persecute him for places, and they were bitterly disappointed when they began to learn how they were thwarted.

As early as the 9th May, when certainly nothing was settled, something got into the *Globe*, a Whig evening newspaper. Next day at two o'clock, as Disraeli was turning the corner of Park Street to see the lady who was going to be his wife, he was caught up by a messenger who sent him racing to Lyndhurst, and he wrote a severe and anonymous letter for *The Times*, to lecture that Queen whom he was afterwards to delight in serving. The Whigs in general talked of harshness and cruelty, of depriving the Queen of the friends of her youth, as any friends of the Queen must be at that period. The Tories talked of mysterious and rather pointless plots and of the Queen having been prepared beforehand, and some of them became so violent that when the time for political dinners came in the winter, they seriously discommoded their cause by talking disloyally.

It would be hard to say what may have been the immediate impression on the great body of public opinion of the rights and wrongs of the case. Some may have felt the appeal of the youth and the sex of the Queen; the picture of H.B. the cartoonist, however, took the Conservative side. Probably in most cases opinion merely followed party lines. Most Conservatives, even the wisest, approved of Peel's actions and, when the time for explanations had come, congratulated Peel both on his own speech and on Lord John Russell's. One Conservative, however, was actually glad that the Whigs were back in office, and to the disgust of his party his opinions crept into a speech that he made in the Lords. Indeed the Duke of Wellington went so far as almost to offer Melbourne's Government his support if Melbourne would do his duty. They talked in the Clubs, says Greville, of the Duke's dotage, but the fact of the matter was that the Duke was always too old or too young for party politics.[1]

§ 5

Melbourne's duty might be hard and doubtful. The Whig leaders' constant phrase, when they took up the seals of office was, that they could not, as gentlemen, do otherwise. Unfortunately even gentlemen are not necessarily successful and efficient, and even gentlemen are not necessarily supported by Radicals. It is true that something had been done to remedy their inefficiency, for earlier in the year John Russell had managed to force Lord Glenelg, his most notoriously ineffective colleague, out of office. Glenelg was succeeded at the Colonial

[1] Hansard, XLVII, 1186.

Office by Lord Normanby, who had retired from Ireland
where Lord Ebrington became Lord-Lieutenant. But
other changes were necessary if the Government was to
become even moderately competent; and whether competent or no the Whig Government still had to settle
those problems which had distressed it before its
resignation.

They were still faced, for instance, by the troubles of
Jamaica and Canada. They managed to deal with
Jamaica by proposing a Bill approximating to the
suggestions which Peel had opposed to their original
measure. It was passed into law when it had been
further moulded by the Lords to suit Conservative desires.
On Canada nothing was settled. The quarrel between
the Ministry and Lord Durham had, in spite of Conservative hopes, come to very little, and the event of the year
had been the production of Lord Durham's report on
the problem of Canada. Roughly speaking, he recommended that Canada should be governed by ministers in
Canada responsible to the Canadians, and also that the
two Canadas should be united in order to swamp the
French majority in the Lower Province. But nothing
was effected in 1839 beyond the passing of a mutilated
Bill to delay the decision and provide further for a
provisional Government. When this Bill came before the
Lords its most active effect was to produce great anxieties
in the mind of the Duke of Wellington. He had heard
that Brougham was concocting a new plan for a flare-up
against the Government, which must destroy them. He
was afraid that other Lords might think it proper to follow
Brougham's views.[1]

The Duke did not want to hurt the Government wilfully, but he still wished to keep their Lordships together
with their eyes open to their dangers, and if possible to
keep them in London during the Session. He still felt
that if they did not act together and resist further invasions
of their property and rights they would each in turn
become a sacrifice to the "new principle." He still

---

[1] Add. MSS. 40,310; 483, 485.

wished the House of Lords to prevent the enactment of fresh mischief. "Possibly I am wrong," said he in bitter sarcasm to Aberdeen who had slipped off home early, "possibly I am wrong. All this trouble and all these efforts may be useless, nay, more, injurious. It may be best to let the country go to the Devil its own way, or according to the guidance of the Government, the Political Unions, the Chartists! With all my heart! I will not desire anybody to stay! I have before now stood, and I can stand, alone, and please God as long as I have strength and voice they shall hear of the mischief they have done and are doing." [1] So, with the passionate and unnecessary resignation of an old man, he turned to his work in a world where he had gained no new hope, where he had lost no old despair.

But the Government had to attempt to do much more urgent work in a world which, if not so tragic as that of the Duke, was at least exceedingly embarrassing. On their return to office it was said that there were signs of repentance among some of the Radicals for the infidelity which had expelled them, yet they were almost immediately confronted by two Radical motions. One was to alter the franchise in the Counties, and the other was Grote's Annual Motion on the Ballot. Lord John Russell resisted the first in the name of the Government, but on the second there was a sad change in his position. It is true that he himself opposed the ballot as he had always done, but after the threat of resignation on the part of several members of the Government it was at last allowed to be an open question.[2] The new liberty only slightly increased the minority in favour of the ballot. But it might be a sign that for all his resolution John Russell was going to truckle to the Radicals, or that the more Liberal Ministers, despite Melbourne, would be able to force the Government from its immobility. Perhaps they might find a more hopeful solution to their troubles

---

[1] Privately printed Corresp. of Lord Aberdeen, 1832–44, p. 153 (Duke to Aberdeen, July 20, 1839).

[2] Spencer Walpole, Life of Lord John Russell, I, 323 ff.

than slow deterioration. But that was for the future. For the moment they had to be content to continue governing a country in which Chartists rioted, education schemes miscarried, the Poor Law had to be renewed and income could not be made to balance expenditure.

The spring had been filled with the bruit of Chartist violence, while on the other side the Government had been making their preparations. In April Napier was put in command of the troops in the Northern Districts; in May the Government issued a proclamation against dangerous meetings, and Lord John Russell circulated a letter authorizing armed associations for the protection of property. Meanwhile local authorities enrolled special constables and arrested Chartists when they had the opportunity. But the agitation neither dominated nor terrified political life. Sometimes it came up before Parliament, sometimes it intruded on Peel; and as was usual in periods of disturbance there was a rumour of an attack from Birmingham on Peel's house near Tamworth.[1] Now and again men would talk of the matter very seriously, even melodramatically, but their minds were perforce generally occupied by other things. The developments of ordinary politics naturally held the thoughts of politicians, and the whole world inevitably supplied subjects to claim the attention of an Imperial Parliament.

To the tribunal of that busy and preoccupied institution the Chartists were desirous of bringing the nation's woes and their own remedies. The Chartist Convention had met for the purpose of petitioning what was ordinarily considered to be the House of Commons, although the Convention was also firmly convinced that they themselves and not the oligarchic assembly were the real People's Parliament. They collected about 1,200,000 signatures to a national petition which they deposited with Attwood for presentation. Then the Convention adjourned itself to Birmingham; while all the time one after another of

---

[1] Add. MSS. 40,426; 417.

the more moderate men resigned from it because they did not like the constant talk of violence and of ulterior measures.

The petition was handed to Attwood on May 7th, but in that day and the days following, the scene was occupied by the Jamaica crisis and the problem of the Ladies of the Bedchamber, so that it was not presented to the House of Commons till the 14th June, and there was no full debate on its matter till the 12th July. Even then the debate was not very satisfactory. A motion of Attwood's raised the question. He spoke of the misery of the country, and tried to urge some sort of compliance with the desires of the petitioners, or at least some consideration for them, and he also tried his best to keep his foolish currency theories in the background. But Attwood was an easy man to destroy in debate, and Lord John destroyed him, attacking at the same time the theory that Universal Suffrage would bring comfort to the labouring classes. He denied indeed the existence of general distress among the labouring classes, using, as so often, the argument of the small deposits in the savings banks, and he denied also their general sympathy with the petition. He was followed by Disraeli.

Disraeli spoke in favour of considering the petition. He agreed with Lord John about the fallacy which pervaded it, that political rights ensured social happiness. But the complaint of a million fellow subjects was worthy some consideration. He diagnosed their grievance as half social, half economic. It was caused, said he, by the succession to power of a class, the middle class, which did not exercise the old local social and administrative duties. To save themselves time, trouble and expense, this class demanded a cheap centralized Government, and this Government caused the discontent in the country by invading the civil rights of the people of England. An example of this was of course the new Poor Law, and he deeply regretted that some of the Tory party had supported the new Poor Law and that they had not opposed everything that tended to centralization. But his invective was not, this time, reserved for his friends. He attacked the Whig Government ferociously and, as he himself complacently believed, effectively.

Disraeli's diagnosis was interesting; in fact he made the most interesting speech in a dull debate. But could the ills of the people be ended by resisting centralization? The speech was made before empty benches, for the Tories, the saviours of the people, were elsewhere, supposing, as Disraeli told his sister, that Chartism would only be a squabble between the Whigs and the Radicals. Peel was in the House during the speech, possibly not approving of what was said of the new Poor Law; but he himself said nothing at all, for apparently he had come down to the House to speak on another matter. All that he did was to vote with the large majority which refused further consideration to the petition.[1]

However, no consideration that the House could have given would probably have satisfied the Chartists, for their demands could not have been conceded. On the rejection of the petition the Convention began futile preparations for a "National Holiday" or rather a general strike, which utterly failed. More important were the riots in Birmingham. On July 4th there was a riot in the Bull Ring at Birmingham, possibly in part caused by the precipitancy with which the magistrates launched upon the mob the police whom they had obtained from London. On July 15th there was another riot in the Bull Ring, which was allowed to develop to great excesses of destruction and arson, and this time the trouble was probably due to the magistrates' inaction. The Conservatives did not forget that the Birmingham magistrates had been appointed by Lord John and were in many cases men of advanced Liberal opinions.

For the Conservatives did not forget that they were in opposition to the Government. They suspected Whig vigour and courage in interfering with Chartists. They delighted in pointing out comparisons between the behaviour of the Chartists whom Whig ministers and

[1] Monypenny, *Disraeli*, II, 64. Hansard, XLIX, 246.

Liberal magistrates were trying to suppress, and the behaviour of Whigs and Liberals when they themselves were agitating; it was with this view, for instance, that Goulburn's brother defended Collins, the Chartist, when he was arrested in Birmingham.[1]   Above all they abused Lord John's appointment of magistrates.   There was even a tendency to oppose the Police Bills which the Government brought in during the Session, to provide police for Manchester or Birmingham or Bolton. Indeed Conservatives felt that the new police arrangements for Bolton and Manchester were probably unnecessary jobs on the part of the Whigs or of the new Corporation.[2]

But there was a counteracting feeling among Conservatives that they ought to support the demands of the Executive.   "We do not oppose," said Peel to his wife, "the measures of the Government requisite for the maintenance of the public peace.   Whigs in opposition would have taken a very different course."[3]   So of all the Conservatives in the Commons Disraeli was the only daring and consistent opponent of the Government's Police Bills, and his opposition was after all only the odd unimportant manœuvre of an independent member.   It was not likely to be imitated by responsible men who had been and would be ministers, but Disraeli had not developed his views from the angle of the Treasury Bench.

In one department, however, the Government's proceedings were likely to raise the profoundest objections in the most ministerially minded statesman.   For three years Spring-Rice had been unable to make his income balance his expenditure.   Each year since 1836 there had been a deficiency, each year the Chancellor of the Exchequer had declared that the difference was small and

[1] *Life and Struggles of William Lovett,* Chap. XII, p. 226.
[2] Add. MSS. 40,427; 103 (Granville Somerset to Peel resp. opposition to Police Bills).
[3] *Private Letters,* p. 164.

temporary, and each year he had proposed no taxation
to meet it.   Meanwhile he had allowed too large an
unfunded debt to accrue, and in 1839 he added to his
embarrassments by trying the expensive experiment of
adopting a penny postage, thereby putting in hazard
about a million and a half of revenue.   The danger of
this he tried to minimize by accompanying his postal
scheme by an absurd and mysterious pledge that the
House of Commons would make good, at some period
in the future, any deficiency which might be occasioned.
No wonder that Goulburn and Peel both thundered at
him and talked of Whigs who had not the courage to
impose or maintain necessary taxation.   It was to speak
about the penny postage and the continual deficits that
Peel had come down to the House of Commons on the
evening on which the National petition was rejected.
Among other things he declared that the Government's
postal scheme and its pledges would probably pledge
the House to a property tax, "and looking," said he, "at
the state of the public interests, and at the high scale of
taxation upon articles which were the elements of manufacture and general consumption, possibly a property
tax might be the wisest to be resorted to in such a case." [1]

That night, on the National Petition, Disraeli had
shown genius and insight in his diagnosis of the evils of
the poor, if his remedy was illusory.   That night Peel
gave a hint of what might be the financial policy of his
Government.   Each was moved and interested and
angered by what was likely to enlist his attention.   One
was the man of ability and the Treasury Bench, the other
the man of insight and peculiar opinions.   It would be
tempting to say that they ought to correlate, that the
powers of each should dovetail with the others' needs.
It would be impossible to say that they would remain
allies.

But as yet Peel and Disraeli could take turns at the
whip-handle and there were many blows prepared for the

[1] Hansard, XLIV, 277.

Government.   At the end of the Session Lyndhurst fitted
a new thong to his scourge and reviewed its achievements.
He spoke terribly of the emptiness, feebleness, the signs
of partisan motives and the incapacity, that he found in
the Government's record; he spoke of promises un-
performed, and of measures introduced and abandoned.
He laid to their charge the Chartist disorders, "for it is
they," said he, "who first roused the people."   Melbourne answered his accusations with spirit, and declared
that the making of laws " is only a subsidiary and
incidental duty of Parliament; the principal duty of
Parliament is to consider the estimates for the public
service, to retrench what is superfluous, to correct what
is amiss, and to assist the Crown with those supplies and
subsidies which it thinks it right and necessary to afford."
He in his turn attacked the House of Lords for obstruction.   Brougham followed, eloquent, damnatory and
angry.   After him came the Duke, criticizing the Government, deploring the weakness of everything.   In fact he
gave voice to his heart cry, "all that he desired now and
had for some years desired was to see a Government in
this country." [1]   Much was said in that debate that was
eloquent, much that was interesting, much that was
genuine.   But not much perhaps that could be construed
into a message of hope for the future fruitfulness of
politics.

§6

Yet they had discussed in that Session what has been
considered the nurse and mother of hope.   The Cabinet
had tried to make good their determination to produce
an improved scheme of popular education.   During the
course of 1839 they called into being a committee of the
Privy Council to control the money which the State
granted towards education.   They tried to produce two
normal schools in which masters for both Church and
undenominational schools could be trained.   They intended to make the reception of a grant carry with it the

[1] Hansard, L, 496.

burden of inspection by the Government, and they announced that they would not in future be as strictly guided as hitherto by the rules under which they had apportioned the grant. In fact they took a few timid steps towards a centralized State-controlled educational system.

They did not take such steps with impunity. To enter into the problem of education in the nineteenth century was like entering among those rocks in India which are tenanted by many millions of vigilant and irascible hornets. The committee of the Privy Council was abused because it was in fact merely a committee of the Cabinet, and through it education was to be put under the control of those who were at the moment the Ministers of the Crown. Men's nerves were not yet dulled to the idea of politically controlled education, and at least to churchmen the proper guardians of the country's education were its Bishops and Archbishops. In the normal schools there was to be some sort of general religious education as well as special denominational teaching, and there was a horrible suspicion that the Scriptures might sometimes be read in the Roman Catholic version. Inspection, though sound in principle, seemed to be intended to lead to the control of the schools inspected.

Even Dissenters were suspicious; but Dissenters' principles in this controversy were likely to be obscured by their politics and by the great need of their schools for the Government's money.[1] However, the Wesleyans, who were unembarrassed by Liberal politics, came forward prominently against the Government's scheme. They resolved against it in conference and promoted petitions against it.[2] They were moved largely by the fear of Rome, and the fear of Rome, as is shown by the tone which *The Times* thought fit to assume and by some of the speeches in the House of Commons,

---

[1] *Kay-Shuttleworth*, p. 83 (Baines to Shuttleworth).
[2] Dr. G. Smith's *History of Wesleyan Methodism*, III, 395. *Minutes of Wesleyan Conferences*, VIII, 514–15.

deeply infected men's objections to the Government's proposals; it was still one of the profoundest emotions that had their grip on the country. Certainly the Church was not likely to be silent. Churchmen had not even the pressing need for funds to silence them and, unlike the Dissenters, they received the largest share in the grants of the old system. The Government inspectors would probably interfere with their National Schools, they could not be content to see the highest control of the education of the country pass into the lay hands of a committee of Cabinet Ministers. Many Churchmen objected to latitudinarian and undenominational teaching. Moreover about the Church there still remained the torn mantle of her official position. She might not claim— indeed she did not claim—to have in her hands the religious education of all the children in England, yet she might still feel after the doctrine, already transgressed, that the State should only extend pecuniary aid to that Church whose Creed the State had acclaimed as the Truth.

So the storm rose and the Government's desires suffered. Petitions poured in to Parliament, there was a great Education meeting in London at which the Archbishop of Canterbury spoke, and even Whig-made Bishops objected to the Government's proposals. The normal schools had to be abandoned because the state of opinion in the country made it impossible to establish them. But since the Government's scheme was largely carried out by orders in Council, it was not often forced to run the gauntlet in Parliament, and practically the only critical vote which the Government had to take was on the appropriation of the necessary grant in the House of Commons. However the Commons managed to have two full-dress debates, one of great length, and two divisions. On the first division the Government's majority was only five and on the second only two. The House of Lords followed the matter up by passing a deprecatory resolution, which Peel had drawn for them.[1]

[1] Add. MSS. 40,427; 78.

They carried it in a body to the foot of the Throne, and did not get a satisfying answer.

The controversy continued in the country, within the National Society itself, or in negotiations between the Bishops and the Ministers. The outcome was that the committee of the Council remained, an amicable agreement was arrived at for the inspection of the schools, and in 1840, after considerable trouble, a concordat was arranged between the Government and the Church. Perhaps it may seem that the incident is too little decisive to be left in the narrative of political history. It gave evidence of Liberal intentions on the part of the Government, it served to demonstrate the strength and suspicions of the Church. But its results were not large and it was settled out of court. Principles were approached and appealed to but not, on the whole, applied. On the one hand it was to be thirty years before there came a real scheme of State elementary education. On the other it may be said that whatever was the Church's strength in the Commons, or her rights as the most important denomination in the country, obviously she could no longer claim with success that she was the Church which the State put forward as Truth, and that she had therefore a right, and an exclusive right, to the State's assistance. The past could not be revived, the future could not be hurried, and the present lay between them, full of confusion and frustration.

But it is this characteristic which makes the problem and the period interesting in the history of Conservatism. It is a twilight period, either early morning or late evening when a man might be hampered by ghosts and assailed by embryos. It is a period troubled and rendered pathetic by ineffective hopes, the hopes of Conservatives.

---

1 *The Life of Sir James Kay-Shuttleworth* (Frank Smith), Chap. III. *Memoir of Bishop Blomfield* (Alfred Blomfield), Chap. X. Halévy, III, 208. Hansard, XLV, 273. XLVIII, 227 ff.; 1332, etc. Add. MSS. 40,426; 442; 447. 40,427; 19, 25.

The Church was still established, yet since 1828 and 1829 Parliament, which was considered to govern State and Church, could be controlled both by Protestant and Roman Catholic Dissenters. Really more important than that, in the present state of opinion in the country, it was possible that legislation in accord with the old principle of Establishment could never again be passed. Ireland was a chaos of theories, and the arrangements in the Colonies could not be made to bear out the position which was claimed for the Established Churches of England or Scotland.[1]

This question of Education raised difficulties of its own. As Gladstone urged in debate, if the State could finance the spiritual instruction of dissenting children, why should it not go further and finance the spiritual instruction of dissenting adults, their chapels and their ministers?[2] It might indeed be asked, whither did the principle of the equality of religions lead? How could the State undertake the teaching of children, when in theory it ought to have no official knowledge of what the Truth was? There was, perhaps there still is, a dangerous paradox in that position.

It was not, however, a very important paradox. In part the State had braved it already in its grant to dissenting education, and in part compromised itself out of its difficulties by confining itself to inspection and subsidy. However, as a paradox it served to confound and confuse Conservatives, and the religious disagreement of the country made education difficult to many men who were not, like John Russell, shallow enough to despise other men's differences on dogma. During these debates Peel confessed himself deeply convinced "of the absolute necessity and of the moral obligation of providing for the education of the people." But he was so much impressed with the problem of dissent that he felt that education in this country could only be effected by the

---

[1] Gladstone, *The State in its Relations with the Church*, Chap. VII.
[2] Hansard, XLVIII, 622 (Gladstone on Education).

voluntary exertions of the Churches themselves.[1]   It was a counsel of despair, and he showed his limitations by not knowing it.   Perhaps he had often no real picture of the problems which sometimes confronted his deep convictions.

Education was but one item in the whole problem which Church Establishment raised for the Conservatives. It is true that even Noncomformists and Liberals were able to accept the fact of the Church's Establishment, and that the Whigs defended it loosely.   All Conservatives could agree that the Church was still in danger; the *Quarterly* had prophesied new virulence on the part of the Dissenters at the beginning of 1839; the malice of Dissenters was detected in these education proposals.[2] The Church was in a state of siege; that was certain. But there were difficulties even inside the walls.   There was the question of the State's rights over the Church. In the Established Church of Scotland there had already been started the Non-Intrusion Movement, which aimed at giving the controlling voice in the appointment to livings to the parishes and not to those who were patrons in the eyes of the law.   In England there was the growth of the Oxford Movement, with its dislike of Erastianism and its insistence upon Catholicity and unchangeable peculiarities of dogma.   Both of these movements inevitably tended to spiritual independence, and could the State possibly protect, foster or sustain where it could not control?   In England, also, the policy instituted by Peel with his Ecclesiastical Commission was bitterly resented and ineffectively opposed by Churchmen.   It was urged that no one, and certainly not the State, had a right to redistribute the wealth of the Chapters in order to supply spiritual aid elsewhere.   For various reasons High Churchmen shrank not from Whigs alone, but from the Erastian Sir Robert Peel.

While the quickened sensibilities of Churchmen, and

[1] Hansard, XLV, 309.
[2] *Quarterly Review*, No. CXXV, p. 274.   Blomfield, I, 266.

especially of High Churchmen, might resent, more and more, invasions of the Church's independence, the quickened consciences of Churchmen might desire more and more the aid which the State could no longer give them. The eyes of many Churchmen were opened to the needs of the ignorant and the neglected. It was an age of Church effort. In 1838 and 1839 there had been very great activity in the matter of Church Education, largely in competition with the desires for State Education. This was under the guidance of young men touched by the Oxford Movement, such as Acland and young Gladstone.[1] In 1836 Bishop Blomfield had launched his crusade for building churches in London. Members of the Scotch Established Church were attempting to extend their activities and reduplicate their parishes. Everywhere men were attempting to remedy the spiritual destitution that everywhere confronted them.

It was natural that both the Churches of England and Scotland should look to the State for assistance in their heavy task. The past was not distant when Parliament had voted money for the building of churches. When he was Minister in 1835, and afterwards, Peel had brought forward the demands of the Scotch Church for State Aid in Church extension. "The line that moves everything in Scotland," said Graham in 1838, "is the Kirk and Church Extension." Inglis, the representative of the old-fashioned High Church school, was anxious to press the same claims for the Church of England.[2] The two Churches would turn to the State to help them minister to the poor, yet would even the Church and King party make any modern Parliament do its duty?

The Scotch demands for State aid were juggled and postponed by the Government in such a way as to frustrate them until the Non-Intrusion Movement began to fill the scene in Scotland, and to dull Conservative

[1] *Memoir and Letters of Sir Thomas Acland* (privately printed). Purcell's *Manning*, Vol. I.
[2] Add. MSS. 40,616; 94 (Graham to Bonham, Oct. 27, 1838). 40,428; 19 (Sir R. Inglis to Peel, Jan. 4, 1840).

hopes and sympathies.   Peel was inclined to believe in
the work of the much abused Ecclesiastical Commission
as a remedy for spiritual destitution in England.[1]   When
he came into power, would he not probably prefer to use
such expedients for Church extension, and thus continuously keep out of sight and out of use the just claims of
any truly established Church to national assistance?   As
a statesman, as a friend to the Church, would he not wish
to avoid exasperating her enemies who were so strong in
the country?   In modern England, to try to act on the
old Church principles might not be feasible, to mention
them dangerous, to dream of them deceptive.   Yet what
was then left for the old Church and King party?

Moreover, both hopes and principles often die too
slowly; they linger as burdens to the brain and as a false
light to the spirit.   There were many who by no means
wished to slur over the question of the Establishment.
The great Dr. Chalmers, as yet of the Scotch Established
Church, gave in London a series of notably attended
lectures on the principles of the Established Churches,
to which Gladstone listened disapprovingly, for he
realized that Chalmer's hazy and enthusiastic mind
glozed over the difficulties of the position.   In 1838
Gladstone tried his hand on the problem, and published
his first book on the State in its relation with the Church,
a book which was most significantly successful.   Gladstone's mind was dominated by the idea of a State with
a conscience and a Church that should be both Established and Catholic.   It was said that Peel wondered
how a man with such a career in prospect should go out
of his way to write books.   When Gladstone stood by
his opinions in the debates on education in the House of
Commons, Peel said later in the debate that he would
not undertake to defend every opinion that had been
advanced.   He would confine himself to the practical
question before the House, rather than consider the
speculative opinions advanced by Gladstone and others.[2]
Perhaps Peel had grown up in an age when no one cared

[1] Hansard, XLV, 869.   [2] *Ibid.*, XLVIII, 666.

for the definition of principles, and had survived to an age when it might be dangerous or even disastrous to define them.   If so Peel might be in his way happier than Gladstone.[1]

No doubt principles need not be defined, even if they cannot or ought not to be eluded. No doubt Gladstone's particular views were confined to himself and other young men equally mediæval, and no doubt his general Church principles were clearer and more extreme than those of the bulk of his party.   Still, apart from the fact that the Church had captivated the imagination of many of the best young Conservatives, the party had certainly consciously rallied to the defence of the Establishment principles.   In 1838 the Duke of Wellington told a Scotch deputation on Church Extension that the real question which dominated politics was Church or no Church.   The party was everywhere recruited from churchmen and supported by clergymen. Was there to be no positive side to it all?

When abysses of ignorance, disorder and sedition were disclosed, the remedy that was apt to suggest itself to the Conservative mind was the provision of more churches and more clergymen.[2]   Church Education and Church ministration to adults were natural vehicles for Conservative social reform, yet it was possible that such things could never again be specifically aided by the national resources.   Would, then, all Conservative philanthropy be confined to voluntary effort?   The success of the Conservative party excited high hopes in the breasts of many of the religious.   Churchmen, Low Churchmen, enthusiastic Protestants, gave the party their votes and their prayers, while Ashley fed Peel with tracts and with sermons, as one consecrated to a holy task.[3]

[1] Chalmers, *Memoirs of Chalmers*, Vol. III and Vol. IV.   Gladstone, *A Chapter of Autobiography*; *State in its Relation with the Church*.   *Gladstone's Life*, by Morley, Vol. I, Chaps. 4 and 5.   *Memoir of James Hope Scott*, Vol. I.
[2] E.g. Add. MSS. 40,427; 319 (Granville Somerset to Peel resp. Chartists, Dec. 13, 1839).
[3] E.g. Add. MSS. 40,428; 233 (Parker, II, 461). 40,483; 1, 4.   *Life of Shaftesbury* (Hodder), Vol. I, pp. 332, 342.

Yet as victory approached and was secured, Ashley admitted privately that he and some of the best religious members of the party had doubts and worse than doubts about their leader.   He has plenty of human honesty, said Ashley, but little of divine faith.   But what future was there for divine faith in the Conservative party? [1]

[1] Halévy, III, pp. 187–97.   *Aberdeen, Life*, by Lady Frances Balfour, Vol. II, Chap. VIII.   *Chalmers* (Hanna), etc., etc., *v.s.*

CHAPTER XI

THE CONSERVATIVE PARTY—1840-41

Perhaps principles have less of permanence in them than have parties. The Conservative party would certainly have a future, whatever part Divine faith would be enabled to play in it. The technical business of party organization and leadership went on, whatever difficulties of principles lay behind it. Some of this was far enough away from Divine faith, and not always closely connected with human honesty, as when Bonham the Whip reported that of the 409 Penryn voters only three did not expect payment.[1] But whatever was the tone in certain constituencies, the Leaders and Whips themselves were honourable men, and their reflections were not exceptionally cynical or sordid. They went about their duties, they speculated on their problems with an efficiency and lack of profundity such as most able men show in the ordinary tasks of life. During the recess Bonham and Graham debated ceaselessly on the state of the registration in various constituencies and on election prospects. Graham told Bonham his fears of what would be the effect on Conservatism of the movement which had started to ravage the Church of Scotland, and they both became deeply engaged on the problem of what would be the Conservative party's chances on a division in the Commons when Parliament met again in 1840.

That calculation could not then be worked out with such certainty as it would be in the twentieth century, although apparently the day of the independent member was already over. There was a fringe of undecided Whigs at one end of the Government's majority and a group of disillusioned Radicals at the other, and parties were so nicely balanced that a few votes might decide the result of a division. The result of various by-elections must be considered and the nature of the division which would force the issue, as also the possi-

[1] Add. MSS. 40,427; 363.

bility of the Government's dissolving either just before or just after a division.   The problem was difficult, and ultimately Graham prophesied a majority for the Government, while Bonham reported to Peel that the Conservatives would have one.   So the situation was close and critical enough to demand thought on thepart of statesmen, perhaps to the exclusion of the problems of Divine faith and the more distant future.[1]

Other matters challenged attention during that recess. The harvest was bad, there were serious difficulties in the financial world which were thought to menace the Bank of England, and much material was provided for the despair and excitement of Graham.   By the middle of August he had decided that unless the harvest was saved none of the precautions which had been taken would avail, but "inextricable confusion must ensue and the grand blow-up be inevitable." [2]   Men's fears are as ill-directed as their hopes; perhaps both serve only to relieve the tedium of ordinary political duty.   The grand blow-up never came, but it cannot be denied that the situation sometimes disclosed features that might well be disquieting to more torpid Conservatives than Sir James Graham.

Since its failures and futilities of that summer, Chartism had to a large extent gone under ground and entered on a curious phase of secret conspiracy and organization. Early in November it produced a mysterious and sinister incident.   Late on the evening of November 3rd the authorities of Newport in Monmouthshire were apprised by terrified refugees that armed bodies of men were gathering in the hills.   At nine o'clock next day about 3,000 roughly armed miners poured into the town.   It was a night attack timed to arrive there at 2 a.m. but delayed by mishaps.   They were routed with loss by the vigour of the local Mayor and a small force of twenty-

---

[1] Add. MSS. 40,616; 132 ff. (Graham to Bonham, constant commentary throughout the winter).   40,428; 13 (Bonham to Peel, Jan. 4, 1840).

[2] *Ibid.* 40,616; 132.

eight soldiers, and their ringleaders were captured. But there still remained the menace and mystery of their proceedings. The ostensible reason for their attack was to release a Chartist prisoner named Vincent, and it was thought that personal hostility to the Mayor had in part directed it. But there was held to be more behind, though its nature has never been made clear. Later on dark and incredible stories of Russian intrigue were propounded; at the time Granville Somerset, writing to Peel from Monmouth where the Newport prisoners were being tried, said that they had proofs of a widespread organization inspired with a desire to obtain the Charter and secure the millennium by force of arms. The labouring population, so said Granville Somerset, had become universally inoculated with treasonable and seditious views, even though they were in enjoyment of abundant wages. He was not the only one to hear the whispers of armed conspiracy abroad. At the same time Graham in Cumberland saw symptoms of quiet preparation. "Their secret machinations," said he, "are far more formidable than their public meetings." Perhaps the time had come for Conservatives to enjoy the luxury of fear in good earnest.

But the sentiment uppermost in Conservative minds was not dismay at the public danger, but condemnation of the Government. The chief ring-leader at Newport, a man named Frost, had been one of Lord John Russell's magistrates, though he had been struck off the list for attending a Chartist meeting. Granville Somerset thought that his position had led the mob to believe that they could come to no harm under his guidance. The Government did not seem to take enough trouble to investigate the organization in Monmouthshire. The Attorney-General appeared to mismanage the trials of the Newport prisoners. There was a technical error in the proceedings which, although it was not allowed to invalidate the verdict and sentence, caused the penalty for treason to be commuted to transportation. But before that was known Graham had constructed a dilemma into which he thought, perhaps it ought not to be said that he hoped, that the Government must fall. They must either execute Frost and alienate the Radicals, or pardon him, to the utter disgust and dismay of every man of property and right feeling. Meanwhile Conservatives constantly repeated among themselves that Chartism would never cease till England had a strong Government, and with or without reason they believed that the country was coming to think so too.[1]

§ 2

Other things happened that autumn which might affect the Conservatives' position. There were changes in the Cabinet. Normanby changed places with Lord John Russell, who thus became Colonial Secretary, and Poulett Thomson went to Canada from the Board of Trade; and Graham pointed out that both Normanby's and Thomson's promotions were direct insults to the interests involved. Spring-Rice, being succeeded by Francis Baring as Chancellor of the Exchequer, was jettisoned into a comfortable sinecure by what seemed to Conservatives the grossest of jobs. Angered by the manner in which these changes were effected, and disliking their political implications, Lord Howick, Earl Grey's son, resigned, to be followed out of office by his brother-in-law Charles Wood, a movement which might easily foreshadow a revolt of the old Whigs from the Government. Finally Macaulay became Secretary of War with a seat in the Cabinet, an event obviously of perilous significance, since he had adopted the Ballot when he was elected to Edinburgh a few months before.

These changes certainly greatly increased the efficiency of the Cabinet, while they might or might not have their results on its majority. Graham noticed signs of discontent among his old Whig friends, but he generously came to the conclusion that the mouths of the Grey section

---

[1] Hovell, *Chartist Movement*, pp. 174 ff. Add. MSS. 40,427; 319, 371. 40,428; 3, 20 (Granville Somerset to Peel); 40,616 *passim* (Graham and Bonham, *v.s.*, etc.).

of the Whig party could be easily stopped up with
patronage. There was, however, one event in 1839
which was bound to affect the Conservatives' future, and
that was the engagement between the Queen and Prince
Albert. It would as a matter of fact clear their path into
office by helping them to surmount the difficulties which
had produced the Bedchamber incident. But the Conservatives were in no very generous mood with regard
to the Queen. The news did not cause them to abandon
their tendency to speculate wildly and to joke maliciously.
Albert was a Radical, he was a metaphysician, he
entertained very stirring and ambitious views, he said
that no tailor in England could cut a coat. Indeed
they said much that was prompted rather by their
wayward imaginations than by their charity or knowledge.[1]

There is little significance in the casual and factious
speculations of politicians. The Prince was as yet an
unknown quantity, but that did not mean that his entry
into English life could be unaffected by politics. Ashley
suspected that the Government would attempt to give
him an unnecessary and unwarrantable revenue, and it
was not likely that the Conservatives would be so blinded
by loyalty as to pass over such a mistake. In the speech
to the Council, in which the Queen announced her
intention of marrying Prince Albert, no mention was
made of Albert's Protestantism, although of course it
was legally necessary that he should be a Protestant.
The omission was criticized by all the Conservative leaders.
It was a departure from tradition and a foolish concession
to liberality. Ashley told Peel that he might say he
knew that the omission was intentional. "Cast aside all
other views," was his advice, "and let us endeavour to
get the Government out on a *Protestant* point. We shall
thus combine the truths of religion (God be praised for it!)
and the feelings of the Country." Then, if Ashley's

---

[1] Parker, II, 414. Add. MSS. 40,341; 141.   40,427; 223, 268, 289.
40,616; 201, etc.

advice was followed, the Conservatives might indeed make a very profitable use of Divine faith.[1]

But Ashley's advice was not likely to be followed. The dictates of Divine faith are simpler than the demands of human statesmanship, and it would be harder for Peel than it could be for Ashley to decide what course to take in 1840.   There was first the question whether he should attack the Government at all.   Fremantle, one of the Whips, was very urgent that he should move against the Government at the time of the Address, to satisfy the party's appetite and secure their attendance, and there was evidence from elsewhere that the party was restless and bellicose.   An article had appeared in the *Quarterly*, criticizing the Conservative Leader's tranquillity.   Bonham spoke to Graham of a tone of desperation among their friends, while Graham feared that men would become weary of hopeless resistance, and would endeavour "to compound with the abominable thing"; by which he apparently meant a Government made up of men who six years ago had been his colleagues.

Peel consulted Graham, Goulburn, Stanley and the Duke on the subject.   Graham was the most eager to attack, and the Duke was the one who most deplored such a movement.   Like a great ship in a sea mist on a windless day he cruised slowly, satisfied with infinitesimal progress, overburdened with the consciousness of dangers on every side, his mind cloaked heavily by his immovable despairs.   He ransacked the world for dangers which would confront Peel's Government.   He thought what he had always thought of the effects of Reform, and they were now aggravated by the fact that the Sovereign was herself the head of the adverse party. He pleaded for delay, but Graham and Fremantle were swift to point out that at any time some difficulties would stand in the way of Peel's Government.   If they were too great for Peel, they must be too much for the dishonest and incompetent men now in power.   It would be impossible to hold the party together much longer

[1] Parker, II, 414.   Add. MSS. 40,427; 268.

without a direct and vigorous attack on their opponents, and, as the Duke would not see, the constituencies were now prepared to return a Conservative majority.

The Conservative Party was doomed to success. If party politics were to go on at all the Duke's despairs had to be overruled as an archaism. Peel was fully conscious that he must risk the dissolution either of the Government or of his party. If he voluntarily attacked the Government he knew that he was bound in honour, if called upon, to attempt to replace it, and he felt that he ought not to let his personal position on the Bedchamber problem affect his policy. There was no escape; the logic of the facts was at last inexorable, and the principle was established that, as Graham said, "the constant legitimate object of an Opposition is the overthrow of an Administration which they consider bad, and hope to replace by a better."

However, wisdom comes only by instalments, and there was more to be learnt or neglected. An Opposition must not only desire to overthrow its adversaries, it must also prepare the country for what should succeed them. In discussing the form of attack to be made on the Government, Stanley told Peel that he did not see that a want of confidence motion "has the peculiar advantage which you seem to attribute to it, of saving us from committal on doubtful points of policy." Perhaps the thought which had crossed Peel's mind did not lack significance.[1]

The necessity of congratulating the Queen on her marriage protected the Address from amendment. Indeed before the Conservatives launched their assault they had not only congratulated the Queen, they had had also the pleasure of teaching her and her Ministers a lesson, for with exterior aid they managed to reduce by £20,000 the revenue granted to Prince Albert. On January 28th the much desired attack was opened in the House of Commons. A substantial county member,

[1] Parker, II, 416 (Add. MSS. 40,310; 308. 40,318; 163). Add. MSS. 40,427; 331, 336, 345, 349, 369. 40,616; 227.

Sir J. Yarde Buller, was put up to move a vote of want of confidence in the Administration. The debate went on for four nights, dealing again and again with the same accusations and counter-accusations. Graham was said to be malignant, Stanley was dashing and aggressive. Macaulay delivered a speech which reads well but was heard badly, Disraeli effected what he complacently called a brilliant guerrilla movement, and as for Peel, Peel did as a matter of fact foreshadow the nature of his Government.

Much had been said in the debate about what would be Peel's fortunes in office. Men had canvassed his dilemma on Irish Policy between his followers and justice, they had even touched upon his possible tergiversation on the Corn Law, and when he came to speak Peel agreed that at the least from considerations of prudence he should answer the questions that had been raised. Consequently when he had sufficiently flogged the Government he turned to the future, and first he declared one unalterable resolution. He would not be the instrument for giving effect to opinions in which he did not concur. He would profess his principles and not abandon them in order to conciliate the support of either side of the House. So he declared his intention to maintain the new Poor Law, protection for agriculture and, looking to Ireland, the principles of Roman Catholic Emancipation. There is no doubt that he seemed in his speech to announce that he would not be the tool of the Ultra-Tories; there is no question that with all the sincerity, openness and eloquence at his command Peel attempted to ensure that there should be no deceiving of the party which should elevate him into power. Future history alone could judge of his success.[1]

But again his destiny was delayed, for the Government managed to defeat the Conservative motion by a majority of 21. Peel was not to try his hand at the hardest task of all in 1840. Nevertheless a line of more active

[1] Hansard, LI, 1017.

opposition had been instituted, and other more successful attacks followed. Graham brought forward a motion against the Government's proceedings in China. Stanley produced a Bill to cure the abuses of which Conservatives complained in the registration of voters in Ireland. It must have pleased even the most restless Conservatives, for night after night they sacrificed their pleasures and came down in large numbers to hear the dullest of subjects debated in the hottest of tempers. The Government opposed and obstructed, but Stanley was able to fight his Bill into Committee. Ten divisions were taken from first to last upon it, on five the Government expended their full force, on one only were they successful. So much time had been taken up by struggle and delay that the Bill had to be dropped when it was part way through its committee. But even this Stanley did with a flourish, and the Bill remained to disgrace the Government's record and menace their future.

Indeed the Government was doomed. Stanley's successes showed that the old Whigs would not be unquestionably loyal to their leaders. The results of the by-elections were full of hope for the Conservatives. The reports from the constituencies favoured them; Bonham reported that even the Radical constituencies in the towns would make common cause with the Conservatives against the Whigs, as long as it was the Whigs who were in office.[1] The Whigs were doomed. Probably it did not much matter that within the next nine months or so the Government were successful in Canada, in China, temporarily successful in the first Afghan war, and strikingly successful in foreign affairs. Saint Luke's summer might brighten autumn, it did not postpone the winter.

Nor was there anything decisive in the divisions among themselves which confused the Conservatives during this year. The first part of the Session was largely taken up by interminable debates on the question of privilege arising from the case of Stockdale v. Hansard. Peel took

1 Add. MSS. 40,428; 13.

up, with some obstinacy, the side opposed to the mass
of his party, and Graham and Stanley followed him in
silence and discomfort.   When a settlement was at last
reached, the Duke made difficulties about passing the
requisite legislation through the House of Lords.   But
there was an end to these troubles; the party could unite
for the assault, and at this stage in the hunt the prey
was not to be saved by quarrels among the pack.

Yet perhaps there was something significant in the
violence with which, so Graham noticed, Peel attacked
his friends when they differed from him, which compared
rather strangely with the studied moderation with which
he attacked the Government.   An old wound often aches
less than a new pinprick, even when the sword has been
in the hand of an enemy and the pin is in the hand of
a friend.   For Peel there may have been something
peculiarly exasperating in even pinpricks from the hands
of political friends.[1]

§ 3

Apart from these troubles in the Commons there were
other Conservative disagreements that year which were
more tragic, if hardly more effective.   The Duke was
now an old man.   He had suffered of late from a series
of sudden attacks or seizures which had greatly alarmed
his friends and his followers.   They constantly repeated
that his life was of national importance.   As Graham
said, if he went, how would they be able to manage the
House of Lords?   But there was no question but that
these attacks had left their marks.   He was now little
more than the bones of a Field-Marshal, and very wasted
and shrunken inside his clothes.   He stooped a good
deal to one side and, though his step was still reported
as being firm, in his saddle he was inclined to sway
unsteadily.   Everywhere were the marks of age; his
face was pale and careworn, his eye less bright.   Whenever he sat down he was inclined to go to sleep, he did

[1] Parker's *Graham*, Vol. I, 291 ff.

H H

not read readily without spectacles and he was very deaf.

It could not be said that his mind had perished, although there were a number of men, whom Greville both sneers at and represents, who were inclined to see signs of senility in the Duke whenever they disagreed with him. He could still think clearly in his own way and be gay and talkative in his own way also. But Greville noticed in him now and again an unreasoning and senile irascibility and as unreasoning a belief that all his influence had gone from him. His large correspondence made him complain of hard work with a bitterness which was probably significant. Even ten years before there had been times when the pressure of affairs had become suddenly too much for him, but then they had been more important affairs than the constant requests of old soldiers for patronage, and it was the pressure of such minor troubles that made him cry out in 1840: "Rest! Every other animal—even a donkey—a costermonger's donkey —is allowed some rest, but the Duke of Wellington never! There is no help for it. As long as I am able to go on they will put the saddle upon my back and make me go!" But then a costermonger's donkey would have been perfectly contented if it were turned out to grass.[1]

The real tragedy of the Duke of Wellington's position was that the time had come when, on the whole, his influence was more important than his opinions. His opinions of course still carried great weight. He had much to do with settling the difficulties about precedence and a possible Regency raised by the Queen's marriage. When he contradicted all that his friends had been saying on the question of China the Whigs quoted him with emphasis and delight. His views had indeed a unique importance. He was a national hero, and one who would undoubtedly rise above the limitations of faction. But there were times when it was his duty to abandon

---

[1] *Conversations with the Duke of Wellington*, Earl Stanhope (pp. 194, 236, 241).

his opinions and surrender his influence into other hands, and such times came in 1840.

In 1840, finally and at last successfully the Irish Municipal Reform Bill was brought before Parliament. There were difficulties in the Commons, but Peel declared himself pledged to its passing, and it went up to the House of Lords.   A little later in the Session a Bill was introduced to lay the foundation of Lord Durham's proposed reforms in Canada by uniting the Provinces of Upper and Lower Canada.   Peel convinced himself that they ought to pass this measure.   He saw, as he said, "less danger in the measure of Union, proposed as it has been by the Crown after ample public notice and assented to by all the Colonial authorities, than in the rejection or delay of the measure." [1]   Consequently in course of time the Canada Bill also went up to the House of Lords.

But meanwhile a storm had blown up in the mind of a hero.   There had been trouble last year when the Duke had thought of rejecting the Irish Municipal Bill; this year matters were worse.   There was an ominous speech on the second reading of the Irish Bill in the Lords. The Duke did not feel satisfied with the working of the two measures, in return for which open municipalities were to be given to Ireland, nor did he like the details of the measure which had been laid before them.   When counsel were heard by the House of Lords against the Bill the Duke was impressed by their arguments.   It transpired that he certainly did not think that he was bound to pass the Bill if it should affect the general interest of the Empire.   On Canada, apparently, his opinions were even more poignant.   The consequences of the union of the Canadas would, he believed, mean separation from the Mother Country, and he would not at the end of a life passed with honour take upon himself

---

[1] Parker, II, 433.   Add. MSS. 40,428; 217, and e.g. Hansard, LIV, 119.

the grave responsibility of inflicting a heavy and a fatal blow upon England.

In June and July matters were critical. At the beginning of June Graham had scented danger and brought Arbuthnot, the Duke's confidant and leash-holder, up to London. Arbuthnot at first reported very unsatisfactorily of the state of the great man's mind. But Graham emphatically impressed on him the danger for the party in an open division on such important matters, and he in his turn let the Duke know what the other leaders thought and wished. Gradually with regard to the Irish Municipal Bill the medicine worked, possibly assisted by Stanley's successes with his Irish Registration Bill. Arbuthnot watched his charge's thoughts turning by degrees to the course which was required of him. By June 12th that danger was over, and Arbuthnot wrote that it could all be left now to the working of the Duke's own mind. The Iron Duke had been lured back into the right path on the Irish Municipal Bill. Except for a few stragglers the House of Lords would now go in the direction which the shepherds desired.

But on Canada matters were more obstinate. The Duke's patriotism was on fire against the fatal union of the provinces. Arbuthnot had told Graham that if the Bill to effect it came up to the Lords he would do his utmost to have it thrown out. To make matters worse the course which Peel seems to have adopted on the matter is incomprehensible and, as far as can be seen, indefensible also. His communication with the Duke beforehand had been probably insufficient. When the Duke's opinions transpired Arbuthnot could not get him to call on the Duke to talk matters over. Peel was cordial but adamant; perhaps he thought they were trying to undermine his determination to assent to the union of the Canadas. It may be that direct argument did not appeal to an old ally of the Duke's as a good method of convincing him, yet it is certain that above all things the Duke liked being called on and consulted. Perhaps Graham was able to bring Peel into communication with the Duke

in the second half of June.   There is no record of it.
The long memorandum which Peel prepared on his
views in July may have been intended for the Duke and
the Peers, and it is true that Peel told Graham that he
had never wavered in his belief that the Duke could not
reject the Canada Bill when he looked into the real state
of the case.   But to have relied solely on the real state
of the case seems to imply either too great a belief in
the power of the truth or too little knowledge of the
psychological effects of civility and consideration.   Unfortunately both defects can exist side by side in the
same man, and both might very likely be found in a
sensitive, self-centred, clear-minded statesman like Sir
Robert Peel.

On June 30th the poor shrunken Duke made a terrific
speech against the measure for the union of the Canadas.
He talked about a growing desire he had observed in the
country to get rid of those colonies and make them
republican.   He told the House that he neither thought
a fitting time had come for a final settlement, nor that
it was necessary to unite the Canadas in order to govern
them, and he begged them not to pass the measure under
the impression that there were no alternatives to it.   They
should pass the measure into committee and there give
it their fullest consideration.   They should look to other
opinions upon it and not to his only, but if the Government persevered theirs be the responsibility.   He himself
would have to say "not content" to this Bill.   And while
he spoke his spirit seems to have lighted up his face
with the fire of an angry patriotism.[1]

He was heard in breathless silence.   His speech
seemed to produce a great impression, "especially the
close, when with an energetic gesture he threw off all
responsibility of the measure from himself, and left it
'in the name of God' upon the ministers."   But glowing
face, breathless silence and patriotic indignation were to
have as much effect on the destinies of the nation as if
they had been the protestations of actors at Drury Lane.

[1] Hansard, LV, 239.   Stanhope, *Conversations with the D. of W.*, p. 249.

They were the luxury of a moment. The House of Lords could not take the settlement of such a problem out of the hands of the executive and the House of Commons, and the unity and discipline of the Conservative party prevented their attempting it. The details of the process are not clear, but on July 5th the leaders learnt that the Duke had yielded. There was a meeting at Apsley House at which apparently he advised the Lords to pass the Bill. In the House of Lords he still showed that he believed that these provinces would not be able to be governed according to the principle of the Bill. The amendments which the Lords were able to make in committee made no difference for him at all, but he now recommended their Lordships to pass it if the Government insisted on having it. He wrote a vigorous protest against the Bill in the Lords' Journal; but, while he could have thrown it out or postponed it, he had allowed it to pass into law.[1]

Peel seemed to suppose that looking into the real state of the case had caused the Duke's surrender. That was not the fact. Lord Ellenborough was nearer the mark when he spoke of the admirable way in which the Duke put aside all his own personal feelings for the good of his party. His personal feeling was undoubtedly that the Canada Bill which he was allowing to pass endangered the retention of the North American Colonies, and that the Irish Bill possibly endangered the connection between England and Ireland. These were severe sacrifices to ask an aged patriot to make for the good of his party, and yet matters would have become impossible if he had not made them. Strangely enough his complete surrender to party was the most patriotic course he could have taken, and a lesser man would probably have not had the self-restraint to take it. When he composed his protest Arbuthnot wrote: "There can be no harm in his recording his opinions, though he don't act upon them." It was a curious position for the victor of a thousand fights, but a man must be in a curious, and tragic, position when

[1] Hansard, LV, 490 and 457.

his influence ought to be more important than his opinions.

At any rate the party was afloat again, whatever it cost the Duke of Wellington.   There were, indeed, difficulties between Peel and the Lords over the amendments they inflicted on the Irish Municipal Bill, but the question was solved by the Government's yielding upon the points in question.   At last the Irish Municipal Bill was passed into law.   1840 had been no sterile year.   In it old complications and new difficulties had been suitably shelved or effectively settled.   They had closed the question of Stockdale and Hansard, they had passed the Canada Bill and the Irish Municipal Bill, and the education question had been adjusted by the concordat between the Government and the Bishops.   In 1840 the enactments which should complete the plan of the Ecclesiastical Commission were carried, and in 1840 the Regency was determined.   In fact the barriers were down, the road was open to the climax and crisis of Peel's career; much more open that it would have been if he had taken office in 1839.   Graham enumerated to Arbuthnot at the end of July how these and other difficulties had passed away, and came to the conclusion that there was no rallying-point left to the Government. The only resources open to them, said he, were either an agitation for a new Reform Bill, which was not desired by the community, or an agitation for the repeal of the Corn Laws, which would divide their party.   So the way was cleared for a Conservative Government or, so Graham said, for a permanent Conservative Government.

Graham seems to have feared that the estrangement between Peel and the Duke would prevent the Duke's forming part of Peel's Government, but that only showed his lack of experience of Conservative affairs.   This trouble was not new, and had never been fatal.   As Aberdeen told Graham, the characters and dispositions of Peel and the Duke were so different that there was little sympathy between them.   Even when they were working together in office this had been apparent.   It would not have the slightest effect on their conduct when they were summoned to act together for the public service. The Duke knew his duty and destiny, and Arbuthnot was soon able to report to Graham that the drift of the Duke's conversation showed that he would be ready to enter Peel's Cabinet. In November there were communications between Peel and the Duke through Arbuthnot. The Duke spoke of the difficulties which stood in the way of their constantly conferring with one another, and made use of his old doctrine to the effect that even when they had not much previous communication they usually found their opinions to agree almost precisely. Peel declared, as he had declared before, "that nothing in private life gives me half as much satisfaction as communicating freely and unreservedly with the Duke of Wellington." In general he did communicate freely, yet there had seemed to be moments when he had denied himself his crowning satisfaction. But perhaps it did not matter, for perhaps necessity and the Duke's view of his duty had combined to provide Peel with a splendid slave.[1]

§ 4

Parliament was prorogued on August 11th, and during the rest of the year the attention of the political world was claimed by a crisis in foreign politics. It was the crisis that was connected with the ambitions of Mehemet Ali, the ruler of Egypt, which seemed to bring the country within measurable distance of war with France. It was Palmerston's first truly typical adventure and at the height of the trouble there was sharp division in the Cabinet, and grave discontent among some of them against Palmerston's policy and high-handed methods. But the Cabinet managed to remain united, although the feebleness of Melbourne's control over his colleagues was amply demonstrated. War

---

[1] Parker's *Graham*, Vol. I, 298 ff. Parker's *Peel*, II, 433 ff. Add. MSS. 40,318; 196 ff.   40,312; 322.   40,416; 220.   40,310; 362.   40,616; 244.

was avoided, and all Palmerston's objects were gained. His success had been great, but it does not appear to have lent any strength to Whig Government in the country. He could humiliate France to his heart's content, but he could not as yet help his friends to win a single by-election in England; and by-elections, not glory, would determine the fate of the Ministry.

Another event in 1840 which was not directly Parliamentary was the beginning of the Repeal Agitation in Ireland. On April 15th, 1840, O'Connell had founded the Repeal Association. The step was logical and inevitable. Repeal had always remained in O'Connell's mind as an inspiring possibility and a probable necessity during all the years when he had determined to give trial to the good will of the Whigs and of England. Naturally, as his friends in England became feeble, his thoughts had turned more and more to agitation for the Repeal, and his Precursors' Society had been intended to prepare the way for it. But his lead was not likely to be followed immediately by all his associates. He had perpetually and angrily to complain of apathy in Ireland itself; the most important man in his following, Sheil, deplored the move, while it must make O'Connell part company with the Whigs. Graham watched eagerly to see whether in any election the Whig Government supported a Repealer, but for their principles' and reputation's sake the Whigs could not have any truck with Repeal; and their Lord-Lieutenant in Ireland definitely and clearly declared against it. Nevertheless this Repeal Movement would in time gather impetus. It would gain enough force to shake all Ireland with tumult, to land Peel in difficulties and O'Connell in prison. This was to be the last great movement of O'Connell's life and it pointed away from England.[1]

Parliament met again on January 21st, 1841. There was plenty of matter to attract attention. Besides

[1] *O'Connell Correspondence*, Vol. II, Chap. XVIII. *Memoirs of R. L. Sheil*, Vol. II, pp. 285 ff., and e.g. Add. MSS. 40,616; 260 (Graham to Bonham, Dec. 11, 1840).

O'Connell's Repeal Movement there was war in China and in Afghanistan, while there were matters outstanding between this country and the United States which might produce war at any time.   But all else was overshadowed by Lord Palmerston's exploits and our relations with France.   Whatever various Conservatives may have thought on the Mehemet Ali question, there was certainly among their leaders a genuine desire not to antagonize France.   Peel himself always showed in this period a deep-rooted antagonism to Palmerston and a genuine anxiety for the cause of peace.   Consequently Peel in the Commons and the Duke in the Lords made appeals for friendship with France, but they had concocted no amendment to the Address on the subject, and the Session began without any sign of intensified party warfare.   Little did men think that it was the lull before the final assault.

Before the battle began the Whigs had to attempt one very difficult piece of work.   The time was approaching when the powers of the Poor Law Commissioners would lapse, and on January 29th John Russell moved a Bill to continue them and to extend them in certain directions.   Naturally to introduce a Bill on such a subject was like turning on a tap, and the debates which followed had their fill of criticism, invective and pathetic instances.   It was all to little purpose, for the Bill eventually had to be dropped owing to the imminence of a General Election; but it is interesting to take note of Peel's attitude.   Of course he supported the continuance of the Commissioners' powers and the Poor Law experiment, but this time he showed that he was not uncritically committed to anything that the Government might propose.   He had been deluged with communications on the subject from various parts of the country, largely from clergymen, and he had endeavoured to find out the truth behind some of the complaints.[1]   In the House he protested against the Commissioners' powers being continued for ten years, and got their term reduced to

[1] Add. MSS. 40,429 (e.g. 231).

five.   He suggested other amendments and spoke with
feeling, quoting Scripture in contradiction to an announcement by the Commissioners that one of the principal
objects of compulsory provision for the poor was "the
prevention of almsgiving."[1]

Cold as Peel seemed, practical and cautious as he was,
he was not always in vote and thought a mere frigid
interpreter of Benthamite principles.   Indeed for that
matter he had certainly blood in his veins and bowels of
compassion in his body, whether this matter of the Poor
Law proves it or no.   But his personality, his passion
and his principles were soon to be tried out in circumstances more illuminating and more fateful than anything
his present position could provide.   For soon the drama
was to quicken its pace and Peel was to take the middle
of the stage with all the limelights turned full upon him.
This year he was at last to become Prime Minister with
an enduring administration.

§ 5

It was in February that the Government began to give
signs of collapse, like the first menacing cracks of a hewn
tree.   At the earliest possible moment in the Session
Stanley had revived the Bill about the registration of
voters in Ireland which he had run so successfully in
1840.[2]   The Government countered with a Bill of their
own which would probably extend rather than restrict
the constituency in Ireland.   After a certain amount of
preliminary fencing the first division on the question was
taken on the second reading of the Government's Bill
on February 23rd, which they carried, but only by a
majority of five.   The division was claimed by the
journalists on both sides as a victory, but it was not an
encouraging victory for the Government.   The real
danger to the Bill would come in Committee, and they
had not much margin to meet their difficulties there;
besides it was clear that in the near future there might

[1] Hansard, LVII, 442.   [2] Add. MSS. 40,467; 1.

well be no Government majority available for any division at all.

For the Conservatives were winning by-elections. Towards the end of 1840 they had even managed to win one in Ireland in the County of Carlow, and in the first nine days of February, 1841, they scored four new successes, at Walsall and Canterbury, in East Surrey and Monmouthshire, and in all but East Surrey a Conservative replaced a Whig. The Whigs won the seat at St. Albans, but the balance was in favour of the Conservatives, and it was obvious that the Government's minute and doubtful majority could not long stand such attrition. Conservatives began to wonder in what way they could extrude a Government discredited, defeated but persistent.

It was not for Conservatives to choose. The Whigs might not keep their majority, but they did keep the initiative. They could change a felon's death into a martyrdom and die for a cause for which they had not lived. It is the method by which other martyrs have falsified the sentence of their condemnation, and there was a cause available which might easily repay its martyrs with a joyful resurrection. The Whigs had done little for Free Trade during the last ten years. They had come into office to some extent under Free-trading auspices. Just before their régime opened the financial reformer Parnell had put forward theoretically and logically the Free-trading programme, and Parnell for a short time had been a member of their Government. Lord Althorp had tried to produce a Budget reforming and moderating protective duties, but he had been too weak to carry it, and after that things had very definitely taken the wrong turning. The Whigs had not preserved for themselves the resources of revenue necessary for any extensive reduction of the duties that were held to oppress trade, and Spring-Rice, as Chancellor of the Exchequer, had neither the strength, ability nor application to set about anything so important. Consequently the Whigs had done less than had been done, empirically and in a practical and piecemeal fashion, by their Tory predecessors under the guidance of Huskisson. And though Huskisson was dead there were still men on the Conservative side of the House who were proud to boast that they had supported him as colleagues. His policy still survived, and all through the period there had been intimations in Peel's speeches that he was anxious where possible to free trade from encumbrances. Whatever happened, when the Conservatives came in there would probably be a considerable simplification and reduction of protective duties.

But since Peel was last in office, Free Trade had become a great deal more dangerous. The cub with which a statesman might play had turned into a lion, self-willed and ferocious. While Peel had been in opposition there had sprung up the Anti-Corn Law agitation, and the Anti-Corn Law men had given Free Trade a new passion and strength and the natural concomitant of passion in England, a religious significance. Since their Parliamentary defeat of 1839 they had redoubled their activities and achieved their successes. The art of organized public agitation was already well developed in England. The Methodist revival had given the type of agitation by public meeting, and the methods of the Anti-Slavery Societies and of O'Connell's various associations in Ireland were useful examples. All these resources the Anti-Corn Law League used to the full. Their organization was extraordinarily good, their meetings were numerous, well managed and well attended, their orators were able and emotional, their lecturers scoured the country. Their seed took root and flourished. Part of the working-class discontent in the country was attracted into the movement, and the Liberalism of Nonconformity and of the manufacturing interests, unsatisfied by the work of the Reformed Parliaments and discontented with the leadership of the Whigs, found in the Anti-Corn Law League its natural focus and its most congenial line of advance. Consequently there was by now in England and Scotland a very large body of important opinion, interested, enthusiastic and angry, ready to put forward Free Trade as a religious dogma.   Its sanctions were divine, its demands could not be questioned and must not be evaded.   Peel with his political and practical mind, with his partial use of a Free-trading policy, and especially with his defence of the Corn Laws, was in the face of these people rather like a partially moral agnostic confronting an organized Church.   His virtues must be obliterated by his damnation.

In 1840 the annual motion in the House of Commons against the Corn Laws was again unsuccessful; but even in the Commons one good piece of work was done.   Peel had pleaded in favour of protection for Agriculture the amount of protection enjoyed by other interests in the country.   The force of this argument was noticed by the Radical Hume, and he determined to do what he could to abolish it.   So he obtained in 1840 the appointment of a Committee on Import Duties, and its report when it was published did all that he could have desired in furthering reform.   It exposed with great power the absurdities and ill-effects of the existing system.   The facts were probably known to the statesmen, on both sides, who had had to consider them when in office, but this report put them clearly and authoritatively before the public.   Incidentally the evidence of the permanent officials showed that on the whole they too held Free-trading convictions.   Altogether the committee produced so effective a document that the Anti-Corn Law League spread it abroad as a manifesto among the people.

However, it could not be long before so important a body as the League had a more direct influence on politics.   If the House of Commons stopped its ears the League might speak to the constituencies.   In 1841 it gave an omen to the Whigs.   The League had determined to support no candidate who would not pledge himself to a total repeal of the Corn Law.   In 1841 came the election for Walsall, and the Whigs sent down as their candidate a young and well-connected guardsman named Lyttelton. Either he would not or could not pledge himself specifically and intelligibly to a total repeal of the Corn Laws, so the League drove him out of the field and put in a candidate of their own, who though too late to win the election, yet ran the Tory candidate very closely indeed.[1] It was an incident that deserved deep consideration in the councils of the Whig party.

But there is every reason to believe that the problems of Free Trade were already receiving attention from the Whigs. Liberal Whigs all naturally now sympathized with the cry for Free Trade, and the most liberal portion of the Government had long chafed at its inactivity on the matter. In 1841 the *Edinburgh Review* echoed the conclusions of the Committee on Import Duties, and the Whig Journal, the *Morning Chronicle*, pressed forward the agitation. Moreover, Free Trade was to be related to another problem to which in 1841 the Whig Government could by no means avoid giving their attention. Since 1837 their financial arrangements had produced deficits on each year. This was probably not due to a falling off of receipts, but to an inevitable increase of expenditure, springing from causes over which the Whigs had no control. Such troubles as those in Canada and China, which were to a large extent the natural growing pains of Empire or of Trade, had helped to use up the money, while it had been necessary to make up some of the arrears in the equipment of the fighting Services. But the Whigs had not had the courage to make proper provision for National Expenditure in their Budgets. The Exchequer was set on decreasing taxation, and Spring-Rice as Chancellor had slurred and fumbled over the matter, and in the end made the situation much worse by his expensive experiment of penny postage. However, the problem was by now in abler hands. In 1839 Spring-Rice, cheerful, talkative and incompetent, had been succeeded as Chancellor of the Exchequer by a much stronger man in Francis Baring.

[1] Prentice, *History of the Anti-Corn Law League*, Vol. I, Chap. XII.

The change was bound to make some difference.
Baring was not likely to be content with a state of affairs
in which deficit succeeded deficit with no other provision for them than a special explanation to prove that
each year's expenditure was exceptional. Consequently
in his Budget of 1840 Baring had asked for additional
taxation. He had added 10 per cent. to the assessed
taxes, 5 per cent. to the Customs and Excise, and had
laid a new duty of 4d. per gallon on spirits. His increased
taxation did not cure his trouble. Owing to the fact
that he would not immediately enjoy its results, he had
foreseen a deficit of £858,000 for the year 1840–1,
but the year did not bear out his calculations and in the
end he found himself actually faced with a deficit of
£1,840,000. For 1841–2 the estimated expenditure
was increased, and even when he had put out of his
calculation all demands which he might consider to
be extraordinary, it seemed that there would still be an
estimated deficit of £1,700,000. How could he meet
such a situation? [1]

The problem was apparently before the Cabinet in
February, 1841,[2] and Baring was able to suggest a
solution. It was of course the thesis of Free Traders
that the yield of a duty could be increased if its rate was
lowered and consumption stimulated. Such possibilities
had been emphasized in the Report of the Committee on
Import Duties. Statesmen could remit taxes and yet
increase receipts, and what more attractive policy could
there be for a Whig Chancellor of the Exchequer desirous
to be Liberal and determined to be solvent? It is not
surprising that Baring laid before the Cabinet, as, some
time before February 9th, he apparently did, a scheme
embodying this principle. The duty on foreign sugar
was to be reduced to 36s. a hundredweight, that on
foreign timber from 55s. to 50s. a load, while that on
Colonial timber was to be raised from 10s. to 20s. He

[1] Buxton, *Finance and Politics*, Vol.I, Chap. II.   Halévy, Clapham,
op. cit.
[2] *Later Correspondence of Lord John Russell*, Vol. I, p. 34.

anticipated from these changes an additional revenue of £1,300,000.[1]

The scheme was attractive, but it presented one obvious objection and one obvious omission. Foreign sugar was slave-grown and under the proposed duty would compete upon more equal terms with the sugar of the British West Indies which was the product of the recently liberated free labour. On the other hand, there was one heavily taxed article of common consumption omitted from Baring's proposals, and that was corn. The Corn Laws were the most obviously unpopular duty of them all, and therefore the most obviously unjust; it was not likely that all would be content at their being passed over when the Government was reducing protection. In 1839 John Russell had been ready to take the risk of meddling with corn, and he was equally brave in 1841. On February 9th he circulated a memorandum declaring that when it was proposed to favour the produce of foreign slavery in order to increase the revenue and obtain cheap sugar, it seemed to him that they could not shut their eyes to the grievous privation attendant on the present monopoly of corn;[2] so he suggested a modified sliding scale. Presumably John Russell realized that as soon as the Ministry touched corn the fat must be in the fire; but of course it has often been realized that the fire may be a more honourable and hopeful position than the frying-pan.

Lord John had suggested, it was for the Cabinet to decide, and how they hammered out their decision is as yet unknown. Indeed it is not quite clear what was before them, for the evidence of what was Baring's first proposal does not seem quite irreproachable. Presumably Melbourne objected; echoes of his opposition seem to penetrate to us; but the history of the Cabinet crisis over Palmerston, in 1840, shows how much enfeebled was Melbourne's control over his colleagues. No doubt the dangerous state of the revenue, perhaps the dangerous

---

[1] Spencer Walpole, *Life of Lord John Russell*, Vol. I, p. 368.
[2] *Ibid.*

state of the Ministry were used as arguments. Probably, as it is reported, Melbourne shouted down the stairs after a Cabinet meeting that he didn't know and didn't care what they were to say about the price of corn but they had better all be in the same story.[1] Certainly they were all in the same story at the end, for the Cabinet at last determined to adopt Baring's proposals —as given—on Timber and Sugar, and on Corn to supersede the sliding scale altogether by a small fixed duty.

It was a dangerous and an important decision and it would be hard to say at what precise moment the Cabinet settled upon it. It seems to have been after the Session opened, for not till then did Baring bring forward as his Budget the proposals from which the scheme had developed. Probably this seemed a suitable time for considering a Budget, especially since men's minds had previously been occupied with foreign affairs. It must be supposed that the Cabinet took some time, after John Russell's memorandum had gone round, to take the important decision of extending their operations to corn, and certainly various enquiries had to be made and information received and discussed. Consequently, it would not be surprising if the Cabinet's deliberations were not completed till a good deal of the Session had passed.

Certainly there had been no chance for their proposal to have been foreshadowed in the speech from the Throne. But such an important decision, so unheralded, aroused the deepest suspicions. It was said that only after the course of the Session had showed the full danger of their position had the Ministry adopted their Budget, and then not as a normal financial proposition but as a foul-weather Budget, a basis on which they could appeal to the people and escape from their difficulties. The charge would be hard to prove. Whatever the Ministry's strength, both Baring and Lord John were intrinsically likely to have proposed what they did when they did. It was likely that the Cabinet would ultimately accede,

[1] Spencer Walpole, *Life of Lord John Russell*, Vol. I, p. 369.

as on other matters, to the desires of its more Liberal section, and especially likely that they would yield at a time when that section could urge the absolute necessity of finding some way out of the financial position; and there was perhaps a general movement of men's minds towards Free Trade. There really seems not to be adequate evidence to prove that this convenient wave of Free Trade was stimulated by members of the Cabinet for their own desperate purposes. Certainly they had had nothing to do with the appointment of the Committee on Import Duties. There is enough to account for every part of this episode without attributing it to the sudden reckless action of Ministerial despair.[1]

Ultimately the question is one of motive, and therefore insoluble. Certainly no motive can be excluded. At whatever point in 1841 the Cabinet made their decision, they could not have put away from their minds the reflection that they were in sore need of a popular movement in their favour. Probably, as is usual in politics, the motives of several of them were mixed and their intentions misty. Men followed their honest convictions and also the promptings of public opinion. They wanted to do the best for the country, and no doubt some of them had a natural desire to strengthen the Government and party whose members they were. Probably some at least of them had at various levels of their consciousness a vision of repairing their damaged popularity, perhaps after an appeal to the people. Yet the Budget was certainly not put forward merely as an election address, without any hope of its being successful in the present Parliament. As late as May 7th, and in the privacy of the Cabinet, neither Baring nor Russell would admit that their proposals had been certain not to pass the Commons.[2] And even after the first defeat of their Budget the Cabinet was undecided whether to resign or dissolve. Lord John Russell was doubtful.

[1] But see Halévy, *Histoire du Peuple Anglais,* Vol. III, p. 325 (Le Budget de 1841 et son histoire).

[2] Broughton, Vol. VI, p. 91 (from *Recollections*).

Yet a dissolution should have formed rather an elementary part of their plan of campaign if it is to be supposed they had ever had a plan of campaign at all.

Whatever Ministers intended, the game went through from the events at the Session's beginning to its climax. On February 23rd there had been the very small majority for the second reading of the Government's Bill for the registration of Irish Voters. On March 1st Lord John got up and proposed that the Bill should be postponed till April 23rd, to give time for the estimates and for the Easter holidays, and also for the Government to gain additional information from Ireland. He gained his point; Stanley had to submit to the postponement, and the Government secured a temporary and insufficient respite. In March they dealt with the Estimates and the Poor Law and with a proposal for the equalization of the various duties imposed in the Colonies themselves, the debates on which showed the interest men took in the Report of the Committee on Import Duties. On April 6th Parliament broke up for the Easter holidays, to reassemble again on April 20th.

The time for the last struggle was at hand, and the skies still frowned on the Government. In the middle of April they lost another by-election. John Walter of *The Times* went down as Conservative candidate and carried Nottingham, which had been hitherto the seat of unsoiled Liberalism. He was a fanatic opponent of the new Poor Law, and his success was due to a violent use of the Anti-Poor Law cry. Stanley, for one, did not approve of a victory which was the "result of a combination with the Chartist faction on the single ground of the Poor Law." [1] It is significant to see Stanley, for a large part of Disraeli's life his colleague and ally, repelled by an alliance which was one of the first foundations of Tory Democracy. Other Conservatives were not so squeamish. Walter was said to be a good candidate if a bad member, which might well mean that

[1] Add. MSS. 40,467; 25 (Stanley to Peel, April 18, 1841).

they disapproved of what he said in the House, but it seemed to go down very well in the constituencies. Certainly it would be a policy of nihilism to refuse any victory that had been won by unreal combinations and distrusted friends, and at that moment victory in general was very near. Indeed so near had it seemed to Peel at the beginning of April that he made Bonham prepare his suggestions for the appointments to office.[1]

At that moment the decisive question was still the Irish Registration Bill. The crucial point in the debates on the subject had been the defection of the ex-Minister Lord Howick, who had voted against the Government upon it. This year he had taken a line of his own, and it was essential for the Government to approximate their proposals to his, but the Conservatives began to realize that the Government's negotiations with him had failed.[2] As soon as Parliament met again, Peel began questioning the Government as to when they could bring on their Bill. Stanley believed that they would still manœuvre for delay, but their answers seemed so positive that Peel brought Stanley back to town, and assembled his friends for the last fight.

The Committee on the Irish Bill was started on April 26th. The Ministry increased the value of what they proposed as a qualification for a vote, presumably in order to placate opposition. Lord Howick tried an amendment, but failed to carry it, and consequently he and his friends had to vote against the main clause of the Bill when the division was taken upon it on April 29th. So the Government was beaten in a full House on a Government measure by 10 votes. But the end was not yet. The Government was determined to develop its financial measures. On April 30th John Russell announced that on May 31st or soon afterwards he would move the House into a Committee on the Corn Laws; when he had finished Baring got up and laid his proposals before the House.

[1] Add. MSS. 40,429; 186, 189 (Bonham to Peel, April 7 and 15, respecting new Ministry and Walter).   [2] Add. MSS. 40,429; 199.

§ 6

The Government's move had not been entirely unexpected. There had been rumours of what was coming, and an uneasiness, like the whisper and flutter of birds in the bushes before a thunder-shower, had preceded the Whigs' declaration. Leading Conservatives had from the beginning viewed the Committee on Import Duties with fear and a strong desire to move cautiously. Before the Session started Goulburn was warned that the Commissioners' report might be the forerunner of a Government attack on the duties on corn, coffee, sugar, etc., and he passed the warning on to Peel. As the Session developed, Goulburn's own suspicion deepened. On April 6th he told Peel that he had noticed in John Russell's speech on the equalization of Colonial duties a premonition of something not yet announced, and said that when he had hinted as much Labouchere, the Whig President of the Board of Trade, had become most menacingly self-conscious.[1] During April Bonham became exceedingly anxious that a mortal blow should be given to the Government before their Budget, "which will, I fear, be attractive but revolutionary in proportion to the desperate position in which they are now placed." [2] The Whig move had been obvious enough for the Conservatives to foresee it, and it seemed to them profligate and menacing as well. When judgment had been passed and sentence nearly executed on these dangerous and despicable Ministers, they might manage to make it all obsolete and to switch matters on to completely new ground. It was as if the prisoner had managed to change the topic while the Judge was putting on the black cap. But worst of all was the chance that it might afford the Whigs, and to more violent than Whigs, to agitate the country.

Free Trade promised men light taxes, better trade and cheap food; such promises are not even argued against

---

[1] Add. MSS. 40,333; 425, 428.   [2] Add. MSS. 40,429; 199.

with impunity.   Moreover, conditions were not going
to be favourable to dispassionate argument.   Not only
were Free Traders using the dialect of religion, not only
had the matter been made a question of human morals,
but it would also be put forward most poignantly as a
question of human suffering.   Bad trade in the past
two years had given a large part of its impetus to the
Free-trading movement.   The Anti-Corn Law men
constantly claimed, and in a great many districts and
occupations it was certainly true, that trade was failing,
that distress had increased and was increasing.   This
meant that the battle would not only be one of economic
argument.   There would also be the inevitable accom-
paniments of a question of distress, the harassing description of individual cases of hardship, the blistering
accusations of callousness and personal responsibility,
the difficulty and pain of trying to fight back to the world
of statistics.   Peel and his friends probably did not
realize to the full the strength of what was stirred up
against them, but they knew enough to be apprehensive
of the easy promises of a desperate Ministry, they knew
enough to imagine how wild might be an election fought
on the basis of bread or starvation, now that the hungry
forties had begun.

And against all this the Conservative leaders could
only have recourse to the austere and unintelligible
virtues of caution and reticence.   For them the matter
could never even have the refreshing and blind simplicity
of a war of principle.   Peel and the other Conservative
leaders were not Protectionists in principle or theory.
Nor was Peel in full theory a Free Trader, he often
spoke strongly against applying a principle without
consideration for the special social and political complications involved.   Nevertheless, his instincts, his boasted
and respectable past as a colleague of Huskisson's, all
taught him to desire the diminution of duties where
possible, and to free trade from encumbrances.   He
could not declare simple war on Free Trade; nor could
he enthusiastically adopt it as it was now presented to

him.   Conservatives must fight this Budget, the child of imprudence and of their enemies.   They must repudiate radically complete Free Trade, they must pay their tribute to their special social and political considerations—which meant that they must maintain adequate protection for agriculture.   Peel's position, therefore, was not simple.   Neither a Free Trader nor a Protectionist, when men attacked him with principles he must answer with particulars.   But, after all, it suited his genius so to do.

If Peel could not produce a principle intact, he felt he must not produce a programme at all.   His instinct was to get into office, to gain the advantage of official information before he even put his thoughts into form. He felt, too, a difficulty in promising a revision of duties the expectation of which must hamper trade, while a very long interval must elapse before he could complete anything at all.   Peel must keep silence even from good words, because good words ought to be weighed carefully and announced cautiously.   Besides, the words of his message might not all be good.

The most serious feature in the problem was the succession of deficits to which the Whigs had submitted. This had long been the nightmare of the Conservative leaders, frequenting Goulburn's bedside in particular. These deficits must cease, yet Peel and his colleagues could not believe in trusting, for the increased revenue, entirely to the speculative produce of a reduction of duties. There must be something more certain to rely upon, and that seemed to mean increased taxation.   The Conservatives seem to have been fully conscious how that suggestion would look when contrasted with the Whigs' pleasant scheme for restoring the national finances. With their pledge to protect agriculture adequately, the vagueness of their hopes to reduce duties and their inward wish to increase the burdens of the people, none of the Conservative promises would seem attractive as alternatives.   Perhaps it would prove the best tactics to say as little about them as possible.   They were tactics particularly suited to Peel's style of speech and skill in manœuvre, and also congenial to Peel's cast of mind.

When the Conservatives heard, on April 30th, of the Government's intentions they were filled both with indignation and with doubt.   They were angry because they felt that the Whigs had shown that they would obstruct any honest attempt that Peel might make to set straight the national finances [1]; but the question was what to do?   They ought to attack immediately, to prevent the Government developing their Budget; but how should they attack without exposing their own intentions?   The matter was under debate among the Conservatives in the early days of May, and Peel wrote a long memorandum giving his views on the subject.[2] He considered in turn the various modes of attack available in the House of Commons.   They might move for a committee on the state of the nation, or put forward a general declaration of want of confidence in the Government, or one with special reference to their financial position.   But to each course objections could be raised, objections which ranged round the great tactical difficulty of the Conservative position.   Each motion in some way involved "the inconvenience of a declaration of your own policy."   Each motion would launch the Conservatives into a direct discussion either on their intentions on what Peel called the two great pending and unsettled questions, the Poor Laws and the Corn Laws, or on their financial policy.   The Poor Laws and the Corn Laws both were exciting and compromising subjects, and as to finance, Peel explained in his memorandum the difficulties inherent in a prospective revision of duties and a prospective menace of increased taxation.   All that he could say was that when in office he would take a loan and consider matters maturely.   Peel had good reasons for wishing to avoid direct question as to his own

[1] Add. MSS. 40,429; 212 (Herries to Peel, May 2, 1841, on Budget).
[2] *Ibid.* 40,425; 425 (Memo. by Peel, undated, and included in Add. MSS. among documents of 1838).

policy; yet was it an entirely unreasonable question to put to an incoming Prime Minister?

Fortunately one possibility had been suggested that was not open to these objections. Lord Sandon had written to Peel pointing out the tactical advantages of an attack on the Government's proposed changes in the sugar duties.[1] Sugar would enable them to avoid a discussion on corn just before the elections, while the case against the Government's new duties would rest on the special ground of the diminution of the protection given to free-grown sugar against that produced by slaves. It would not involve the discussion of any ordinary economic considerations. Such reasoning seems to have attracted Peel, and his memorandum concludes with an apparent approval of Sandon's suggestion. So sugar was chosen and announced as the point at which the Conservatives would attack the Government's proposals.

It was on May 7th, when the House was moved into a Committee on Ways and Means, that Sandon moved an amendment raising the question of slavery against the Government's sugar proposals. The debate went on for eight nights, full of repetitions. The case for the special protection of the West Indies, where the slaves had been so recently enfranchised, was argued to the full and supported by some of the usual opponents of slavery. But of course other questions could not be wholly excluded, and when Peel spoke on the last night of the debate he did not confine himself to sugar and slavery. He diagnosed and minimized the commercial distress in the country, spoke of the support he had given to Huskisson and of his preference for a sliding duty on corn. He rubbed in the failure of the Whigs' finance in the past, and harped on the fact that he would not and ought not to be expected to declare his views on financial measures and customs duties before he had maturely considered matters with the assistance of official information. Indeed he seems to have regarded the Government's proposals as a mere attempt to extract his opinion. It moved him to

[1] 40,429; 214 (Sandon to Peel, May 2, 1841).

humour. "Can there be a more lamentable picture"—
he asked—"than that of a Chancellor of the Exchequer
seated on an empty chest—by the pool of bottomless deficiency—fishing for a Budget?—— I won't bite," said he.
"Then he giggled," said Hobhouse the Whig Minister,
"as if he had said something exceedingly funny."[1]   But
Hobhouse had good reason to be annoyed and the laugh
or giggle was certainly with Peel, for Sandon's amendment was carried in a full House by a majority of 36.

The victory was startling; it was not decisive.   The
Conservatives had avoided fighting their battle on the
most important question raised, the question of corn
It was not likely that all would be content with such
evasion.   Indeed the more foolish agricultural Conservatives had been lashing their sides with rage because
the sugar duties had been selected as the point of attack.
They wanted to fight the battle on corn, and they dreamed
of wonderful schemes for the popularization of the Corn
Laws such as an assemblage of Irish labourers in the
Spa Fields to be addressed then and there by Lord
Stanhope.[2]   Much more important than these excita-
tions was the fact that the Whigs were naturally extremely
unwilling to die feebly on a side issue, and the Whig
Ministry still retained the initiative.   They could decide
whether to resign immediately or to fight on and perhaps
dissolve in the end.   There were technical difficulties
in dissolution, and Melbourne held that there were strong
constitutional objections to it.   Others of the Cabinet
also seemed to have disapproved or been doubtful, but
favourable reports had come in as to the effect in the country of the Ministry's proposals.   Most of Melbourne's
colleagues began to turn against him, and when, on
May 19th, the day after their defeat, he took his Cabinet's
decision on the subject they voted nearly unanimously
in favour of dissolution.[3]   It was to be a fight to a finish.

[1] Hansard, LVIII, 639.   Broughton, Vol. VI, 25.
[2] Add. MSS. 40,429; 302.
[3] Broughton, VI, 26.   *Letters of Queen Vict.*, I, 281 (Melb. to Queen,
May 19, 1841).

It was not, however, intended to dissolve immediately; they meant to bring forward the Corn Laws and make the Tories show their colours. On May 20th members crowded into the House to hear Ministers announce their resignation or at least explain their intentions, and they were dumbfounded to hear the Chancellor of the Exchequer quietly announce that he would move the House into committee on the usual annual sugar duties, which would have lapsed unless renewed. Peel turned as pale as ashes, said the malevolent Hobhouse. If so he must have turned as white as milk in a moment, for, on being questioned, Lord John Russell announced that he intended to bring forward the question of the Corn Laws on Friday, the 4th of June.

The Conservatives had probably expected the manœuvre, they must certainly prevent it, so they countered by a direct vote of want of confidence, which Peel moved on May 27th, before John Russell's date for the Corn Laws. Another interminable debate followed, this time lasting five nights. Peel made full use of an advantage which he had foreseen, in his memorandum, would come from his having already defeated the Government on sugar. He based his case not so much on questions of policy, as on the fact that it had been already amply demonstrated that the Government had lost the confidence of Parliament. Once more he refused, against protest, to describe what his policy would be in office. They knew, he said, his principles; he had declared them on the great constitutional questions that had been raised, on the ballot, the extension of the suffrage and the rest; they knew them on Church matters. It was only on financial questions that he ought to be silent. Unfortunately it was only financial questions that interested Parliament at that moment. Even about finance Peel had said something. He had practically told Parliament that when he had got into power he would take a loan and then think, maturely. With regard to the Corn Laws he said often enough that he desired adequate protection for agriculture, and that he preferred a sliding scale.

It was preposterous that he should be asked for details and figures.[1] No doubt he was right, but the figures which he refused were without question the essentials of the situation.

But Peel's intentions referred to the future. The only question for the moment with Conservatives was whether they would gain enough votes to carry their motion. It seemed doubtful enough. Probably on the former vote some of the Whigs interested in slavery and sugar, or antagonized by their friends' Corn Law proposals, had voted with the Conservatives or abstained; on the question of confidence they would rally to the Ministry. At three o'clock on the morning of Saturday, June 5th, the division was taken amid very great excitement. The Whips had made every effort conceivable, the House was packed and no one knew which way the vote would go. The Conservatives were told first, and then the Whigs came in from their lobby. They had a lord in a wheeled chair, who was in a state of drivelling idiocy, and men jumped up on their benches with cries of shame as this figure, inhuman and completely unconcious, was counted for the Government. A moment later the tellers managed to struggle through the crowd and come up to the table; and Fremantle, the Conservative Whip, was on their right hand. It was the symbol of victory. The Conservatives went mad with delight, they roared, they stamped, they threw their hats in the air, they clapped their hands and they shouted again when Fremantle read out the numbers, 312 Conservative votes had been cast to 311 Whig, Government had been defeated by one vote.[2]

It had been very close. It might well have been a momentary Whig success, for it was said that while the Tories had voted or paired every man, five or six Whigs were absent without an excuse. But it was enough.

---

[1] Hansard, 3rd Series, Vol. LVIII, 803, 1231.
[2] Grev., *Vict.*, Vol. II, p. 11. Broughton, Vol. VI, p. 33. Morley's *Gladstone*, Book II, Chap. VII, Section IV.

The Government had been beaten, and the country would probably soon be entrusted to the mystery of Peel's mature considerations. Of course there was still the election to come; the Whigs intended to appeal from the Commons to the people, and the rest of the Session was mainly occupied in clearing up, except perhaps for a little sparring about the motives with which the Government had produced their Budget. John Russell, it is true, managed to use the opportunities of debate to hammer out a little of what he had meant to say on the Corn Laws, but Peel made no comment beyond saying that since those were the arguments he had selected they were probably his best. John Russell, gallant and able as he had shown himself to be, could do no more. The Ministry could produce no more of their programme. Parliament was dissolved by Proclamation on June 22nd, and the tumult began.

It was not this time a very angry tumult. There does not seem to have been any worse disorder than usual, even though the people were judging between starvation and cheap bread. Men bribed, and accused each other of bribery, they intimidated, and accused each other of intimidation, much as they had ever done before. There is little to show that there was anything to choose between the two parties in the guilt of corruption, or that elections had changed their character much since before the Reform Bill. There were riots, bands, and high-sounding and rather vague speeches from the hustings. Electors were as usual abducted and disguised, or kept drunk and under lock and key till polling day, and as was fit, considering the cause of the election, the big and little loaf were carried about on poles above the crowds. As at other elections, the voice of the people seemed to alternate in many cases between a howl and a hiccup.

The Whigs spoke much of the promises of their new Budget, and were many of them inclined to abuse monopolists. The Tories talked a very great deal of the inefficiency of the Whig Government and many of them

defended the Corn Laws.   A French observer noticed
signs of doubt and hesitation in all the proceedings, caused
by the abrupt change of emphasis which had taken place
in politics.[1]   The parties had been organized to fight
over Constitutional matters and the problems of Ireland,
and now the centre of importance was Free Trade and
corn.   Men's speeches, he held, showed that they were
cautious and mystified.   He probably does not take
sufficient account of the tradition of circumlocution in
British politics.   Yet it seems clear that the suddenness
of the Government's change did in some way confuse the
election.   There is evidence that a few Conservative
supporters in the towns were attracted by the proposal
of a small fixed duty on corn,[2] and there were probably
Whigs whom it alienated.   There were strong doubts
abroad of the Whigs' sincerity and of their ability to
implement their promises.   It was felt that were Peel
to take office he would propose and carry many schemes
of importance to the commercial interest, which the
present Ministers dared not broach or could not carry.[3]
After all, the Government's record was bad and their
conversion both precipitate and convenient, while Peel's
reputation for ability, if not for sincerity, was very good
indeed.   It is always hard to speak with veracity about
movements of opinion, but there was in 1841 quite
probably a movement in the country towards strong
government and Sir Robert Peel.

Peel would always be strong; the question was what
he would do.   Consequently it is important to see what
account he gave of himself on the hustings, even if there
was little in his speech that it would have been difficult
to expect.   Fairly early in his speech he launched into
a careful discussion of the questions raised by the Government's Budget.   He perfectly admitted that restrictions

---

[1] Duvergier de Hauranne, *Revue des Deux Mondes*, Aug. 1, 1841, Vol.
XLIX. "De la dernière session du Parlement anglais et du prochain ministre."
(An admirable account of the whole crisis.)

[2] Add. MSS. 40,429; 275, 293 and 295.

[3] E.g. Add. MSS. 40,429; 245.

on trade were objectionable, unless clearly justified by
the necessity of protecting great existing interests; and
he then went on to give the special reasons in favour of
the protection of corn and sugar. With regard to corn
he was peculiarly elaborate and able, showing knowledge
and judgment, and continually through that part of his
speech he referred to the question of manufacturing
distress, and of the privations and miseries it involved.
He said he knew distress to exist at Nuneaton. He
expressed his desire to alleviate it. He diagnosed it, and
ascribed it to temporary causes. He denied its attribu-
tion to the Corn Laws, and he limited its extent by
statistics of shipping and exports. Yet when all was
done, neither interest, sympathy, analysis nor explanation
would abolish it altogether. It would remain, gaunt and
eloquent of suffering and of menace, to haunt Downing
Street and to disturb the long working hours of a newly-
appointed Prime Minister.

Corn and sugar occupied much of his speech; they
did not occupy it all. He had time in which to attack
the Government and to refer to his own party. He
talked of his party's unity and yet had to complain, a
short time afterwards, that the Government would
attribute to him the opinions in the addresses of other
Conservatives. He talked of the objects with which he
had founded his party, how he had seen the needs of
a party not disposed to resist necessary changes, but
determined to maintain the institutions of the country
on their ancient foundations—a statement which was
greeted apparently by tremendous cheering. But any
statement that Peel had chosen to make at Tamworth
would have been cheered to the echo. It was not an
audience ever likely to criticize the sufficiency of Peel's
party ideals.[1]

Nor was it ever in the least likely to refuse him his
seat in Parliament, and he was left at liberty to devote
himself to assisting other elections. It was indeed a
heartening sight to which he could turn his eyes. Every-

[1] *The Times*, June 29.

where the Conservative cause was prospering. Everywhere it was plain that the Government had not raised the country by their proposals. It is true that the Anti-Corn Law League had determined to support the Whigs when they had no candidate of their own. Probably they did not believe in them very heartily; certainly their help was not enough to prevent Conservative success in many manufacturing and commercial constituencies.[1] For instance, notable Conservative gains were reported in the West Riding, in Westminster and in the city of London, where John Russell came in with difficulty as the last of the four candidates elected. In other large places the Conservatives held their ground. No doubt each case was very largely affected by local conditions.[2] But perhaps more general factors were also at work. Perhaps the Conservatives were still helped by the feeling against the new Poor Laws, and perhaps to a small extent by the distrust, among Chartists and operatives, of the motives and intentions of those who demanded the repeal of the Corn Laws.[3] As the *Annual Register* said, the cry for "cheap corn" could be met by the cry of "low wages."[4] Unfortunately that answer was not going to weather well, at least in the immediate future.

But it is often dangerous to adduce general causes for the results of elections. Parties seem often to advance and retreat like the irrational and irresistible tides. Certainly there had been no violent Tory reaction; there was nothing which could form the focus for Tory enthusiasm. All that there had been was a gradual revival of Conservative influence and a continual decrease of confidence in the Government. The result of the election was due not to any single cause but to the history, both local and imperial, of the last ten years. But it was enough. At all points the Conservatives scored a gain

---

[1] Morley, *Life of Richard Cobden*, Vol. I, Chap. VIII, p. 172.
[2] See Prentice, *History of the Corn Law League*, Vol. I, Chap. XV, p. 224.
[3] E.g. Add. MSS. 40,485; 75 (Peter Power, Secretary of Handloom Weavers in Manchester, to Peel, July 6, 1841).
[4] *Ann. Reg.*, 1841 ("History of Europe," p. 146).

KK

on their figures in the previous Parliament. The smaller boroughs seem to havè disappointed Graham, and of course in them the issues were most personal and confused. Nevertheless, the Conservatives reported a distinct gain on their previous figures for the cities and boroughs of England. In Scotland they were probably hampered by the Scottish Church question, and perhaps by mismanagement, and their gain on the balance was infinitesimal. In Ireland their gain was greater, but it was in the counties of England that their most striking successes occurred. The farmers were frightened by the Anti-Corn Law cry, and there still continued unchecked that spreading of Conservative influence in the counties to which every election since 1832 had borne ample testimony. Consequently, taking the lowest calculation, the Conservatives gained 22 seats on what they had previously held in the English counties.

It was indeed enough. There were some unforeseen losses, some unfortunate complications, but altogether the Conservatives had utterly routed their adversaries, and at the end of it all the Whips could calculate with pride, and with but slight exaggeration, that there would be a majority of eighty for the Conservative Government of Sir Robert Peel.[1]

Parliament was not to meet till August 16th, and the interval was partly occupied by Peel in discussing the financial problem with Goulburn, Graham and Stanley, for he was now near enough to office for the mature considerations to begin. There was also, before Parliament met, some disagreement on the part of a small group in the party about reappointing the Whig Speaker. Peel got round it by consulting the leading Conservative members, who almost universally agreed with him. However, the affair had repercussions. There was violent

---

[1] Add. MSS. 40,617; 23–40 (Graham and Bonham). 40,476; 18 (Report from Fremantle). 40,485; 1–106 (General), etc., etc. *Ann. Reg.*, "Hist. of Europe," Chap. VII. *The Times,* June and July.

talk in the Carlton and an angry anonymous letter in *The Times* which Bonham, Arbuthnot and Granville Somerset unjustly but significantly put down to Disraeli.[1]   It was only a passing cloud, and a very small one at that, at the most not bigger than a man's hand.   When the time came, the party attended joyfully and confidently to pass an amendment to the Address and dispatch the Whigs to the Hell prepared for Governments defeated and driven back into futility.   Naturally, on such an occasion, the most important speech was to be made by the man who was going to be Prime Minister, but before that another and perhaps a more significant speech had been delivered by a new member.   Richard Cobden, who had been returned for Stockport, made his maiden speech in this debate.   He spoke ably and impressively and with concentrated force against the Corn Laws, dwelling much on the sufferings of the people, and attacking the doctrine that wages followed the price of corn.   He caught his opponents' attention.   "Stanley scowls and Peel smiles at me," so wrote Cobden to his brother, "both meaning mischief."   But the mischief was not all to come from the side of Stanley and Peel.[2]

When Peel spoke it was the fourth and last day of the debate, and he followed not his new enemy Cobden, but his old scourge, Daniel O'Connell.   He spoke as one girded and braced for great office.   He touched on foreign politics and dealt with Free Trade, Timber, Sugar and Corn, naturally saying nothing intrinsically different to what he had said many times before.   He still refused to give the details of his measures, and among his other arguments the question of the people's suffering again crept in.   He commented on the accounts of suffering given by members on the other side of the House.   If such distress could be cured by the abolition of the Corn Laws he would recommend straightway that the landed interest should surrender them.   But he could not convince himself that the Corn Laws were at

[1] Add. MSS. 40,487; 7. 40,484; 20.
[2] Morley's *Cobden*, Vol. I, p. 180 (Cobden to F. Cobden, Aug. 29, 1841).

the bottom of the trouble. With a huge population concentrated on manufactures, with the disturbances abroad that from time to time checked trade, with the vagaries of the development of industrialism, he was afraid that no effectual remedy could be devised against the recurrence of such distress. So he went on from such subjects to the Constitutional reasons for the Government's resignation.

His speech was able; it was not novel, for he could say nothing new till he faced the House as Prime Minister. What impressed his contemporaries most was the way in which he spoke out about his party. Men's minds were always full of the contrast between Peel and the Tory extremists, which formed a delightful pasture for scandal-mongers, moralizers and prophets. His decision not to oppose the Whig Speaker had been applauded on the ground that it would have been a fatal beginning if Peel had been thwarted at the outset by the Ultras. In this speech there were various resolute passages. He declared, for instance, that he would not accept the support of the agricultural interest, if it had been given on the condition that he bound himself to the details of the existing Corn Law. But at the end came the passage which most men remembered. He was dissociating himself from the extreme Protestants of Ireland. He would neither gain office nor retain it, he said in emphatic phrases, by favouring such opinions. "If I do accept office," said he, "it shall be by no intrigue —it shall be by no unworthy concession of constitutional principle—it shall be by no unnatural and factious combinations with men (honest I believe them to be) entertaining extreme opinions, but from whom I dissent. If I accept office, it shall be by walking in the open light and in the direct paths of the Constitution. If I exercise power, it shall be upon my conception—perhaps imperfect—perhaps mistaken—but my sincere conception of public duty." [1] These were brave and sincere words, and at that moment there was not the slightest danger of

[1] Hansard, LIX, 39.

their antagonizing his most extreme ally. But all the same, no traveller can promise himself open light to the end of his journey; direct paths sometimes lead at last to abrupt precipices, and sincerity is not an adequate substitute for some knowledge of the road ahead.

But gloomy prophecies are always ungracious. If Peel had work to do, he also had work completed. In a way the Conservative Party had already served its purpose. It had faced the full blast of Reform, it had survived and helped to stay its violence. The Reform Bill was over and done with, and the House of Lords seemed unimpaired: Conservatives could still talk of it as independent. The Church had stood firm against the tempest. After all that had been planned against it, it remained unbroken, unsubdued and best of all unplundered. Even the Church of Ireland had been saved as a charred brand for another burning. The restless spirit of constitutional innovation had been damped down till it was disreputable and futile, while the established institutions of the country stood erect and mysterious on their ancient foundations. The work was complete. It was for these things that the Conservative Party had been founded, and these things were secured; perhaps the people's happiness was a separate question.

The Conservatives had performed their task and they had beaten their adversaries. The Whig reign was over; the Government was finally beaten at three o'clock on the morning of August 28th, by 91 votes. It was better for everyone. As the Whig Reformers' vigorous youth had perished almost out of remembrance, so now their long dotage was completed and they could begin to forget it. They had been, by no means entirely through their own fault, such a danger to the reasonableness of politics as was only possible for a morally weak Government. For while strength will soon probably immolate itself for good or for evil, weakness may well sneak into a kind of desperate immortality. Now Whig Ministers were relieved from their burden, and many of them felt grateful. Now Peel could start to work hard and to consider maturely, and the Party he had forged could be put to the test. Now the country would gain a real Government, and where impotence had miserably existed men would see the reality of strength.

On August 30th Peel went down to see an unhappy Queen. This time there could be no hitch. The question of the ladies of the Bedchamber would not occur again. Peel in his strength could ask for less and be refused nothing, and the danger had been prepared against by secret negotiation. So all went smoothly and on September 4th the new Ministers were appointed. Peel was Prime Minister in fact at last.

§ 7

On August 30th, between three and four o'clock in the afternoon, a travelling barouche with four horses passed through the streets of Windsor on its way to the Castle. It carried a man to the starting-point of the five most important years of his life. Sir Robert Peel was going to undertake the nation's destinies. That he wholly liked the prospect as he sat there seems doubtful. In the immediate future he had an interview with a young woman who probably disliked him personally, and certainly resented his errand. All would go right, but all might not be comfortable, and perhaps even an eminent statesman may know what it means to feel shy. A little further ahead was the glorious prospect of governing the country. Peel knew what that meant; he had governed the country before. Before this he had been made the hopeless target for the importunities of all human cupidity, vanity, and folly, and he had learnt by experience that great place attracts the ceaseless attention of petty men. Before this he had learnt that the office of Prime Minister would often mean for him ten, twelve or more hours of work a day, that it would cut him off from his happy home life, his house at Drayton, his boys, and worst of all from the wife to whom he still gave the ardour of a lover. And this was what awaited him at

the end of his drive.   If he had time to review the matter
while he sat in his carriage, he possibly felt, not self-
distrust, but distaste at the gift which was to be put into
his hands, the terrible gift of power.

On the whole Peel had not consciously sought for
power.   At times, it is true, he permitted himself to confess in his speeches a carefully sterilized ambition, an
honourable ambition that he might deserve well of his
country and earn the praise of posterity.   No doubt this
did represent some sort of emulous emotion somewhere
in his mind.   Also Peel's ability and his courage unquestionably prompted him toward a task that demanded
their exercise; especially when the need seemed pressing
and the circumstances stirring.   He had shown this in
the troubled years that had immediately followed the
Reform Bill, most noticeably when in 1834 he had
accepted with such spirit a hopeless mandate from an
imbecile King.   But after 1835 the press and stir of
things had departed, a Conservative Government was a
proved impossibility and the desire for it, wherever it
still existed among the Conservatives, was factious,
selfish and inconsiderate and exactly calculated to excite
all Peel's most deep-rooted antipathies.   The ambition
for office and power had seemed to be, at the least,
irrelevant to his duties as leader of the Opposition.   All
his life it had seemed to him a suspicious emotion.

The desire for power may be too shallow a feeling for
a man to entertain; it may also be too profound for him.
To hunger for power implies unfulfilled wishes, and,
maybe, more reputable wishes than for place or for
patronage or a specious importance in the eyes of the
public.   What unfulfilled wishes had Peel?   The institutions he had defended were secure, the enemies he had
opposed were impotent.   Peel's desires were satisfied,
and Peel was satisfied with his desires.   No doubt he
was glad to provide the country with a more competent
Government, and especially to supplant Whig inefficiency
over the national finances.   But what really important
and urgent dream was there in Peel's heart to make

him yearn for and rejoice at his chance of shaping his
country's destinies?

Perhaps a man's principles should prompt him to
desires outside his immediate necessities. No such
promptings were likely to come from Peel's political
principles. They had been on exhibition too long.
They had always been defensive, they were inclined to
be formal, and he knew all their practical limitations.
By 1841, they had been cut into convenient lengths and
had become slightly desiccated, like museum specimens.
In 1841, Peel still announced without addition that the
objects of his Party were to preserve the institutions of
his country. The ideal was irrelevant, though natural.
It was not very likely to expand Peel's desires and
designs.

Perhaps Peel is not to be blamed. Probably it is
inevitable that if political issues change, party principles should lag behind them. No doubt the succession
of practical problems that confront even a leader of
opposition is such that the consideration of anything
but the immediate present is rendered exceedingly difficult. Probably it would be hard to ask any honest
hard-working statesman to have either vision or desire.
But was there not something lacking in Peel's mind?
He was content with the routine of politics. He went
from Drayton to the House of Commons and from the
House of Commons back to his beloved Drayton, he
read about the French Revolution, he commented on the
follies of the Government, intent all the time on the politics of the moment, and seldom raising his eyes to the
circle of the horizon, to strain and see the realities of
the world outside. He was content to hold or decide
upon his various opinions without considering their
implications and contrasts. He was satisfied often with
what was unreal and formal. Above all he was satisfied with the sterile and respectable purities of an honourable ambition. He was content to do his work with a
blurred background, pollarded principles and no very
ardent or extensive desires.

It is idle to speculate on what would have happened if Peel had been different during these later years of opposition.   He might have refreshed his Party's ideals, he might have provided himself with material for different decisions on various subjects.   He might possibly have controlled more surely the course of events and have been less at the mercy of the future.   But it would be untrue to pretend that he would certainly have been much more successful, or that he would have escaped the fate reserved for him.   Perhaps he was clear-sighted rather than far-sighted, but when he was in office the most important problems of the country would infallibly come within the range of his strong and capable hands.   The difficulties inherent in a Prime Minister's lot would strike fire out of him.   The Country, if not the Party, would have the benefit of his labours.   It was an able and an honest man that was being carried along in that barouche, a cold and commanding middle-aged figure. Probably he was not thinking of his destiny at all but with what office he could satisfy which of his colleagues. Yet it was an important moment when Peel drove up to Windsor Castle and went in to see the Queen.

BIBLIOGRAPHY

SOURCES IN BRITISH MUSEUM

Peel Papers. Add. MSS.· 40,301 to 40,617. (Only systematically read after the date 1832.)

N.B.—This includes the Bonham Papers, Add. MSS. 40,616 and 40,617.

Privately Printed Aberdeen Papers.

PRINTED BOOKS

Aberdeen. The Earl of Aberdeen, by Lord Stanmore. London, 1893. The Life of George, 4th Earl of Aberdeen, by Lady Frances Balfour. 2 vols. London, 1922.

Acland. Memoirs and Letters of Sir Thomas Dyke Acland, by A. H. D. Acland. (Privately Printed.) London, 1902.

Albert, H.R.H. Prince. The Life of H.R.H. the Prince Consort, by Sir Theodore Martin. 5 vols. London, 1878–80.

"Alfred" (S. Kydd). History of the Factory Movement. 2 vols. London, 1857.

Alington, Cyril Argentine. Twenty Years; being a study in the development of the party system between 1815 and 1835. Oxford, 1921.

Althorp, Viscount. Memoir, by Sir Denis Le Marchant. London, 1876.

Argyll. The 8th Duke of Argyll, Autobiography and Memoirs. London, 1906.

Arnold, Thomas, D.D. Life and Correspondence, by A. P. Stanley. London, 1853.

Bagehot. Biographical Studies. Edited by R. H. Hutton. London, 1881.

Bathurst, Earl. Report on the Manuscripts of Earl Bathurst. Hist. MSS. Commission. London, 1923.

Blackburne, Francis. Life of the Right Hon. Francis Blackburne, late Lord Chancellor of Ireland, by his Son. London, 1874.

Blomfield. Memoir of Bishop Blomfield, by his son Alfred Blomfield. 2 vols. London, 1863.

Brougham, Lord. Life and Times, by Himself. 3 vols. Edinburgh, 1871.
Lord Brougham and the Whig Party. A. Aspinall. Manchester, 1927.
Life, by Lord Campbell. London, 1869.

Broughton, Lord. Recollections of a Long Life. Edited by Lady Dorchester. 6 vols. London, 1909–11.

Bright, John. Life, by G. M. Trevelyan. London, 1913.

Buckingham and Chandos, 2nd Duke of. Memoirs of Court of George
    IV. 2 vols. London, 1859.
    Memoirs of the Courts and Cabinets of William IV and Victoria.
    2 vols. London, 1860. [Referred to as Courts and Cabinets.]
Bulwer-Lytton. Life of Edward Bulwer, First Lord Lytton, by his
    grandson the Earl of Lytton. London, 1913.
    England and the English. E. Bulwer-Lytton. London, 1833.
Butler, J. R. M. The Passing of the Great Reform Bill. London,
    1914.
Buxton. Memoirs of Sir Thomas Fowell Buxton, Bart. London, 1848.
Carlyle, Thomas. Chartism.
Chalmers. Memoirs of Dr. Chalmers, by William Hanna. 4 vols.
    Edinburgh, 1849–82.
    Lectures on the Establishment and Extension of National Churches.
    Glasgow, 1838.
Church, Richard William. The Oxford Movement, 1833–45. London,
    1891.
Clapham, J. H., Litt.D. An Economic History of Modern Britain
    (The Early Railway Age). Cambridge, 1926.
Clarendon. Life of the 4th Earl of Clarendon, by Sir Herbert Maxwell.
    London, 1913.
Cobden. Life of Richard Cobden, by John Morley. London, 1881.
Colchester. Diary and Correspondence of Charles Abbot Lord Col-
    chester, edited by his son Lord Colchester. 3 vols. London,
    1861.
Creevey, T. The Creevey Papers, edited by Sir Herbert Maxwell.
    2 vols. London, 1904.
Croker. Correspondence and Diaries. Edited by L. J. Jennings.
    3 vols. London, 1885.
Dickens, Charles. Sketches by Boz.
Disraeli. Life of Benjamin Disraeli, Earl of Beaconsfield, by W. E.
    Monypenny and G. E. Buckle. 6 vols. London, 1910–20.
    Correspondence with his Sister, 1832–52. London, 1886.
    Coningsby. Sybil, or the Two Nations, Etc.
    Runnymede Letters. London, 1885.
    "What is He?" and "A Vindication of the English Constitution."
    London, 1884.
Dod, Charles Roger Phipps. Electoral facts from 1832 to 1852, im-
    partially stated. London, 1852.
Drummond, Thomas. (Under-Secretary in Ireland, 1835–40), by
    Richard Barry O'Brien. London, 1889.
Durham, J. G. Lambton, Earl of. By Stuart J. Reid. 2 vols. London,
    1906.
    Lord Durham's Report on the Affairs of British North America,
    edited with an introduction by Sir C. P. Lucas. Oxford, 1912.
Eldon, Lord. Life and Correspondence, by H. Twiss. 3 vols. Lon-
    don, 1844.

Ellenborough. Political diary, 1828–30, edited by Charles Lord Colchester. 2 vols. London, 1881.

Ellesmere, *see under* Wellington.

Froude, Hurrell. Remains. 4 vols. London, 1838–9.

Gladstone, W. E. State in its Relations with the Church. London, 1838.

Church Principles Considered in their Results. London, 1840.

A Chapter of Autobiography. London, 1868.

Life, by Lord Morley. 3 vols. London, 1903.

Graham, Sir James. Life, by Charles Stuart Parker. 2 vols. London, 1907.

Life and Times, by McCullagh Torrens. London, 1863.

Grant, J. Random Recollections of the House of Commons from the year 1830 to the close of 1835. London, 1836.

Random Recollections of Lords and Commons. 2nd Series. 2 vols. London, 1838.

Portraits of Public Characters. 2 vols. London, 1841.

Gregory. Mr. Gregory's Letter Box, 1813–30, edited by Lady Gregory. London, 1898. [Concerned with Ireland.]

Greville, Charles. A Journal of the Reigns of King George IV and William IV, edited by Henry Reeve. 3 vols. London, 1874.

A Journal of the Reign of Queen Victoria from 1837 to 1852. Vol. I. London, 1885.

The Letters of Charles Greville and Henry Reeve, 1836–65, edited by A. H. Johnson. London, 1924.

Grey, Charles, Earl. Correspondence with Princess Lieven, edited by Guy Le Strange. 3 vols. London, 1890.

Lord Grey of the Reform Bill. G. M. Trevelyan. London, 1920.

Grote, George. The Personal Life of George Grote. Harriet Grote. London, 1873.

Halévy, Elie. Histoire du Peuple Anglais au XIX Siécle. 3 vols. 1912–23.

Article on Chartism in Quarterly Review. Vol. 236.

Hatherton, John Littleton, 1st Lord. Memoir a Correspondence Relating to Political Occurrences in June, 1834, edited by Henry Reeve. London, 1872.

Herbert, Sidney Herbert. Lord Herbert of Lea a Memoir. 2 vols. 1906.

Herries, John Charles. Memoir of Public Life, by Edward Herries. 2 vols. London, 1880.

Hook. Life and Letters of Walter Farquhar Hook, by W. R. W. Stephens. 2 vols. 1878. [Concerned with the Church.]

Hope-Scott. Memoirs of James Robert Hope-Scott with Selections from his Correspondence, by Robert Ormsby. London, 1884.

Houghton, Lord. R. Monckton Milnes: Life, Letters and Friendships, by T. Wemyss Reid. 2 vols. London, 1890.

Hovell, M. The Chartist Movement. Manchester, 1918.

Huskisson. William Huskisson and Liberal Reform, by Alexander Brady. Oxford, 1928.

Hutchins, B. L. and A. Harrison. A History of Factory Legislation. 3rd Edition. London, 1926.

Kay-Shuttleworth, Sir James. Life and Work, by F. Smith. London, 1923.

Lovett, William. Life and Struggles. London, 1876.

Liverpool, Lord. Life and Administration of, by C. P. Yonge. 3 vols. London, 1868.

Lyndhurst. Life, by Sir Theodore Martin. London, 1883.
Life, by Lord Campbell. London, 1869.
The Victorian Chancellors, by J. B. Atlay. Vol. I. London, 1906.

Macaulay, Thomas Babington, Lord. Life and Letters, by Sir G. O. Trevelyan. London, 1876.

Manners. Lord John Manners and His Friends. Charles Whibley. Vol. I. London, 1925.

Manning, Cardinal. Life, by Edward Sheridan Purcell. London, 1895. Vol. I. [Concerned with religious education.]

Martineau, Harriet. The History of England during the Thirty Years Peace. 2 vols. London, 1849–50.

Melbourne, William Lamb, 2nd Viscount. Papers, edited by Lloyd C. Sanders. London, 1889.
Memoirs, by W. M. Torrens. 2 vols. London, 1878.

Moore, T. Memoirs, Journal and Correspondence, edited by Lord John Russell. 8 vols. London, 1853–6.

Molesworth, Sir William, Bart. Life, by Millicent Garrett Fawcett. London, 1901.

Mozley, Rev. J. B. Letters, edited by his Sister. London, 1885.

Mozley, Rev. Thomas. Reminiscences of Oriel College and the Oxford Movement. 2 vols. London, 1882.

O'Connell, Daniel. Correspondence of Daniel O'Connell, edited by W. J. Fitzpatrick. 2 vols. London, 1888.
The Life of Daniel O'Connell, by M. Macdonagh. London, 1903.

Palmer, William. A Narrative of Events connected with the Publication of the Tracts for the Times. London, 1883.

Palmerston. Life, by Henry Lytton Bulwer. London, 1870. 2 vols.
Palmerston, by Philip Guedalla. London, 1926.

Parkes, J. Parkes of Birmingham, by Jesse K. Buckley. London, 1926.

Parker, see under Peel.

Peel, Sir Robert, 2nd Bart. Memoirs, by the Right Hon. Sir R. Peel, published by the Trustees of his Papers, Lord Mahon and Sir E. Cardwell. 2 vols. London, 1856.
Memoir of Sir Robert Peel, by Guizot. London, 1857.
A Sketch of the Life and Character of Sir Robert Peel, by Sir Lawrence Peel. London, 1860.
See Bagehot's Biographical Studies.
Peel, by J. R. Thursfield. London, 1891.

Sir Robert Peel from his Private Papers, edited by Charles Stuart Parker. 3 vols. London, 1891–99.

Sir Robert Peel, by the 8th Earl of Rosebery. London, 1891.

Private Letters of Sir Robert Peel, edited by George Peel. London, 1920.

Sir Robert Peel, by Miss A. A. W. Ramsay. London, 1928.

Place, Francis. Life, by Graham Wallas. London, 1918. [Revised Edition.]

Prentice, Archibald. History of the Anti-Corn Law League. 2 vols. London, 1853.

Raikes, Thomas. A portion of a Journal kept by Thomas Raikes. London, 1856.

Private Correspondence with Duke of Wellington, etc., edited by his Daughter. 4 vols. London, 1856–8.

Roebuck, J. H. Life and Letters, edited by R. E. Leader. London, 1897.

Russell, Lord John. Life, by Spencer Walpole. 2 vols. London, 1889.

Early Correspondence of Lord John Russell, 1808–40, edited by his son Rollo Russell. 2 vols. London, 1913.

Later Correspondence, 1840–78. Vol. I. Edited by G. P. Gooch. London, 1925.

Recollections and Suggestions, 1813–73. London, 1875.

Shaftesbury, Anthony Ashley-Cooper, 7th Earl. Life and Work, by Edwin Hodder. 3 vols. 1886.

Lord Shaftesbury, by J. L. Hammond and Barbara Hammond. London, 1923.

Sheil, Richard Lalor. Memoir, by R. McCullagh Torrens. 2 vols. London, 1855.

Shelley, Frances, Lady. Diary, 1787–1817, edited by R. Edgcumbe. London, 1912.

Sidmouth, Lord. Life and Correspondence, by the Hon. George Pellew. 3 vols. London, 1847.

Smith, Sidney. Works. London, 1859.

Letters to Archdeacon Singleton. London, 1837–9.

Stockmar, Ernst Alfred Christian Freiherr Von. Memoirs, edited by F. Max Müller. 2 vols. London, 1872.

Sydenham, Lord (C. E. Poulett Thomson). Memoirs, by George Poulett Scrope. London, 1843.

Temperley, Harold. Chapter XI, Volume VIII, Cambridge Modern History.

Victoria, Queen. Letters. A Selection from H.M. Correspondence between the years 1837 and 1861, edited by A. C. Benson and Viscount Esher. 3 vols. London, 1908.

The Girlhood of Queen Victoria, a selection from H.M. Diaries between the years 1832 and 1840, edited by Viscount Esher. 2 vols. London, 1912.

Walpole, Sir Spencer. A History of England from the conclusion of the Great War in 1815. New Edition. 6 vols. London, 1890.

Warren, J. "Ten Thousand a Year." 2 vols. 1884. (Description of manners inside the House of Commons and of an election.)

Wellington, Arthur, Duke of. Despatches, Correspondence and Memoranda, edited by his son (in continuation of the former series). 8 vols. London, 1867–80. [They cover from Jan., 1819, to December, 1832.]

The Life of Wellington, by the Right Hon. Sir H. E. Maxwell, Bart. 3rd Edition. 2 vols. London, 1900.

Notes of Conversations with the Duke of Wellington, 1831–51, by Philip Henry, 8th Earl Stanhope (Lord Mahon). London, 1888.

Personal Reminiscences of the Duke of Wellington with a Memoir of Lord Ellesmere by Alice Countess of Strafford. London, 1903.

Wellesley, Richard Colley, Marquess. The Wellesley Papers: The Life and Correspondence of Richard Colley Marquess Wellesley, 1760–1842. 2 vols. London, 1914.

Whateley, Richard, D.D. Life and Correspondence, by E. J. Whately. 2 vols. London, 1866.

PERIODICALS

Annual Register, Blackwood's Edinburgh Magazine, Edinburgh Review, Quarterly Review, Revue des Deux Mondes, Morning Chronicle, Standard, Times, Punch (from 1841).

NOTE ON REFERENCES.—"Parker" always refers to C. S. Parker's *Sir Robert Peel*. "Private Letters" to *Private Letters of Sir Robert Peel*, by George Peel. "Grev." to the journals of Charles Greville—up to Chapter VIII to 1st part (George IV and William IV), afterwards 2nd part (Victoria). *"Courts and Cabinets"* to *Memoirs of the Courts and Cabinets of William IV and Victoria*, by 2nd Duke of Buckingham. Where there is more than one book on one subject in the bibliography, if it is not otherwise stated it is the first book which is referred to in the notes.

INDEX